THE CULTURAL SECTOR AND SUSTAINABLE ECONOMIC DEVELOPMENT

The cultural sector plays an important role in sustainable economic development and creates economic activities, opportunities for entrepreneurship and jobs, adding to the attractiveness of cities and contributing to the development of tourism. *The Cultural Sector and Sustainable Economic Development: Innovation and the Creative Economy in European Cities* offers both a theoretical and practical analysis of the contemporary approach to culture and innovation, with special emphasis on the relationships among culture, innovation and the economy.

Sustainable development, itself, balances environmental protection, culture, social progress, the economy and stability today and for the future. The book's key theme is the role and possibility of culture as a laboratory, with a strong supporting subtext on innovative practice. The text provides an eclectic mix of possibilities that reinforce and underscore the full innovative and complex potentials of culture. It is a cross-disciplinary volume presenting case studies that cover the main theme of cultural ecosystems in a very broad sense, highlighting the relationships that could lead to a sustainable system where economy and culture are the main players. It proposes and maps the European perspective of urban cultural development and suggests that the successes and challenges of European cities under consideration may offer guidance on best practices for urban development in other distant cultural contexts.

This book is written in such a way that it can be used as a summary for a cultural professional, a reference text for an academic or for actors in local development and cultural policy at European, national, and local levels.

Biljana Mickov, PhD, is a cultural researcher who holds a PhD from University of Reims Champagne - Ardeen, France.

Routledge Advances in Regional Economics, Science and Policy

Designing Smart and Resilient Cities for a Post-Pandemic World
Metropandemic Revolution
Anthony Larsson and Andreas Hatzigeorgiou

Political Geography of Cities and Regions
Changing Legitimacy and Identity
Kees Terlouw

The Economic Geography of the Car Market
The Automobile Revolution in an Emerging Economy
Edited by Bartłomiej Kołsut and Tadeusz Stryjakiewicz

Worker Mobility and Urban Policy in Latin America
Policy Interactions and Urban Outcomes in Mexico City
David López-García

Cities Learning from a Pandemic
Towards Preparedness
Edited by Simonetta Armondi, Alessandro Balducci, Martina Bovo, and Beatrice Galimberti

Urban Change in Central Europe
The Case of Kraków
Jacek Purchla

Clusters and Sustainable Regional Development
A Meta-Organisational Approach
Evgeniya Lupova-Henry and Nicola Francesco Dotti

The Economics of Affordable Housing
Alexander Styhre

The Cultural Sector and Sustainable Economic Development
Innovation and the Creative Economy in European Cities
Biljana Mickov

Evolutionary Urban Development
Lessons from Central and Eastern Europe
Katarzyna Sadowy

For more information about this series, please visit: www.routledge.com/series/RAIRESP

THE CULTURAL SECTOR AND SUSTAINABLE ECONOMIC DEVELOPMENT

Innovation and the Creative Economy in European Cities

Biljana Mickov

Routledge
Taylor & Francis Group
LONDON AND NEW YORK

First published 2023
by Routledge
4 Park Square, Milton Park, Abingdon, Oxon OX14 4RN

and by Routledge
605 Third Avenue, New York, NY 10158

Routledge is an imprint of the Taylor & Francis Group, an informa business

British Library Cataloguing-in-Publication Data
A catalogue record for this book is available from the British Library

Library of Congress Cataloging-in-Publication Data
Names: Mickov, Biljana, author.
Title: The cultural sector and sustainable economic development : innovation and the creative economy in European cities / Biljana Mickov.
Description: Abingdon, Oxon ; New York, NY : Routledge, 2023. | Series: Routledge advances in regional economics, science and policy | Includes bibliographical references and index.
Identifiers: LCCN 2022035837 (print) | LCCN 2022035838 (ebook) | ISBN 9781032373676 (hardback) | ISBN 9781032373683 (paperback) | ISBN 9781003336648 (ebook)
Subjects: LCSH: Cultural industries--Europe. | Sustainable development--Europe.
Classification: LCC HD9999.C9473 E8565 2923 (print) | LCC HD9999.C9473 (ebook) | DDC 338.4/77--dc23/eng/20220901
LC record available at https://lccn.loc.gov/2022035837
LC ebook record available at https://lccn.loc.gov/2022035838

ISBN: 978-1-032-37367-6 (hbk)
ISBN: 978-1-032-37368-3 (pbk)
ISBN: 978-1-003-33664-8 (ebk)

DOI: 10.4324/9781003336648

Typeset in Bembo
by SPi Technologies India Pvt Ltd (Straive)

For the success in writing this dissertation, I would like to especially thank my wonderful parents Blagoje and Ljiljana Mickov (née Ljubojević), and my thesis director, Fabrice Thuriot.

CONTENTS

List of Figures *x*
List of Tables *xi*

1 Introduction 1

Hypothesis 2
Methodology of the Thesis 2
Objectives and Questions of the Research 3
Background and Research 7

2 About Cities Today 10

Plan for Culture in Cities 12
Why Innovation is Good for Cities 16

3 Culture, Innovation, and Development 20

Cultural Policy Analysis 20
Networking and Innovation 23
Building Creative Space, a New Way of Thinking, New Ideas… 33
Culture and Innovation in the Open City 41
Building Open Space as Works of Art 43
Technologies and Innovation as Programs in Cities 43
Transformations: Digital Art in an Urban Environment 46

4 The Environment and Sustainable Development 51

Culture, Innovation, and Climate Change 53

Part I
Local Government and Innovation 59

Introduction 59

5 Innovation in Local Governments – Culture Policy 63

Innovation in Local Governments 63
Experimental Government 78

6 Innovation and Development of Creative Industries 83

Creative Industries and Innovation 83
The Public Policy of Economy and Creative Industries 90
The New European Agenda for Culture 91
The Creative Industries 95
The Cultural Economy 97
A Smart Cultural Sector Makes for Inclusive Cities 105
The Creative Cities in Europe 106
Spillover and Cross-Innovation in Creative Industries 108
The Creative Industries, Innovation, and Territories 111
The Creative Economy – Future 114

Part II
Culture and the Creative Economy 121

Introduction 121

7 Economic and Social Value of the Cultural Sector 123

Ecology of Culture 125

8 Case Studies – Research (Local Governments, Cultural Institutions, and Organisations throughout Europe) 129

Introduction 129
Case Study Research 139

9 The First Focus Group of the Qualitative Research 147

City of Stockholm 147
City of Glasgow 149

City of Edinburgh 154
City of Dublin 155
City of London 162
City of Turku 163
City of Eindhoven 164

10 The Second Focus Group of the Qualitative Research 176

City of Rome 176
City of Bologna 182
City of Barcelona 188
City of Brussels 195
City of Marseille 196
City of Reims 199
City of Grenoble 200
City of Mannheim 202
City of Dortmund 205

11 The Third Focus Group of the Qualitative Research 218

City of Bratislava 218
City of Novi Sad 219
Cities of Kiev/Moscow/Eindhoven 222
City of Belgrade 223
City of Gabrovo 226
City of Zagreb 227
City of Skopje 229
City of Krakow 230
City of Ljubljana 232
City of Budapest 234

Part III
Analysis of Case Studies in Europe **247**

12 Discussion 263

13 Conclusion 267

Bibliography 274
Index 283

FIGURES

1 *Elements that Make up the Sustainable Development of Society.* 21
Jordi Pascual, "Cultural Policies, Human Development and Institutional Innovation: or Why We Need Agenda 21 for Culture," in *Sustaining Cultural Development: Unified Systems and New Governance in Cultural Life*, ed. James Doyle and Biljana Mickov, (London: Routledge Publishing, 2013), 58.

2 Eurostat (Statistics Explained). *Persons Employed by Economic Activity*, 2018. Available at: https://ec.europa.eu/eurostat/statistics-explained/index.php?title=File:Persons_employed_by_economic_activity,_EU-28,_2008-2017_(index_2008%3D100).png&oldid=421913. 98

3 Eurostat (Statistics Explained). *Evolution of Indicators for Different Sectors of the Economy*. Available at: https://ec.europa.eu/eurostat/statistics-explained/index.php?title=File:Evolution_of_indicators_for_different_sectors_of_the_economy,_EU-27,_2012-2017_(index_2012%3D100).png&oldid=475446. 99

4 *Growth of the UK's Creative Economy.* 102
Bakhshi, Hasan, Alan Freeman, and Peter Higgs, *A Dynamic Mapping of the UK's Creative Industries* (London: Nesta, 2013). Available at: http://www.nesta.org.uk/publications/dynamic-mapping-uks-creative-industries.

5 Department for Digital, Culture, Media & Sport (DMCS). *The UK Creative industries – Value*, 2018. Available at: http://www.somersetculture.org.uk/blog/research-facts/creative-industries-facts-statistics/. 102

6 City of Stockholm, *Budget expenditure for 2018*, 2018. Available at: https://start.stockholm/. 149

TABLES

1 The First Focus Group of Research. Author: Mickov, Biljana. 2021 170
2 The Second Focus Group of Research. Author: Mickov, Biljana. 2021 211
3 The Third Focus Group of Research. Author: Mickov, Biljana. 2021 240

1

INTRODUCTION

The book offers a theoretical and practical analysis of the contemporary approach to culture and innovation, with a particular emphasis being placed on the relationship between culture, innovations, and the economy as an indispensable sustainability factor, while it is clearly stated that a cultural ecosystem inevitably incorporates the economy.

> The evaluation of cultural projects in cities is based on realistic and practical experiences of international organizations, universities and activists. They represent a dedication of city councils to integrate culture into the process of sustainable development, both on local and global level.[1]

To attain sustainability, the economy has to produce the values on which it is based, which take into account the culture of the specific environment. The economy is dynamic when it is adapted to local resources—in the cultural context it is based on the values of the local environment, and is therefore self-sustainable.[2] Cultural activism plays an important role in sustainable economic development and creates economic activities, entrepreneurship and jobs, adding to the attractiveness of cities and contributing to the development of tourism.

Economic models[3] have a tendency to prioritize rapid development which tends to be unsustainable in the long run and is generally not beneficial to local environments. The cultural and the economic factors of the environment must be taken into account and developed in parallel. In the same document, it is emphasized that

> Economic models that aim at cultural sensitivity need to engage in implementation practice that includes collaboration, cooperation, trade and donations. All economic models are based on specific cultural values. An effective link between the public, market and cooperative economy, together with the reciprocity among them, is essential to achieving a decentralized, environmentally balanced development.[4]

DOI: 10.4324/9781003336648-1

The cultural ecosystem should not be treated as merely a segment of the economy, but rather as a system that contains the economy. Therefore, the interconnectedness of cultural systems and other segments of sustainable development must be taken into account. It is essential to distinguish artists and professionals in the cultural sector, ensure access to their work, promote corporative responsibility and implement adequate support for cultural projects. There are a range of mechanisms for cultural project support, such as microloans and sponsorships. Cities and regions should maintain mixed economic programs that maximize donations for cultural projects. Partnership between people from the cultural and business fields is also important, together with systemic innovations and knowledge transfer. "Tourism needs to be linked to this cultural ecosystem, by means of implementing cultural routes. Business organizations such as chambers of commerce possess special programs related to cultural politics of cities."[5] When it comes to the development of cities and regions, a priority has to be made to restore public spaces for cultural happenings and art-related activities that would represent the social unity of a city, as well as strengthening the city's cultural identity based on a network of cultural entities and associations.[6] Clearly, it is this network that forms a basis for the promotion and implementation of ambitious cultural policies on a city level. The thesis points out that an essential factor in the promotion of urban change, an innovative cultural profile of the city has to be defined, together with the transformation and opening of new cultural institutions. This would mark the particular contribution of the cultural sector to economic development.

Hypothesis

The empirical hypothesis of this dissertation is that the elements we investigate are consequentially related. The relations between culture, social development, the economy and environmental sustainability are causal-consequential and thus they have to be balanced. When there is a change in relation to cultural policy, there are also impacts on the social and economic aspects of society. The cultural sector is equally as important as the economic, social and environmental dimension of sustainable development, and has to be included among the dimensions that support sustainability.

Methodology of the Thesis

In terms of method, the thesis is based in part upon a qualitative study, centered around the cultural policy dimensions of public cultural governance, comprising 30 interviews conducted with professionals and focused on several major themes: the place and role of innovation; new modes of governance; relationships with the environment; the changing role of institutions; the impact of economic and tourism issues; and professionalization and education. The aim was to study a diversity of examples according to the relevant criteria in relation to the object of research: the size of the cultural sector, the size of budget and staff, the type of funding and status, the presence or absence of an administrator, the location in an urban, suburban, or rural setting, and so on. The interviews will be partially directive, based on an interview guide. We will analyze the responses case by case, then globally. This research tries to clarify the relationship between culture, innovation, and economy through the case studies. We will analyze innovation facilities based on new technology, creative industries, and institutional research. Through its multidimensional approach and the flexibility between different perspectives (going from in-depth interviews with the relevant actors of the case studies from direct observations), this methodology seeks to point, as closely as possible, to the interaction between culture and innovation.

Objectives and Questions of the Research

The aims and objectives of the research are:

- To explore recent developments in cultural policy making and the experiences of people working within the sector throughout a variety of regions and cities.
- To explain how the need for innovative effective cultural policy in contemporary culture is increasing due to movements in society that are inevitably impacting both the arts and, equally, cultural institutions themselves.
- To show that good cultural policies enhance democratization and development.
- To examine how cultural institutions are becoming much more open and innovative than they used to be and how these institutional changes go hand in hand with social changes that thereby allow them to take an active role in that process.
- To bring about the development of new innovative skills within the cultural sector with the intention of continuing knowledge advancement and the exchange of experience within cultural practice.
- The development of innovative cultural policy and strategy, town planning, cooperation models between countries, population inclusion, audience analysis, art education and interaction, which are all necessary for the successful management of contemporary culture.
- The improvement of art education that can be facilitated by the evolution of cultural institutions into centers for art education through the provision of educational programmes that can ensure a permanent audience, which has access to a means by which it can make its own impact on the development of cultural policy.
- To investigate how contemporary culture can provide important insights into modern life and how it connects aspects of popular culture, modern civilization and developmental technology.
- To clarify the significance of innovative cultural institutions. Art institutions must become emphatically open innovative spaces for both artists and society as a whole in order to achieve a wider context.

Culture is a fundamental element within society and is the main aim of the United Nations Educational, Scientific and Cultural Organization (UNESCO).[7] Culture is a necessary part of the development of the individual's worldview and it allows people to question the seemingly immutable certainties that appear to exist within communities of place and shared heritage. Innovative cultural development is also important. Contemporary culture speaks directly about the important questions of our time and to the changing landscape of global identity.

It is needless to emphasize the importance of cultural development. In its essence contemporary culture itself speaks about the crucial questions of our time and the immense changes in the environment of global identity.[8] Sustainable development stands in direct correlation with the cultural policy and strategy of a particular city or region. The indispensable role of cultural policy is to encourage the structuring of cultural projects (art projects and equipment, for example) that can have a powerful impact on society.[9] Cultural policy enables an equitable apportionment of cultural facilities in a particular city or region; it makes it possible to clearly balance the impartial reasons that may exist either in favor of or against the support of certain cultural projects; and, finally, to encourage artistic creativity and innovation. Sustainable cultural development at both regional and national levels in a modern society must be transversal. All dimensions of the city or territory (social, educational, economic, touristic) are interconnected and culture has to be connected with each of them. By means of clear cultural policy, sustainable cultural development should incorporate modernization, digitalization and technologically sophisticated media.[10] It has to take into consideration the presentation of culture that aims to facilitate cultural exchange between contrasting communities while simultaneously preserving the specific characteristics of place, traditional values and architectural heritage.[11]

The goal of securing better access to sustainable development can be reached through the provision of good cultural policy, more effective management between national and international partners, and also through projects such as this, which aim to support research and generate the production of new ideas.[12] Investments in research projects are absolutely necessary in the cultural sector, particularly in the form of conferences, forums, and seminars. In order to ensure future development and attain certain levels of stability it is vital to present new models that can be implemented, especially in strategic cultural planning. This early part of the twenty-first century, and perhaps this decade in particular, will almost certainly be an epoch of networking that will give rise to the advancement of myriad agendas and platforms that will seek to further cultural research and development. Networking provides the space in which information turns into knowledge and knowledge into innovation, making it the laboratory of the present. Despite the fact that the maintenance of contacts and networks can be demanding and requires permanent communication, it also denotes positive work and the possibilities for further development that exist based on the experience of other cultural practitioners working in contrasting environments.

Accordingly, the networks that exist both within and between regions and cities have evolved to become more conceptual, programmatic, and organizational in order to cater to this new kind of cultural sector management; managing these three elements of cultural sector networking brings with it certain complexities.[13] We still require some room for research and laboratory-style experimentation. The local becomes global, and one of the reasons for this is the technological advancement of recent times which compels us to share, exchange, and communicate. There are now some platforms available to cultural managers that are incredibly inexpensive, yet they have the ability to enable global improvements in cultural management through the exchange of innovative models and their transfer into other environments, which can then be implemented at a local level. Without these new technologies, we cannot expect artistic creativity to maintain the high standards of innovation required of it in order to achieve balanced development across the various sectors of society. As we will see, the platforms, agendas and networks that are involved have, within themselves, become conceptual and programmatic and they are an organized trilogy that can enable new methods of governance in the cultural sector. However, the effective management of the tripod of this new governance system is an exercise filled with intricacies.[14]

The majority of cities have based their cultural policies on four key principles: cultural identity, cultural diversity, creativity, and the participation of citizens in cultural life.[15] Now more than ever, we need dedicated places for interchange, centers of transference, spaces for experimentation, and cultural laboratories. The thesis advanced in this book explicates new activities in cultural policy and the systems employed in various cultural organizations by educated professionals who have been involved in these processes within their own cultural environments. We need cultural policies that support the structuring of cultural projects, which can, in turn, exert a real influence on all aspects of a society; to ensure the appropriate distribution of cultural facilities within a city or region; to refine objective reasons for maintaining, withdrawing, or withholding support for projects on a case-by-case basis; to foster artistic creation; and to give artists the opportunity to work in suitable conditions so that they may inspire the development of new ideas and change within society.[16]

The challenge of good cultural policy today in communities of place and in contemporary society as a whole is to be transversal. All aspects of society are linked and both culture and cultural policy need to relate to each of them. We have to create a variety of high-quality conditions for artists, for artistic diffusion, and for circulation. We need to create good conditions for mutual resources that will better integrate cultural workers at all levels: local, national, European and international.[17] The cultural development strategies of cities should ensure that cultural policies are observed and interwoven throughout all public policies. Programmes that will encourage greater public participation in cultural life have to be developed specifically with this goal in mind. Substantial investment in research projects exploring the possibilities of culture is necessary and the introduction of new measures, especially in the area of strategic planning, that will ensure further development, is paramount.[18] The overall objective of cultural policy is to create favorable conditions for the creation of harmonized cultural development that is capable of contributing to the sustainable development of its society or community. The creation of an active cultural policy opens up the area of cultural development for communities of place in a new and contemporary manner. The challenge is to abandon old methods and ways of thinking and instead initiate and introduce new thinking. There is no doubt but that the creation of a new and functioning system of cultural development should begin immediately. The findings of this thesis clearly call for the repositioning of culture from the edge to the center of society in order to enable a different way of thinking. They also indicate the need to switch from a vertical approach to more horizontal governance and, because of this, we determine that the managerial element could contribute to the process of focusing on culture as the torchbearer of cultural and social developments. Cultural policy relates to the decentralization of decision-making and budgetary affairs by recognizing creative originality and defending the principle of citizens' right to culture.[19] This can be promoted through the advocating of digitalization and digital access in cultural projects that support both local and global cultural heritage. Permanent innovation is crucial and the use of new technologies can facilitate the availability of culture to all citizens.[20] Achieving a sympathetic cooperation between cultural and educational policies is important for society. The role of educational programs is to organize the principle of culture as a creative tool that will result in the development of creativity and it is related to a great extent to the increase of knowledge in society.

The real benefits of this for citizens include increased knowledge and the opening up of new methodologies and skills. Our future is not only globally intertwined, but increasingly urban.[21] Over the next twenty years, Africa and Asia will see by far the fastest growth in urban settlements. In Africa alone the growth in population will equal the entire current population of the United States and this growth, rather than centering on large cities, will instead look toward small and medium-sized towns and cities to take on the responsibility of receiving and looking after these millions of new urban dwellers. Moreover, as the world's urban population grows, the interdependence that exists between town and countryside will become increasingly apparent. We know, of course, that the challenges facing city leaders differ from place to place, and from country to country, and that those in low-income countries face problems and stresses on a vastly greater scale. But we share many common goals as well as problems, and are united in a common determination to make our urban world a better, more inclusive one.[22]

The future city of 2030 constantly inspires and nurtures creativity and innovation while cultivating knowledge, the appreciation of heritage and memory.[23] This city will also strive for excellence and creativity in its cultural programs, giving full recognition to the role of its artists. It will place a high value on education, at all levels and for all ages, endowing its children and adults with the skills, knowledge, and attributes they require to succeed. It will foster and promote culture, the essential "fourth pillar" of the sustainable city, for culture is at once an expression of the human spirit, a means of bringing people together across divides and a powerful factor in the city's economic and social life and development.

Background and Research

This thesis aims to understand processes *from the Innovative Culture Policies to the Economy and Innovation* and to exchange knowledge of innovation and experience between different cultural institutions and environments in Europe and the UK. It is crucial to highlight the concept that clearly shows a vertical connection between different experiences of innovation regarding strategic plans for the development of culture, which in effect reinforce a horizontal cultural organization regarding innovation policies.

"Joseph Schumpeter defined innovation as encompassing new products, processes, raw materials, management methods and markets."[24]

This thesis shows both local and regional cultural policies and examines how the relationship between innovation and new design contributes toward raising standards while also stimulating development, new thinking, and the relationship of local governments toward cultural institutions. It also investigates the significance of networking, the value of collaborative partnerships, developments in the field of creative industries and, lastly, provides an evaluation of specific innovative cultural projects. This thesis encompasses a wide range of case studies dealing with topics of innovative sustainable cultural development in different cultural institutions in cities and regions. It also includes various examples of cultural innovation with respect to the environment, combined with theories and practice of innovative development contributed to by leading professionals specializing in this area. It is needless to emphasize the importance of innovative cultural development. At its essence, contemporary culture itself speaks about the crucial questions of our time and the immense changes in the environment of global identity.

Innovation stands in direct correlation with the cultural policy and strategy of a particular city or region. Cultural policy's role is to encourage the structuring of cultural projects (art projects and equipment, for example) that can have a powerful impact on society. Furthermore, cultural policy enables an equitable apportionment of cultural facilities in a particular city or region; it makes it possible to clearly balance the impartial reasons that may exist either in favor of or against the support of certain cultural projects; and finally, to encourage artistic creativity.

> Innovative cultural development at both regional and national levels in a modern society must be transversal. All dimensions of the city or territory (social, educational, economic, touristic) are interconnected and culture should connect with each of them. By means of clear cultural policy, innovation has to incorporate contemporary innovative approach, digitalization, new ideas, creative processes and technologically sophisticated media. It should also take into consideration the presentation of culture which aims to facilitate cultural exchange between contrasting communities while simultaneously preserving the specific characteristics of place, traditional values and architectural heritage.[25]

In order to ensure future innovation and attain certain levels of stability, it is important to present new models that can be implemented, especially in strategic cultural planning. We need, more than ever, dedicated places for interchange, centers of transference, spaces for experimentation, and cultural laboratories. The objective of this thesis is to present examples of innovative cultural policy in action and the experiences of its practitioners.

In the network society, relationships have changed radically between creation and the audience; in addition, however, a range of factors (access to information and communication technologies) have participated toward creating a new reality. Everyone can now be both creator and receiver of culture at the same time. Cultural practice has diversified and, as a result, the positions that a person or group can adopt have multiplied.[26] The idea of cultural consumption cannot be based on only one type of cultural practice; instead it is important to be diverse and that is essential for cultural development. Cultural practice includes all kinds of processes and activities, ranging from the most basic and popular to the most skilled; from the most amateur to business projects and including a wide range of community or associative initiatives. Culture is complex. And cultural wealth, just like natural wealth, is based on complexity and diversity. The evolution is also observed in culture.[27]

The head of the culture department of the city of Barcelona, Jordi Marti, said that cultural policies need to aim toward expanding educational options for cultural and artistic practice.[28] The educational profile of cultural policies adds to the cultural aspect of educational policies. However, these kinds of cultural policies are not only made by departments for culture. They are the policies of educational cities, and also policies supporting creation. Without raising awareness and providing an introduction to artistic languages, there is no aesthetic education or diversity in artistic practice. In that case, the cultural industries cannot reach their full potential.

Notes

1 United Cities and Local Governments (UCLG), Culture 21 Actions: Commitments on the role of culture in sustainable cities, (Bilbao: UCLG, 2015), accessed May 6, 2020, http://www.agenda21culture.net/documents/culture-21-actions
2 UCLG, "Agenda 21 for Culture." Culture 21 action, 2015, accessed May 6, 2020. http://www.agenda21culture.net/
3 UCLG, "Culture 21: Actions."
4 Ibid.
5 Ibid.
6 Esteve Caramés, "Barcelona's Cultural Policies Behind the Scenes New Context, Renewed Strategies," in *Sustaining Cultural Development, Unified Systems and New Governance in Cultural Life*, ed. J. E. Doyle and B. Mickov (London: Routledge Publishing, 2013), 29–35.
7 The United Nations Educational, Scientific and Cultural Organization (UNESCO), UNESCO in Brief - Mission and Mandate, accessed May 6, 2020. https://en.unesco.org/about-us/introducing-unesco
8 UCLG, "Agenda 21 for Culture."
9 Biljana Mickov and James Doyle, "Introduction," in *Sustaining Cultural Development, Unified Systems and New Governance in Cultural Life*, ed. J. E. Doyle and B. Mickov (London: Routledge Publishing, 2013), 1–16.

10 Ibid.
11 Ibid.
12 Ibid.
13 Mickov and Doyle, "Introduction."
14 Ibid.
15 UCLG, "Agenda 21 for Culture."
16 Ibid.
17 Jordi Pascual, "Cultural Policies, Human Development and Institutional Innovation: or Why We Need Agenda 21 for Culture," in *Sustaining Cultural Development: Unified Systems and New Governance in Cultural Life*, ed. J. E. Doyle and B. Mickov (London: Routledge Publishing, 2013), 55–66.
18 UCLG, "Agenda 21 for Culture."
19 Ibid.
20 Pascual, "Cultural Policies, Human Development and Institutional Innovation: or Why We Need Agenda 21 for Culture."
21 UCLG, "Agenda 21 for Culture."
22 Ibid.
23 Pascual, "Cultural Policies, Human Development and Institutional Innovation: or Why We Need Agenda 21 for Culture."
24 Joseph Schumpeter, *Capitalism, Socialism and Democracy* (New York: Harper, 1950), https://en.wikipedia.org/wiki/Joseph_Schumpeter
25 UCLG, *Culture 21 Actions*; Culture 21 Actions. is a key guiding document on culture and cities. It highlights the interdependent relationship between people, culture and sustainable development. Very practical and useful, it promotes 9 commitments (or 'themes') and 100 actions. It is being used by cities all over the world.
26 Jordi Martí Grau and Carles Giner Camprubi, "If the Agenda 21 for Culture is the Answer, What was the Question?" in *Report 5: Cities, Cultures and Developments. A Report that Marks the Fifth Anniversary of Agenda 21 for Culture* (Barcelona: UCLG, 2009), 44–54. Biljana Mickov and James Doyle, "Introduction," in *Sustaining Cultural Development, Unified Systems and New Governance in Cultural Life*, ed. J. E. Doyle and B. Mickov (London: Routledge Publishing, 2013).
27 Ibid.
28 Ibid.

2

ABOUT CITIES TODAY

In his book *The Fragile City*, the theoretician Charles Landry "writes about the ideal city where people can live, work and be inspired by culture."[29] He states that, "since the Renaissance City, many have proposed ideals, from the Garden City, to the Radiant City and, more recently, the Green City or New Urbanism." He notes that, when we look at the city in which people have a central role in cultural policy, the expectations of people depend on their stage in life, personal preferences, the opportunities they have, their needs or desires, their lifestyle and their ambitions.[30] For him, cities are perfect places for life and they are places of communication and networking, interaction and moving around; the outside world is accessible, and one feels like a part of a bigger, more extensive web. "They are places to self-improve, learn and reflect. They are places of inspiration."[31] The conditions for life for all kinds of moods and interests are well catered for.

"They are emotionally pleasing." He writes that great places have a good balance:

> They are alive and vibrant yet provide spaces for calm and tranquility. The great city has clarity of purpose and it knows where it is going. It is a blend of hardware (its physical fabric like streets buildings and parks), software (its activity base like its enterprise, its cultural life or its shopping experiences), and how it is organized, managed and governed.[32]

In his research on deferent cities throughout Europe and the world, Charles Landry concludes that "some vast cities are wonderful and livable, while others are depressing.

Some smaller cities are a delight and convenient and others are small-minded and depressive. The cultural sector is the main chain that can make city life good for the people."[33]

DOI: 10.4324/9781003336648-2

In his book *Psychology and the City*, Landry states that "the cycle of influencing and being influenced by the city impacts our mind, and our emotional state impacts the city with untold effects."[34] It is astonishing that psychology, "the study exploring the dynamics of feeling and emotion, has not been taken sufficiently seriously as an urban discipline, not only by psychology itself but also urban decision makers, since it seeks to understand why we act the way we do."[35] People are those who define the city and they have personality, identity, and make the city. "There are psychological consequences to our adaptation to 'homo urbanis' and the cities that will do best may be those most able to connect the ancient as well as modern parts of ourselves."[36]

The digitized city is already here; technology is fast developing and citizens have work on digitalization processes through the city services, culture, design, and life. "Digitalization is changing society and social life, culture, connectivity, the economy and cities."[37] "Smart city ideas or evolving collaborative governance models are just some responses to digitalization through which improvements to our quality of life are possible by making life more citizen-centric, more local, more convenient or efficient."[38] Cities matter like never before in spite of increased virtual interactions. "The volume, velocity and variety of instantly available data streams combined the 'anytime, anyplace, anywhere' phenomenon changes how we interact with space, place and time."[39] "Technology has to be driven for people's use and not the reverse, but at the same time the cities, citizens and the variety of urban leaders have a once in a lifetime opportunity to rebuild our cities in a different way."[40] With open data space, we can build more democracy in our hand as well, to be certain that we can do more for our life in the cities. "Theoretically, the Creative City idea was first established by Richard Florida."[41] Since then, there has been a lot of thinking and redefinition of the idea of the Creative City and how it can be developed. "He established the concept of the creative class and its implication for urban development in the cities."[42] On the other hand, Charles Landry concludes that

> creative city making seeks to address the escalating crisis cities face that cannot be solved by a business-as-usual approach, including the challenge of living together with great diversity, addressing the sustainability agenda and how cities can rethink their roles and purpose in a changing world to persevere economically, culturally and socially.[4344]

Creativity is going to flourish before innovations, to develop as well as to solve urban problems and to create opportunities.

> It is a new form of capital and a currency in its own right. Creativity has broad-based implications in all spheres of life. The creative economy is not the only important factor; it includes social innovators, business people or bureaucracy.[45]

Cities need to create the conditions for people to think, create, be innovative and act with imagination.

> Today, the personality of many cities is their 'culture of engineering', which the citizens have to build and create in every sense of the phrase. Many cities have been trying to find a way to set up the best cultural policy through learning and understanding contemporary cultural processes.[46]

Plan for Culture in Cities

In one moment, cultural polices became the priority for many cities in Europe and also around the world. Defining culture means defining oneself and defining cultural policies also means defining oneself.[47] The *Agenda 21 for Culture* is the first document that shows that new culture policy is possible for cities. The Agenda 21 for Culture project was set up in 2004, and shows the importance of planning culture, especially in the long term. From this point of view, citizens play a central part in cultural policy and their cultural practice. The important thing is how good cultural policy impacts people's lives, their feelings, how they interact with the institution they visit, and what kind of knowledge they can obtain from these visits. *Cultural Practice*: In the network society, relationships have changed radically. Consumption and creation have become the new reality. Everyone can now be both a creator and receiver of culture at the same time. Cultural practice has diversified and, as a result, the positions (active, passive, as emitter, as receiver, etc.) that a person or group can adopt have multiplied.

Diversity: Cultural practice includes all kinds of processes and activities, ranging from the most basic and popular to the most skilled; from the most amateur to business projects, including a wide community or associative initiatives. Culture is based on both complexity and diversity. Obviously, these kinds of cultural policies are not only made by departments for culture. They are the policies of educational cities, and also policies toward supporting creation. And without support of creation, there is no space for risk, experimentation, rehearsal, mistakes, etc. The question is: what about cultural industries? Without education and without creation, there would only be one option: to remain consumers of what is produced by hegemonic cultural industries.[48]

Agenda 21 Culture: Local cultural policies need to have their own theoretical framework in the city. The *Agenda 21 for Culture* provides cultural management, cultural policies, and planning with a theoretical corpus and a common view of culture. Any practice (professional, political, academic, and social, etc.) that seeks to be recognized needs this background.[49] In *Agenda 21 for Culture*, the approaches and positioning of actors working together have achieved a great deal of maturity. Local cultural policies achieve a high degree of centrality and the *Agenda 21 for Culture* is a force for the unity of the cultural sector in the city.

The Agenda 21 for Culture in the City

The *Agenda 21 for Culture* presents a guide for cultural action and a global perspective as a link of cooperation networks. Cities are places that bring together the majority of cultural actions produced by human beings. Cities localize a global dynamic and, at the same time, globalize local dynamics. This means that the cultural policies of cities are connected with the construction of a planetary society, and this is the main innovation of the *Agenda 21 for Culture*.[50] Thus, the *Agenda 21 for Culture* is a device that connects with the world.

> Agenda 21 for culture's power comes from its ability to connect with these other devices for cultural policies. In Barcelona, this has created a singular geometry. The Agenda 21 for Culture needs to be seen in a geometry that also includes cultural planning processes (the Libraries Plan in 1998, the Cultural Sector Strategic Plan in 1999, and the *Nous Accents* Strategic Culture Plan in 2006), the main instruments for cultural policies (the Institute for culture, the constellation of consortiums set up with other governments and civil society).[51]

Cultural planning can help us to think about the goals of cultural policies and Agenda 21 for Culture is radical in terms of cultural policies. The network of cities is committed to certain values.

Open City: If we look the city of Barcelona as an example of the implementation of good cultural policy practice, the next step for its development is the participation of citizens in the open city government.[52] Digital rights and democracy provide a chance for Barcelona's digital citizens to make decisions. For example, the Decidim project provides an experimental, "open, secure, and free" platform for gathering ideas and testing their viability. The ideas that survive this test of collective intelligence can then be implemented by the city with the support of the people. The new network has been started with the cities that protect digital rights globally. What is happening and what is current is that cities agree on common principles in coordination with the EU and the United Nations Human Settlements Programme (UN-Habitat). What matters is universal and equal access to the Internet, digital literacy; privacy, data protection and security; transparency, accountability and non-discrimination of data, content and algorithm; participatory democracy, diversity and inclusion; open and ethical standards of digital services that include the cultural sector.

A theoretician and professor based in the United Kingdom, John Holden, has written about the role of culture in the global city. He states "that cities are places that are culturally and financially active, right here and right now: they combine the making of money with the making of meaning."[53] These are cities that people actually want to move to; places where history and news are made, and where living artists thrive. He writes that,

> in the West, the role of the traditional arts in the life of cities seems to be changing. In the nineteenth and twentieth centuries, any city with ambition wanted to host a world class museum, an orchestra, and maybe an opera house. Usually there is a question to the politicians—what value do the arts and culture provide for the place—the city?[54]

Holden pointed out that answering these questions is made more difficult than it otherwise would be, because "we are collectively in a muddle about some of the important terms in the debate, especially the words 'culture' and 'value'."[55] "Cities without the arts do not have a progressive economy or social and political sustainability."[56] The suggestion is that cities have to improve their cultural sectors and adapt to contemporary changes. For a long time, "art forms such as opera, ballet, poetry, etc. were considered the arts. For a long time, the arts were considered elitist."[57]

John Holden writes that

> The meaning of culture has to be radically rethought because two things have happened. The first is an obvious one: and that is that the old notion that somehow particular forms of culture are inherently better than others—by which we mean that they are more capable of bearing intense meaning—that idea has been untenable for quite some time.[58]

We have to rethink the relationship between the arts and the rest of culture.

> The second imperative for a reconsideration flows from a much more recent and much more fundamental shift in the way that the cultural system works. The old understanding of high art and popular art as separate entities is no longer relevant; instead, they are completely intertwined.[59]

Holden concludes that,

> Funded culture is the type of culture that needs support from governments or philanthropists. This type of culture is defined not through theory but by practice: what gets funded becomes culture. Therefore, who makes these decisions about what to fund, how those decisions are made, and hence who gets to define this type of culture, is a matter of considerable public interest—all of these are intensely political questions?[60]

Commercial culture is market-driven:

> Home-made it is defined by an informal self-selecting peer group. The decision about the quality of what is produced then lies not in the hands of an expert, but in the hands of those who see, hear or taste the finished article.[61]

The really revolutionary technological innovation has been the internet. The internet has enabled people to use culture to communicate, collaborate, and make money in ways that are entirely new.

It has changed the possibilities for all types of culture and all forms of cultural expression within it, presenting a wealth of new opportunities (such as new audiences). However, it has also set some questions—what to do about intellectual property.

> The revolutionary technology has also changed the role of culture in people's lives. Instead of being passive consumers of culture, nowadays we all take on positions as producers and consumers, authors and readers, performers and spectators all of the time.[62]

This all creates the sense of individual and collective identity and people define themselves by what they choose to watch, read, and listen to. All of these processes explain why culture has become more important to cities and why culture has become increasingly important in the world of politics and policy. New technology is completely changing the way of doing and creating. "This is crucial to the ecosystem of humans. Connectivity between cities is important in terms of economy and creative industries as a driver of those industries. In many cities, smart public sector investment is driving private sector prosperity."[63]

We are all familiar with the idea that physical infrastructure, such as roads and water pipes, are an essential component of building a city. "We can, by extension, comprehend the need for physical cultural infrastructure like museums and concert halls. What is less familiar, but now equally important, is the idea of investing in the less visible infrastructure of connectivity."[64]

"Cities need to constantly form new connections in order to regenerate and renew themselves. They need stimulus and diversity."[65] "The cities of today are dynamic, rapidly evolving organisms of change and recognize culture as one of the pillars of development."[66] In the cities of the future, ideas are the basic materials. In order to keep creative people, cities need to work on this and strategically built creative capacity for the city. The development of technology and the support of creative ideas makes a city attractive to people. In this condition, an innovative urban environment can develop. "The majority of cities have to become a prominent center of different activities, especially those related to the economy, culture and politics. At the same time, the relations between urban and rural realms remain symbiotic and balanced."[67]

Contemporary urban landscapes reflect the ever-increasing pace of changes, driven by place-specific conditions and globalization. Cities, their authorities, professionals, cultural managers, and citizens try to wrestle with the situation within the framework of economic, social, cultural, and environmental transformations. Therefore, the question of the mechanisms by which different social, economic, historical, cultural, and physical conditions coincide in the formation of space and/or its transformation is of great importance for urban researchers, cultural researchers, practitioners and policy makers. *Valuing the role of culture in regeneration* is really important—cultural projects can help change the image of an area, give local people (particularly young people and other vulnerable groups) access to a wider range of opportunities, generate local pride, and build social cohesion. "Culture creates the norms of behavior that build social capital. In turn, social capital underpins the relationships and transactions that make a city and its economy function and thrive."[68] The policy approach is that the job of city governance is to *enable* people to be a part of culture and to improve their ability to learn from culture, and to create the culture of today and the future.

It is about drawing attention to the capacity of people to use cultural places for themselves. It is also about viewing these activities as educational tools and planning decisions supporting cultural activity for both citizens and visitors. The city will flourish socially and economically. The conclusion is that city governments can make a rich cultural life for everyone.[69]

Why Innovation is Good for Cities

We need to create good conditions for mutual resources that will better integrate cultural workers at all levels.[70] Programs that will encourage greater public participation in cultural life have to be developed specifically with this goal in mind. Substantial investment in research projects exploring the possibilities of culture is necessary and the introduction of new measures, especially in the area of innovation and strategic planning, that will ensure further development, is paramount.

The challenge is to abandon old methods and ways of thinking and instead to initiate and introduce new innovative thinking. There is no doubt but that the creation of a new and functioning system of cultural innovative development has to begin immediately. The findings of this thesis clearly call for the repositioning of culture from the edge to the center of society in order to enable a different way of thinking. They also indicate the need to switch from a vertical approach to more horizontal governance and because of this we determine that the managerial element could contribute to the process of focusing on culture as the torchbearer of cultural and social developments.

Innovation and Cultural Policy

Permanent innovation is crucial and the use of new technologies can facilitate the availability of culture to all citizens. Achieving sympathetic cooperation between cultural and educational policies is important for society. The role of educational programs is to organize the principle of culture as a creative and innovative tool that will result in the development of creativity and, as such, is strongly related to the increase of knowledge in society.

The real benefits of this for citizens include increased knowledge and the opening up of new methodologies and skills. By expanding the provision of cultural facilities, people are provided with better access to cultural institutions at all levels of society with the aim of promoting confidence in cultural facilities and self-confidence amongst children, students, teenagers, adults and the elderly.[71]

The ability of culture to provide a platform for expression that can lead to social change is evident in the development of educational programmes in cultural institutions and this can make a positive impact on formal and informal education systems in the future. The benefits for participants are largely learning outcomes that may include an increase in knowledge and understanding, the acquisition of skills, a change in attitudes and values, enjoyment, inspiration, creativity, activity, personal behavior and progression. The positioning of cultural parameters within urban planning and the establishment of regulations that govern the aesthetics of public facilities and collective properties can lead to innovation. This would include plans for micro units in urban areas through visibility studies, thus ensuring innovative cultural facilities in urban and rural areas. Innovative cultural policy brings many new elements to the city's cultural structure. Connecting cultural institutions at various levels across different sectors in the town in turn results in a more stable level of innovation. "By adapting new ideas, municipal staff would be prompted to begin considering the new cultural guidelines. Undoubtedly, the active approach elicits a strong argument for supporting creative activities within cities."[72] It is also important that a process of cultural decentralization is begun in most cities, as the significance of strategic planning in cultural development has been recognized as an innovative urban policy instrument, with priorities encompassing facility maintenance, digitalization, various components of the urban community, a variety of cultural events, and support for the development of cultural industries (especially publishing).

"Our future is not only globally intertwined, but increasingly urban. In the next 20 years, Africa and Asia will see by far the fastest growth in urban settlements."[73] Moreover, as the world's urban population grows, the interdependence that exists between town and countryside will become even more apparent. The future city constantly inspires and nurtures creativity and innovation while cultivating knowledge, the appreciation of heritage and memory. This city will also strive for excellence and creativity in its cultural programmes, giving full recognition to the role of its artists. It will place a high value on education, at all levels and for all ages, endowing its children and adults with the skills, knowledge and attributes they require to succeed. "Culture is at once an expression of the human spirit, a means of bringing people together across divides and a powerful factor in the city's economic and social life and development. The growing role of cultural institutions as contributors to development in local areas has enormously enriched their missions and is driving them to assume new responsibilities and adopt fresh management rules which may be described as follows:

- In addition to their recognized role in attracting cultural tourism, cultural institution must strive to satisfy the needs of local audiences and communities in terms of the development of social capital.

- By assuming such responsibilities, museums and local governments become close partners, jointly defining new objectives and weaving new business models."[74]

International researchers on art, public culture, creative education and urbanism explain the role of cultural institutions in contemporary society.

The integration of art academies within university structures and the new-found centrality of creative economic discourses have generated a renewal of interest in art education on the part of policy and planning elites, and a renewal of critical debate among educators themselves.[75]

There has also been a marked increase in the visibility and the volume of educational activity by cultural institutions such as museums, concert halls, theatres, arts centres, galleries, and arts festivals. They constitute one part of a diverse "informal" educational sector where a wide range of different educational models are being utilized and contribute to the development of creative industries.

Notes

29 Charles Landry, *The Fragile City* (Gloucestershire: Comedia Publisher, 2014), 5. https://charleslandry.com/panel/wp-content/themes/twentyeleven/books/Fragile-City.pdf
30 Ibid.
31 Ibid.
32 Ibid.
33 Ibid.
34 Charles Landry, *Psychology & the City: The Hidden Dimension* (Gloucestershire: Comedia Publisher, 2017), 4. https://charleslandry.com/panel/wp-content/themes/twentyeleven/books/Psychology-and-the%20City.pdf
35 Ibid.
36 Ibid.
37 Charles Landry, *The Digitized City: Influence & Impact* (Gloucestershire: Comedia Publisher, 2016), 4. https://charleslandry.com/panel/wp-content/themes/twentyeleven/books/Digitized-City.pdf
38 Ibid.
39 Ibid.
40 Ibid.
41 Richard Florida is an American urban studies theorist focusing on social and economic theory. Florida is best known for his concept of the creative class and its implications for urban regeneration. This idea was expressed in Florida's most famous book *The Rise of the Creative Class* (New York: Basic Books, 2002).
42 Ibid.
43 Charles Landry is an author, speaker and international adviser on the future of cities best known for popularizing the Creative City concept. His book *The Creative City: A Toolkit for Urban Innovators* became a movement to rethink the planning, development and management of cities.
44 Charles Landry, *The Civic City in a Nomadic World* (Rotterdam: Nai010 Publishers, 2017), 9.
45 Ibid.
46 Ibid.
47 Jordi marti Grau and Charles Giner Camprubi, "If the Agenda 21 for Culture is the answer, what was the question?", 44–54. Biljana Mickov and James Doyle, "Introduction," in *Sustaining Cultural Development, Unified Systems and New Governance in Cultural Life*, ed. J. E. Doyle and B. Mickov (London: Routledge publishing, 2013).

48 Ibid.
49 Ibid.
50 Ibid.
51 Ibid.
52 Decidim Barcelona, accessed April 5, 2020, https://www.decidim.barcelona/
53 John Holden, "How We Value Arts and Culture," in *Sustaining Cultural Development, Unified Systems and New Governance in Cultural Life*, ed. James Doyle and Biljana Mickov (London: Routledge Publishing, 2013), 17–29.
54 Ibid.
55 John Holden, *The Future of the City* (Chicago: University of Chicago, 2011), 17–29.
56 Ibid.
57 Ibid.
58 Ibid.
59 Ibid.
60 Holden, "How We Value Arts and Culture".
61 Ibid.
62 Ibid.
63 Ibid.
64 Ibid.
65 Edward Glaeser, *Triumph of the City* (New York: Penguin Press, 2011), Intrudaction 7.
66 Art Forum, *Innovation and Creativity in Europe*, Brussels, 2009. Available at: www.encatc.com, http://www.cityfutures2009.com/PDF/89_M_Kostres_Atanackovic_Jelicic.pdf
67 Ibid.
68 Holden, "How We Value Arts and Culture".
69 Holden, "How We Value Arts and Culture".
70 UCLG, "Agenda 21 for Culture."
71 Ibid.
72 Ibid.
73 Ibid.
74 Ibid.
75 Ibid.

3

CULTURE, INNOVATION, AND DEVELOPMENT

Cities and regions should, through a process of exchange, evaluate projects with partners in order to develop new innovative models. The networks that cities and regions create have to be made sustainable in the long term through the implementation of specific action plans. This can be sustained with the development of strategic partnerships and participation at national and international levels.[76] A partnership strategy have to be set up for projects following active policies to reach a level of stability. To achieve new ideas in cultural development, partnership and network are key elements and each project must, above all, have an innovative context. This could become a platform through the cooperation of working groups, projects, activities, and events. We would like to emphasize that specific action plans in the following areas would be very useful for cities: the development of educational programs (to develop art education practice) in a culture of partnership; the development of projects relating to urban design (developing feasibility studies for micro-parts); and the development of cultural industries' projects (entrepreneurship in culture). Creativity and innovation are the core of capability in culture. Traditional models are no longer feasible. In any case, innovation is an important part of cultural policy in the contemporary, post-industrial world that has been seriously impacted by changes in global culture, which now see top positions being given to creative industry innovators and representatives.

Cultural Policy Analysis

We think that culture has to be a part of public policies in every city. The local horizontal level needs to be developed even more than the vertical (centralized) level, which is an old model and no longer sustainable. The traditional governance

DOI: 10.4324/9781003336648-3

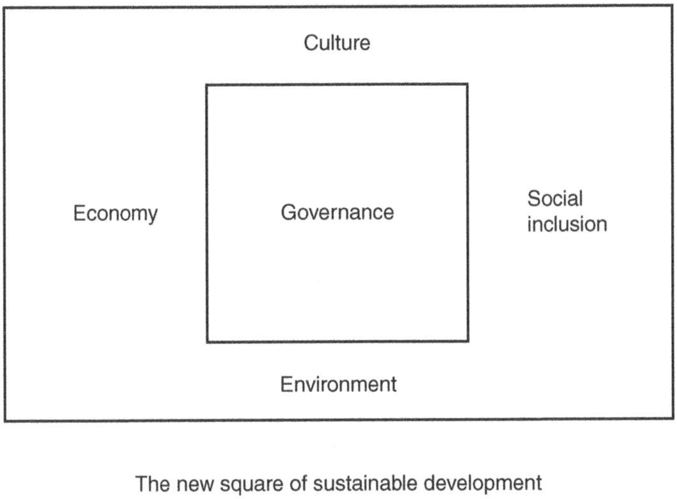

FIGURE 1 *Elements that Make up the Sustainable Development of Society.*
Source: Jordi Pascual, "Cultural Policies, Human Development and Institutional Innovation: or Why We Need Agenda 21 for Culture", in *Sustaining Cultural Development: Unified Systems and New Governance in Cultural Life*, ed. James Doyle and Biljana Mickov (London: Routledge Publishing, 2013), 58.

of the cultural sector needs to adopt a new, more horizontal approach that links cultural workers at different levels in different sectors and different locations. Here is the square of sustainability:[77]

The important cultural policy is:

- The innovative political response to culture, which requires changes in the way that cultural funders and cultural organizations conduct their business.
  The old model of funded, or high, culture could be marginalized as the elite preoccupation of a small minority, commercial culture could be dismissed as mere entertainment, and home-made culture could be patronized as being merely amateur. However, when they are placed together, they become "the second ecosystem of humankind."[78] All those elements are interconnected – then we can start to appreciate the wider value of culture in and for society. Culture should be less focused on serving the professional needs of the artistic community in order to recognize the growing needs of the wider community and how these could be explored through cultural programming.

Local governments disseminate models of financing through:

- The allocation of grants and subsidies but also the provision of practical support, advice, discussion, and cooperation between institutions as well as individuals in various forms.

- It is evident that public participation has an important influence on the cultural institution's role as mediator.
- Digitalization of not only the arts administration but also the presentation of arts in museums, art organizations, etc.
- Building the city as a laboratory, knowledge becomes the new "fuel" for regional development. It is "SMART" (Specific, Measurable, Achievable, Realistic, Time- based, Tech and Digital, Open City).
- To implement tolerance, dynamic development, interaction, pragmatism in creativity, business, and culture is of interest to all of us. Creativity is our response to systems that are changing very fast because of new technology.
- Developing intellectual property rights that have important economic value. *Creativity is the core of capability in culture.* Traditional models are no longer feasible.
- Creativity in any guise is an important part of innovative cultural policy in the contemporary, post-industrial world which has been seriously impacted by changes in global culture, and which now sees top positions being given to creative industry innovators and representatives.

> To be sustainable, an economy has to give thought to the values on which it is based, and take into account the resources, cultural and otherwise, of the surrounding environment. Economies have the greatest legitimacy and dynamism when they are adapted to local resources.[79]
>
> Cultural activities play an important role in comprehensive and sustainable economic development. They allow the renewal and creation of economic activities, boost entrepreneurship and employability, make up an important part of the attractiveness of places, and contribute to the development of tourism. A sustainable use of cultural resources is respectful of core values and should contribute equally to cultural and economic development. Economic models that aim to be sensitive to culture should consider implementing practices that rely on collaboration, cooperatives, trading, and donations. Given the direct positive effects generated by cultural activities, a sustainable cultural ecosystem must reinvest resources into local culture. While doing so, close attention should be paid to the cultural initiatives that are the weakest and have the lowest profile. Examples include artistic education centres, grassroots organizations, minority expressions of identity, and cultural mediation.[80]

Action Plan:

1. Local economic development strategies take the cultural economy into account and work with its participants to ensure that it is a key economic sector of the city or region.
2. Contributions by the public, civic, and private cultural sectors to the local economy, including their direct and indirect impact on the creation of wealth and employment, are analyzed regularly.

3. Appropriate contractual and salary conditions for people working in the cultural sector, as well as the recognition of author's rights and neighboring rights, are guaranteed by law.
4. There is information and training on author's rights, shared production models and new distribution systems.
5. Employability programs cover cultural knowledge and skills.
6. There are a variety of financing mechanisms for non-profit cultural projects, such as microcredits, venture capital, and sponsorship programs.
7. The local government promotes public or mixed economic programs that increase donations to, or volunteering for, cultural projects.
8. There are partnerships between people active in the cultural sector and businesses, such as through residencies or other systems of innovation and knowledge transfers.
9. The value in maintaining traditional local trades and crafts (including the development of innovation, as required) is recognized.
10. The local tourism model is sustainable, balanced across the region, connected to the local communities and interactive with the cultural ecosystems.
11. Corporate social responsibility programs explicitly include projects in the area of culture and engage with the cultural values of the population and local culture.
12. Local business organizations, such as the chamber of commerce, have specific cultural policies and programs.

Networking and Innovation

> Organizations recognize that they have to invest in people, helping them stay alert and current, understanding new trends and new developments. For the creative city this is paramount: placing people in the right position and in a progressive environment offers greater opportunity for creativity and innovation. Formal and informal networks are key to the creative impetus; hearing, listening and learning from others forms new ideas in ourselves. The biggest challenge of networking has always been time; however, the growth in professions and social networks offers the creative city the tools to make networks successful. These proactive connections are particularly suited to the close confines of city living, offering as they do the opportunity to make ideas real by being able to act on them and connect immediately.[81]

Innovation carries with it the notion of intent—an intent to improve upon something else, to create something new.

> It gives everyone the impetus to consider the potential to make a better life. The creative is about a differential in thinking processes: Being creative is seeing the same thing as everybody else but thinking of something different. This is creativity: to take existing actions, objects and concepts and combine them in different ways for new purposes; the action of combining previously uncombinable

> elements. Creativity let loose in the city has the power to generate new ideas and solutions to everyday problems and challenges. Creativity translates talent and vision into an external reality that is driven by a new dynamic. Creativity is now, more than ever, part of the fabric of our existence and takes place unavoidably inside our own personal, social and cultural boundaries.[82]
>
> The innovation of people and professionals in culture, education and business sectors of a certain society are capable of making a quick change and responding to new challenges. Technology is developing extremely fast and it must be a tool for creative people. We have to use it for implementations of new ideas. The networks are virtual and at the same time material. The networks are the platform for innovation.[83]

The networks are the base for new systems of the future. There are many networks of cities, entrepreneurs, artist, culture works, etc. Therefore, if we want to make a change and build our region or city, we have to make a strong balance between networks, local strategic plans, and implementation. In that case, the people who work in regional and local governments have to have a big role in the innovative change of society. Still, in many countries culture and innovation are not a priority and they are not considered a really powerful tool. However, this position of culture is slowly changing and step by step culture is becoming an equal part of state systems.

> Direct networks among governments on a horizontal level (position of the local governments), institutions and education systems as well as NGOs can overrun a lot of gaps in culture and the creativity sector and bring connectivity with other sectors such as business, health and education. The cultural sector has to be brought from the outskirts to the center of societal development.[84]

The "bottom-up" strategy that cities try to implement in their environments shows a wide development of the cultural sector as well as networking with no governmental organizations.[85] That is a key strategy for sustaining development in the local-city environment. One of the cities in Europe that adopts this strategy is the city of Eindhoven, a medium-sized town with a constant innovative development process. However, if we look at the "city of Barcelona, we will see the systematic local development of culture based on a strategic plan for culture."[86] They have a systematic management approach for cultural development.

> We would like to point out that local development does not mean the loss of input by the state government. It only means that cultural development is equable. The governments that want to maintain sustainability have to be related to economy, social inclusion, culture and the environment. It is a basic approach that has to have progressive development. Every city has to find the best way to change and face new challenges. The answer to that is to "be extremely innovative and try to implement your ideas".

A strategic plan for culture, which has to be evaluated after a few years with an analysis of results, is becoming increasingly important. It is also important that a regional government has strategic plans for the cities in the region in relation to the cultural sector. Regional-city context is key for development at state level.[87]

Strategic plans for culture (urban plans, cultural managers) in the city are important for the development of creativity. It is crucial for a city to have well connected cultural institutions with a local cultural department, since those cultural institutions, art organizations, and galleries present the ecosystem of the city. In this field, we will include libraries as well.

> Cultural institutions such as galleries (public and private), museums, art organizations and creative centres play a crucial role in the cultural ecosystem and have to be connected from a local level. Again, that brings us back to the network of cultural institutions at the local-city and regional level. Exchange of experience among institutions, such as a presentation of activities, better approach to the public, digital forms of presentation, and educational processes for professionals and visitors, are elements of basic materials necessary for the development of creativity. Investments in research for conferences and debates in governmental departments for culture that have support the sector with a clear definition of implementation and formatting new models of art and culture to institutions in the city is crucial. The aim is to place culture at the heart of the development of society.[88]

Innovation will develop if we build systems that can include people who develop their creative skills. Creative people are present everywhere: in art, business, and architecture, small and big companies. Innovative ideas are an original value for business, art, and culture. Also, new, innovative ideas are a response to the fast-changing times we are living in at the moment. Change is actually an essential ingredient for any innovative project. But we need to have the ability to be agile and make changes quickly and it is important to listen to your own feelings too, and on this basis, make decisions regarding which way to go. In that sense, the competition becomes stronger but the quality of innovation is much better.

> An important issue is also how people become happier in creative processes. Citizens have a new opportunity for changes and success. We make a good system for creative and innovative development, including new models of institutions such as creative centres or creative quarters in the city and we are heading towards progress and development of innovation and creativity. This is extremely good for citizens. Social inclusion in these processes is important and we have to set up good cultural management to attract people to be active participants. It is not enough to make a simple analysis of potential visitors, but to point out the importance of marketing in the public sector.[89]

To attract citizens to cultural events, we have to make a good program and we have to feel what people like and listen to their needs. Therefore, visitors are significant and the processes of involving them in cultural activities need to have a systematic approach. We have to find a way to attract them, as well as feel their needs. We cannot be passive viewers; instead we have to be innovative in order to include more people in cultural activities. It does not matter if it is a museum, theatre, or a city library.

> Interesting programmes, educational programmes and attractive information are elements that can get more visitors involved. Mutual trust between cultural professionals and citizens has to be built in order to serve and feel what the citizens expect from us.[90]

It is important to understand what kind of feelings they have and how to make them interested in being a part of artistic expression. That means not only entertainment, but also a learning process and innovative development (for professionals and citizens).

> The right and clear information is the main tool necessary to get people informed about the happenings in the cultural field in their city. If we look at that task from a managerial position, it is clear that a complete digitalization of the sector can make information accessible. In order to attract citizens to cultural activities through institutions and open space artistic projects, we have to provide good information (marketing). There are so many different kinds of exhibitions, festivals, theatre shows needy of the right audience. We believe that it is crucial to make a good balance between cultural projects and citizens' interest.[91]

In the words of Esteve Caramés:

> Contemporary information and communication technologies can play an important role in the formation of a broad audience for cultural projects, for which the formation of a large audience is no longer the only priority. The promotion and encouragement of participation in culture are now considered the common, higher goal of cultural projects. This means that culture project has to develop new services to achieve highest possible degree of availability. The services designed to promote unique cultural events taking place in cultural facilities, and opening clubs or custom spaces for the activities associated with the programme, as well as providing greater support for open events and leisure activities.[92]
>
> Citizens no longer go to the public theatre or concert halls regularly to listen to philharmonic orchestras, nor to museums. Life has become faster on every level and in every sector. The right kind of information to the right kind of people is a very important way of increasing audience numbers and

> getting more funding. Cities have to make a brand of their cultural offerings (production or service) and keep improving them. A good story that connects with citizens needs emotions combined with quality service and will attract more visitors. This is the process of changing cultural behaviour.[93]

We have to work for the mutual benefit of developing innovation for citizens and building the city through culture.

> Cultural policy has to be part of the public policy. Culture is the fourth pillar of sustainable development.[94,95] Therefore, culture must be implemented in all public policies. We believe that the development of relationships between citizens and cultural activities is essential. A good relationship starts and continues through different stages of growth (step by step) of the relationship, to higher levels of trust. Mobility through cities is very often a contemporary process. Economic and political integration makes a sustainable future with diversity. We have to be aware that national cultural institutions that are mostly recognized in the city focus themselves on a broader public than the elitist, local ones. Cultural institutions and their management are engaged in their own mission, cultural impact and social position. All mobility makes the city more of a creative space for people.[96]

"In each city, the key players must be the strongest cultural institutions, those with a model of cultural infrastructure, institutions that can inspire and make a brand. The classical, 'local' institutions belonging to the dominant culture"[97] have to redefine their sense of tradition. Many innovative strategies come from smaller cultural organizations as a challenge and opportunity to grow, increase their impact and make new alliances and partnerships. Those small cultural organizations have a big influence on classical national institutions as well. It is very obvious that many creative centres are becoming more relevant in models of management and artistic performances than classical institutions and are used as an innovative training point for classical cultural institutions.

> Artistic projects run by creative organizations and creative people who are changing the city environment, including people from different communities of the city, are important. In these projects, there are three significant issues. One is a change of living space; the second is the development of creativity and the third one is artistic work. Urban art projects have involved people and artists to renovate their living space. This cultural activity is clearly dealing with aesthetics and creativity. It is about getting together to play with scattered ideas. The streets have become an "art centre" and a part of a public service project. It is evident that art is going out of buildings in order to serve the citizens and at the same time giving opportunity to artists to use open spaces for their artistic work.[98]

Cultural projects need to be positioned in the city, but also in the region.

> The connectivity between city and Regional cultural projects is important as well. It is a way of developing creativity through art and culture in the city and region surroundings. It is important to build a cultural structure with an objective to support artistic creation in the region in order to support cultural development. Professionals have to connect artistic creation in the region and support artistic creative processes among artists, inhabitants and the environment. Such projects are very often seen in France but also in other parts of Europe.[99]

Artistic projects based and made in the region have attempted to give an answer to problems such as the integration of art regarding heritage, transformation of the landscape, environment, city/countryside connectivity, etc.

> This role of connectivity between contemporary artistic creation and the landscape/environment makes it possible to initiate new steps of artistic creation in the region. Urban art projects are also run by cultural organizations with the aim to support involving the inhabitants in artistic creation. It is the development of synergies between the actors and the emergence of new projects and cultural structures.[100] Creative centres have a mission to build and develop creative industries. Those centres are prepared to be places for new research projects in arts and culture. Most creative spaces are open to develop the creative industries sector and bring new job opportunities.[101]

The term "creative industries" describes businesses with creativity at their heart—for example, design, music, publishing, architecture, film and video, crafts, visual arts, fashion, media, advertising, literature, and the performing arts.

> The use of empty space for creative industries is more than just a trend for the cities. Indeed, this is a way to connect and make creative economy through research and practice of creation. The cities and regions that have understood the power of creative industries for their economy and job potential have to put the development of cultural and creative economy as an essential pillar of development. Those cities try to develop creative space and locations. Also, they have become known as cultural places.[102]

These elements are essential in developing important processes for the creative industry:

> A working space for artists, creative people and innovative management in a creative quarter make all processes successful. It involves culture, urban development and economy, but also education. With creative quarters, the concept of urban development is evident and integrative.[103]

Again, the local and regional governments are important parts, in addition to cultural offices, business and planning:

> A visible urban space is a space where creative urban work is connected with the local environment in which creative industries are an integral part of creative urban areas of cities. Usually, the urban plans in larger cities in Europe change and make creative quarters in empty spaces and buildings (former factories) in order to regenerate the city. This is the quarter in the city that is undergoing a process of change. Urban regeneration is also part of the work of cultural policymakers in local and regional governments who support and make creativity visible in different parts of the city together with urban planners.[104]

Creative businesses move more quickly to international markets than many other forms and often use the Internet to do so. Digitalization is important because of online services. The creative industries have the potential to regenerate economies and create jobs and wealth as well as to develop creative work for people. Cultural industries are defined by UNESCO as "industries that combine the creation, production and commercialization of contents which are intangible and cultural in nature; these contents are typically protected by copyright, and they can take the form of a good or a service."[105] The creative industries are at the crossroads of the arts, culture, business and technology. All these activities are intensive in creative skills and can generate income through trade and intellectual property rights. UNCTAD (the United Nations Conference on Trade and Development) has introduced the topic of the "creative economy" in the world's economic and development agenda. The creative economy is an emerging concept dealing with the interface between creativity, culture, economics and technology in a contemporary world dominated by images, sounds, texts and symbols. The Global Alliance promotes cultural diversity by strengthening the capacity of cultural industries to produce and distribute goods and services and help them gain access to national and international markets.[106]

It is important to make a balance between horizontal and vertical governmental approaches if we are talking about creative industries.

> The creative industries have to be understood in a sense of how we see the concept. Understanding creative industries at the level of individual cultural products or services allows for a more flexible approach to creative industries. Cities, regions and countries have to define their public policy on creative industries. The economic contribution of the creative industries is simply too large to be ignored. Public support to creative industries must be based on different principles and goals than support to traditional arts, cultural heritage and libraries. In order to be creative, cities, regions and countries shall require defining cultural policy on creative industries and specific measures in terms of public support in the production of particular products or services.

> Without considerable financial, industrial, and technological resources the main economic resource is human capital, creativity, innovation. Therefore, development of creative industries has to include as many people as possible from the world of art, particularly the nongovernmental cultural sector.[107]

We have to focus on developing those creative products and services that represent a market and correspond to the specific features of the environment and to the resources available to you. In doing so, do not neglect digital technologies. We have to listen to what the artists and everyone involved in culture in your environment have to say about creativity.

> The attitude is that we cannot expect economic regeneration without the development of creative industries, since in the present world there is no economic progress without the development of technology. The creative industries are a component of technological development and products of the creative industries are delivered to the consumers through technological instruments. The specific high value products or services that are attractive to consumers have to be defined and creative people have to be included. They need to be in a position to deliver such products and services. Another important matter is that we cannot develop creative industries without new technologies.[108]

We are supporting a creative economy of artists, performers, and filmmakers that contribute to a more sustainable society. The cities of today are dynamic, rapidly evolving entities of change, placing culture in the position to be one of the pillars of development. The future development of the city based on urban development, culture and planning will be clear, ensuring sustainable development of the city.[109]

In the cities of the future, ideas are the basic materials for developing creativity and for the future. If any city needs to keep the creative people, they need to work on it and strategically built the creative capacity for the city.

> The development of technology and support for creative ideas makes a city attractive to people. In this condition, an innovative urban environment can develop. Most cities have to become a prominent centre of different activities, such as the economy, culture and politics. At the same time, the relations between urban and rural realms remain symbiotic and balanced.[110]

Contemporary urban landscapes reflect the ever-increasing pace of changes, driven by place-specific conditions on the one hand, and the homogenizing influences of globalization on the other. Cities, their authorities, professionals, cultural managers, and citizens try to wrestle with the situation within economic, social, cultural, and environmental transformations. New city-images, thus, are often characterized by a lack of coherence and identity and need to be restructured in order to meet the real needs of the local communities.

Therefore, the question of the mechanisms of how different social, economic, historical, cultural, and physical conditions coincide in the formation of space and/or its transformation is of great importance for urban researchers, cultural researchers, practitioners, and policy makers.

> Recognize that a city is in competition—especially in attracting sustainable, wealth-generating companies, creativity and enterprising individuals. Setting and managing a strategy to make a city attractive, creative, and innovative, user-friendly and distinctive is crucial. Work together across sectors and professions—successful economic development, and linking disadvantaged people to the new opportunities it creates, need long-term commitment and genuine collaboration between many agencies and interests. Give power and resources to city authorities—since city-regions compete; it is at this level that strategic control needs to be exercised.[111]

The local authorities have to clearly accept responsibility for both urban regeneration and the future development of their metropolitan areas. They also have access to resources to match their responsibilities.

> Spread the benefits of regeneration and economic development throughout the community—people in all parts of the metropolitan area need to feel that they benefit from the development of the city. Value the role of culture in regeneration—cultural projects can help change the image of an area, give local people access to a wider range of opportunities, generate local pride and build social cohesion. The aim is to highlight the need to plan and design places that can accommodate and adopt changes. Modern cities have a big advantage in mixing different cultures. Diverse teams of people offer new skills to creativity, which in combination might produce new innovation. Diverse cities are better equipped than homogeneous ones for the global economy and they adapt better to change.[112]

In Germany, for example, the way of thinking is that success at the level of local and regional economics will also be influenced by creators to the cities.[113]

The cities need to be open and diverse in order to attract creative people. The local governments have to provide a positive atmosphere and good environment for creators and citizens. Franco Bianchini, in his research into the Intercultural City, pointed out the Diversity Advantage:

> In North America, for example, diversity has been regarded a source of progress, opportunity and advantage, since the private sector is a leading sector in these countries. It is important to support ideas for intercultural approach as a way of providing power for towns and cities in general. We have to look at advantages of intercultural societies and not only cultural but social, economic and political ones.[114]

> The cities with such a concept will prosper and advance as well as confirm their position locally and globally. Today, the cities are most likely to have a more urban image. They provide a more international atmosphere with a frame that provides more business, culture and creative perspectives. A cosmopolitan city is a model of a city where there is a constant dialogue. In these cities, one of the important functions is local governing and managing. The city have to be built by a town planner and cultural managers based on a good policy.[115]

The city has to develop street design, security, tolerance, and urban space management. This is a city whose population has a wide variety of cultural attitudes.

> The citizens of that kind of city has to be part of the process of city making. This city is a place of their history, emotions and memory. The different skills and competencies for the city are given by multiculturalism which gives positive processes. We call these cultural competencies. That city has new ideas under an intercultural approach and needs to be made on the streets. The different cultures mostly have to engage cultural space. The innovation of those cities goes to the creativity and its model of diverse policy. The significant element of development is the openness of a society. The cross-cultural economic, social, cultural and civic networks are important in order to establish culturally mixed business associations, social clubs, political parties and movements and make a positive cultural representation.[116]

The openness of public space is a democratic resource.

> It means open access to facilities such as libraries and cultural institutions in the city center and cultural participation in public space. Cities have to encourage the flow of ideas, knowledge, resources and people beyond professional, institutional and cultural innovation. Those cities have a much better position in this ever-changing world. The modern economy seeks open societies in the city and those cities have a greater advantage than the less open ones.[117]

The cities that understand all these elements can act through adaptation of innovation and build a creative space for citizens.

> Networking with other cities based on partner cooperation in cultural policy should include a clear definition of one's own cultural requirements while looking for the common denominators of cultural legacy with other professionals, with the aim of improved cooperation. The cities through exchange, evaluate projects with partners in order to develop new models. The networks

that cities are creating have to be made sustainable in the long term through the implementation of specific action plans for developing creativity.[118]

The development of projects depends on a number of factors such as active support, engagement, mobility and so on; however, it can also be sustained with the development of strategic partnerships and participation at national and international levels. With all this, the cities can make a good base for the developing creativity in the urban space. What is important is that we make the city a laboratory for the citizens.[119]

Building Creative Space, a New Way of Thinking, New Ideas...

"Making creative and innovative space is a necessity. Fast changes in the system, the informational system, education and life makes us creative. Namely, the answer to acceleration is creativity and innovation."[120] Sustainable development, when it comes to the cultural sector, is practically the creation of a system, a plan that enables a constant and continuous development of the cultural sector. When we say sustainability in culture, it means that every city or region and country needs to have a certain cultural policy that is implemented in practice. In addition, every environment—the city—needs to have a strategic plan that positions the culture in the center and relates it closely to the economy. Such a strategic plan includes cultural participation in urban planning, digitalization, involvement of contemporary management in culture, etc.

Each environment has to improve the cultural sector through a plan and in a balanced way. Time itself simply forces us to make such movements. That is sustainability, and, of course, we do it not only for art and culture, but for society as well. Of course, by culture, social sustainability is achieved too. They are mutually developmentally complemented and we think this is excellent. Culture is the fourth pillar of the sustainable development of a society besides economy, social inclusion, local authorities, and the environment. We definitely live in times that make us intensify the participation in culture for citizens as well and by doing so we intensify the creativity that is increasingly dominant in the lives of all of us, all being conditioned by the development of technology.

> We all need innovation, both the professionals in culture and citizens. Innovation is a necessity of contemporaries. Citizen participation is important on several levels; cultural institutions are no longer of the close type we are used to. They are open and active institutions that give a special contribution to human development. First of all, the educational character is very dominant, and in stepping out of the established systems of work, citizen participation is important.[121]

The rapid development of technology makes us creative because systems change quickly. An individual, creative idea has its economic value. Networks are one of the crucial elements and the new elite will be composed of the people who are in the networks and the ones who are the consumers.

> Research in culture is important, but the processes that respond to the given moment must be contemporary research processes. Research opens the development of the new models of functioning for the managers of culture institutions, curators, programme editors, etc. The exchange of ideas leads to developing new models, thus, the professionals in the cultural sector and the citizens themselves who take part in the process can prosper.[122]
>
> Creative industries are an economic resource and they should be seen as such. Creative industries are a substitute for industry, they inherently have an economic potential, and in every environment, they exist through publishing, museum work, film, design, new media, etc. The bottom line is that their potential is recognized through public policy.[123]

Contemporary production exists in more or less all environments; creative ideas enable us to achieve traditional products that have a more contemporary form.

> For example, the digitalization of a classical traditional museum gives a completely new insight into the cultural heritage and production. If we observe the people in the culture sector, their way of thinking and their mindset and knowledge, what definitely lacks is a more contemporary approach, the exchange of ideas in the European context, research projects, a balanced relationship between politics and the professionals in the cultural sector.[124]

Moving culture from the outskirts toward the center is more than important. Of course, it could all develop more quickly, but we think that even the small steps mean a lot considering that, here, the culture sector hasn't been supported in the last ten years.

> The Louvre Museum in Paris implements modern art in its programme, combining modern art with the classical. Particularly, they included a "dance" show in the Museum programme, all for better public access. This exists in bigger museums in Europe. For example, the Prado Museum in Madrid works a lot on management and they are successful.[125]

To clarify: what is significant is a concept of cultural policy that clearly shows a vertical connection between different experiences against a plan for cultural development that actually strengthens a horizontal cultural management, through cultural policies of regions and cities, as well as the relationships between urbanization and new design in raising the standard and boosting development, new thought, the attitude of local authorities toward cultural institutions, the significance of networking and partner cooperation, as well as development in the field of creative industries and evaluating projects in culture.[126]

Modern times and this decade will certainly be a time of networking, agendas, and platforms that consider the development and research in culture.

> This is the space where information is turned into knowledge and knowledge into innovations—the laboratories of the present moment. Keeping these contacts and networks alive is difficult and it requires permanent communication, but it also represents positive work in modern times as well as the possibility of development based on the experience of other environments.[127]
>
> That is why the platforms, regional and city networks become conceptual, programmatic and organizational for the new management of the cultural sector. Managing these three elements in the cultural sector brings a certain complexity. We still really need the space for research and laboratories. Otherwise, we cannot expect artistic creation to sustain innovation and standard, and the balanced development of the society.[128]

Intersectoral cooperation is the essence; connecting sectors gives a new quality, and nothing is separate. For example, the sector of urbanism of a city has to work closely with the cultural sector. These two sectors are naturally connected. The same goes for the university and the institutions of a city, environmental protection and museums—by setting up exhibitions about environmental protection in museums, we contribute to "lobbying" for projects in this area, new technologies and cultural institutions, web portals and the media. The right to culture influences human development and interculturality as an integral part of democratic societies. Through citizen participation in the cultural sector, the democratization of a society is increased. Culture is a segment that creates conditions for peace and contributes to essential democratization.

Professor John Holden, one of the leading experts and a guest professor at the University of London, formerly the manager of DEMOS, made a critical statement about cultural policy at a lecture in Novi Sad: "Culture policy is a closed conversation among expert. What culture needs is a democratic mandate by the public…"[129] The civilian part of a society can have the initial force; that is, it can influence local authorities to set a trend for art and culture to be a service for citizens, something that is there for them. Cultural policy is formed in the interest of the citizens; it is not restrained to the circle of professionals. A greater participation of citizens in this project is important—a democratization. Curators have been making exhibitions in museums for themselves; but it is simply no longer the case, and, in addition, the professional taste they have to get more involved and be closer to the audience. We vote for the citizens.

Cities have to make certain plans for digitalization systems of their cultural institutions.

> A system with one unique website of the city that will connect all cultural institutions, organizations and cultural activities is more than enough and an excellent move toward digitalization. With this system, we are getting better

> services for citizens and professionals. The digital frame of culture is at the contemporary time the "material world." If we proceed with just the simple digitalization of each cultural institution individually, it will mean nothing unless there is a system of network connectivity at the city level. The best example is the City Council of Barcelona and their website Barcelona Culture.[130]

The website clearly shows information on the city of Barcelona's culture digitalized, including: art, architecture and design, performing arts, science, music, festivals and traditions, museums and heritage, literature and libraries, cinema and audio-visual experiences. In one word, it is the city and its culture.

What we achieve with this:

- Contemporary presentation of culture facilities
- Better access to the cultural offer
- Good access for citizens and professionals
- Network of culture that is a good presentation for international access

For example,

> the Bologna City Council has been creating a framework that can collect and share 3D models and all the useful knowledge of the city. This is an excellent platform of knowledge and memory of the city. It is dedicated to the area of the city and, with geo and time-referenced data, would handle the already existing historical, archaeological, artistic and architectural 3D models, making them available to the community for a new cross platform.[131]

This digitalization can lead to the production and distribution of open-source platforms/software, as well as the creation of a virtual environment that can share and reuse knowledge and resources. It is a tool for the development of the cultural sector. This can be an excellent digital form that takes full advantage of the resources available and made available in the future. A certain number of files with geographical, historical and contemporary data on the city have to be created. The Virtual Museum Transnational Network is a funded network of excellence that aims to provide the heritage sector with the tools and support to develop virtual museums that are both educational and long-lasting.[132] The virtual world is very material. The purpose of such a portal would be to collect and share 3D models and useful background knowledge necessary for their creation. The educational section of the portal, which will be opened to national and international users, can host thematic sectors, with PDF files and videos, where participants can discuss specific issues with other members. This example can be a good model for any city. Of course, every city has to find its way in the process of digitalization, connecting through websites and portals that can help access and build a new tool for culture development.

The need for creative space is increasing:

> On the one hand, it is a consequence of cultural institutions evolving, that is, coming out of the existing frames, while on the other hand, technological development, especially in Western Europe, has left numerous industrial buildings abandoned; therefore, creating the need for redefining space and its functions.

However, in my opinion, forming creative centers have to be seen only pragmatically in service of the citizens. Cultural centres should not be seen as merely social centres, which of course they are, but by no means are they only that. In our region, there is such a tendency which is, in my opinion, surpassed. It is smart to think that creative ideas provide a special contribution to the urban development of cities, but also provide a new product—the idea that represents a new human resource. Cultural and creative ideas are the fourth pillar of the sustainable development of a society.[133]

Positioning cultural parameters are important in terms of urban planning and adopting regulations on the aesthetics of public space and public property. Participation of cultural objects in an urban territory would be ensured. Building our urban environment is actually building a better world for all of us in Europe. Cultural participation has a special place. That is why we need a joined politics of urban development. A successful city is a city that has been positively planned to ensure that the infrastructure, services, and investments take their place in coherence with the urban design, and is creative for living in.

Cities have to develop business life and the design of spaces and public services for citizens. Much more creative, greener, and more compact cities in regions can influence better living conditions. In existing creative centers, the activities are as follows:

- education (workshops, seminars, etc.)
- promotion of existing products (for example, designer products)
- connecting creative companies in a city with economic and art organizations;
- publishing

Implementation is even more important and through combinations within creative industries, we receive new products that are innovative. "Creative centers" Apple, Google, IBM, etc., actually have a product.

> If we take into account that the whole industrial production has moved to Asian countries, Europe is making a new product with its creative ideas. Creative centres are places for making these creative industries, opening new workplaces. Creative work fulfills humans and enriches their lives. Creativity is a part of us that makes us human.[134]

Plans made at the levels of the city, the region and the republic represent a part of the politics which has to be implemented.

> The development of culture is a consensus between the political actors on the stage. The plan always has to be compliant with the present moment, thus it has to be composed by experts. The environments, by which we mean the cities and regions that do not manage culture or do not put it in a priority position, should be aware that they are not making good decisions for the environment they live in. Culture is no longer without powerful influence on development at a global level.[135]

What is it that we can do? It is crucial to realize that we have to change and accept the exchange of ideas and knowledge via networks. Networks are creating the new "elite" professionals in the cultural sector.

UNESCO[136] adopted the first declaration on cultural development (2001) and later a convention on cultural development (2005)—a convention was adopted that was later ratified in the countries of the European Union. Culture can no longer be seen as an unimportant goods/commodity and the public sector can create special mechanisms that will define its social value.

The context is now very different from the technological perspective, all the way to the development of new systems.

> Nowadays, if we take a look at the audio-visual sector, film and TV are no longer enough—there are new platforms such as Amazon, Google, Facebook, etc. The only way to implement the integration of the cultural sector with all social segments is through the re-education of people working in the cultural sector. They need to show inter-sector cooperation as a necessity and culture as an integral part of public policies. Creative processes are a necessity and they have to be directed towards creating a high-quality lifestyle that integrally contains culture.[137]
>
> The directions of connecting: the implementation of a plan for culture, the economy and urbanism has to connect with the cultural sector, support the development of the creative industries, prioritize the attitudes of the local, regional authorities, permanently educate professionals and citizens, and keep up with technological innovations. These elements are necessary for development. Cultural organizations, as well as the other sectors of society are in a transition to the new system of management, that is, more effective functioning. Now is the time to think about new ways of functioning and financial systems. The question arises—can we save and at the same time improve the quality of the offer in culture. How do we restructure the institutions of culture so that they can function better and what is the actual role of a manager in culture in terms of those structural changes? [138]
>
> Cultural institutions have to ask themselves several important questions. What is the value of the cultural institution and why and who for does the

> institution implement its activities? Does it need relationships with other sectors and what are the roles of technology and digitalization? One of the ways of functioning is to use corporative management, cooperation is important for the cultural sector, the competition and networking with other actors, public and private at the same time. The institutions of culture and organizations need to evaluate the structure, the mission, finances, activities within local communities and the audience as well as the relations with the authorities in order to define a management strategy which will take them into the future.[139]

Institutions run in such a way have to evaluate both their internal and their external vision.

> Many institutions nowadays conduct their activities of internal visions related to the artistic product. In museums, this internal vision has been made by the curators who are occupied with the collections and exhibitions in the museum. That option is no longer enough—organizations have to focus their actions and be real players in society for the benefit of the citizens and use the art as the essence of the changes in a society. By combining financial and intellectual resources, museums do not have to act alone in times of crisis. The strategy of internationalization has a positive influence on a museum's business model and it increases its own resources and makes them financially sustainable. The point is not to apologies for public cuts in culture, but to have a long-term vision.[140]

Museums are supposed to be brands with good-quality contents whether regarding cultural heritage or the modern concept. Business models, such as shops within museums, tourism, and a digital approach, have to be developed. All these measures can contribute to the stability of museum operations and, by doing so, build the institution itself. Interesting business models are being developed in the sector of culture. For example, electronic books are a part of new activities such as digitalization, electronic distribution, and thus they are becoming indisputably important players in the chain of the publishing sector. Creating new models of functioning is necessary; therefore, every institution and sector, with the help of experts, has to find new systems so that their work remains sustainable.

> International partner cooperation represents a very important segment of presentation and production of culture in an international context. Having in mind how active cultural diplomacy is nowadays, it plays a very important role in foreign and domestic affairs. What is local becomes international and global and, in that context, the presentation of culture of any state should be regarded as an integral and equally important part of the presentation of other cultures.[141]

An artist and his work have to be presented with several innovative managerial aspects on an international level, which is growing in popularity, in order to raise the standard of domestic culture and to improve the impact of positive presentation internationally.

> We would like to emphasize the importance of stronger presentation of culture in relation to international institutions and individuals who can affect the positioning of it. There is a need for active cooperation with modern networks, organizations, and individuals who take part in the development of culture, such as the Agenda 21 for Culture as well as with expert planners in culture who act within the European and world framework, with leading managers in culture and researchers.[142]

It is necessary to move the limitations of cultural activities with resources that are within our budget and create possibilities for additional funds. Maintaining such contacts and networks is difficult and demands permanent communication but definitely presents the positive work of today and a possibility for development based on experience of other territories. It is important to emphasize that there have been advances towards our goals throughout the region and the city but more intensive involvement is still necessary.

"Ways of representing our culture through innovative ideas of managers in culture are essential due to several segments:"[143]

1. Strategic position in relation to international factors
2. Raising the standard of presentation of our art and culture
3. Establishing and raising new standards of cultural relations at an international level
4. Strengthening relations between international factors and our culture/cultural diplomacy

More than ever, the phenomenon of today requires personal analysis, which can only be achieved through access to cultural activities, as well as their practice. The implementation is extremely important and we need to demonstrate it through concrete examples. If freedom and human development include culture, public institutions need to establish laws and policies and later programs and projects that will enable all citizens/residents and international partners to guarantee the possibility of achieving human development in general, the culture. That is why our cultural policy[144] has to be clear and the implementation create opportunities not provided by any other public sector. "Cultural policy is based on the so-called intrinsic values of cultural and artistic activities, which include concepts such as memory, creativity, critical knowledge, rituality, excellence, beauty, diversity (and maybe some others)."[145]

However, the question is how to represent culture in the process of creating public policy if it is built exclusively on the three pillars and none of which is culture?[146] Development of society rests on three pillars, namely, the pillar of the economy, the pillar of society and the pillar of ecology, whose role is to take care of the environment.

> As activists and agents in the field of culture, we need strong metaphors and images in order to raise awareness of the cultural dimension as an essence for human development, and at the same time to provide a solid role for cultural representation in public activities. It is a tough job for anyone to represent the interests of culture without building connections and good relationships with other areas of government.[147]

The technological revolution requires that we examine the mechanisms of production and accessibility of cultural goods and services. One important initiative is to promote the idea of organizing the management at the global level that would have greater competence in the field of public culture. European countries should simultaneously be a member of the "International Network of Cultural Policy," and the two cultural associations of civil society: the "International Network for Cultural Diversity" and "Coalition for Cultural Diversity." which prompted UNESCO to become the center of conversation in this area and open space for these activities.

Culture and Innovation in the Open City

Technology and innovation in settlements have always served the design and function of many processes that take place in them in a number of ways, and during the entire course of history there has always been a goal to improve and innovate—not just to change something momentarily, but also to mark places, events, time, and people. Professor Darko Reba noted that

> A great number of issues is linked to technology and innovation in the open spaces of cities; primarily, there is a desire for a specific identity that should be distinguished from the other, and then there is the durability of elements that need to be technologically designed so that the weather does not affect their appearance, as in numerous examples of elements and city segments that have lasted for thousands of years.[148]

Innovation and technologies are also becoming connected in the contemporary city landscape:

> Technology and innovation in artistic elements that occur in open urban spaces are certainly a topic not only related to decoration, especially today, when art cannot be created without technological innovations that enable reaching high achievements in various fields of culture. Perhaps the key topic related to technology and innovation in cities is certainly related to someone who makes decisions that something new will happen in open spaces.

> Sometimes it is the client, or an investor who can be one person or an institution, and sometimes it is the society, be it at the level of a small part of the city or the entire city, or a larger spatial unit such as the region, all the way to the entire country.[149]

It is common in developed societies to organize various programs, fairs, and events that should reflect the latest technologies and solutions available at a certain stage of development, thereby contributing to the wide distribution of new knowledge.

> Special topics are certainly technologies and innovations in the field of movement and traffic in cities; however, due to the volume of works and the orientation towards pedestrians as the most significant users of their open spaces, the study will not deal with this segment of technology.[150]

Technological innovations in cities often become their most significant identities; one example is the Eiffel Tower,[151] which, after the great world exhibition of technological innovations, became perhaps the most important symbol of one of the cultural centers of Europe. The quest toward the sky has always been the objective of every culture and society; today, technology and innovation have enabled humankind to reach heights that previous civilizations could not have even dreamt of—the highest building today is more than 800 meters tall, forming a completely different silhouette and panorama of the city. The different elements in cities have an innovative approach to city life.

> One of the most important elements of cities that always include modern technology, innovation, culture, and art, are clocks in public areas. They can only have the function of showing the exact time; they can also present other information, like astronomical movement of heavenly bodies. However, most often in significant public spaces they make artistic and technologically innovative solutions that should depict the culture of the community.[152]

Perhaps the most interesting example is the astrological clock on the main square in Prague.[153] Similar clocks have become the identity of spaces in Venice and London, Novi Sad, and Belgrade, as well as being found in many other cities.

It is evident that through the city, public spaces simultaneously connect history, technology, and art.

> The connection between technology and art in open urban spaces is a relation which has historically greatly influenced the character and atmosphere of public areas, creating relationships that could sometimes obtain the title of masterpieces—this is the goal of every creation, and in the cities, it is probably the greatest and most sublime ideal. Works of art in cities cannot exist without the materials and connections from which they are created; for them to be shaped, technologies enabling this are required. Materials installed in

> cities have changed throughout history and they have improved in line with innovations and opportunities, always directly related to knowledge and science, with the aim of creating a relationship that can and should receive the attribute of art.[154]

Art is crucial for the city and if the city has different art forms in public spaces, it is a benefit for city life.

> The discoveries in the treatment of materials, and the research of their features has enabled numerous technological innovations, followed by the creation of city elements that have become a part of the artistic culture of the epoch to which they belong. What we do know is that such works, throughout history as well as today, represent points towards which millions of visitors from around the world gravitate, wanting to experience the power and blend of innovative technologies of previous times and arts.[155]

Building Open Space as Works of Art

Since Ancient Rome, and other past civilizations, emperors have wanted to build open spaces of the city during their reign to reflect all the splendor and energy of their power, as well as the technological, innovative, and artistic capacities they possessed. It is no big secret that they always wanted to be surrounded by the most important scientists and artists, who were encouraged to create the most prestigious and magnificent works possible.

> Today, in the open spaces of Rome, one can see forums – squares that were supposed to celebrate social life during ancient times. In this way, they introduced the latest developments, but they also cultivated people's spirit by acquainting them with the latest innovations and art. This practice has remained to this day, and we have often seen the open spaces of cities become stages of technological and innovative approaches through the redesign of their elements, while new innovative technologies in lighting, incorporating visual communications, transform certain elements of the city, increasingly invading and occupying open city spaces, as well as the attention and emotions of users.[156]

Technologies and Innovation as Programs in Cities

Every society throughout history has represented technology and innovation in open city areas in different ways. Sometimes these were exhibitions, fairs, and parades organized in order to present the latest developments. In open as well as in enclosed spaces, numerous programs for the presentation of technology and innovation, the latest scientific and technological achievements, are organized, clearly demonstrating the progress and innovation in specific areas of life.

> In addition to programmes that are organized in the squares and streets, every major city has a space for fairs that serves to present achievements in different fields, often including convention centres for scientific conferences, organized to present the latest technological knowledge. At construction fairs, innovative technologies in this area are always presented, having a great influence on the open spaces of cities. Furthermore, fairs related to other techniques and technologies, especially information and communications technology and electrical systems, are programmes that allow the population to learn about the latest developments in areas that increasingly alter modern cities.[157]

Information technology for modern city life connects many aspects of the lives of citizens.

> Some of the most important areas of life for each resident are leisure and entertainment; to fulfill this part of their needs, all major cities have open spaces such as amusement and theme parks. These programmes should enable exceptional impressions and emotions of visitors, and such feelings are usually related to technological innovation systems and entertainment devices. In these kinds of programmes, technologies improve in high speed, and it is in every park's direct interest to be innovative and interesting, with a specific identity, in order to attract more visitors. From the phenomenon of Disneyland that spread from the USA across Europe and Asia, to amusement parks such as the Prater in Vienna or Tivoli in Copenhagen, that has existed for 175 years, technology and innovation serving entertainment is constantly improving and evolving.[158]

This industry occupies more and more open space in contemporary cities. In the era of working hours that often last more than eight hours, everyone in the city needs to have fun and entertainment in a variety of ways, and modern technology and innovation in this industry are progressing in great steps.

History is always connected with modern times.

> Even today in cities, we can see and feel the amazing technological advances of former civilizations that stopped existing thousands of years ago, through their buildings and cities that remain standing to this day. Such parts of cities undoubtedly prove that the technologies used by former builders were intended for building structures with a very long lifespan.[159]

It is duration that is one of the most significant facts related to each technology, since persistence in time is set as the primary fact in building cities and the relationships between their elements in open public spaces.

> Looking at Athens or Rome today, as well as a large number of old cities around the world and their numerous buildings lasting for a long time after

> the disappearance of their culture, we cannot help but wonder how technologically advanced they were and committed to connecting construction with advanced technologies and innovations that were constant and frequent during that time as well. They have left such achievements that even today, despite the fact that we have mastered much more advanced technologies, we cannot clearly interpret and understand, nor penetrate all their secrets.[160]

Perhaps the most essential issues when dealing with technologies, innovations, and the arts in the open spaces of the city are the following: why, how, where, and for whom to work and build? This issue probably has been considered at the beginning of the study; however, due to the importance of the topic, it is raised at the end in order to clearly know from whom and what it all begins and ends. Often, the answers to these set questions are not clear, but we believe that the purchasers—those who paid for the construction of open spaces and their elements—together with the builders of former times, had a goal to demonstrate and prove their technical skills and knowledge, not just to themselves and their contemporaries, but also to numerous generations to come.

> It is clear that, throughout history, there have always been people who commissioned works of art. When they were intended for open city spaces, that person was always someone who had the power to rule and decide what should be built. The name of the person who commissioned has changed through the course of history; sometimes it was a pharaoh, emperor, king, tsar, etc. Today, they are presidents, mayors or people in power from various government and community levels that have the will, culture and ethics and can order or decide about building works of art in residential areas, always using the latest technologies and possibilities, and of course, skills of the artist. They have the same intentions as their predecessors from the epochs that have passed, and that is leaving a trace of their reign or personality.[161]

This approach has remained in a number of societies to this day, and we can witness that numerous cultures, whenever it comes to building and designing open urban spaces, want to do their best to reflect the time in which they live and work, as well as the achievements in technologies and art.

> To simplify, staying in any public space, if we want to read and observe, we can understand many elements installed in these spaces, and certainly the technologies, innovations and arts that people used in order to build and design. Whether those who have the power to decide on the layout of open spaces are always ready to include the latest technology and the most valuable art of that time, is only a question of their ethics and morals. In the modern age, technologies greatly shape the character and atmosphere of open spaces.

> We are witnessing new elements appear on streets and squares daily, having not only adequate performance, but also an artistic quality due to their technological and innovative character. For example, the fountains that exist in city areas—a tradition remaining since ancient times—can now be utilized with modern technology in order to shape water in very interesting and unusual ways.[162]

There are more and more elements of open spaces whose change is enabled by technologies, either in form or some other features.

> An interesting example is certainly the market Schouwburgplein in Rotterdam, where the public lighting is in the shape of large port cranes, with the possibility of moving vertically, enabling visitors to create an atmosphere according to their own sensibility and depending on the programmes and events happening at the market. The mobile stage in Hamburg, on the Reeperbahn, is another example of how modern technology enables programmes to be run in a way completely adapted to their nature. The analyzed topics relating to technologies and innovations in open urban spaces, such as identity, art, programmes, duration, leisure, entertainment, and commissioners, display all the complexity of including new elements into public areas.[163]

We believe that the issues analyzed are oriented toward qualities provided by technologies and innovations for pedestrians, who constitute the largest number of urban space users.

Transformations: Digital Art in an Urban Environment

The artist and educator Hugh McElveen stated that,

> Understanding the transformative role and power of public space is important in order to appreciate the evolution of contemporary society and the lives of its citizens. Real public spaces are managed by the state that believes people are a priority.[164]

Bill Gates famously dreamt of a computer in every home. With a computer now present in every pocket, it looks like his dream grossly underestimated the presence of digital media and its transformative power.

> The linear point-to-point communication of the tracks of the industrial revolution has been replaced by the web like an array of the almost infinite connection points of the digital revolution. The artists use the city as a canvas—audience as viewer, audience as participant. As engagement deepens, the audience is transformed from a passive observer to an active collaborator, to

> make the participants co- operate, and co-ordinate their movement. Collaborations happen across ages and cultures creating social interactions.[165]

Through unexpected interactions participants find themselves in situations of different emotions, further adding to an acute awareness of society's power structures.

> The artists also look at the audience as an interpreter. Mapping explores the overlapping of digital and physical worlds through online activity. Some types of mapping seek to develop social collaboration while others draw attention to our individual existence. Mapping seeks to give citizens a new way of navigating familiar public space. These maps deepen communities and create new spatial understandings, challenging concepts of ownership while transforming the use of the city.[166]

Audience engagement (viewer, interaction, orientation and activism) all develop an awareness of the issues concerning artists and society.

> The increasing mobilization of the audience has the potential to further the issues artists are concerned with. As such, the audience becomes an essential element enabling the artist to realize their goals. This new role is closer to interactive art than participatory art, as the audience engages with the work's distribution, not its creation. By determining their own contribution to the debate, these amateur artists have gone from interacting with to producing participatory art.[167]

Digital technologies are presently transforming the audience from passive consumer to active producer.

> Apart from the benefit to society, there is also a positive support for the individual amateur artist.
>
> In other areas, new technologies such as augmented reality (AR) and artificial intelligence (AI) have started to transform our relationship with public space and each other. It appears that developments are beginning to run faster than civil society can moderate them. Pokémon Go-related crime clearly shows that the developers did not envision the anti-social uses of the game.[168]

Art, technology, public space, and citizens weave a very rich and constantly changing tapestry.

> Artists seek to question our relationship with and understanding of the use of space, formalist art concerns in the 21st century city, the place of art and technology in empowering citizens and how technology builds relationships. Participation and interaction with digital technology, art and public space ultimately become the text that transforms the citizen.[169]

Notes

76 UCLG, "Agenda 21 for Culture," accessed May 6, 2020. http://www.agenda21culture.net/
77 Ibid.
78 Jordi Marti, "If Agenda 21 for Culture is the Answer: What Was the Question," in *Sustaining Cultural Development, Unified Systems and New Governance in Cultural Life*, ed. James Doyle and Biljana Mickov (London: Routledge Publishing, 2013) 37–43.
79 UCLG, "Culture 21: Actions."
80 Ibid.
81 Biljana Mickov, "Networking and the Creative Impetus," in *Creative Cities: Vision & Execution*, ed. James Doyle and Biljana Mickov (London: Routledge Publishing, 2019) 1–2.
82 Mickov, "Networking and the Creative Impetus," 1–2.
83 UCLG, "Culture 21: Actions."
84 Ibid.
85 "Bottom-up" planning allows for ideas for policies and different projects at any level in the government structure, up to and including the development of those ideas.
86 Barcelona Cultura, "Barcelona Institute of Culture," accessed May 10, 2021. http://barcelonacultura.bcn.cat/en/culture-institute
87 UCLG, "Agenda 21 for Culture."
88 UCLG, "Agenda 21 for Culture."
89 UCLG, "Agenda 21 for Culture."
90 James Doyle and Biljana Mickov, "On Creativity", in *The Creative City: Vision and Execution* (London: Routledge Publishing, 2015).
91 Ibid.
92 Doyle and Mickov, "On Creativity"; Esteve Caramés is Head of the Culture Program at the Barcelona Culture Department, City of Barcelona.
93 Ibid.
94 UCLG, "Agenda 21 for Culture."
95 Culture is a goal in the post-2015 development agenda.
96 Doyle and Mickov, "On Creativity," 183–213.
97 Ibid.
98 Doyle and Mickov, "On Creativity," 183–213.
99 Ibid.
100 La chambre d'eau, accessed May 10, 2021, www.lachambredeau.com.
101 Ibid.
102 European Center for Creative Economy, accessed May 10, 2021, www.e-c-c-e.de
103 Ibid.
104 Ibid.
105 "Creative Industries definitions," David Parrish, accessed May 10, 2021, https://www.davidparrish.com/creative-industries-definitions/; the United Nations Educational, Scientific and Cultural Organization (UNESCO) is a specialized agency of the United Nations aimed at promoting world peace and security through international cooperation in education, the sciences, and culture.
106 David Parrish, accessed May 10, 2021, www.davidparrish.com
107 Doyle and Mickov, "On Creativity," 183–213.
108 Ibid.
109 UCLG, "Agenda 21 for Culture."
110 Doyle and Mickov, "On Creativity," 183–213.
111 UCLG, "Agenda 21 for Culture."
112 UCLG, "Culture 21: Actions."
113 European Center for Creative Economy.

114 Jude Bloomfield and Franco Bianchini, *Planning for the Intercultural City*, (Bournes Green: Comedia, 2004). Franco Bianchini is Professor of Cultural Policy and Director of the Institute for Research on Culture and the Creative Industries at the University of Hull, UK.
115 Ibid.
116 Ibid.
117 Ibid.
118 Esteve Caramés, "Barcelona's Cultural Policies Behind the Scenes New Context, Renewed Strategies," in *Sustaining Cultural Development, Unified Systems and New Governance in Cultural Life*, ed. James Doyle and Biljana Mickov (London: Routledge publishing, 2013), 29–35.
119 Ibid.
120 Doyle and Mickov, "On Creativity."
121 Ibid.
122 Ibid.
123 Davor Buinjac, "Creative Industries" in *Sustaining Cultural Development, Unified Systems and New Govermance in Cultural Life*, ed. James Doyle and Biljana Mickov (London: Routledge Publishing, 2013).
124 Doyle and Mickov, "On Creativity."
125 Doyle and Mickov, "On Creativity."
126 Ibid.
127 Ibid.
128 Ibid.
129 John Holden, *How We Value Arts and Culture* (Lecture, Museum of Contemporary Art Vojvodina, Novi Sad, Serbia, 2010). John Holden is a writer, speaker, and cultural commentator. Holden is currently a Visiting Professor at the University of Leeds, an Honorary Professor of Hong Kong University and an Associate at the think-tank Demos. He is the author of many works, including *The Ecology of Culture, Publicly Funded Culture and the Creative Industries, Influence and Attraction and Democratic Culture*, and is co-author of *Cultural Diplomacy and The Cultural Leadership Handbook.*).
130 Barcelona Cultura, "Barcelona Institute of Culture."
131 "Open Data," Comune di Bologna, accessed May 15, 2021, http://dati.comune.bologna.it/
132 Virtual Museum Transnational Network, accessed May 15, 2021, www.v-must.net
133 UCLG, "Agenda 21 for Culture."
134 Buinjac, "Creative Industries."
135 Ibid.
136 Ibid.
137 Doyle and Mickov, "On Creativity."
138 Ibid.
139 Ibid.
140 Ibid.
141 Ibid.
142 Ibid.
143 Ibid.
144 Cultural policy represents government actions, laws and programs that regulate, protect, encourage and financially (or otherwise) support activities related to the arts and creative sectors, and culture, which may involve activities related to language, heritage and diversity. The idea of cultural policy was developed by UNESCO in the 1960s.
145 UCLG, "Agenda 21 for Culture."
146 Ibid.
147 Ibid.

148 Darko Reba, *Culture and Innovation in Open City* (Lecture at the Conference on Culture and Innovation, Institute of Culture Vojvodina, Novi Sad, Serbia, October 29, 2019).
149 Ibid.
150 Ibid.
151 The Eiffel Tower is a wrought-iron lattice tower on the Champ de Mars in Paris, France. It is named after the engineer, Gustave Eiffel, whose company designed and built the tower.
152 Reba, *Culture and Innovation in Open City*.
153 The Astronomical Clock in Prague, an expression of high art that includes technologies, innovations and knowledge in a number of areas, has become a leading tourist sight in the city.
154 Reba, *Culture and Innovation in Open City*.
155 Ibid.
156 Ibid.
157 Ibid.
158 Ibid.
159 Ibid.
160 Ibid.
161 Darko Reba, Milica Vračarić, and Olivera Marković, "Cultural Developments Planning and Innovations at Urban Open Spaces," in *Progress: Laboratory of Culture21–Innovation in culture sector* (Belgrade: Službeni glasnik, 2020).
162 Ibid.
163 Ibid.
164 Hugh McElveen, "Transformations: numérique et art dans un environnement urbain (Urbain, Humain, Art et Technologie)," Digital transformation of art in an urban environment (Urban, Human, Art and Technology), in *dans Innovation Culturelle et Transformation des Villes*, ed. Biljana Mickov et Fabrice Thuriot (Paris: L'Harmattan, 2019), 213–233.
165 Ibid.
166 Ibid.
167 Ibid.
168 Pokémon Go is a popular augmented reality mobile device game that uses the phone camera to place Pokemon creatures on the user's screen. The user catches Pokémon creatures to build a collection.
169 McElveen. "Transformations: numérique et art dans un environnement urbain (Urbain, Humain, Art et Technologie)."

4

THE ENVIRONMENT AND SUSTAINABLE DEVELOPMENT

In 1983, the World Commission on Environment and Development—which had been tasked with preparing an environmental perspective to the year 2000 and beyond—linked environmental issues to economic and social development.[170]

> The Millennium Development Goals (MDGs) were an ambitious agenda for reducing poverty and improving lives, with specific goals and targets set for 2015: to eradicate poverty, achieve universal primary education, promote gender equality, improve maternal health, combat diseases; ensure environmental sustainability, and develop a global partnership for development.[171]
>
> Human activities use "natural" spaces and biological resources such as agricultural heritage. Spaces and resources are bearers of culture partly as reminders of history, practical knowledge, and identity and they contribute to values (urban or rural landscapes). The knowledge people have of their surrounding ecosystems is of significant value. Throughout time, human practices have shaped urban and rural landscapes.[172]

"The specific goals to ensure environmental sustainability are to integrate the principles of sustainable development into country policies and programs, and reverse the loss of environmental resources."[173] At the United Nations Conference on Environment and Development in 1992 and in Agenda 21, the international community agreed to establish a "World Summit on Sustainable Development (WSSD) on a Plan of Implementation."[174]

"The goals are to reduce poverty, change unsustainable forms of consumption and production, protect the natural resource base of economic and social development, and achieve sustainable development in a globalising world."[175]According to this analysis, traditional knowledge should be recognized and used to better understand how cultures and ecosystems interact, and with academic knowledge,

DOI: 10.4324/9781003336648-4

how they impact the ecosystem. "These forms of knowledge must be developed and shared in order to promote ecological thinking and the values of sustainable development."[176]

Cultural diversity and natural diversity are closely related.

> Local governments play an essential role in ensuring the consideration of climate change, as well as promoting knowledge and capacities in dealing with this global challenge. Local governments can promote access to the resources necessary to develop healthy, organic forms of food production. Cultural actors also contribute to raising awareness of different environmental concerns and the promotion of more sustainable uses of natural resources.[177]

Research suggest the following points:

- Cultural factors are integrated into local environmental sustainability strategies.
- Local cultural policies explicitly recognize the connections between culture and environmental sustainability (climate change, risk prevention, sustainable use of resources, fragility of ecosystems).

History and culture are included in the promotion of the production and consumption of local products.

a. Gastronomy is recognized as a constituent element of local culture.
b. The local government takes steps to facilitate and promote citizen initiatives for the sustainable use of public spaces.
c. The local government establishes programs to preserve and spread traditional knowledge and practices that contribute to the sustainable use of natural resources.
d. The local government recognizes the cultural importance of natural spaces with specific programs.

It is important that cultural organizations that receive public support evaluate their environmental impact and carry out ecological activities. There are platforms that link public and private civil society organizations that work in the areas of culture and the environment.

> The increased scale of economic activity and the consequent increased impact on a finite Earth arise from both major demographic changes—including population growth, shifts in age structure, urbanization, and spatial redistributions through migration.[178]

"Various types of natural capital—often in conjunction with other forms of capital—and human labor provide ecosystem services."[179] The destruction of natural capital can result in negative impact on human well-being.

"The integration of the economic–ecological model can generate an understanding of the impact of economy to the ecological system. Achieving sustainable development will require changes in human behavior and actions regarding the environment."[180] Humans are a social species. Economics has been led individually, but from the social science perspective it is clear that social interactions influence individual choices. Sustainable development is not just about sustainability in the sense of how to maintain the environment. "The work in environmental sciences focuses on environmental sustainability and economy is part of this action."[181] The challenge of achieving sustainable development is large and pressing.

> The big number of on-going changes to Earth's systems could cause potentially large negative consequences for human well-being. We have to understand the environmental, social, and economic dimensions of sustainable development, which will require a greater integration of economics, social sciences and the natural sciences. There is an urgent need for more rapid integration of social and behavioral disciplines with sustainable development.[182]

Culture, Innovation, and Climate Change

The persistence of cultural heritage, and of culture in general, is significantly related to environmental conditions and all its factors. The study of climate as a mean state of weather above a place is one of the most important in the field of modern environmental research. The consequences of climate change, perhaps the greatest challenges faced by humanity, are very diverse and, among other things, concern cultural heritage. The solution to some of the current and potential impacts can be found in its adaptation to climate change.

> Climate is the average state of the atmosphere or the average state of the weather above a certain place in a certain period, taking into account the average and extreme deviations.[183] Changes in recent history are observed in the light of human impact on the environment, mainly through the adverse effects of air pollution and the emission of gases, the greenhouse effect and global warming.[184]
>
> The impact of climate change and global warming correlates with various natural and social phenomena such as the rising sea levels, impact on fresh water resources, impact on agriculture and food supply, changes in ecosystems, impact on human health and impact on cultural heritage.[185]

"Assessing the impact of climate change on cultural heritage often involves the analysis of complex interactions between natural, social, and thus cultural factors within this complex topic."[186] "Insisting on this approach of 'integrated wholes' makes sense not only because the amount of qualitative and quantitative evidence is greater, but also because these factors are inseparable."[187] In an attempt to inform the debate, the project on the "Impact of Global Climate Change on Material Heritage and Cultural Landscapes" (NOAHS ARK), funded by European Union funds, was implemented in the period from 2004 to 2007.

The goals of the project were as follows:

- determining the meteorological parameters and changes that were most important for tangible cultural heritage;
- forecasting and description, based on the results of research into the effects of climate change on European soil in the next 100 years;
- developing strategies to mitigate and adapt historic buildings, sites, locations, monuments, and materials that are likely to be most affected by climate change; and
- providing electronic sources of information and tools for managers and strategies.The results of the project appeared after its implementation in the form of a publication entitled: "Atlas of Climate Change Impact on European Cultural Heritage."[188] The project reached a number of conclusions, including the following:

"The analysis of factors influencing cultural heritage mainly results from the knowledge on the increase of air temperature on a global level, which is then reflected in changes in humidity, floods, weather conditions, and hurricanes."[189] The range of temperature changes is wide, depending on the geographical position of a place and the season: "Temperature affects the speed of chemical reactions and the time during which the surface of a monument will remain wet, which ultimately reflects the tendency of metal surfaces to corrode."[190] The influence of temperature on material cultural heritage is especially evident in the knowledge that the key segment of the artistic value of a monument is in its surface layer: "Water can affect historical materials and structures in all their phases, and when it acts together with temperature or other climatic elements, it can lead to a worsening of the condition or even complete destruction of a cultural monument."[191]

"Rising temperatures both globally and in individual regions could affect higher water losses on the Earth's surface due to evaporation. Also, in regions with an increase in precipitation, higher evaporations will be noticeable."[192]

"Despite the pronounced emphasis on air temperatures, some research has confirmed that, according to the climate change scenario, water is actually the main threat to cultural heritage (rain, floods, storms), especially in the case of European cultural heritage."[193] Rising sea levels are one of the biggest challenges faced by those seeking to preserve cultural heritage.

> This is an equal threat to: (1) the heritage of coastal areas and (2) the heritage that has already been submerged. In the case of rising water levels, a scenario of transformation of the first into the second type of heritage is also possible.[194]

"Cities with their built facilities are always a kind of human response to adaptation to weather and climate conditions, which prevail in their environment or a given climate."[195]

> In addition to the impact on people and their health, climate change has a great impact on the urban heritage of cities, with the assessment that architecture, especially in the case of historic buildings, is in danger due to natural and anthropogenic influences.[196]

"Cultural landscapes and cites could completely disappear with rising sea levels."[197] "An important tool in the fight against climate change is adaptation or adaptation to new circumstances."[198] Despite the fact that the topic of the impact of climate change on cultural heritage, as one segment of the overall impact of the same changes on the environment in the 21st century, has been affirmed as research in scientific and practical terms, it still does not attract adequate public attention.

> Climate change is a very complex process and we cannot predict in detail the climatic conditions in the future. However, we can develop some consensus on a possible scenario, based on observations, knowledge, expertise and professional intuition. It is clear that changes are underway.[199]

Cities are affected by climate change and there are critical places for experimentation and innovation—the "urban laboratory" is increasingly connected with cultural policy makers and environmentally focused projects.[200]

> Collaboration between city departments is taking place everywhere, aligning diverse strategies, projects and engagement initiatives. Cities are increasingly recognizing that action on environmental sustainability is an essential component of local resilience as well as a platform for new ideas, entrepreneurship and innovation.[201]

"The COVID-19 crisis is impacting all dimensions of our lives: public health, labor systems, social interaction, political debates, the use of public spaces, the economy, the environment, and the cultural life."[202]

> COVID-19 is hitting cultural life. Libraries, memorials, community centres, museums, and all cultural venues have suffered several weeks of lockdown; some of them are still closed and some are getting ready to reopen with physical distancing measures. Performances, festivals, parades, carnivals, and intangible heritage events have been cancelled. The digital presence of cultural institutions and organizations has exponentially grown. What we need is a post-COVID-19 recovery phase by continuing to work, learning and supporting each other in terms of ideas and recovery plans.[203]

Notes

170 United Nations University (UNU), "The Environment and Sustainable Development," accessed May 9, 2021 https://archive.unu.edu/esd/ESDtext.pdf
171 Ibid.
172 UCLG, "Agenda 21: Actions," 24–25.
173 Ibid.
174 Ibid.
175 Ibid.
176 Ibid.
177 Ibid.
178 Paul Ehrlich and John Holdren, "Impact of Population Growth," *Science* 3977, no.1971: 1212–1217. https://faculty.washington.edu/stevehar/Ehrlich.pdf
179 Stephen Polasky, Catherine Louise Kling, Simon Levin, Stephen R. Carpenter, Gretchen C Daily, Paul R. Ehrlich, Geoffrey M. Heal, and Jane Lubchenco, "Role of Economics in Analyzing the Environment and Sustainable Development," *Proceedings of the National Academy of Sciences* 116, no.12 (2019): 5233–5238. Accessed May 9, 2020, https://www.pnas.org/content/116/12/5233
180 Jason Shogren and Laura Taylor, "On Behavioral-Environmental Economics," *Review of Environmental Economics and Policy* 2, no.1 (2008): 26–44. Accessed May 10, 2020 https://ideas.repec.org/a/oup/renvpo/v2y2008i1p26-44.html
181 Ibid.
182 United Nations University (UNU), "The Environment and Sustainable Development."
183 Dušan Dukić, *Klimatologija*, (Beograd: Geografski fakultet, 2006).
184 John Houghton, *Global Warming. The Complete Briefing*, (Cambridge: Cambridge University Press, 2006).
185 George Ochoa, Jennifer Hoffman, and Tina Tin, *Climate: The Force That Shapes our World and the Future of Life on Earth*, (London: Rodale International, 2005).
186 Augustin Colette, *Case Studies on World Heritage and Climate Change*, (Paris: UNESCO World Heritage Centre, 2007).
187 May Cassar, "Sustainable Heritage: Challenges and Strategies for the Twenty-first Century," *APT Bulletin: Journal of Preservation Technology* 40, no. 1 (2009): 3–11.
188 Cristina Sabbioni, Peter Brimblecombe, and May Cassar, *The Atlas of Climate Change Impact on European Cultural Heritage, Scientific Analysis and Management Strategies*. (London: Anthem Press, 2012).
189 Dario Camuffo, *Microclimate for Cultural Heritage* (Amsterdam: Elsevier, 1998).
190 Ron Hamilton and Helen Crabbe, "Environment, Pollution and Effects," in *The Effects of Air Pollution on Cultural Heritage*, ed. John Watt, Johan Tidblad, Vladimir Kucera and Ron Hamilton (New York: Springer, 2009), 1–28.
191 Ibid.
192 Houghton, *Global Warming. The Complete Briefing*.
193 Cristina Sabbioni, May Cassar, Peter Brimblecombe, and Roger-Alexandre Lefèvre, *Vulnerability of Cultural Heritage to Climate Change* (European and Mediterranean Major Hazards Agreement (EUR-OPA), Strasbourg, 2008, November 20).
194 Elena Perez-Alvaro, "Climate change and underwater cultural heritage: Impacts and Challenges", *Journal of Cultural Heritage* 21 (2016): 842–848.
195 UNESCO, *Case Studies on World Heritage and Climate Change* (Paris: UNESCO World Heritage Centre, 2007).
196 European Commission, *Preserving Our Heritage, Improving Our Environment, Volume I – 20 Years of EU Research Into Cultural Heritage* (Luxembourg: Publications Office of the European Union, 2008).
197 Michael Hall et al., "Climate Change and Cultural Heritage: Conservation and Heritage Tourism in the Anthropocene," *Journal of Heritage Tourism* 11, no. 1(2015): 10–24.
198 Mark Maslin, *Global Warming. A Very Short Introduction* (Oxford: Oxford University Press, 2004).

199 Jim Perry and Charlie Falzon, *Climate Change Adaptation for Natural World Heritage Sites - A Practical Guide*, World Heritage Papers Series, no. 37 (Paris: UNESCO World Heritage Centre, 2014).

200 World Cities Culture Forum, *Culture & Climate Change* (2017), accessed May 15, 2021, http://www.worldcitiescultureforum.com/assets/others/WCCF_Report_June_28_FINAL_v4.pdf

201 Ibid.

202 "#CULTURECOVID19," Agenda 21 for Culture, accessed May 15, 2021, http://www.agenda21culture.net/culturecovid19

203 Ibid.

PART I

Local Government and Innovation

Introduction

The role of local governments is to consider the ways in which they can organize themselves, manage services, work with stakeholders, engage with citizens and be as innovative as possible. It is important to change citizen attitude towards local government, change the central government's attitude towards the local government and change the innovative nature of local government work.[204] It is also important to try to implement as many innovations as possible to be useful for citizens and communities and to define the interconnection between culture and economy, creative industry sectors, and innovative culture policy. Innovations in local governments are divided into two groups that are interconnected: one group refers to technological innovations that are later transferred to smart cities, regions with the role to help citizens to improve living conditions;[205] the second group refers to social innovations that are also in service of the citizens themselves.[206] Social and technical innovation in local governments is an important part of cultural policy in the cities. All innovations have to be adapted to citizen needs in the urban space.

The need for innovation is in line with the changes that are happening with the development of technology—in that sense the social response and human beings must follow the changes. The innovations have to be in the service of the citizens. In this context, local governments play a major role, perhaps even greater than that of central governments. Innovation should be democratic, whether technological or social, and must correspond to each other.

Social innovation in culture refers to new processes that more effectively reflect citizens and respond to their needs, as well as enabling them to make better use of resources and have better accessibility. Inspiring projects of social innovation have to be supported on a government level.[207] Social innovations are new ideas that

DOI: 10.4324/9781003336648-5

meet social needs, create social relationships, and form new collaborations through different networks, organizations, and projects.

It is important to build an ecosystem in cities that improves social innovation through different parts, by mapping and looking for new ideas to strengthen the ecosystem of social innovation.[208] Democracy is an essential basic condition of the participation of citizens in public decision-making. The city governments have to promote dialogue between citizens and their national governments and international institutions.[209] Local governments also have to have a multi-level governance framework (governing in dialogue with civil society and the private sector), developing cross-level or horizontal forms of governance (that integrate the cultural dimension into public policy), and demanding the construction of vertical governance frameworks.[210] Local governments have to promote the participation of everyone in the creation, implementation, and evaluation of public policies, including cultural policies. The city governments have the responsibility and equity, both between the centers and peripheries in terms of innovation policy. In addition, the city governments promote local diplomacy and participate in international cooperation in the area of culture, as an indispensable tool for creating human solidarity and exchange.[211] Local governments are laboratories for testing effective and appropriate solutions to global problems. City policy has to connect the cultural and educational sectors, as one of the important developmental processes in the cities. The city government has to give a local strategy regarding educational policy and cultural policy.

In that case, a local government makes a local platform or network that brings together public, civic, and private actors in the fields of culture, education, and lifelong learning. The cultural institutions that receive public support provide educational activities for formal and informal environments. Schools and education centers and associations take part in cultural creation, distribution, and activities and creativity training.[212] Artistic education, such as music, visual arts, performing arts, and multimedia, among other disciplines, is provided in local schools at all levels, and is accessible to people. There are cultural innovation programs for people that promote social inclusion and knowledge of cultural codes, as well as digital environments. Public projects generate permanent forums for the consultation, negotiation, and regulation of goals and methods, with the participation of all the parties involved, as well as both citizens and policy makers. Policies or programs operate to support the participation of citizens in the management of cultural institutions, programs, and events.[213] Training programs in the field of culture are supported by local governments to strengthen non-governmental organizations (NGOs), associations and other civil society organizations that contribute to cultural life. Further, cities build the frameworks to foster collaboration for cultural policies between local, regional, and national governments.

Technical innovation refers to all digital resources for the collection of data that can be used to address citizens' needs. This includes data collected from citizens, devices, buildings, and assets that are then processed and analyzed to monitor and manage traffic and transportation systems, supply networks, information systems, schools, libraries, hospitals, and other community services.[214]

Notes

204 Mark Evans et al., *Innovation in Local Government: Defining the Challenge, Making the Change* (Australian center for Local Government; Sydney: University of Technology, 2013).

205 The smart city is an *urban area* that uses different types of electronic methods and sensors to collect data. This includes data collected from citizens, devices, buildings, and assets that is then processed and analyzed to monitor and manage traffic and transportation system, utilities, water supply networks, *waste, information systems*, schools, libraries, hospitals, and other community services.

206 Social innovation is an opportunity for cities to empower their citizens, by creating new opportunities, promoting social inclusion and generally addressing the various existing social needs.

207 "Social Innovation," European Commission, accessed May 9, 2021, https://ec.europa.eu/growth/industry/policy/innovation/social_en

208 Ibid.

209 UCLG, "Culture 21: Actions."

210 Ibid.

211 Ibid.

212 Ibid.

213 Ibid.

214 European Commission, "Smart cities," accessed May 9 2021, https://ec.europa.eu/info/eu-regional-and-urban-development/topics/cities-and-urban-development/city-initiatives/smart-cities_en

5

INNOVATION IN LOCAL GOVERNMENTS

Culture Policy

Innovation in Local Governments

The creative economy is considered the economic contribution that the cultural and creative industries make to cities and countries.

> At EU level, CCIs are defined as including the following areas of activity: books, newspapers and magazines, music, performing arts, TV, film, radio, video games, visual arts, architecture, advertising. A 2014 study by Ernst & Young Global limited (EY) shows that the creative economy's contribution to the GDP of the Union is 4.2%, employing 7 million people (nearly 2.5 times more Europeans than the automotive industry). Such figures may suggest that the presence and development of cultural and creative industries constitutes a main economic driver for a city and a region, and because of their high content of creativity, CCIs contribute significantly to spin-offs such as, for example, youth employment.[215]

In the creative industries, there are permanent crossovers between the commercial and non-commercial sectors.

> The examples are: Designers, or people working in advertising, look for inspiration in art galleries or museums for their new products; visitors want to see a city after reading an inspiring book or seeing a movie set in that location. Video game developers work together with illustrators and story-tellers to develop their creations. This is why cities with vibrant cultural ecosystems upstream are also the places where CCIs thrive downstream. This is also where urban and image transformation initiatives such as the European Capitals of Culture can have an impact. To date, the ECoC title has been

DOI: 10.4324/9781003336648-6

> awarded to nearly 60 cities in 30 countries with the programme becoming a key platform for city positioning and a catalyst for economic and cultural regeneration.[216]

Research and development in the sector of creative industries is more than crucial, particularly because of local development in the cities and regions. Academics are trying to show more research in this field. One of the main points for local development and innovation is networking and the exchanging of ideas between professionals in the public sector. Their influence on the policy makers for innovation is significant. It is important that we build the capacity for local development in the cultural sector with regard to innovation policy.

> Capacity building is also about facilitating learning and the exchange of experience among those involved in the sector, in order to explore the key areas of culture and creative industries': building resilient creative ecosystems; creative industries for inclusive development; governance and funding; raising awareness of creative resources.[217]

There have been a significant number of case studies on the contribution of culture through creative industries in the economic sector.

At the European level, there is a growing literature matched by evidence that cultural activities and especially the creative industries can drive the economies of this continent forward and help communities respond to the challenges of globalization.

> At the global level the literature emphasizes the fact that the economy at large is increasingly innovation led, and innovation has become a key competitiveness indicator. In this context innovation is understood as a system capable of going beyond traditional forms of technology and R&D into a multidisciplinary and cross-sectoral activity. In part, this is also because today's economy is characterized by a "customization" of products and services, the success of which relies greatly on the unique aesthetic, symbolic and socio-cultural elements of such products. Consumers are keener on brands which are associated with a particular set of values and often prefer to buy memorable experiences or sensations.[218]

Innovation is the main part of cultural policy today. Cultural economist Pier Luigi Sacco convincingly argues that what we are witnessing today is a "culturalization" of the economy where culture becomes a key asset at the top of every kind of value chain.[219] In particular, an unprecedented access to web-based production technology capable of allowing professional treatment of text, still and moving images, sound and multimedia at very cheap prices is one of the key components of this scenario. In addition, the ease of communication, coupled with the social fragmentation of post-industrial society into social groups, lifestyle communities, networks of affiliations—all seeking identity and belonging—creates a climate in which not only new taste, but also new values, can arise.[220] The cultural expert John Holden has highlighted the question of values in cultural activities. In his work he argues that in order to shift away from the simple dual notion of culture being discussed as an economy, a more useful way is to look at culture not as a mechanism but as an *organism*.[221]

> Taking this kind of an ecological approach to culture concentrates on relationships and patterns, on the messiness and dynamism of the cultural system. Approaching culture as an ecology offers a richer and more complete understanding of the topic because it concentrates on showing how ideas transfer, monetary value flows, and product and content move to and from, and in-between, the funded, self-made and commercial subsectors. It also reveals new career patterns together with the skills needed to thrive in this system.[222]

The important view regarding innovation and the cultural ecosystem is that it is not sufficient to consider innovation only through research and development; attention should also be paid to social links that can create new ideas and businesses. In this way, an ecosystem is formed in which everybody is working in a mixed model. Creativity works in a system of relationships and it is connected with the cultural sector to produce spillovers in which the economy exists.[223] The impact of culture on creativity is also significant, as

> The KEA 2009 report examines the contribution that culture and the creative industries make to the wider economy, and features a series of recommendations for the better integration of culture and creativity into EU-wide strategy and policy. Among their recommendations there is a proposal to establish a European Culture-based Creativity Index, which would introduce a rationale for including indicators related to culture-based creativity into existing socio-economic indicator schemes, such as the European Innovation Scoreboard and other frameworks, with a view to highlighting the socio-economic impacts that culture can have on local development. This framework contains indicators grouped across what they see as six pillars of creativity (human capital; technology; the institutional environment; the social environment; openness and diversity). The report also makes a number of suggestions and recommendations on how to make the most of culture, creativity and creative resources in education, regional development, EU policies for mainstreaming culture-based creativity, supporting enterprises, fostering social impacts.[224]

The local and state governments can also take action in relation to this topic:

> The importance and competitive advantage identified within the cultural and creative sector has prompted European, local and national governments to develop targeted business development services, investment programmes and

> cluster initiatives. This level of attention from governments is based on the "exceptionalism" of creative and cultural businesses, and measures have been designed to tackle challenges such as the need to balance the creative with the commercial, the independent with the corporate, the cultural with the managerial. However, the application of these measures at local level has in some cases resulted in the adoption of unsophisticated, linear, "cookbook-like" strategies which have neglected (or even undermined) the unique qualities of local cultural and creative ecologies. Thinking holistically about local development means taking a more nuanced approach to creative city strategies, an approach that is sensitive to local cultures and differences, and is capable of grasping the gaps, the needs, and the potential within each ecosystem.[225]

KEA conducted a study on local ecosystems and the influence of digitalization as innovation.[226]

> The study opens with a reflection on how all steps in the value chains of the cultural and creative sectors (from creation to consumption) have been influenced by new digital solutions, generating new opportunities for innovative practices and increased interaction with audiences (which become actors and producers).[227] Another effect is that the boundaries between creative value chains and other value chains are becoming more blurred. The study also argues that the downside in this otherwise positive scenario is that digitization has also brought a greater risk of piracy as well as more pressure on existing models of value creation and remuneration for the people working in these sectors.[228]

The explanation of spillovers in the creative sector has also been clearly defined by researchers:

> The knowledge spill-overs (e.g., when creative professionals move into other sectors bringing useful ideas, technologies and ways of working with them). The creative firms and activities generate a vibrant urban climate that attracts skilled workers and encourages collaborations. The research suggests that it is best to support existing clusters rather than engineer new ones. In particular, it recommends the undertaking of systematic mapping of local ecosystems of clustering in order to discover whether latent clusters are in existence in a particular location. The benefits of collecting such evidence are clear. If a latent cluster is uncovered somewhere in a locality, then working out its internal dynamics, and taking the necessary steps to support and grow the cluster is the next strategic move.[229]

The crucial point is that cities need to think smart, in a few directions:

> The cities need to be smarter in tackling issues of mobility, the quality of the environment, housing, urban texture, education and work. Our argument

> is that, in order to respond to these trends (and challenges), cities need to mainstream creativity across the whole system (i.e., they can't just put in place unsystematic interventions, such as creating a media cluster, or implementing a public art project, or a place branding strategy in isolation from other initiatives that are local development related). In other words, they need to put in place an architecture of integrated interventions and interconnected actions capable of responding to local needs while activating local resources, collaborations, partnerships and funding.[230]

The interaction between local community-supported events and local policy events make a synergy of ideas for the future on the local level.

> As well as provoking discussion on constructive, rather than confrontational grounds, these events (e.g. brainstorming on perceptions, spirit of place, urban feel etc.) were also instrumental in discovering new resources, talent, opportunities, and provided a platform for new collaborations and partnerships.[231]

The following conclusion is that,

> The development of funding, clustering, incubating, training and the negotiation with governments about fiscal mechanisms are also part of the remit of such agencies. They also in some form provide transversal models of new governance which are worth considering for their ability to take calculated risks in the implementation of pilot actions across the whole of the creative ecosystem. Such mechanisms work in partnership, thus bringing new stakeholders and ideas to the table, and together can help a city to establish the ground for a shared vision about local development priorities.[232]

Networking also has a strong impetus on local culture actors:

> Networking is also about learning from other places, so taking delegations of civic leaders and high-level local stakeholders (e.g., chambers of commerce reps, tourism managers, business leaders, together with cultural and creative practitioners) on study visits is a good way of broadening views on particular issues and boosting confidence in creative strategies processes. Hosting conferences or high-profile events for a local, regional and national audience can also have a positive effect.[233]

Creative tourism also has an important role in the development of the local economy:

> Economic impacts and social and cultural spill-overs can be generated also through creative tourism, defined by Raymond and Richards as 'that which offers visitors the opportunity to develop their creative potential through active

> participation in courses and learning experiences which are characteristic of the holiday destination where they are they are taken' (2000). This particular segment of tourism offers advantages for places because, by its very nature, it creates a diversification of the tourist offer without much investment—just by optimizing the existing tangible and intangible heritage. It also increases profitability across the existing cultural ecology because it creates a new and diversified demand, and, last but not least, it has a positive effect on the self-confidence of the local people thanks to this new interest in their culture and traditions. This in turn can re-energise entrepreneurship and business capacity, as well as inducing innovation of products and experiences at local level.[234]

Cities and places benefit from innovative approaches, especially from creative tourism. Visitors can find places that are unique in terms of what they can offer to tourists, visitors and local inhabitants.

> The cities engage visitors in participating in the experience of producing, enjoying and consuming local products, particularly through a network of bio-retailers, and the enjoyment of high- quality gastronomy. The city has embarked on a programme of rediscovery of its traditions and is committed to promoting creative tourism as a key element in local sustainable development.[235]

The crucial approach is innovation in the way that the local government operates in connecting cities, places, tourist, visitors, professionals, policy makers and inhabitants.

> Supporting creative ecosystems is also about understanding what is already in the territory, perhaps in the form of industries, skills and ways of doing that are culturally embedded in a location (albeit in a reduced form due to deindustrialization). Bringing such broader "cultural" capacity back to life through support for new and innovative products is one way not only to provide opportunities for employment, but also to put a city or a region in the visible map. It is also worth mentioning here that initiatives to capitalize on strengths, such as the quality of place (e.g. landscape, topography, nature, countryside), could help to launch sustainable creative rural economies. In this context, viniculture and gastronomy stand out as activities with high growth potential, representing a new economic dynamic in an alliance between agriculture and tourism.[236]

The revitalization of cities, in order to coordinate with innovation, becomes one of the main projects of local governments.

> Building resilient creative ecosystems also features proposals for the implementation of urban regeneration and revitalization programmes, the objectives of

> which have to ensure there is an adequate and balanced provision of creative spaces (i.e., workspaces, co-work spaces, hubs, artists' studios etc.), cultural buildings, retail, lifestyle and night time venues. The practice of transforming derelict town centres or former industrial quarters started in the 1990s when the Basque capital of Bilbao reinvented itself as a city focused on services and in particular on culture, seen as a key factor for economic growth and development. Since then, many cities large and small in Europe and outside have benefitted from the adoption of a similar approach.[237]

One such example, made by the local government, is the Barcelona Art Factories program.

> This programme of Art Factories, developed since 2007 in a network of ten spaces, is as an initiative of Barcelona City Council, coordinated by the Directorate for Programmes at Barcelona Arts Council. The initiative seeks to strengthen and increase support for creation as a prime condition for better cultural development of the city. Underpinning the project was a mapping which looked into a number of former industrial spaces around the city and into the uses that were made of such venues. Today, up to new 30,000 sq. meters have been transformed in order to host cultural and artistic incubators in close cooperation with the local cultural sector. The Barcelona Art Factories model is interesting because it goes beyond traditional paradigms of access to culture by building bridges with other professional networks (educational, social, business, academic). It aims to offer young creative talents the opportunity to improve their skills and take their first steps towards professionalization. In addition, Barcelona Art Factories promote a new model of management that eschews the usual trend of top-down local government-led actions. Here the city works directly with the different groups that run the facilities, and they are the ones that shape, structure actions and projects on the ground.[238]

The revitalization of former industrial areas of city centers has been a policy agenda for enhancing local cultural and creative ecosystems for at least thirty years. This has helped the city create a new identity by thinking creatively about its resources, people and places. To make social innovation for many cities, it is crucial to put the citizens in the center of cultural development. The important thing is to have citizen engagement in the local cultural policy in the city. Improving local movement to innovate is of great significance. "Innovations in communities create a self-sustaining cycle that benefits the cities/towns and the businesses within."[239]

Innovation implies new ideas that make a difference: "The creation and implementation of new processes, products, services and methods of delivery which result in positive social and/or economic outcomes for the citizenry."[240] The specific responsibilities of local governments are closely linked to cultural policy innovation. For instance, Agenda 21 for Culture,[241] created by the Barcelona City Council,[242] has adopted a new document that talks about a new approach to government policy and innovation:

> They have agreed that local governments are on the front line in the defense and promotion of cultural rights as fundamental human rights. Local democracy is an essential basic condition of the participation of citizens in public decision-making. Local governments can also promote dialogue between citizens and their national governments and international institutions.[243]

The document also concludes:

> that local governments are applying multi-actor governance frameworks (governing in dialogue with civil society and the private sector), developing cross-cutting or horizontal forms of governance (that integrate the cultural dimension into public policy) and demanding multi-level or vertical governance frameworks (allowing them to coordinate and collaborate with other levels of government).[244]

The innovative approach of the document is reflected in social innovation policy that local governments have to promote:

> the participation of everyone in the creation, implementation, and evaluation of public policies, including cultural policies, and aim to facilitate cultural democracy. In addition to rights to culture for all citizens, local governments have the responsibility of guaranteeing spatial equity, both between the centres and peripheries of cities, and between cities and rural areas, paying special attention to indigenous communities.[245]

In the following document, the local government has essential actors in international processes, ensuring that the voices of citizens are heard on the world stage. Local governments promote local diplomacy and participate in international cooperation in the area of culture, as an indispensable tool for creating human solidarity and exchange: "They are especially well-placed to take into account and address the unique situations of less developed regions in their international cooperation work."[246]

The Culture 21: Action's document advocates the importance of two governing principles: "good government" and "shared government." It has three dimensions: multi-actor governance, including the public and private sectors; civil society, transversal or horizontal governance, covering different areas of public policy; and multi-level or vertical governance, between different levels of government. The transversal integration of culture into local sustainable development strategies requires the recognition of the shared nature of culture and its central place in the construction of public spaces in which people can explore, experience, and learn. The shared responsibility of all participants in multi-actor governance is innovative.[247] As well as local governments, it is necessary for civil society organizations, private organizations, and individuals to be recognized as key actors in public debates, in establishing priorities, in developing policies, and in managing and evaluating programs.

> Local governments have to be able to take on different roles as leaders, financial supporters, facilitators and, sometimes, just as observers. They have to accept overall responsibility for creating an enabling environment for sustainable development and cultural participation. In doing so, local governments must identify obstacles to citizen cooperation, and promote shared methods and goals between different parties.[248]

Over-institutionalization risks the unbalancing of cultural ecosystems just as much as privatization.

Ensuring the right to participation in cultural life requires that the cultural dimensions of all policies are taken into account.[249] The local governance of culture has to include opportunities for citizens to participate in cultural mapping (that is, in identifying cultural resources and relationships) and strategic planning of priorities and key actions, as well as their evaluation.

> Balanced governance encourages the establishment of participatory forums, either public (like local councils on culture), or independent (established and run by civil society). Governance of culture has to be supported by coordination mechanisms across different departments with responsibilities in cultural areas, as well as multi-level governance frameworks that help facilitate coordination among local, regional (where applicable), and national governments.[250]

In the document *Culture 21: Actions*, the local government implements a cultural policy based on the Agenda 21 for Culture and Culture 21: Actions, bringing together public, civic, and private initiatives for joint projects:[251]

a. The local government promotes cultural planning at the neighborhood or district level.
b. The local government creates public forums whose aims are to steer local cultural policy, such as local councils on culture that include public, private and civil society participation.
c. Public projects generate permanent forums for the consultation, negotiation, and regulation of goals and methods, with the participation of all parties involved, and that have to be characterized by foresight and the dynamics of reflexivity. Also, the "cultural institutions that receive public support are transparent, accountable, and evaluate the public services they provide; citizens are represented on their boards."
d. Programs and institutions in receipt of public support develop and practice gender equality.
e. Policies or programs operate to support the participation of citizens in the management of cultural institutions, programs, and events.

f. The local government recognizes and supports management practices that are representative of local culture, and develops specific and appropriate management practices for common goods.
g. An independent civil society platform, or network of civil society organizations that includes citizens and cultural professionals from all sectors is established."[252]

The innovative approach is the relation between local government, culture, and the economy.

> To be sustainable, an economy give thought to the values on which it is based, and consider the resources, cultural and otherwise, of the surrounding environment. Economies have the greatest legitimacy and dynamism when they are adapted to local resources. Cultural activities play an important role in comprehensive and sustainable economic development. They allow the renewal and creation of economic activities, boost entrepreneurship and employability, make up an important part of the attractiveness of places, and contribute to the development of tourism. However, economic models that prioritize quick, short-term economic impact at the expense of longer-term sustainability have driven the abusive exploitation and undermining of local cultural resources, resulting in the loss of identification of inhabitants with their local area. A sustainable use of cultural resources is respectful of core values and should contribute equally to cultural and economic development. Economic models that aim to be sensitive to culture should consider implementing practices that rely on collaboration, cooperatives, trading, and donations.[253]

The initial document, approved by local governments at a meeting in Bilbao, points out that all economic models are based on specific cultural values and choices.[254] Effective links between the public, market, and cooperative economies, and the forms of reciprocity between them, are essential to achieving people-centered, ecologically balanced economic development.

Cultural ecosystems cannot be treated as a mere footnote in the economy; on the contrary, they sustain it. The document *Culture 21: Actions* focuses on the interconnectedness of cultural ecosystems with and between other dimensions of sustainable development that have to always be taken into account.[255]

> In the cultural sphere, as in all areas of production, it is necessary to recognize artists and cultural professionals, ensure access to their works, promote corporate responsibility, and provide an adequate range of support mechanisms for cultural projects. Given the direct positive effects generated by cultural activities, a sustainable cultural ecosystem has to reinvest resources into local culture. Tourism is one of the economic powers for local governments and the local tourism model is sustainable, balanced across the region, connected to the local communities and interactive with cultural ecosystems.[256]

Corporate social responsibility programs must explicitly include projects in the area of culture and engage with the cultural values of the population and local culture. Local business organizations, such as the chamber of commerce, have specific cultural policies and programs. In that case, the economic and cultural ecosystem is sustainable.

The UK Innovation foundation based in London, NESTA, published a report on innovation culture policy in the government in which it stated that: "The 21st-century public servant is expected to be adept at change. The best of them will have access to the tools of an innovator and embrace a growth mindset which looks outwards to new possibilities."[257] This report highlights 20 tools[258] designed to help you bring ideas to life to change lives from within government. "This includes tools that generate ideas, tools for developing, or tools that support system change. Some of the tools exploit new technologies like data analytics, collective intelligence and people-powered public services."[259] The tools that NESTA has set up for support innovations are: Data analytics, Collective intelligence, Technology for democratic engagement, Prototyping, Experimentation, 100 Day Challenges, Testbeds, Innovation labs, Challenge prizes, New ways of using money, Behavioural insights, What Works Centres of evidence, People powered public services, Impact partnerships, Digital technologies to enhance services, Anticipatory regulation, Data governance, How to develop an innovative mindset, How to change operating models, and How to use structures to promote innovation.[260]

The report highlights the local government's new role:

> The primary motivator has been governments around the world seeking out a new role, moving away from the paternalistic institutions that did things to and for people, and towards a role as facilitators of new solutions for places and economies. These changes require a reimagining of the public sector, which in turn requires government innovators. Being an innovator inside or alongside government can feel isolating. The 20 tools are proven to help innovation flourish inside government, based on our work over more than a decade in UK local and central government, as well as with more than 30 international governments. So, whether you are a delivery manager or a policymaker, whether you work in national or local government, whether your role is externally or internally facing, this Report is helpful There are many ways to bring good ideas to life. Nesta's experience is that many innovators, especially in government, lean on just a few tools, rather than picking the best one for the job.[261]

In the NESTA report, it is also explained that data analytics can also innovate how the governance operates.

> For instance: earlier intervention and prevention: using predictive analytics, public services can move from the standard mode of addressing failure after it happens, to early intervention and prevention. For example, by analyzing trends of what happened in the past, why it happened and what is likely to

> happen, it is possible to identify buildings at risk of fire or road networks at risk of serious accidents, and take early action to reduce risk and costs. Faster and better decision-making: By bringing together complete, reliable and timely information, frontline teams and organizations can optimize their way of working, making more informed and impactful decisions at the same time.[262]
>
> For example, the use of dashboards that collate multiple sources of information means that everyone from police inspectors to social workers can have complete, real-time data on the progress of a child at risk to improve their decision-making. Resource targeting and personalization of services: By having a better understanding of individuals or groups of people, agencies are able to target resources at the areas most in need, or even tailor services based on the needs of their citizens.[263]
>
> Collecting, storing and using data to turn it into meaningful insight is complex in government. Data is often held in different public sector agencies (e.g., councils, police forces, job centres, regulatory bodies etc.), but it's hard for anyone to put all the pieces together to see what the big picture shows, and there are important ethical and legal constraints on sharing data.[264]

Collective intelligence is one of the innovation methods for local governments, and the NESTA report highlights its importance.

> The growing interest in new ways of using collective intelligence—using information, ideas and insights from citizens. Over the last few years, many experiments have shown how thousands of people can collaborate online, analyzing data or solving problems, and there's been an explosion of new technologies to sense, analyse and predict. The results of this can be seen in things like Wikipedia, like Wikihouse; or the spread of citizen science in which millions of people help to spot new stars in the galaxy, observe nature.[265]

In recent years, cities have been using online platforms to encourage citizens to propose ideas, comment and sometimes vote on how money is allocated. One of the European examples is the city of Barcelona, which established a digital platform for citizens under the DECIDIM[266] project. The report gives a few examples that parliaments are also experimenting with better ways to mobilize citizen expertise, for example, through select committees. The next step for governments is to use collective intelligence to address problems such as climate change or culture. Every government can work more successfully and mobilize more brains, data and computers to help it.[267]

The NESTA report highlights that the innovation labs consist of teams of professionals that can solve the challenge:

> Innovation labs are teams or units within government charged with making innovation happen. These multi-disciplinary teams are given dedicated resources to direct towards solving specific problems in a given time frame.

> They also often have a broader role of promoting innovation methods and cultures. All governments can struggle to find the resources and time to invest in the future when they are responsible for delivering the services that people rely on today. Building dedicated innovation labs can create much needed space for innovation by providing the time, structures and capabilities required. Innovation labs—often referred to as innovation teams, funds or units—have helped to change how governments around the world tackle challenges using experimental methods, by multidisciplinary teams, to tackle both social and public issues. Nesta set up its first public services lab in 2009 and since then has run labs (such as the HealthLab and Innovation Growth Lab), convened labs from around the world and documented how they work.[268]

The report found that innovation labs have to be focused on

> scanning for and identifying key issues, priorities and tasks, developing ideas that impact on these areas, testing solutions and creating routes into larger scale impact or systems change. Today there are many labs using different methods to try to solve social problems, both within and beyond government. Most famous perhaps is the "27e Région" in France and SITRA in Sweden. But in the last 10 years many more governments have established labs including Colombia, Mexico, South Korea and the UK Government's own Policy Lab.[269]
>
> The lab for transforming public policy is "27e Région", which conducts action-research programmes to test new innovation methods for designing public policy involving all public stakeholders. To this end, it mobilizes the capabilities of multi-disciplinary teams composed of designers, idea generators, and social scientists from many fields (ethnography, sociology, participant observation) and engages in ground-level actions (do-it-yourself projects, adult education actions, etc.). Both these approaches prioritize the concrete experience of users, civil servants and citizens to serve as the starting point for re-examining public policy.[270]

The innovation labs are most effective when:

> They have dedicated resourcing and support from the senior decision-makers in both political and officer positions of power, they work on time-limited challenges, understanding that part of their role is to seed change in the culture of their parent organisation.[271]

We live in a time in which the participation of citizens in decision-making processes is more than necessary. In the report, NESTA explains that,

> There is growing dissatisfaction with the limits of overly top-down, technocratic public services that no longer fit well with people's increasingly complex lives, nor with systemic challenges like social isolation, child poverty and

> long-term health conditions. Public services are experimenting with new ways of involving more citizens in the design, decision-making and implementation of public services to achieve better outcomes. This includes a wide spectrum of activities from civic activism to meaningful consultation to involving skilled volunteers in the delivery of support services. Over the last decade people powered approaches have been at the heart of Nesta's government innovation work. People power offers the public sector: new resources to achieve social goals including the giving of time, money and insights by beneficiaries, family members and communities, new expertise and knowledge, direct from patients, customers and users to compliment professional expertise.[272]

Innovation leads to changes in the way societies respond to social challenges:

> The capacity of central teams and units within governments is vital to the effectiveness and creativity of government, and in particular to how successfully they can innovate. Yet many are organized in inefficient ways that reflect both the goals, and the means, of the past. In order to promote innovation and achieve better outcomes, the centres of government—whether transnational, national or local—have to be organized to fit the methods and priorities of the 21st century.[273]

NESTA is

> focused on how governments can best support innovation and adaptation to changing environments. Five elements stand out: organizing leadership roles that fit the strategic priorities of the government: these leadership roles help ensure that innovation is coherent and strategic, resource mobility: ensuring that resources can be shifted quickly and that enough is being invested in public and social innovation (not just science innovation) to guarantee a pipeline of future options. People mobility: an ability to create temporary teams to work on problem-solving and ideas (as well as crises), helped by platforms that cut right across government (rather than staff being 'owned' by departments), central teams focused on strategy and innovation (including innovation labs): Although much of the work of innovation needs to be done as close to the ground as possible, central teams are vital not just to tackle cross-cutting issues but also to signal culture change.[274]

Innovation practices help local government organizations focus on economic and community development:

> These definitions recognize the process of introducing new things or methods. It is this process of introducing new things or methods into local government management and organization that motivates this research. Importantly,

> what is it that facilitates and sustains the innovation process, and how can this process be encouraged in other local government organizations. Definitions Rogers (1998) makes the important distinction between innovation and invention. The innovative organization does not need to have invented the new product or process they adopt.[275] Innovation is as much about the way new ideas and products are brought to effect as it is about the uniqueness of the original concept. The difference between innovation and invention is an important distinction for this research. Local governments do not have to have invented a new product or service to be innovative.[276]

The leading process to sustained economic and community benefit is a far more important innovative process.

> Kirton suggests that some individuals are more likely to innovate than others.[277] If these individuals are well placed within the organization hierarchy they are less constrained by others less likely to innovate. In specific situations individual differences will be less important than the interactions between situational and personal characteristics. Clearly there is an important relationship between individual and organizational characteristics affecting the development of a culture of innovation. Innovators look for, and work with, the waves of political, social, economic and technological change occurring in their environment. They adopt an open and engaging strategy learning as much as they can about what drives change and how they might come to work with it, rather than fighting a fruitless rear-guard action to restore things to the way they were in some idealized past.[278]

The support of research for new ideas by innovators entails the need for experimentation. They need to have freedom in their organization to experiment.

> Building innovative capacity is a conscious strategy to qualitatively improve the human capital that is the organisation's employees. The key words are building and capacity. Innovative capacity must be built in an organization, and where one starts to build will be different for different organizations. The idea of building something suggests that a plan, or a picture of the finished product is in the builder's mind. In organizational terms having such a picture goes to the heart of the innovative organization. Optimistic managers with a vision of the future, of what is possible in organizational terms, are key drivers in building innovative capacity. Building capacity refers to this process of enabling people to acquire and to develop new insights into the way they work and problem solve. While absorptive capacity refers primarily to individual learning, building innovative capacity refers to organizational learning.[279]

In the book *International Entrepreneurship in the Arts*,[280] the relations between creativity and innovation are defined. Innovation implies "newness" in a product, service, or process, or alternatively a more efficient way of doing things. The question is: is innovation a result of a "flash of genius," or is it systematically motivated?

"Innovation is an economic or social rather than a technical term. Innovation is specific tool of entrepreneurs." P. Drucker.[281]

Experimental Government

> The idea that governments have to be experiment isn't new. China has a very old tradition of testing ideas out before taking them to scale. Nineteenth-century reformers in the West, inspired by the achievements of science, often advocated a deliberately experimental approach too.[282]

But this idea has never been all that enthusiastically embraced. The public aren't keen to be guinea pigs. Politician's fear being crucified for the failures and given no credit for the successes.

> Yet the benefits of experimentation are huge, as this report confirms. Far better to test ideas out on a small scale rather than on a whole nation. Far better to let promising ideas improve before they are imposed on everyone. And far better to find out quickly if apparently brilliant ideas that work well on paper do not work well in practice.[283]

These arguments for experimentation help to explain why there is now much more use of formal and less formal experimental methods around the world, from welfare to education, health to justice. But there is still uncertainty about what method to use and when, and whether, for example, the methods that work in clinical trials are always going to be appropriate for the work of government. The report also covers the question of how to fit experiments into the daily life of public organizations.

> In some discussions of this issue there is an unhelpful polarization between purist advocates of randomized controlled trials, who see them as the only truly valid source of knowledge about what works, and others who reject them outright. Both positions risk being equally simplistic, and equally blind to the often-subtle evidence about evidence. RCTs can be immensely useful, particularly in fields where they are uncommon. But as medicine and healthcare have discovered, they are far from being panaceas, and are often most useful in combination with other kinds of evidence. They are only one tool; they are not always the best tool; and they are not well-suited to testing many types of policy.[284]
>
> Breakthroughs in transforming public services only come from a willingness to push at boundaries, to take risks, and, sometimes, to fail. If the government is to play a role in innovating, it is essential that it does so in the expectation that some of what it does may well fail, and that when things are not working, they will be stopped.[285]

Experimental government is not about trying things out in a haphazard way. It needs to be done in a way where we can genuinely learn from those experiments and adapt.

> Indeed, governments experiment all the time—rolling out new policies on the populace, but without really learning if they are doing any good. The Russian Soviet 'experiment', for example, was not really an experiment at all. The government could not really evolve, test different approaches and set up feedback loops. The reality was that Soviet central planners had a 'pathological inability to experiment', creating some disastrous command-and-control industrial policies.[286]
>
> In the face of political pressures and the urgency to deliver results within short timetables, experimentation can be sidelined. That is why we are calling for a genuine ethos of experimental government. It requires a degree of humility and openness to risk and failure. We usually do not know exactly which policies will work. Experimental government is a way of finding out.[287]

An experimental approach is also vital in moving beyond a static "evidence-based policy."[288] Evidence can sometimes only reflect what worked in the past – or in other countries. Focusing on what seemed to work in the past reinforces the *status quo*. We need to constantly strive for new alternatives and new knowledge to meet current challenges. When dealing with any open complex system about which there is missing information and substantial uncertainty, the best way to discover is to probe and experiment.

> In the area of business innovation policy, for instance, experimentation is more effective than old-school industrial policy of command-and-control—where government knows best, picks winners, and rolls out business-support policies with little idea if they will succeed or not. The superior approach is to embrace uncertainty, and for government to have an innovation policy which actively experiments with business to create valuable (open) data and intelligence. As Bakhshi, Freeman and Potts state, "Innovation policy... can turn up knowledge of opportunities faster, it can spread this knowledge faster, and it can dramatically reduce the social cost of repetitive failure.[289]
>
> Experimental government means avoiding an approach where everything is well and truly fixed from the outset. As the author of a UK government report on piloting, the late Professor Sir Roger Jowell said, we need a "spirit of experimentation, unburdened by promises of success.[290]

Many experiments need to start small, so as to limit the political and economic cost to a government of a trial that fails.

> The advantage of an experimental approach is that you can be 'innovative and cautious at the same time ... try things out in an overly tentative manner',

according to a US position statement on social policy experimentation funded by the MacArthur Foundation. You can test your new idea and, if it fails, it is only on a limited scale, limiting damage.[291]

Experimental government should happen either locally and regionally, not just at the national level. Sub-national, local, or city government offers a ripe opportunity to rigorously test out different approaches to policies, programs, and practice.

Testing out new policies by state governments is commonplace in the US. Their federal structure enables individual states to mount their own fairly large-scale experiments to test the likely impact of a proposed new policy or delivery mechanism or both.[292]

Several scholars of China's economic rise have stressed the important role of experimentation.

What has been so surprising is that so much of this flexibility has taken place in the extremely inflexible institutions of the Communist party-state. The approach to experimentation in China's party-state is very different from other democratic countries. It does not use the small-scale pilot projects seen in Europe and the US. China has used bolder experiments that have impacted China-wide national policies, such as more positive approaches to private business after bottom-up experimentation.[293]

According to the Australian Centre of Excellence for Local Government,[294]

local governments should adopt these principles in innovation: the search for public value, the use of appropriate problem-solving language, recognition that every idea matters, problem-solving involving everybody, creating interdisciplinary teams of problem-solvers with effective disciplinary integration, the importance of community of practice (encompassing stakeholder and citizen participation) at all stages, experimenting—searching widely for new ideas and tolerating failure.[295]

The book *Innovation in Local Government: Defining the challenge, making the change* highlights the importance of understanding effective local government leadership in the context of a broader vision for localism.[296] And the future local governance needs to: safeguard public sector legitimacy and community values, create a clear strategic vision for the community, win the trust of local citizens, manage complex processes of change, build strong working relationships with citizens, solve critical governance issues from climate change to the representation of women, deliver innovative and effective citizen- centered services, be equal partners in governance, lead with personal and professional integrity, and set the agenda of local government reform.[297]

Notes

215 OECD, *The Value of Culture and the Creative Industries in Local Development* (2018), accessed April 10, 2020. https://www.oecd.org/cfe/leed/2018-SACCI-Handbook.pdf
216 Ibid., 11.
217 Ibid.
218 Ibid., 13.
219 Pier Luigi Sacco, *Culture 3.0: A New Perspective for the EU 2014–2020 Structural Funds Programming* (European Expert Network on Culture [EENC], 2011).
220 Ibid.
221 John Holden, *Capturing Cultural Value: How Culture Has Become a Tool of Government Policy* (London: Demos, 2004); John Holden, *Cultural Value and the Crisis of Legitimacy* (London: Demos 2006).
222 OECD, *The Value of Culture and the Creative Industries in Local Development.*
223 Holden, *Capturing Cultural Value.*
224 KEA European Affairs, *The Impact of Culture on Creativity* (Brussels: Author, 2009).
225 OECD, *The Value of Culture and the Creative Industries in Local Development.*
226 KEA European Affairs, accessed April 20, 2020, https://keanet.eu/
227 KEA, *Mapping the Creative Value Chains: A Study on the Economy of Culture in the Digital Age* (Luxembourg: Publications Office of the European Union, 2017).
228 Ibid., 19.
229 Ibid., 20.
230 OECD, *The Value of Culture and the Creative Industries in Local Development.*
231 Ibid., 22.
232 Ibid., 25.
233 Ibid., 26.
234 Ibid.
235 Ibid., 28.
236 Ibid., 29.
237 Ibid., 30.
238 Barcelona Art Factories programme, accessed April 18, 2020, http://www.bcn.cat/fabriquesdecreacio/ca/
239 Steve Glaveski, "Innovation in Local Government," Collective Campus, accessed April 18, 2020, www.collectivecampus.io/blog/innovation-in-local-government
240 Mark Evans, Chris Aulich, Anne Howard, and Megan Peterson, *Innovation in Local Government: Defining the Challenge, Making the Change* (Australian Center for Local Government; Sydney: University of Technology, 2013).
241 UCLG, "Agenda 21 for Culture."
242 UCLG, "Culture 21: Actions."
243 Ibid.
244 Ibid.
245 Ibid.
246 Ibid.
247 Ibid.
248 Ibid.
249 UCLG, "Culture 21: Actions."
250 Ibid.
251 Ibid.
252 Ibid.
253 Ibid.
254 The document Culture 21: Actions was approved on March 18 to 20, 2015 in Bilbao, in the framework of the first Culture Summit of UCLG.
255 UCLG, "Culture 21: Actions."
256 Ibid.

257 NESTA, *"20 Tools for Innovating in Government,"* 2019, accessed April 20, 2020, https://media.nesta.org.uk/documents/20_Tools_Innovating_Government.pdf
258 Ibid., 4.
259 Ibid.
260 Ibid., 1.
261 Ibid., 6.
262 Ibid.
263 Ibid.
264 Ibid., 10.
265 Ibid., 18.
266 Decidim Barcelona, accessed April 5, 2020, https://www.decidim.barcelona/
267 NESTA, "20 Tools for Innovating in Government".
268 Ibid.
269 Ibid., 58.
270 "A Lab to Transform Public Policies," La 27e Région, accessed April 21, 2020, http://www.la27eregion.fr/en/
271 Ibid.
272 NESTA "20 Tools for Innovating in Government."
273 Ibid.
274 Ibid.
275 Mark Rogers, *The Definition and Measurement of Innovation* (Melbourne: Melbourne Institute of Applied Economic and Social Research, 1998).
276 Evans et al., *Innovation in Local Government.*
277 Michael Kirton, "Adaptors and Innovators: A Description and Measure," *Journal of Applied Psychology* 61, no. 5 (1976): 622–629.
278 Ibid.
279 Peter Senge, *The Fifth Discipline: The Art and Practice of the Learning Organisation* (New York: Doubleday, 1990).
280 Lidia Varbanova, *International Entrepreneurship in the Arts* (London/New York: Routledge, 2016).
281 Peter Drucker (1909–2005) was one of the most widely-known and influential thinkers on management, whose work continues to be used by managers worldwide.
282 Jonathan Breckon, *Better Public Services Through Experimental Government* (London: Alliance for Useful Evidence, 2015).
283 Ibid.
284 Ibid.
285 Ibid.
286 Ibid.
287 Ibid.
288 Ibid.
289 Hasan Bakhshi, Alan Freeman, and Jason Potts, *State of Uncertainty, Innovation Policy Through Experimentation* (London: NESTA, 2011).
290 Ibid.
291 Ibid.
292 Ibid.
293 Ibid.
294 Evans et al., "Innovation in Local Government."
295 Ibid.
296 Ibid.
297 Ibid.

6

INNOVATION AND DEVELOPMENT OF CREATIVE INDUSTRIES

Creative Industries and Innovation

In the study on the Economy of Culture in Europe,[298] it is written that:

> Culture is ideally positioned on the cusp between the economy and the political sphere. Compared to other sectors of the economy, culture has an additional dimension—it not only creates wealth but it also contributes to social inclusion, better education, self-confidence and the pride of belonging to an historic community. Culture is also a powerful tool to communicate values and to promote objectives of public interest that are broader than wealth creation.[299]

In the following excerpt, the study explains the role of culture in European societies:

> Culture performs multiple social and political functions. These have often served as justifications for cultural policies at national levels which have gained an increased relevance in a globalized and multicultural world. Indeed, culture can be regarded as an "ambassador" and as a vehicle for European "values" (tolerance, democracy, diversity, and pluralism, etc.) and its "way-of-life." Europe has succeeded in establishing the principle of cultural diversity as a tenet of international law and in establishing those cultural products are not mere merchandises, but deserve specific treatment. But culture is more than a banner for European "values".[300]
>
> It acts as a catalyst for intercultural dialogue within Europe, as well as with the rest of the world. Distributors of films, books or sound recordings give citizens the opportunity to experience the culture of others. In a multicultural world culture has a role to play in exemplifying the peaceful and

DOI: 10.4324/9781003336648-7

> enriching dimensions of exchanges between populations. Culture is also a lever for territorial and social integration. The Bilbao Guggenheim Museum opened up the Basque country to the world and reintroduced Bilbao into modernity. "Brownfield sites, when they are vested with cultural activities, bring a new economic and social life to our cities. Culture is powerful tool to re-integrating the socially excluded, providing them with the opportunity to set up and fulfil their own project, acquire new skills that can be transferred into other sectors of activities and recover self-confidence.[301]

The European Union has been built through the economy and market. In this perspective, Europe can create minimal economic solidarity amongst European nations. It is particularly important to assess the value of the cultural and creative industries to Europe's economy.

Research and development play an important role in this sector. The importance of digital technology has been significant for Europe. The study of the Economy of Culture in Europe also points out the fact that,

> So far the focus of the Lisbon Strategy[302] has been on ICT uptake and network development as well as on research in technology. Technology has been given prominence over other factors that stimulate economic and social growth in Europe. Culture and creativity suffer from an image problem and their economic role needs to be articulated if the sector is to gain better exposure amongst decision makers.[303]

The importance of culture for our societies has been recognized as significant. The reasons are numerous, as the Study of the Economy of Culture in Europe explains:

> The situation of marginalization in the cultural sector is changing. It has been triggered by the following factors: The contribution of culture to the economy has gradually been acknowledged, in particular with the development of the cultural industries. Culture contributes directly to the economy as it provides products for consumption, namely the cultural goods and services embodied in books, films, music sound recordings, concerts, etc. In addition, long-term structural changes in our societies give more importance to culture as a product of consumption. The demand for an ever-greater number of diverse cultural products is indicative of post-modern consumer behavior: consumers seek to differentiate themselves by appropriating the signs and values that mark specific products. This trend is being reinforced by the average level of education: as it increases, so does the demand for culture. Considering income availability, the richer our societies become, the more immaterial our consumption patterns become. When basic needs are covered and satisfied, consumption is increasingly a cultural statement. This trend is reinforced by the increase in availability of leisure time that can be devoted to cultural activities. All these social trends converge in sustaining an increasing

> demand for cultural content consumption and for cultural participation. It is also increasingly acknowledged that the benefits culture brings to European economies are wider than the mere consumption of cultural goods: culture is indirectly used by many non-cultural economic sectors as a source of innovation. "Creativity" is a complex process of innovation mixing several dimensions such as technology, science, management, and culture. Culture provides tangible as well as intangible assets consisting of artistic heritage, processes, references, and skills that interact with other skills and resources to foster innovation.[304]

Some European states have been analyzing the commercial value of creative industries without necessarily attempting to analyze their cultural and social values. Those countries are developing programs to turn creativity into industrial successes. The study also confirms that creative industries are growing and increasing the national income in the upcoming years.

> Leading State is the UK which set up a Creative Industries Task Force and published the Creative Industries Mapping Documents in 1998 and 2001. On the basis of its initial findings the British Government states that the creative industries are now bringing in 8% of national income and employing 5% of the workforce. Since 1997 the output of the creative industries, according to the UK government, has grown by up to 20% a year, compared with less than 6% for the economy as a whole. Again, according to the UK Trade Secretary, the creative economy is growing at 8% per year. It accounts for one in five of all jobs in London and £ 11.4 billion of UK's balance of trade "well ahead of the construction industry, insurance and pensions, and twice that of the pharmaceutical sector". The creative industries are now bigger than the financial services sector in the UK.[305]

In the study on the Economy of Culture in Europe, under the section on the economy of cultural goods and services, an explanation is given of the relationship between the traditional sector, which is understood as a non-economic "work of art," and the creative industries:

> Traditional art sectors (such as visual arts, dance, drama, opera, museums, etc.) have tended to be confined to a non-economic approach. The output of these sectors is generally referred to as "works of art" rather than "cultural goods and services". Their main function was considered as pertaining to the "enlightenment" of the people: the pleasure in enjoying the beauty of a work of art, the historical and educational value attached to it and the philosophical & political dimension they encompass. The economic value they entail is often not regarded as important. These sectors are also seen as "subsidized" sectors, public subsidies being justified by the non-economic and non-profitable nature of the works of art. And yet, their economic value

> is increasingly acknowledged. The arts field is a powerful tool for local development. It is a sector of growth and a catalyst to the dynamism of creative cities. It acts as a soft location element in a local economic policy aimed at triggering the establishment of companies and talented people. It helps reinforce social integration and ensures territorial cohesion. It is a successful driver to attract tourists. Cultural industries produce market and distribute cultural goods aimed at mass reproduction and mass consumption. Consumption does not take place on the spot, as for works of art: these products are aimed at being disseminated and exported. The economic dimension is here more obvious. New technology is a powerful driving force that is increasing the economic potential of the cultural and creative sectors.[306]

We are living in a time of creativity. Traditional models are no longer feasible. Innovation actually improves creative processes. The European Union Study explains that,

> Creativity combining some or all of the following dimensions: ideas, skills, technology, management, production processes as well as culture. Creativity has the ability to benefit almost all economic sectors. In this context, culture is not analyzed as a source of final consumption (as in the case of films, books, music, cultural tourism, etc.) but as a source of intermediate consumption in the production process, most of the time the final products being functional (to the contrary of works of arts or to the output of cultural industries). For example, culture can be used as a source of heritage, providing elements of creativity to other economic sectors—heritage is thereby continuously renewing itself. This is the case when a piece of music is "sampled" to create a new one, or when old images or famous characters of our literature are used to create multimedia artworks or entertainment.
>
> 37 Culture will provide specific skills, working methods and codes that will be transferred into other sectors of the economy and combined with other skills. The creative imperative in a post-industrialized economy to foster innovation Until recently, the two essential parameters of competition were price and technology. Today, consumers are flooded by a market full of products with similar prices and technical performance. A good product can easily be copied at a lower cost. One traditional (but socially disruptive) response to increased competition, and to the downward pressure on costs, is to shift a significant share of value-added and labour-intensive production activity abroad, allowing for the production of the same products at lower costs. Alternatively, the situation can be addressed by fostering competitiveness, growth and income within Europe, through an optimal use of "creativity". Competition triggers, in addition to techno-economic knowledge, the need for increased quality and differentiation to gain a competitive edge. What increasingly matters today, and constitutes a distinctive competition parameter, lies in the immaterial dimension generated by creative people,

> skills, ideas and processes; in other terms, creativity. The cultural sector, its entrepreneurs, its employees and artists which are the main sources of this creativity.[307]

The European Union Study on the European Economy of Culture also defines the

> territorial dimension of culture and creativity—"glocality" and it means that creativity constitutes a response to some of the economic challenges of globalization, it requires initiative and organization at a local level. To put it another way, creativity is both global and local—hence the term "glocality". This feature of localization is a positive aspect of creativity: not only does creativity nurture economic competitiveness but it helps retain talent (and corresponding jobs) locally.[308]

In his book on the Creative City, American researcher Richard Florida argues that conventional assumptions about the relationship between investment, technology, human capital, and growth are not the same as traditional ones.

> He says that creative firms will increasingly follow the talent (which he labels "the creative class") because creative people look for cultural amenities and because creative people and resources are more difficult to replicate. In other words, the spatial dimension and the interactions generated on a limited territory are crucial for creativity to emerge and contribute to the economy. A virtuous circle can then be nurtured, because these creative people once concentrated on a territory will create synergies and fruitful collaborations, thereby fostering further creativity.[309]

A creative city is a city where artists are part of the professional class, where the city has a long-term development plan; it is a place with a unique cultural identity not found anywhere else. Where the word "authentic" is more than a prefix for the latest restaurant. It is a city that can clearly demonstrate the connection between creativity and innovation and knows how to leverage the full economic potential of the cultural economy. The creative city is an illusion, a mechanism for describing a better way of living. It is an aspiration as much as a reality, a template for what might be. The creative city is an outline of a city we all want to go to, but no one is 100% sure of how we are going to get there.

In his preface to *The Creative City*, Peter Hall notes that, "British city economies are in structural crisis."[310] Not much has changed since then. The creative city is an illusion, as much a talking point for urbanists and city planners as is the Smart City or the Digital City. Economic stability needs more than the weaving together of ideas; it needs a new economic paradigm, beyond, or built on top of, the capitalist framework. It needs values that extend beyond money. Rights that embrace all citizens and equity at every level. It needs to be ethical, sustainable, and fun. A Creative City needs to think in terms of generations, not years.

According to the NESTA research report on the creative industries,

> The most influential definition of the 'creative industries' was given by the Department for Culture, Media and Sport's Creative Industries Taskforce in 1998 (DCMS, 1998). The taskforce defined them as based upon activities which have their origin in individual creativity, skill and talent, and as having the potential for wealth creation through the generation and exploitation of intellectual property. The Creative Industries include: advertising, architecture, arts & antiques market, crafts, design, designer fashion, film, music, performing arts, publishing, software and computer service, computer games (interactive leisure software), radio & TV.[311]

The research report provides a basis for thinking that

> Some creative industries do design or produce physical artifacts. Most often, "the physical work is the vehicle for conveying the idea" rather than playing the purely functional role of an "ordinary economic good."[312] The value of the artifacts is usually overwhelmingly based on the "content," their cultural meaning, or the experiences they help create. Many creative industries produce "information products," and this means that they can often be made available in digital form.[313]

In addition, the report concludes that,

> the goods and services have unusual properties. Most can be consumed repeatedly. This provides opportunities for innovation—digital content may be put together in new ways, through music remixes, new DVD box sets or as internet or mobile phone downloads. But such opportunities also present economic challenges. This raises issues for intellectual property rights (IPRs).[314]
>
> There is in general limited scope for patenting (except for certain aspects of software, and some developments of technology in the processes of creative firms), but copyright, trademarks and design rights may be invoked. Enforcing IPRs—and establishing their reach in an evolving information environment—is a highly contentious topic. Indeed, the debate is both promoting and being reshaped by technological and organizational innovation.[315]

In the research report *Hidden innovation in the creative industries*, it is concluded that many information goods and services require consumers

> that can understand and process the information provided; and the consumers' experience of creative goods and services is highly informed by their consumption of related works, prior knowledge, and changing tastes. In this environment, creative products resemble a 'service experience'. Indeed, some

> commentators argue that the 'experience economy' is a more appropriate term than the 'service economy'. In the terms of services: many creative products are services, and many that are technically goods are used in a service context. Services of many sorts frequently involve performance, where the staff help to create the consumer experience—vconsider for example hotels and restaurants. One feature of many services is that production and consumption are largely co-terminous: the service is produced and consumed simultaneously, at the same time and in the same place. A theatre performance has this in common with a theme park visit.[316]

The literature on the topic provides a classification of services. Innovation in the creative industries is not based solely on aesthetics and content.

Aesthetic innovation is not the only form of innovation in the creative industries. In the following thesis, by analyzing the case studies, we can find many aspects of innovation that have less to do with new creative content than with other aspects like production or presentation processes.

In a study of creative industries, NESTA

> focuses less on 'product innovation' than on creative approaches at the strategic and organizational level of businesses. Five important areas of innovation are singled out:
>
> - innovating into new markets (e.g., moving from clothing to construction, from entertainment to education)
> - disrupting the value chain through digital technologies (by cutting out existing distributors and retailers)
> - building on diversity (drawing on ethnic minorities and global cultures)
> - moving from being IP (Intellectual Property) producers to IP owners (generating ongoing revenues from their creative content, for example by enabling material to be used in a wider range of commercial formats)
> - collaborating to compete (co-production of new ideas with customers, enabling the development of competitive new products).[317]

The few dimensions are seen as "hidden innovation" and likely to be common within the creative industries.

> These four dimensions are described as: Cultural Product—the product that carries the cultural meanings and information content (a film, videogame, stage performance, sculpture, or set of design specifications); Cultural Concept—the information 'content' of the product, such as characters, narratives, representations of tangible objects, or less tangible ideas. Delivery—how the product is made accessible to consumers and User Interface—how the consumer interacts with the product to gain the experience that is the outcome of the creative activity.[318]

It is important to understand innovation in a set of creative industries where many innovative activities exist.

The Public Policy of Economy and Creative Industries

The term creative industries have various definitions and needs to be analyzed.

> The European Union report on "Models of ICT Innovation. A Focus on the Cinema Sector" concludes that, "Over the last two decades, the term creative industry has been widely used in the academic literature and in public relations. The term, however, remains unclear. It makes it difficult, in particular, to adequately characterize the dynamic technology and innovation in the field of media and culture."[319] To address this gap, the first chapter of the report seeks to specify the types of industrial systems that exist in the creative industries. To this aim, it develops an assessment and a critical discussion of existing works, feeding them with emblematic cases and comparative empirical data. This first part characterizes the different types of innovation." [320]
>
> The observations serve to emphasize that Research & Development is not globally invested as such, and structured in the creative industries; it exists nonetheless both in terms of physical infrastructure and applications. In the most technical creative industries, innovative initiatives succeed in finance; technology specialist companies exist and are sometimes large.[321]
>
> Also that in Europe, the seminal definition of creative industries came from the UK: the Department for Culture, Media and Sport Creative Task Force formalized the definition of creative industries as 'those industries which have their origin in individual creativity, skill and talent and which have a potential for wealth and job creation through the generation and exploitation of intellectual property'.[322,323]

The following excerpt of the European Union report on models of ICT Innovation. "A Focus on the Cinema Sector" notes that

> a decade later, creative industries are still described as "a mixed bag" by Deutsche Bank Research (2011). The ESSnet-Culture report notes in a similar fashion: "The concept is used in various documents and it is not standardized.[324] The report adds "Not only can the notion of 'creativity' not be statistically measured but" also the notion of 'industries' has different meanings, ESSnet-Culture strongly recommends when speaking about creative and cultural industries, to clearly mention the sectors that are covered."[325] The coverage of the resulting grouping of industrial activities under one banner is impressive and shows that the historical aggregation of a variety of domains under one same category has not made it easier observing research and development or the innovative processes in and across those industries,

gauging their economic weigh, analysing their commonalities or differences or measuring their spillovers in the rest of the economy. The same applies for the media and content industries, a subset of the creative industries.[326]

The European Union report on "Models of ICT Innovation. A Focus on the Cinema Sector" (2015) also explains that,

> The concept of Creative and Cultural Industries (CCIs) is often used by different stakeholders, especially by policy makers (in different fields of economic or social policy) and, in particular, when economic data on CCIs are presented. The concept is used in various documents and it is not standardized. It also extends to different realities (creative industries, creative goods, creative economy, creative cities, creative regions, creative class etc.) and covers different cultural sectors in academic documents or national strategies. Starting from a core set of relatively basic cultural fields (heritage and fine arts in general) and broadening it to wider activities (publishing, audio-visual, design, architecture) and peripheral fields (software, telecommunications, ICT), the CCIs' notion often seems generic and broad and does not merely include cultural/artistic creation. Not only can the notion of 'creativity' not be statistically measured but also the notion of 'industries' has different meanings, ESSnet—Culture strongly recommends when speaking about creative and cultural industries, to clearly mention the sectors that are covered.[327]

Research and technical innovation takes place outside the creative industries and its supported by information and communication technology (ICT).[328] The study shows the important role played by numerous smaller-sized companies in content-related technology innovation. The creative industries are not the main focus of R&D (research and development), Bakhshi et al. suggest that: "Experimentation and innovation in content and form are inherent to the arts." Being an "inherent form" of the arts does not necessarily allow confusing creative experimentation with R&D. The Frontiers Economics 2006 report emphasizes that they cannot all be grouped under a single definition when thinking about policy (Frontiers Economics, 2006: 8).[329] The report defines three main industry groups: "production industries, characterized by the production of physical or tangible products (for example the production of CDs in the music industry); service industries providing services to customers (for example architecture); and arts and crafts."[330,331]

The New European Agenda for Culture

> The New European Agenda for Culture has been created to build cohesive societies and offer a vision of an attractive Europe. It aims to harness the full potential of culture to help build a more inclusive and fairer Union, supporting innovation, creativity and sustainable jobs and growth.[332]

"The New Agenda will make a synergy between culture and education and strengthen links between culture and other areas."[333]

> It will also help cultural and creative sectors overcome the challenges and grasp the opportunities of the digital shift. The European Council has now tasked the EU to do more in this area and to examine further possible measures addressing, among others, the legal and financial framework conditions for the development of cultural and creative industries and the mobility of professionals of the cultural sector.[334]

The European Agenda for Culture has a few strategic objectives in which the economy and culture play a central role.

> The New Agenda has three strategic objectives, with social, economic and external dimensions.
>
> Social dimension—harnessing the power of culture and cultural diversity for social cohesion and well-being.
>
> - Foster the cultural capability of all Europeans by making available a wide range of cultural activities and providing opportunities to participate actively.
> - Encourage the mobility of professionals in the cultural and creative sectors and remove obstacles to their mobility.
> - Protect and promote Europe's cultural heritage as a shared resource, to raise awareness of our common history and values and reinforce a sense of common European identity.[335]

The New Agenda points out that cultural participation brings people together.

> Culture is an ideal means of communicating across language barriers, empowering people and facilitating social cohesion, including among refugees, other migrants and host populations. Under the 2007 European Agenda, policymakers and practitioners have agreed ways of using participatory arts to promote understanding, empower people, and increase self- confidence.[336]
>
> Culture is a transformative force for community regeneration. The successful 30-year history of the European Capitals of Culture demonstrates this, as do cultural infrastructure projects funded by European Structural and Investment Funds. The European Year is spotlighting the transversal contribution of heritage to European societies and economies. There is a new, adaptive approach to shaping our built environment—and it is rooted in culture.[337]

From the following document of the New European Agenda for Culture, it is clear that, "Cultural participation also improves health and well-being. 71% of Europeans recently surveyed agreed living close to places related to Europe's cultural heritage can improve quality of life."[338] And research confirms that cultural access is the second most important determinant of psychological well-being, preceded only by the absence of disease.

> But social and financial barriers to cultural participation remain, despite cultural organizations' efforts to adapt to changing patterns of cultural consumption and composition of the population. So, a new approach is proposed with cultural capability as the guiding principle. This means making available a wide range of quality cultural activities, promoting opportunities for all to take part and to create, and strengthening links between culture and education, social affairs, urban policy, research and innovation.[339]

The document highlights the clear link between education and participation in culture.[340] "Cross-sectoral action on Cultural Awareness and Expression—one of the eight key competences recognized at European level—will be explored in the context of the revised Key Competence Framework for Lifelong Learning."[341]

> There is also consensus on the need for transferable competences and skills, which stimulate creativity and critical thinking. The Commission has supported the work of the Organization for Economic Co-operation and Development (OECD) on how to teach, learn, and assess creative and critical thinking, which is now the innovative domain for the program for International Student Assessment 2021 (PISA). This focus on creative and critical thinking have to be extended to all levels of education and training, in line with the shift in approach from STEM (Science, Technology, Engineering and Maths) to STEAM, including the Arts.[342]

The main targets of development are cities and regions in Europe. Therefore, the New Agenda for Culture in Europe is exploring models of innovation. "Cultural and creative sectors have huge capacity for experimentation, anticipating trends, and exploring models of social and economic innovation. Cities and regions are natural partners":[343] at the forefront of culture-led development thanks to greater local autonomy, the attraction they exert on high-talent individuals, and their proximity to their inhabitants' needs and potential.

> Culture and tourism are powerful drivers of economic activity. Cities that invest in culture can reap substantial rewards, attracting more jobs and human capital than other comparable cities, as shown by the Cultural and Creative Cities Monitor, developed by the Commission's Joint Research Centre.[344]
>
> In rural areas, restoration and upgrading of cultural and natural heritage contributes to growth potential and sustainability.[345] Integrated management of cultural and natural assets encourages people to discover and engage with both. To increase participation, greater circulation of European artworks and of professionals in the European cultural and creative sectors is required.[346]

The document highlights the connecting factors of the economic dimension.

> Economic dimension—supporting culture-based creativity in education and innovation, and for jobs and growth.
>
> - Promote the arts, culture and creative thinking in formal and non-formal education and training at all levels and in lifelong learning.
> - Foster favorable ecosystems for cultural and creative industries, promoting access to finance, innovation capacity, fair remuneration of authors and creators and cross-sectoral cooperation.
> - Promote the skills needed by cultural and creative sectors, including digital, entrepreneurial, traditional and specialized skills.[347]
>
> The facts are that, Culture and creativity are important assets for the economy. Culture contributes directly to jobs, growth, and external trade. EU cultural employment increased steadily between 2011 and 2016, when it reached 8.4 million. There is a EUR 8.7 billion trade surplus in cultural goods,[348]

"and cultural and creative sectors are estimated to contribute 4.2% to EU gross domestic product."[349] "Innovative economic sectors also need creativity to maintain competitive advantage. Urban and rural communities increasingly rely on culture to attract employers, students and tourists."[350]

Cooperating with other sectors helps generate innovative solutions, including in information and communication technology, tourism, manufacturing, services, and the public sector. They have a transformative power for the cultural ecosystem. This is built through education and training, cities and regions, and cultural and creative industries, and makes for a more sustainable culture ecosystem.

The cultural and creative industries increase growth and jobs, the environment that enables better creation, better finances, opportunities, skills, and internationalization.

"The New Agenda builds on ongoing policy work, particularly on entrepreneurial and heritage skills."[351]

> Professionals in the cultural and creative sectors require a broad mix of digital, traditional, transversal and specialized skills. The New Agenda prioritizes a cross-sectoral approach to EU collaboration, as digitization and co-creation continue to break down artistic and economic boundaries. This will be complemented by specific initiatives in the most mature sectors, to support more effectively the rich diversity of European cultural expressions. The New Agenda enables culture to be promoted more effectively as a vector of identity and cohesion, a driver of socio-economic development, and a factor directly nurturing peaceful relations, including through the people-to-people contacts resulting from education and youth projects, with a particular focus on the Western Balkans and Enlargement countries.[352]

"The Commission also plans to use the Agenda to emphasize the cultural dimension of sustainable development and to help implement the UN 2030 Agenda for Sustainable Development."[353]

The Creative Industries

The creative industries include any project, product or service that simultaneously meets the following two conditions:

1. It has to have creative value (in the case of cultural artifacts this pertains to cultural, artistic value).
2. It has to have economic (commercial) value.[354]

> The creative industries are indeed conceived as an array of cultural and creative activities, making it much easier to statistically measure the economic results of these activities compared to a situation in which we declare any individual product or service within any cultural activity as belonging to the creative industries. Thus, we see how this definition is permeated by the logic of official statistics.[355]

"In general, statistics play a huge role in the public promotion of the importance of creative industries."[356] Along these lines, the phenomenon of "creative statistics" is also quite frequently encountered as a result of the desire to arrive at the best possible statistical data.

> The contribution of the creative sector to the Gross Domestic Product (GDP) and the number of people employed in this sector depends on how broadly the data is captured. The more that different activities and occupations are included in the calculation, the higher the percentages. Hence statistical minds contribute in their own way to the continuous spreading of these notions about the creative industries. But once we accept the fact that the creative sector is extremely important to the economic development and creation of new jobs, it no longer matters whether statistics will yield the result of 2, 3, 4, 5 or more per cent of the total GDP being contributed by the creative industries. In other words, defining and managing public policy on creative industries is not and should not be the product of any official statistics.[357]

"To return to the definition: if creative industries are approached from the level of a single product, the entire mind-set for their understanding and operation is changed. This approach, after all, is more closely in touch with reality."[358]

> The problem with definitions is also that they create a false image of some universal and ubiquitous situations. Quite contrarily, creative industries cannot be discussed if they are extracted from their context—and this applies not

only to national but often to their local context as well. For what is creative or commercial in one environment may not even exist in another. Even within national borders, considerable differences often exist in the conception of what is subsumed in culture and thus in creative industries.[359]

When discussing creative industries, the issue of mapping and creative clusters can hardly be avoided. In practice it appears that compiling mapping documents and forming creative clusters is an inevitable step in the pursuit of the concept of creative industries. Mapping is also quite often an introduction into the establishment of clusters.[360]

Creative clusters are based on the idea that the concentration of similar economic activities in a certain area has beneficial effects by itself. The world is teeming with business, industrial, technological and other clusters that existed even before the ideal of creative clusters appeared.[361]

Urban development planners are often obsessed with the urge to plan clusters like Silicon Valley in California. However, Silicon Valley has remained in a league of its own to this day. To put it briefly, we have no guarantee that the development of the creative sector will actually be promoted and fostered if creative people are concentrated in a so-called 'creative hub' or a creative zone. After all, we live in the digital age and physical space is not as relevant today as it used to be.[362]

Creative Industries and New Technologies

We wish to add a couple of words on the relationship between creative industries and new technologies.

> Simply put, if you wish to develop creative industries, then new technologies cannot be ignored. The creative sector goes hand in hand with the information and communication technology (or ICT) sector. Creative industries generate audio, video and other contents for all sorts of digital gadgets. The ICT sector has already become a dominant economic sector. The future lies in digital economy. There is no alternative. The main gap between developed and less developed countries is in fact technological development. Under- developed countries live in an analogue world, while the developed ones live in a digital world. Hence, if we are to bridge this gap we must not lag behind in technological development. We cannot develop creative industries without new technologies.[363]

- Understanding of creative industries from the level of individual cultural products or services allows a much broader and more flexible approach to creative industries than the currently predominant concept, which focuses on entire activities.
- Cities, regions and countries have to define their public policy on creative industries. The economic contribution of the creative industries is simply too large to be ignored.

- Public support for creative industries have to be based on different principles and goals than support to traditional arts, cultural heritage and libraries (the so-called "field of core arts").
- "In order to be creative, cities, regions and countries shall require
  a) a defined cultural policy creative industry; and
  b) specific measures in terms of public support in the production of particular products or services."[364]
- Without considerable financial, industrial, and technological resources, the main economic resource is human capital, creativity, innovation. Therefore, the development of creative industries should include as many people as possible from the world of art, particularly the non-governmental cultural sector—that is, of course, if they are willing to take part.
- Do not copy the models of other cities. Rather, you should focus on developing those creative products and services that represent a niche market and correspond to the specific features of the environment and resources available to all. In doing so, do not neglect digital technologies.

If we decide to enlist consulting services, do not forget the fact that knowledge of the creative industry is also a type of industry in which profits are made, just as with any other commodity.

> This is witnessed not only by the broad interest of consultants but also by the interest of international organizations that tend to export their concepts and methodologies to places around the globe. In addition to the British Council referred to above, the pack includes UNESCO, the Organization for Economic Cooperation and Development (OECD), the United Nations Conference on Trade and Employment (UNCTAD), the World Intellectual Property Organization and others.[365]

The Cultural Economy

Innovative practice with a new idea of business opportunities will succeed in the cultural sector.

> The key theme is one of possibilities, of the potential contained within the cultural economy as a business—a business sector that, by its nature, is based on innovation and imagination. This core theme remains consistent throughout the thesis and connects institutions throughout Europe. Possibilities and examples will reinforce and underscore the innovative and complex potential of the cultural economy.[366]

This thesis is an abstract for cultural entrepreneurs, a reference for academics or in the context of planning and development for resilient and sustainable economic growth.

"The tourism sector is the 'industry' that uses cultural heritage to the greatest extent as support for its backbone activities like hotel accommodation, transport and catering."[367]

Dr. Nypan's report "Cultural Heritage Monuments and historic buildings as value generators in a post-industrial economy places an emphasis on exploring the role of the sector as an economic driver."[368]

This report can be considered a handbook, giving the tourism field some ammunition,—something to refer to. Twenty facts that back up the case for the cultural economy are presented below.

> Culture is the main driving force for tourism, and is one of Europe's most successful industries, representing 5.5% of the EU GDP. In 2005, 1.171 million people were employed in the sector of cultural tourism. In 2004, 5.885 million people worked in the cultural and cultural tourism sectors, equivalent to 3.1% of the active employed population across the entire EU. The average annual growth in cultural employment is higher than in total employment.[369]

The tourism sector generates 5.5% of the EU's GDP in 2015. The tourism sector employs more than 13 million people in 2016.

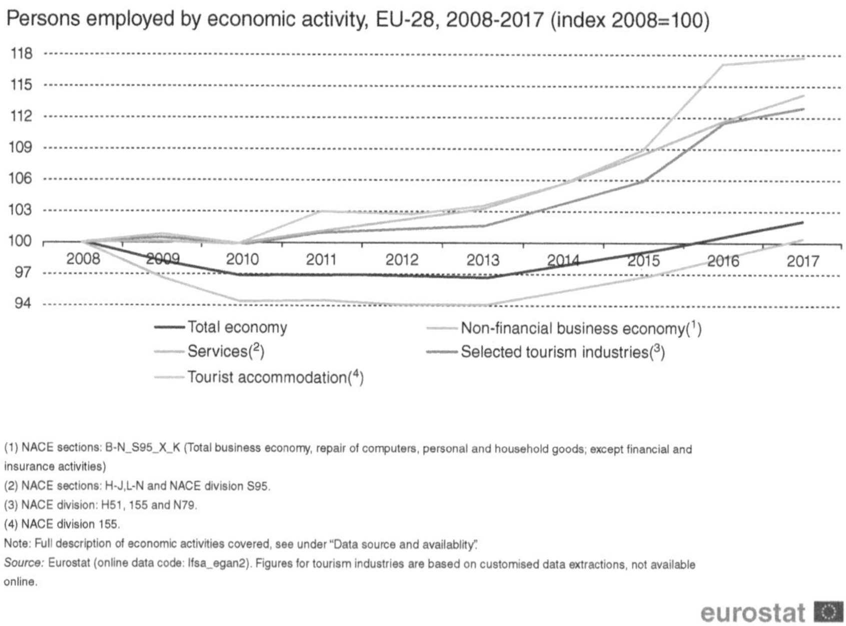

FIGURE 2 Eurostat (Statistics Explained), *Persons Employed by Economic Activity*, 2018. Available at: https://ec.europa.eu/eurostat/statistics-explained/index.php?title=File:Persons_employed_by_economic_activity,_EU-28,_2008-2017_(index_2008%3D100).png&oldid=421913

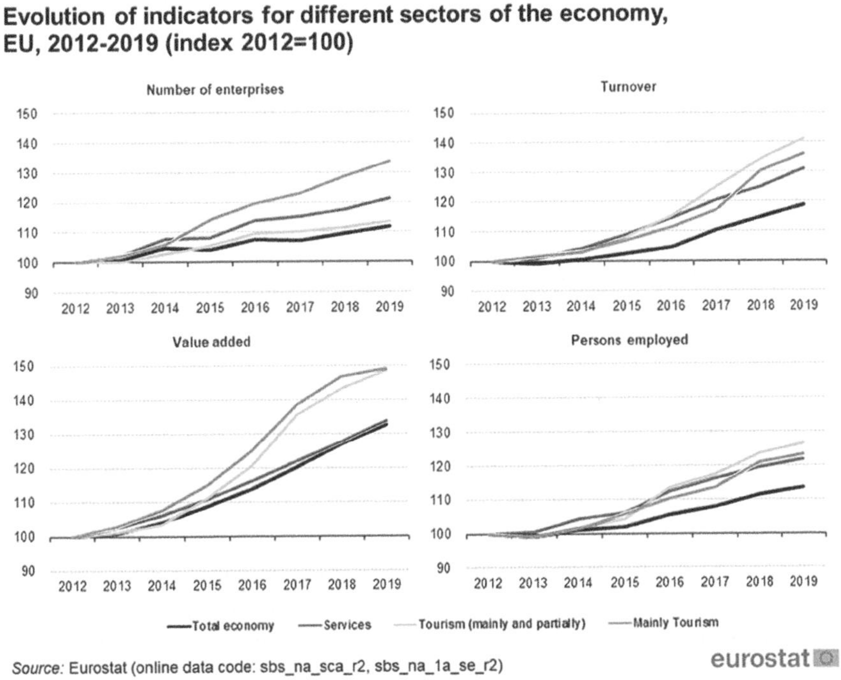

FIGURE 3 Eurostat (Statistics Explained), *Evolution of Indicators for Different Sectors of the Economy*. Available at: https://ec.europa.eu/eurostat/statistics- explained/index.php?title=File:Evolution_of_indicators_for_different_sectors_of_the_economy,_EU-27,_2012- 2017_(index_2012%3D100).png&oldid=475446

In France, the most important castles and abbeys alone are responsible for €15.1 billion profit per year in 2006. (http://ehhf.eu/sites/default/files/EU_DIRECTIVES_BOOK_2006.pdf)

Tourism in the heritage sector accounted for 176,800 pin-off jobs, direct jobs of 43,880 and conservation/maintenance jobs of 41,714. Documenta, a modern art exhibition that takes place every five years in the city of Kassel, 194,176 inhabitants with a €22 million budget, attracted 650,000 visitors, or over three times the population of Kassel. The overall direct impact of documenta on the city of Kassel is estimated at €58,185,000 in 2002.

Since it opened its doors in 1997, the Guggenheim Museum Bilbao has recorded over 8 million visitors, of which more than 60% were foreigners. The total amount generated indirectly to feed the tourism sector represented over €139 million in 2005.

Berlin is the most important destination for city tourism in Germany. In 2004, it was valued at €13 million providing employment to 145,000 people.

The total operating expenditure reported by all European Capitals of Culture is €737 million and the total capital expenditure €1.4 billion, making the total expenditure over €2 billion. Taking this total expenditure into account, the most conservative estimate of the total expenditure attributable to ECoC in the period 1995–2004 would be €3 billion.

> According to recent estimates, more than 8 million jobs are directly and indirectly sustained by the cultural heritage sector in Europe.
>
> In 2011, Travel & Tourism generated $2 trillion in direct GDP. The Travel & Tourism sector is three-quarters the size of the global education, communications, and mining sectors.
>
> With the addition of indirect and induced economic impacts, the total GDP impact of Travel & Tourism was $6.3 trillion in 2011.
>
> In terms of employment, the importance of Travel & Tourism is even more pronounced.[370]

With 98 million people directly employed in 2011, the Travel & Tourism industry GDP will grow at an average of 4.2% per year over the next decade (2012, World Travel & Tourism Council, The Economic Advantages of Travel & Tourism), greater than the 3.6% average annual growth expected for the total global economy.

Tourism generated 10% of all UAE (United Arab Emirates) exports (including oil) and 15% of all of Turkey's exports in 2011. Finally, the contribution of the cultural sector to global GDP is more than double that of the automotive industry and one-third larger than the global chemicals industry.

MKW Wirtschaftsforschung GMbH (https://www.mkw.nrw/), who wrote a report on the Economy of culture in Europe and economy of tourism also completed a study for the European Commission on the "Exploitation and development of the job potential of the cultural sector in the digital age."[371]

Finally, EU statistic and New European Agenda[372] has strong economic dimensions:

- To promote the arts, culture and creative thinking in formal and non-formal education and training at all levels and in lifelong learning.
- To foster favorable ecosystems for cultural and creative industries, promoting access to finance, innovation capacity, fair remuneration of authors and creators and cross-sectoral cooperation.
- To promote the skills needed by cultural and creative sectors, including digital, entrepreneurial, traditional and specialized skills. "Culture and creativity are important assets for the economy."[373]

> Culture contributes directly to jobs, growth and external trade. EU cultural employment increased steadily between 2011 and 2016, when it reached 8.4 million. There is a €8.7 billion trade surplus in cultural goods, and cultural and creative sectors are estimated to contribute 4.2% to EU gross domestic product. Innovative economic sectors also need creativity to maintain competitive advantage. Urban and rural communities increasingly rely on culture to attract employers, students and tourists.[374]

Culture, the arts, creativity and creative industries are interdependent.

> Combining knowledge and skills specific to cultural and creative sectors with those of other sectors helps generate innovative solutions, including in information and communication technology, tourism, manufacturing, services, and the public sector.
>
> To tap into this transformative power, the Commission proposes to focus on three specific ecosystems: education and training, cities and regions, and cultural and creative industries themselves, in order to create supportive environments for culture-led innovation.[375]

NESTA's *A Manifesto for the Creative Economy*, published in 2013, proposed a new methodology ('creative intensity') to present estimates for what is perhaps the UK's greatest competitive strength, namely its creative economy—a term we use to describe "those economic activities which involve the use of creative talent for commercial purposes."[376,377]—that is, those where jobs involve a high degree of creativity.[378] "We showed that the creative economy employed 2.5 million in 2010, or 8.7% of the UK workforce, and had grown at four times the rate of the workforce as a whole. In gross value-added terms, we estimated that it accounted for at least 9.7% of the economy, suggesting that productivity in the creative economy was over one-tenth higher than in the UK as a whole.[379] A central component of this creative economy are the creative industries. Defined as "those sectors which specialize in the use of creative talent for commercial purposes,"[380] they have exceptionally high levels of creative intensity—the percentage of their workforce that are in creative occupations—and are a bellwether for creativity and innovation in the wider economy. They accounted for a massive 5.3% of UK gross value added in 2010, higher than financial services, advanced manufacturing, and construction.[381]

> The historical success of the UK's creative industries reflects a strong domestic market for creative products and services, a business environment that is supportive of foreign trade and inward investment, a historical openness to migrant cultures, and a pool of outstanding creative talent.[382]

They have furthermore been boosted by the UK's natural advantages, including the global reach of the English language.

> But supportive government policies have also played a role, including a strong education system, a competition and intellectual property regime which, at least in the analogue age, has struck a balance between providing incentives for creativity and checks on market concentration, and a deep commitment to the arts and culture.[383]

Digital technological progress has brought with it considerable disruption for creative companies, however, requiring them to develop new capabilities and in many cases to revamp their business models. Policy makers also need to refresh their analysis of how to support the creative industries and be prepared to make changes. "The opportunity lies in harnessing the productive potential of new technologies to expand further the reach of the UK's creative economy and to increase the growth of its creative industries."[384]

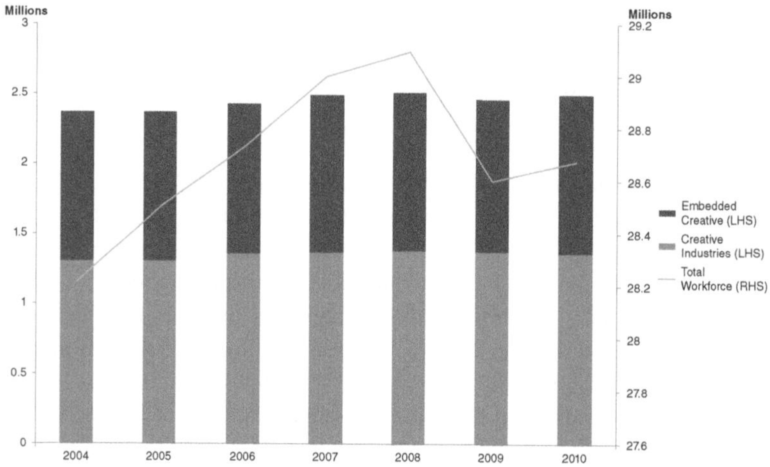

FIGURE 4 *Growth of the UK's Creative Economy.*

Source: Hasan Bakhshi, Alan Freeman, and Peter Higgs, *A Dynamic Mapping of the UK's Creative Industries* (London: Nesta, 2013). Available at: http://www.nesta.org.uk/publications/dynamic-mapping-uks-creative-industries

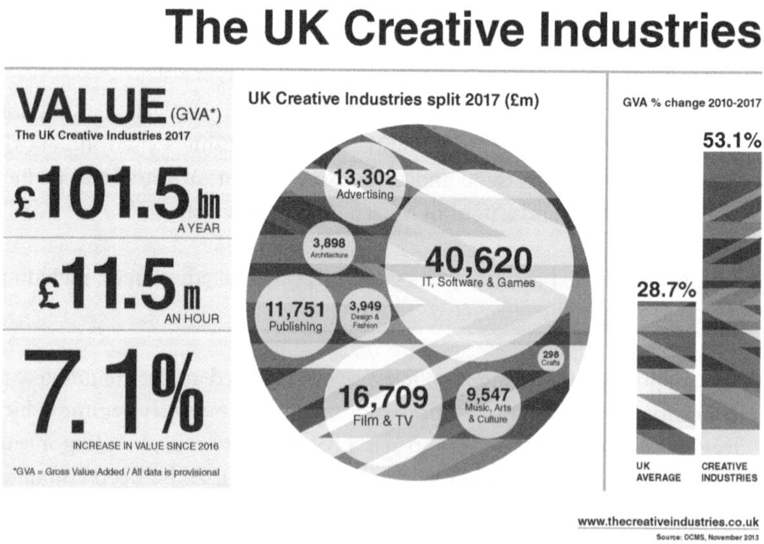

FIGURE 5 Department for Digital, Culture, Media & Sport (DMCS), *The UK Creative industries – Value*, 2018. Available at: http://www.somersetculture.org.uk/blog/research-facts/creative-industries-facts-statistics/

Culture and the Economy - The Business of the Arts

Innovation is to become an enabler for arts organizations to approach potential funders and stakeholders in a visible and transparent way. "Through great governance, innovative approach enables arts organizations to showcase their accountability, transparency and stewardship, and through this alignment to produce great art that inspires."[385]

Our society needs to enable both the arts and business sectors to truly fulfill the needs of its citizens. Both sectors can enhance each other's performance, by enabling thinking in the full potential.

> The funding for arts comes with demands for greater transparency and better corporate governance. Corporate governance requirements are one of the intersection points between culture and business; this intersection point is where common principles and practices can be used and enhanced by both sectors.[386]

Producing and enabling good art is the primary goal and measure of success for all arts and cultural organizations.

> Attempts to quantify the output of arts organizations or to identify value for money indicators are of limited benefit and burdensome to many arts organizations. What is important, however, is that arts organizations in receipt of public monies can justify the expenditures and show some transparency and accountability. This is useful for those same organizations when they are seeking further funding. It is important for the arts sector as a whole to show that it is well run, with a minimum of financial mistakes or scandals.[387]

To think of or to treat the cultural economy as a business would be to deny its inestimable intrinsic importance as a producer of art for its own sake—as a making of meaning in modern society and as a way of helping people find meaning in their individual lives.

> It is important for arts organizations to optimize their ability to attract funding. In all cases the funder was less concerned with artistic output (this was a prerequisite for application) than they were that their funding would be well used, and used for the purpose for which it was given, in a fully transparent way. Good governance has very specific advantages for the arts sector. First, the sector as a whole need to avoid scandals such as those we have suffered in the for-profit sectors. This is important because almost the entire arts and cultural sector depends either partially or wholly on some external funding, and funders demand value for money.[388]

While the principles may be the same, there are particular problems, concerns and issues in implementing and maintaining a good governance program that are specific to arts organizations.

> For example, arts organizations do not use profit as a primary measure of success. Instead, the quality and impact of the artistic output, or the achievement of values and mission, may often be used. These success criteria require that arts organizations need special treatment in the consideration of corporate governance.[389]

"The good corporate governance looks like—some basic standards."[390]

- a functioning board of independent directors
- a timely annual report
- frequent board meetings
- strategy vision and mission
- statement of a corporate governance code of practice
- generally accepted accounting practices
- identification of major stakeholders and funders
- identification of major stakeholders and funders
- transparent information on the company website.

The arts business sectors can not only use each other; they can also learn from each other's thinking and work practices.

> Certainly, this has led to the conclusion that corporate governance is necessary, even for small companies. It is especially necessary in a sector that receives funding from public funds. Public funding demands accountability and particularly transparency; recent scandals have made it clear that funders and taxpayers lose confidence in the whole sector when any lack of transparency occurs.[391]

Many talented and creative people work in the arts sector. It is through best standards for corporate governance that these people will get funding, and indeed additional funding, for their organizations.

> Arts and cultural organizations can be small by global standards and the level of sophistication of corporate governance for these organizations can be low because governance standards are basic; nevertheless, the same principles apply, and only the implementation varies. The public are demanding standards and accountability of the governance and this is clearly demonstrated by the vociferous reactions to any improprieties or wastage of monies within the funded sectors.[392]

The future is bright for arts organizations. There is a growing interest in the sector and what it can contribute to thinking, which may pull the world out of cyclical recessions and into a more sustainable model.

A Smart Cultural Sector Makes for Inclusive Cities

In the digital age, cultural institutions are transforming and maximizing community connections and expertise alongside new technologies to promote citizenship, new world skills, entrepreneurship, and business development.

We have to think about citizens and users of cultural institutions in a new way—as mobile, digitally accessible, yet unique and focused on receiving the service that they want whenever they want it. Technology gives them the opportunity to build a new relationship.

We are changing so fast as human beings, in terms of the way we communicate, learn, and interact. We are getting increasingly demanding in an expectation economy that is customer-led and data-driven. Today the job is creating "experiences," equalizing access and skills around the new and fast-developing technologies from 3D printing, robotics, coding, and circuit making to self-publishing and augmented reality. It is about creating virtual reality experience enabling ordinary people to see and experience the works of art worldwide.

Social media means that we can all now contribute and learn from each other very quickly (but also that we can receive and distribute fake news). Expectations of our physical spaces and digital services are also linked. However, many people still have stereotypical images of those working in the cultural sector and regarding what they do and that must change. As we find our voice, we need to change our attitude and become comfortable with it.

> We are very poor at promotion and marketing; library services almost always offer much more than people understand. We know the role is about merging physical and digital excellence, technology and learning, but also the creation of innovative employment, social enterprise or regeneration spaces.[393]

Future cultural institutions will need to incorporate new designs, philosophies, technologies, spaces, and practices to provide the services people expect. In the future, customers will be able to self-issue items within cultural institutions using apps. Where a service has no security in place, the customers will be able to scan the barcode to issue the item to themselves.

An entrepreneurial approach to developing new paid-for products, services, and spaces will improve audiences and impact trends in usage, appealing to new audiences. Cultural institutions of the future are your meeting place, your learning space, and your assured information resource. Cultural services across the world must familiarize themselves with new technologies. The big facilitator in all of this will be "the platform." "To get there, it will require the development of technological and social platforms, the existence of a central core of workers and skilled individuals connected to that platform who can provide services to customers worldwide."[394] Cultural institutions of the future will be one of the very few free public spaces that you and your community can nurture, design, build around, and own. Now is the time to replicate the "physical" access, value, and trust we have in cultural institutions in excellence in the digital world. If cultural institutions are to evolve rapidly enough to meet that challenge, they will have to make radical changes to their digital offer, changes that will at the same time revitalize physical visits and non-user perceptions of relevance. In addition to developing many of these innovative models, there are potential efficiencies of scale by delivering and extending regionally and nationally.

The public cultural institutions of the twenty-first-century must become learning and digital hubs—one-stop destinations for test driving and learning about the latest technology, equalizing access and skills around the new and fast developing technologies from coding, circuit making, self-publishing to augmented reality. "They have to be experiential, entrepreneurial, experimental spaces where access to technology enhances opportunities to learn, work and create."[395]

The Creative Cities in Europe

The Creative Cities Monitor report connects the cultural and economic development of cities:

> Culture is now recognized as being a competitive and resilient economic sector as well as having broader impacts: for example, as an attractor of creative talent and a catalyst of economic, technological and social innovation and change. The potential of the so-called 'cultural and creative sectors' (CCS) is best realized and demonstrated at city level, for three main reasons. First, while cities have historically been at the centre of innovation and change, in recent decades they have acquired an even greater role in socio-economic development due to the high concentration of people and economic activity they favour.[396]

The specific relation between cities and regions in Europe, the local development of the cultural sector, and horizontal connectivity with cities is significant. "The local autonomy has increased over time to enable cities better to address specific opportunities and challenges."[397] "Last, but not least, geographical clustering, a prominent feature of the cultural and creative sectors,"[398] often generates positive externalities in the areas where they are located, ranging from improved image and reputation and increased numbers of tourists to greater social pride and revitalized local economies.

> Recognizing and promoting culture and creativity is seen as particularly critical in low- and middle-income cities, as the key to inspiring the artists,

> entrepreneurs and innovators who will help take these cities to the next stage of their development. In smaller cities, networks of arts and culture can help maximize economic returns on the production of place-specific and high-value-added products (e.g. arts and crafts), while promoting citizen engagement and community building. Rural areas are also becoming significant sites of culture and creativity, often through the bottom-up initiative of civil society.[399]

The following document researches small and medium cities, placing culture and creativity in the center of local development.

> Several city-level authorities, including in former industrial cities such as Glasgow, Nantes and Essen (counting fewer than 600,000 inhabitants) or even in smaller cities such as Mons (with around 100,000 inhabitants), are therefore putting investment in culture and creativity at the centre of their local development strategies to support policy objectives ranging from urban regeneration and economic diversification and rejuvenation to job creation and social innovation and cohesion. The role of public policies is crucial in maximizing the positive effects of culture and creativity and avoiding potential traps—such as 'Cities, which want to be innovative, to flourish and to offer wealth and employment to its inhabitants, feel that they have to adapt to arenas in which knowledge and creativity can develop.[400]

When we look at the statistics represented in the report,

> The cultural and creative sectors (CCS) contribute 4.4% of GDP and employ more than 8 million people, representing almost 3.8% of total employment.[401] Between 2008 and 2011 employment in the CCS was resilient to the economic crisis, growing by 0.7% in comparison with a drop of 1.4% in employment in the overall economy.[402] The level of education of those employed in cultural fields stands out. Slightly more than 60% of people working in culture in the EU had a tertiary education, almost double the figure for the total working population (33%). Catalysts of creativity and innovation Combining artistic, business and technological creativity, CCS naturally trigger spillover effects in other industries. CCS foster growth in sectors such as ICT (by fuelling content and boosting the demand for cutting-edge consumer electronics and telecommunication devices) and tourism (by enhancing the attractiveness of places).[403]

The monitoring cities report recognizes the level of innovation in cities.

> More generally, culture and creativity contribute to innovation, which is increasingly driven by non-technological factors such as creativity, design and new organizational processes or business models. The use of design in

> manufacturing industries, for instance, increasingly enhances the value of products, services and processes. It is estimated that firms spending twice the average amount on creative inputs such as design or media content are 25% more likely to introduce product innovations.[404]
>
> CCS are also an engine of social innovation, helping to address major societal challenges, such as inclusive development, demographic change and cultural diversity. For example, in partnership with urban developers, CCS can contribute to the design of more inclusive urban spaces to counteract segregation. In cooperation with schools, they can contribute to developing creative skills and critical thinking as well as a risk-taking attitude—valued skills and qualities in a knowledge-based society."[405,406]

The research report concludes that:

> The ideal Cultural and Creative City in Europe is a mix of eight cities mostly of small and medium size. The ideal Cultural and Creative City in Europe would have the Cultural Venues & Facilities of Cork (IE), the Cultural Participation & Attractiveness and the Creative & Knowledge- based Jobs of Paris (FR), the Intellectual Property & Innovation of Eindhoven (NL), the New Jobs in Creative Sectors of Umeå (SE), the Human Capital & Education of Leuven (BE), the Openness, Tolerance & Trust of Glasgow (UK), the Local & International Connections of Utrecht (NL) and the Quality of Governance of Copenhagen (DK). Of these eight cities, five have fewer than 500,000 inhabitants, namely Cork, Eindhoven, Umea, Leuven and Utrecht.[407]

The report also finds that,

> Culture shapes our identities, aspirations and relations to others and the world. Culture in its manifest forms—built and immaterial heritage, but also cinema, music or books—has great capacity to promote social cohesion and integration, through regeneration of neglected areas, creation of locally rooted jobs and promotion of a sense of community across cultures and generations. The soft power of culture has long been employed by states as a tool to assert their presence internationally and to boost their 'soft power' to attract talent. European excellence in sectors such as fashion, design, cinema and music are a strategic asset in the effort to shape an attractive image of Europe, to promote European core values, including peace and inter-cultural dialogue, and to strengthen Europe's capacity to attract talent from around the world.[408]

Spillover and Cross-Innovation in Creative Industries

In this section, we will define the processes of spillover and crossover in creative industries: "Creative industries have become a major focus of industrial policy throughout Europe."[409]

> In the recent decades the world has been moving at a faster pace. For Europe and other parts of the world, the rapid roll-out of new technologies and increased globalization has meant a striking shift away from traditional manufacturing towards services and innovation. Spillover effects and cross-innovation are popular terms in today's innovation policy debate. However, following the debate one cannot help feeling that it is not that clear among the stakeholder in the debate what is actually meant by the two terms and that there is confusion about the difference between these two terms.[410]

The terms "spillover" or "spillover effects" imply that a condition in one particular area has an effect on a different area:

> What happens in one industry affects other industries. Spill-overs in the context of innovation policy called knowledge spillover. This is eventually nothing else than the exchange of knowledge between individuals that can be a starting point for the development of new products, services and processes.[411]

On the other hand, the term cross-innovation debates about spillovers.

> While spillovers describe effects that result from knowledge transfer, cross-innovation leads to spillovers and should be understood as a managed innovation process that facilitates interdisciplinary entanglement of products, services and trends or in other words the entanglement of complementary knowledge (spillovers are not necessarily the result of such a structured approached, they can also happen by coincidence).[412]

Cross-innovation happens in two ways: through the transfer of knowledge and communication between industries and through the promotion of cross-industry cooperation.

> Cross-innovation is about transferring existing technologies, systems, concepts or general principles from one industry to another industry in order to solve problems or answer questions experienced in that industry. This can happen through technologies, patents, specific knowledge or business models. Cross-innovation is a specific form of open innovation which means that in order to benefit from this approach companies need to revisit their innovation processes to make sure that both internal and external ideas are considered when developing new products, services and processes.[413]

Cross-innovation is linked to a specific process: the transfer of solutions or ideas from outside the industry and the Inside-Out process: the search for one's own ideas and solutions in other industries.[414] The conclusion is that cross-innovation depends on innovation processes and, as a result, depends on policy. The European

Commission has made a clear differentiation between industries. It defines creative industries as

> industries which use culture as an input and have a cultural dimension, although their outputs are mainly functional. They include architecture and design, which integrate creative elements into wider processes, as well as sub-sectors such as graphic design, fashion design or advertising. To be differentiated from this are cultural industries including industries that are producing and distributing goods or services which at the time they are developed are considered to have a specific attribute, use or purpose which embodies or conveys cultural expressions, irrespective of the commercial value they may have. Besides the traditional arts sectors (performing arts, visual arts, cultural heritage—including the public sector), they include film, DVD and video, television and radio, video games, new media, music, books and press.[415]

"This concept is defined in relation to cultural expressions in the context of the 2005 UNESCO Convention on the protection and promotion of the diversity of cultural expressions."[416]

> The German Minister of Economic Affairs concludes that, culture and creative industries comprise of all cultural and creative enterprises that are mainly market-oriented and deal with the creation, production, distribution and/or dissemination through the media of cultural/creative goods and services. They include eleven core branches: music industry, book market, art market, film industry, broadcasting industry, performing arts market, design industry, architectural market and press market. Similar categorisations are used in other European countries, e.g. Austria.[417]

Cultural and creative industries are commonly considered market-oriented and an integral part of the economy.

> Creative industries are very much open to collaboration along the entire value links. They are also very much customer and service-oriented which helps to access internal innovation processes of suppliers and clients. This contributes to spillovers to and cross-innovation between other branches within the creative industries and to other industrial sectors. The comparatively weak relationships between creative industries and traditional industrial sector suggest a potential for innovation. Key to unlocking this potential is that new approaches, techniques and thought processes develop in traditional industries.[418]

The European Commission's Green Paper was published in 2010:

> The creative industries are a specific industrial sector with specific needs of assistance both in terms of access to funding (both private and public

investments) and business development. There is also consensus that the promotion of spill-overs and cross-innovation are important key elements on the policy agenda. But in the first place it is not about the implementation of innovation voucher schemes as suggested in the European Commission's Green Paper.[419]

The Creative Industries, Innovation, and Territories

The chapter's aim is precisely to show how open innovation contributes to the construction of creative accessibility.

> The first factor relates to agglomeration effects resulting from the combination of industrial dynamics and territorial dynamics of cultural and creative activities. A second factor is the economy of contribution that tends to appear as a new pattern of economic and social regulation in most of the activities concerned.[420]

In the following report, the first factor is that,

> creative industries can often be characterized as territorialized industries. Their territorial anchoring constitutes a structural characteristic, with a strong influence on the innovation process, and on the conditions of valorization of cultural goods. Value creation in these industries often depends on local properties. The growing influence of the creative industries is primarily based on the development of creativity, innovation and entrepreneurship eco-systems; on the availability of the factors of production; on the nature of the relationship with the cultural practices; and on the effectiveness of public policies.[421,422]

The conclusion is that:

> Four types of interactions can be identified: the relationships between creative activities from the same industry and activities from other creative industries for which the needs in terms of competence are the same; the relationships between the creative industries and the users; the relationships between these industries and the other activities in the territory; and finally, the connections with public and private institutions. Also, the open innovation puts forward the convergence between activities and territory, not only because there are new talents, entrepreneurs, creative assets, and relevant public policies, but also because the city asserts itself through the development of its contributive capacities, as a creative city.[423]
>
> Therefore, the city becomes an open innovation platform, going beyond the definition of an augmented city born out of digital technology. The following developments are devoted to analyzing this specific organization, by

> which open innovation in creative industries tends to combine territorial dynamics and contributive dynamics.[424]

The cultural and creative industries are activities within the urban territory. "The creative industries must use creativity, culture, talents, as localized assets."[425] And these creative assets themselves may result in a kind of absolute advantage. "This assertion may seem paradoxical in the sense that culture and creativity appear to be shared values, like a flux that goes from one space to another."[426]

At the economic level,

> the territorial anchoring of creative industries and the intensification of the effects of innovation sharing that it allows, result in the creation of a differential advantage of location. This advantage can be analyzed as the counterpart of the specific organization of the industries that are dominated by strong location constraints. These industries benefit, for this reason, from property rights entirely or partially conceded to dedicated assets. As a result, there is a value transfer in favor of situated activities, a type of differential rent, which allows for the covering of a part of the development cost of the activities. The value transfer depends on the conditions in which the innovation is shared, the quality of the assets, and the attractiveness of the creative projects that make up the territorial advantage. Different reports and studies highlight the links between territorial advantage and innovation in creative industries.[427]

The open innovation in cultural and creative industries can be seen as a part of a territorial advantage. The prospect of public and private institutions is to create a long-term competitive advantage that turns into a differentiation advantage.[428]

> Territorial collectivizes less seek to have a greater competitive advantage in the same cultural or creative activities than to mobilize relevant activities to be differentiated from the other territories. With highly differentiated cultural goods, they aim to attract and retain investments, and so to foster job creation. These activities are the combined result of technical, cultural and artistic competence. They also meet the cultural needs observed in many cities. And they must cope with complex organizations.[429]
>
> The economy of contribution and public policies can have an influence on these organizations. The non-market relationships are likely to override market relations. This means that the development of open innovation networks converges with the development of cooperative models.[430]

If we consider intellectual property rights,

> the results of innovation sharing are in a certain manner protected by the conditions in which the territorial integration of creative activities takes place.

> Three main phenomena may be underlined, that can appear as a protection against the predatory behavior of other actors, coming from outside the territorial organization.[431]

In the following report, intellectual rights regulation can be noted.

> In a collective metropolitan context that has all the basic capacities, such as the infrastructure, workforce, financial resources, and accompaniment structures, it is possible to mutualize an important part of the intellectual property protection costs, including through specific public policies. Then, the specialization of localized activities tends to unite the actors and produce a club effect that comes with an implicit recognition, a reputation effect, made to ensure trust between the members. Besides this, there is a third phenomenon: the progressive transformation of generic assets into specialized assets in the context of the location of creative industries. This phenomenon tends to internalize a part of the open innovation process between the situated actors, and thus to complexify the access to knowledge and skills for the actors from outside the territory.[432]

The conclusion is that,

> The territorial advantage helps to promote capital development in creative industries. The location of assets tends to compensate for risk factors. In this respect, the sharing of innovation is similar to information sharing. But the positive effects induced by the flow of information are not the only ones in question. Some economic factors can also be analyzed in reference to the specific characteristics of creative industries.[433]

The economic influence of open innovation, combined with the agglomeration effect, tends to decrease the fixed and sunk costs.

> These costs are often very high in creative activities, notably because of the considerable fixed costs for production of cultural goods and the expense of research projects, such as experimental work in the artistic field, and the production of prototypes in the digital arts, software, games, multimedia or design.[434,435]
>
> In the same context, the territorial advantage and open innovation contribute to absorbing the rise of capital-intensive investments, by modifying cost structure, and ceteris paribus, to improving competitiveness of localized cultural and creative activities. Both phenomena are at the root of an equalization that partly allows creative industries to compensate for the risks they are exposed to using joint progression of internal economies of scale, through productivity gains, and external economies of scale, through market share gains.[436]

The Creative Economy—Future

Ideas have become a major driving force in the creative economy today, especially in this digital age in which the distribution of ideas is accelerating:

> Ideas move faster now than they ever have, and digital disruption is forcing the invisible hand of the market, but the physical world still has several practical barriers. On the one hand, the digital age is revolutionizing the marketplace and democratizing access on both commercial and consumer ends. On the other, unequal geographic balance of trade, logistical roadblocks, policy gaps, and inadequate infrastructure persist, limiting access to these goods and services.[437]

Digital distribution is enabling the development of the market in an extremely rapid manner.

> A case in point is the publishing industry and newspapers. Newspapers, originally considered a creative good, have flipped to offering a creative service, as online media outlets expand driven by digital news subscriptions and online advertising. Similarly, the music industry, which for decades focused on hardware, tapes and CDs, has transitioned to digital downloads and online streaming, also a creative service. These shifts are not without knock on effects – often impacting the nature of work, ownership, and particularly in the creative industries, royalties. As we move toward a more connected, integrated, and creative future, these are a few of the megatrends on the horizon.[438]

Thus, it can be seen that the intense interaction between creative ideas and digital worlds is rapidly becoming a reality.

> The symbiosis between the creative and digital worlds should come as no surprise. Creative content interlaces with, and gives visual life to, the digital world. It thus stands to reason that the digital environment would be the fertile ground from which a more integrated, synchronized creative economy could operate, by pulling on the many levers of the creative industry: writing, design, video, software, music, publishing, photography, performance art, games, research and development (R&D).[439]

Digital distribution seeks to reshape the creative industries. We are living in the age of creativity—the new digital world is the real world.

Notes

298 KEA, *The Economy of Culture in Europe* (Bruxelles: KEA European Affairs, 2006).
299 Ibid.
300 Ibid.

301 Ibid.
302 "Glossary: Lisbon Strategy," Eurostat Statistics Explained, European Commission, accessed April 5, 2020, https://ec.europa.eu/eurostat/statistics-explained/index.php/Glossary:Lisbon_Strategy
303 KEA, *The Economy of Culture in Europe.*
304 Ibid.
305 NESTA, *Creative Growth: How the UK Can Develop World Class Creative Businesses* (London: NESTA, 2006); KEA, *The Economy of Culture in Europe.*
306 KEA, *The Economy of Culture in Europe.*
307 Ibid.
308 Ibid.
309 Richard Florida. *The Rise of the Creative Class* (USA: Basic Books publisher, 2019).
310 Charles Landry and Franco Bianchini, *The Creative City* (London: Demos, 1995).
311 Ian Miles and Lawrence Green, *Hidden Innovation in the Creative Industries*, Research Report (London: NESTA, 2008).
312 David Throsby, *Economics and Culture* (London: Cambridge University Press, 2001), 104.
313 Miles and Green, *Hidden Innovation in the Creative Industries.*
314 IPR is short for Intellectual Property Rights, also known as the rights to intangible property.
315 Miles and Green, *Hidden Innovation in the Creative Industries.*
316 Ibid.
317 NESTA, *Creative Growth: How the UK Can Develop World Class Creative Businesses.*
318 Miles and Green, *Hidden Innovation in the Creative Industries.*
319 Pierre-Jean Benghozi, Elisa Salvador, and Jean Paul Simon, *Models of ICT Innovation. A Focus on the Cinema Sector. European Union Report* (Luxembourg: Publications Office of the European Union, 2015), 9–14.
320 Ibid.
321 Ibid.
322 "Department for Digital, Culture, Media & Sport (DCMS)," Government of the United Kingdom, accessed March 30, 2020, https://www.gov.uk/government/organisations/department-for-digital-culture-media-sport/about
323 Pierre-Jean Benghozi, Elisa Salvador, and Jean Paul Simon, *Models of ICT Innovation. A Focus on the Cinema Sector. European Union Report* (Luxembourg: Publications Office of the European Union, 2015), 9–14.
324 Eurostat, *ESSnet-Culture Final Report* (Luxembourg: Eurostat, 2012), 57, accessed April 5, 2020, https://ec.europa.eu/assets/eac/culture/library/reports/ess-net-report_en.pdf
325 Ibid.
326 UNCTAD, *Creative Economy Report 2008 – The Challenge of Assessing the Creative Economy: Towards Informed Policymaking* (Geneva: UNCTAD, 2008), accessed April 5, 2020, https://unctad.org/en/docs/ditc20082cer_en.pdf; UNCTAD, *Creative Economy Report 2010 – Creative Economy: A Feasible Development Option* (Geneva: UNCTAD, 2010), accessed April 5, 2020, https://unctad.org/en/Docs/ditctab20103_en.pdf
327 Eurostat, *EssNet Culture Final report.*
328 Information and Communication Technology – ICT – sector is made up of the manufacturing and services sectors whose main activity is linked to development, production, commercialization and intensive use of new technology.
329 Frontiers Economics Comparative Analysis of the UK's Creative Industries, report to the DCMS, (2006). Available at: www.eukn.org/dsresource?objectid=149334&type=org
330 Hasan Bakhshi, Radhika Desai, and Alan Freeman, *Not Rocket Science: A Roadmap for Cultural R&D* (London: Mission Models Money, 2010).
331 Hasan Bakhshi and Erin McVittie, "Creative Supply Chain Linkages and Innovation: Do the Creative Industries stimulate Business Innovation in the Wider Economy?" *Innovation: Management, Policy & Practice* 11, no. 2 (2009): 169–189.

332 European Council, Bratislava Declaration and Roadmap, 2016, Accessed April 7, 2020, www.consilium.europa.eu/en/press/press-releases/2016/09/16/bratislava-declaration-and-roadmap/
333 European Commission, *The New European Agenda for Culture* (2018), https://ec.europa.eu/culture/policy/strategic-framework_en
334 European Council Conclusion, 2017, Brussels, accessed April 7, 2020 https://www.consilium.europa.eu/en/press/press-releases/2017/12/14/european-council-conclusions-external-relations/
335 Ibid.
336 "Intercultral Dialogue," European Commission, accessed April 7, 2020, https://ec.europa.eu/culture/policy/strategic-framework/intercultural-dialogue_en
337 Davos Declaration, 2018, accessed April 7, 2020 https://www.newsd.admin.ch/newsd/message/attachments/51119.pdf
338 Ibid.
339 Nick Wilson, Jonathan Gross, and Anna Bull, *Towards Cultural Democracy: Promoting Cultural Capabilities for Everyone*, (London: King's College London, 2017).
340 European Commission, *The new European Agenda for Culture.*
341 European Commission, *Cultural Awareness and Expression Handbook* (Luxembourg: Publications Office of the European Union, 2016).
342 European Commission, A *Renewed EU Agenda for Higher Education*, COM/2017/0247 final (Brussels, 2017), accessed April 7, 2020. https://eur-lex.europa.eu/legal-content/EN/TXT/?uri=COM%3A2017%3A247%3AFIN
343 Cultural Heritage in Action, accessed April 8 2020, http://www.cultureforcitiesandregions.eu/
344 Valentina Montalto et al., *The Cultural and Creative Cities Monitor: 2017 Edition* (Luxembourg: Publications Office of the European Union, 2017) https://ec.europa.eu/jrc/en/publication/eur-scientific-and-technical-research-reports/cultural-and-creative-cities-monitor-2017-edition, accessed April 8, 2020.
345 ENRD, *Factsheet on Arts and Culture in Rural Areas*, accessed April 8, 2020, https://enrd.ec.europa.eu/sites/default/files/nrn5_arts-rural-areas_factsheet.pdf
346 European Commission, *The New European Agenda for Culture.*
347 Ibid.
348 "Category: Culture", Eurostat, European Commission, accessed April 8, 2020, https://ec.europa.eu/eurostat/statistics-explained/index.php/Category:Culture
349 Ernst and Young, *Measuring Cultural and Creative Markets in the EU* (Paris: Ernst & Young, 2014).
350 European Commission, *The New European Agenda for Culture.*
351 Including through European Entrepreneurship and Digital Competence Frameworks (EntreComp, DigComp).
352 European Commission, A credible enlargement perspective for and enhanced EU engagement with the Western Balkans, COM(2018)65 final, Strasbourg, 2018, accessed April 8, 2020, https://eur-lex.europa.eu/legal-content/EN/TXT/?uri=CELEX%3A52018DC0065
353 European Commission, *The New European Agenda for Culture.*
354 Davor Buinjac, "Creative Industries."
355 Davor Buinjac, "Creative Industries."
356 Ibid.
357 Ibid.
358 Ibid.
359 Ibid.
360 Ibid.
361 Ibid.
362 Ibid.
363 Ibid.
364 Ibid.

365 Ibid.
366 James Doyle, "An introduction to the Cultural Economy" in *Culture, Innovation and the Economy*, ed. Biljana Mickov and James Doyle (London: Routledge publishing, 2019), 1–2.
367 Ibid.
368 Trond Nypan, *Cultural Heritage Monuments and Historic Buildings as Value Generators in a Post-Industrial Economy* (Oslo: Directorate for Cultural Heritage, 2006).
369 Ibid.
370 Ibid.
371 KEA, *The Economy of Culture in Europe*.
372 European Commission, *The New European Agenda*.
373 Ibid.
374 Ibid.
375 Ibid.
376 Hasan Bakhshi, Ian Hargreaves, and Juan Mateos-Garcia, *A Manifesto for the Creative Economy* (London: Nesta, 2013).
377 Based as it is on relatively standardized labor force survey statistics and on the official occupational and industrial classifications, this method puts within our sights the prospect of internationally comparable statistics, an essential requirement for evidence-based national policymaking.
378 Hasan Bakhshi, Alan Freeman, and Peter Higgs, *A Dynamic Mapping of the UK's Creative Industries* (London: Nesta, 2013).
379 Bakhshi, Hargreaves, and Mateos-Garcia, *A Manifesto for the Creative Economy*.
380 Ibid.
381 Ibid.
382 The Work Foundation, *Staying Ahead: The Economic Performance of the UK's Creative Industries* (London: The Work Foundation, 2007).
383 Ibid.
384 Ibid.
385 Penelope Kenny, "The Business of Arts Cconsultancy: A Personal Analysis of the History, Growth and Opportunities for Business in Arts Consultancy," in *Culture, Innovation and the Economy*, ed. Biljana Mickov and James Doyle, (London: Routledge publishing, 2018), 7–10.
386 Ibid.
387 Ibid.
388 Ibid.
389 Ibid.
390 Kenny, "The Business of Arts Consultancy".
391 Ibid.
392 Ibid.
393 Liz McGettigan, "Smart Libraries Make Smart Communities Make Smart Cities," in *Culture, Innovation and the Economy*, ed. Biljana Mickov and James Doyle (London: Routledge publishing, 2019), 45–51.
394 Ibid.
395 Ibid.
396 Montalto et al., *The Cultural and Creative Cities Monitor: 2017 Edition*.
397 The local specificities of creative industries, particularly those based on local cultural, artistic, linguistic and natural resources. Source: UNESCO (2013 Special Edition). *Creative Economy Report - Widening Local Development Pathways*.
398 Ibid.
399 Montalto et al., *The Cultural and Creative Cities Monitor: 2017 Edition*. The Cultural and Creative Cities Monitor focuses on cities (or densely populated areas). However, some small cities of around 50,000 inhabitants are included in the Monitor, which may offer some insights into the performance of sparsely populated areas.
400 Ibid.

401 TERA Consultants, *The Economic Contribution of the Creative Industries to EU GDP and Employment*, 2014. In 2010, the European Commission in its European Competitiveness Report estimated its contribution at 3% of GDP and 6.5 million people employed.
402 Source: Eurostat (EU-Labour Force Survey).
403 Montalto et al., *The Cultural and Creative Cities Monitor: 2017 Edition.*
404 NESTA, *Creating Innovation: Do the Creative Industries Support Innovation in the Wider Economy?*, 2008.
405 There is also some suggestive evidence that arts education matters for innovation. In OECD countries, arts graduates are commonly involved in product innovation. Source: OECD (2013). *Art for Art's Sake: The Impact of Arts Education.*
406 Montalto et al., *The Cultural and Creative Cities Monitor: 2017 Edition.*
407 Ibid.
408 Ibid.
409 Thomas Lämmer-Gamp, *Creative Industries, Policy Recommendations - Promotion of Cross-Innovation From Creative Industries* (Berlin: Institute for Innovation and Tehnology, 2014).
410 Ibid., 3.
411 Ibid., 5.
412 Ibid., 4.
413 Ibid., 5.
414 Ibid., 6.
415 Ibid.
416 UNESCO, *The 2005 Convention on the Protection and Promotion of the Diversity of Cultural Expressions* (Paris: UNESCO, 2005).
417 Ibid., 7.
418 Ibid., 7.
419 European Commission, *Green Paper Audit Policy: Lessons from the Crisis*, COM (2010) 561 final, Brussels, 2010, accessed April 9, 2020, https://www.europarl.europa.eu/meetdocs/2009_2014/documents/com/com_com(2010)0561_/com_com(2010)0561_en.pdf
420 Phillipe Béraud, Viviane Du Castel, and Frank Cormerais, "Open Innovation, Economy of Contribution and The Territorial Dynamics of Creative Industries," *Journal of Innovation Economics & Management* 2, no. 10 (2012): 81–105.
421 Joseph Rykwert, *The Seduction of Place* (Oxford: Oxford University Press, 2000); David Hesmondhalgh and Andy Pratt, "Cultural Industries and Cultural Policy," *International Journal of Cultural Policy* 11, no. 1 (2005): 1–14.
422 Béraud, Du Castel, and Cormerais, "Open Innovation, Economy of Contribution and the Territorial Dynamics of Creative Industries."
423 Charles Landry, *The Creative City: A Toolkit for Urban Innovators* (London: Earthscan, 2000); Chris Gibson and Natasha Klocker, "Academic Publishing as a Creative Industry, and Recent Discourses of Creative Economies: Some Critical Reflections," *Area* 36, no. 4 (2004): 423–434; Allen Scott, "Creative Cities: Conceptual Issues and Policy Questions,"*Journal of Urban Affairs* 28, no.1 (2006): 1–17.
424 Béraud, Du Castel, and Cormerais, "Open Innovation, Economy of Contribution and the Territorial Dynamics of Creative Industries."
425 Andy Pratt, "The Cultural Economy. A Call for Spatialized 'Production of Culture' Perspectives," *International Journal of Cultural Studies* 7, no. 1 (2004): 117–128; Richard Florida, *Cities and the Creative Class* (New York: Routledge, 2005).
426 Béraud, Du Castel, and Cormerais, "Open Innovation, Economy of Contribution and the Territorial Dynamics of Creative Industries."
427 Ibid., 14.
428 Bernard Pesqueur, Le tournant territorial de l'économie globale, *Espaces et sociétés* 1-2, no. 125-125 (2006): 17–32.
429 Allen Scott, *The Cultural Economy of Cities* (London: Sage, 2000).

430 Béraud, Du Castel, and Cormerais, "Open Innovation, Economy of Contribution and the Territorial Dynamics of Creative Industries," 15.

431 Ibid.

432 Ibid., 22.

433 Harold Demsetz, "The Theory of the Firm Revisited," in *The Nature of The Firm: Origins, Evolution and Development*, ed. Oliver Williamson and Sidney Winter (New York: Oxford University Press, 1991).

434 Olivier Bomsel, Anne-Gaëlle Geffroy, and Gille Le Blanc, *When Internet Meets Entertainment: The Economic of Digital Media Industries* (Paris: Presses de l'Ecole des Mines, 2006).

435 Béraud, Du Castel, and Cormerais, "Open Innovation, Economy of Contribution and the Territorial Dynamics of creative Industries," 25.

436 Ibid., 26.

437 United Nations Conference on Trade and Development (UNCTAD), *Creative Economy Outlook: Trends In international Trade in Creative Industries* (2018), accessed April 10, 2020, https://unctad.org/en/pages/PublicationWebflyer.aspx?publicationid=2328

438 Ibid., 15.

439 Ibid.

PART II

Culture and the Creative Economy

Introduction

The economy encourages creativity and innovation growth and encourages people to be authentic. Investors in creative economies directly influence people, places, and industries that cross-connect ideas, jobs, citizens.

> The creative economy is growing and supporting the creators who are building the future of our communities and economies. The economy has given direct positive effects generated by cultural activities; a sustainable cultural ecosystem must reinvest resources into local culture.[440]

New ideas bring innovation in terms of the social value for the economy. Cultural activities play an important role in sustainable economic development. The creation of economic activities makes an important part of the attractiveness of places, and contributes to the development of tourism. The sustainable use of cultural resources is respectful of core values and should contribute equally to cultural and economic development.[441] Economic models are based on specific cultural values. Effective links between public, market, and cooperative economies are essential to achieving ecologically balanced economic development. The collaborative economy is based on the creation of common spaces where users make exchanges through platforms that allow them to acquire and give using technologies that facilitate the generation of trust, confidence, and information reciprocity with low transaction costs and coordination.[442] "Thanks to new technologies, new types of jobs are being created."[443] Many of these new occupations require a high level of creative skills, have a marked entrepreneurial character, and benefit from low initiation and marketing costs.[444]

The interconnections of cultural ecosystems with, and between, other dimensions of sustainable development must always be taken into account. Cultural

DOI: 10.4324/9781003336648-8

activities create positive effects, and the cultural ecosystem itself must invest in existing resources. "The local tourism model is sustainable, balanced across the region, connected to the local communities and interactive with the cultural ecosystems."[445]

> Cities can be described as dynamic systems, which flourish, stagnate and decline as a result of the interaction of the main actors in the urban arena: households, firms, and the government. Governments adapt to these changes, or foster them in the desired direction.[446,447]

The city has a double layer of networks: the global network of places, such as banking, publishing, media, tourism, education; and the local network within the metropolitan areas.

One of the leading theorists on creative economy value, John Howkins, popularized the term "creative economy" in 2001.[448] Howkins' creativity includes all kinds of creativity, art, or innovation and the creative economy occurs wherever individual creativity is the main source of value.

In 2019, UNTCAD experts defined that the creative economy has both commercial and cultural worth, and that the dual value has led governments worldwide to focus on expanding and developing their creative economies and stimulating prosperity.

> Design and visual arts are among the highest performing sectors with fashion, interior design in developing economies. The creative industries—which include architecture, arts and crafts, marketing and advertising, media and publishing, research and development, software, computer games, and other core creative work—are the lifeblood of the creative economy.[449]

Notes

440 UCLG, "Culture 21: Actions."
441 Ibid.
442 Albert Cañigueral, "Hacia una economía colaborativa responsable," *Oikonomics* 6 (2016): 16–27.
443 Ibid.
444 Thor Berger and Carl Benedict Frey, *Bridging the Skills Bap* (London: Institute for Public Policy Research, 2006): 40–42.
445 Ibid.
446 Leo Van den Berg et al., *A Study of Growth and Decline* (UK: Pergamon Publishing, 1982).
447 A. J. Reuvers, J. W. A. van den Berg, and, C. A. Smolders, "Formation of Membranes by Means of Immersion Precipitation: Part I. A Model to Describe Mass Transfer During Immersion Precipitation," *Journal of Membrane Science* 34, no. 1 (1987): 45–65.
448 John Howkins is a British author and speaker on Creative Industries, particularly the development of this economic sector. He is visiting professor, University of Lincoln, England, and vice dean and visiting professor, Shanghai School of Creativity, Shanghai Theater Academy, China.
449 "Global Creative Economy Shows Resilience, Growth – Report," UNTCAD, accessed May 8, 2021, https://unctad.org/news/global-creative-economy-shows-resilience-growth-report

7

ECONOMIC AND SOCIAL VALUE OF THE CULTURAL SECTOR

Recently, the network of cities Agenda 21 for Culture adopted a document based on research on cities, concluding that cultural activities play an important role in the achievement of comprehensive and sustainable economic development.[450] "They allow the renewal and creation of economic activities, boost entrepreneurship and employability, make up an important part of the attractiveness of places, and contribute to the development of tourism."[451] A sustainable use of cultural resources is respectful of core values and should contribute equally to cultural and economic development. "Given the direct positive effects generated by cultural activities, a sustainable cultural ecosystem must reinvest resources into local culture."[452]

Cultural and creative processes have a strong impact on people's welfare and health. They make it possible for individuals and communities to explore their histories and sense of identity, promote the development of new meaning in their lives, and give them greater freedom. The document also points out that,

> Active participation in cultural life is one of the key aspects in social inclusion. It provides the motivation and possibility of increased civic participation, lends cultural visibility to minorities, fosters mutual recognition and cooperation between different generations and cultures, boosts employment, and improves a city or region's security and image. Culture is an important means for establishing new social spaces and for developing new collective meanings.[453]

In an article, British cultural historian Richard Hewison analyses the situation in terms of the creative economy in the UK.[454] "The creative economy was an invention of the 1980s."[455] It was understood that artists, writers, composers, directors, and performers employed in the significantly titled "not-for-profit" sector were in fact creating profits and indirectly in terms of the cultural consumption they generate in the form of local and international tourism. Nonetheless, the

DOI: 10.4324/9781003336648-9

creative industries, which are more to do with consumption than creativity, do exist, and have to be taken seriously. "Rethinking the relationship between our publicly-funded institutions and the private sector will not harm the creative economy. In fact, it will stimulate it, not by commanding creativity, but creating the conditions in which it will flourish."[456]

That means not supporting the not-for-profit sector for its own sake, but instead because it has a social role that is far more important than its economic one. He concludes by emphasizing that

> we have to think of the arts as part of the public realm, that space where private and public interests meet and where their conflicts can be resolved, where the local can find accommodation with the national, and where there are institutions that are not driven solely by the profit motive, but by the idea of a greater public good. We should worry less about the creative economy, and rebuild the public realm. From the ground up.[457]

The EU points out that,

> In its Green Paper[458] "Unlocking the potential of cultural and creative industries", factory floors are progressively being replaced by creative communities whose raw material is their ability to imagine, create and innovate. All formulations of the Knowledge or Information Society highlight the increasing importance and centrality of the symbolic dimension in social and economic relationships.[459]

In the study "Main connections between cultural and creative activities and the socio-economic space,"[460] professors at the University of Valencia explain the relations between cultural and creative activities and the economy.[461] The study provides an overview of cultural rights in the economic system, how culture brings values to development, the relations between culture and development and innovation models. The study concludes that cultural policies clearly belong to intelligent and inclusive growth.

> Cultural values are one of the elements that determine our behavior and the way we perceive the world. In fact, it is our set of values that sets the objectives of the institutions we create in order to articulate our life in society. Therefore, all our institutions are the result of our hierarchy of values and a consequence of our cultural architecture.[462]

From the findings of the study,

> we can observe that the satisfaction of cultural needs is the main purpose of any economic system and that the set of values derived from the cultural sphere shapes the rest of the socio-economic space. The role of an economic

> system is to fulfil the desires, wishes and objectives of a community. Once the basic material needs have been covered, the next group of needs are those related to the individual or collective cultural dimension.[463]

Cultural rights, as a substantial part of human rights, constitute the dimension of the value of culture. "Culture is valuable because it makes us inherently human."[464] Cultural values are much more in line with the concept of sustainable development and concepts like commons create new values in the economic and social space.[465]

> Recently, cultural values like cooperation, solidarity, transparency or responsibility are being reclaimed. These new values are spreading through conventional social spaces, but also through new ethics on the Internet. The cultural district with a creative component is a district in which creativity is a relevant input in the production process of symbolic goods and services.[466]

The Frontier Economics report on the impact of spillovers from the creative industries on the economy of the United Kingdom, "Creative Industry Spillovers", explains their impact on the wider economy:[467]

- Knowledge spillovers—new ideas that benefit firms
- Product spillovers—new products that are used to benefit
- Network spillovers—benefits of networked firms.

Societies, social diversity, and multiculturalism generate new ideas and forms. Richard Florida remarks that creative people like all this social diversity, so places considered diverse tend to produce and attract creative people in the Creative City.[468] It is crucial that human capital be implemented through the networks of cities and territorial networks with research, education, and innovation.[469] Potts and Cunningham conclude that the creative industries are not a sector, but rather a structural part of the innovation of the economy as a whole.[470] Culture leads the transformation process in the economy and is considered a public good in a dynamic sense.

Ecology of Culture

The term "cultural ecology" has been used in anthropology since the 1950s; it means the study of human adaptation to the social and physical environment. But the use of the word ecology in relation to the cultural sector is a recent phenomenon. Two reports from 2004, published almost simultaneously on both sides of the Atlantic, although written without any contact between the authors, use "ecology" as a metaphor.[471] This may not be the first connection between ecology and the cultural sector; after this, however, the idea that the cultural sector can be thought of in terms of ecology has become more widespread. In *The Art of Living*, John Nell uses the terms "funding ecology" and "art and cultural ecology" quite freely,[472] and the UK Department of Culture, Media, and Sport uses the term "artistic ecology" in Our Creative Talent.[473] In February 2011, the Minister of Culture of the United Kingdom, gave a speech entitled "Creative Ecology", which he defined as "an alliance between subsidized and commercial art; professional and volunteer arts; arts and creative industries."

Many have given a concise look at what "cultural ecology" means. For example,

> how the arts and creative industries interact and what impact they have on economic and social well-being. How different parts fit together. (Barbican Centre, London); Everything that comes from an idea: art, literature, music, film, narrative, design-driven manufacturing; High art or urban culture or medieval culture.[474]

Samuel Jones, of the Tate Modern gallery (London), gave his response in terms of the links between culture, society and politics:

> You cannot participate in society without a cultural voice. Culture is a type of record created by choice. A healthy cultural ecology is an environment in which people feel safe and are able to contribute to that record and in which they feel a sense of belonging and find an audience. This means that people create culture, that subcultures can thrive, and that society cannot be run with a firm idea of what culture is. At any given moment, certain elements of cultural ecology will be valued more than others. In the seventeenth century it was tulips, today it is the artist, Jeff Koons.[475,476]

Treating culture as ecology:

- In a natural ecosystem, everyone is equally important because some could not exist without others. All parts of the cultural system are interdependent and, in this sense, equal and equally valuable.
- The phrase "ecology of culture" means that culture is a collective phenomenon, with unequal elements that come together to produce a whole; where "audience" creates culture just like "artists."[477]
- The concept of ecology helps us to see our position in relation to culture. Like the natural ecosystem, the cultural ecosystem is not separate from the people. Culture is a process of constant formation, in which our attitudes and decisions are shaped by what we see, read, create, and listen.
- The description of the approach to natural ecology by the naturalist Denis Owen in *The Science of Ecology* can be equally applied to cultural ecology.

> The economics and ecology are subjects in which intuition also plays an important role and, although both subjects are treated in a rigorous mathematical way, the question is whether this has indicated to us something we did not already know.[478]

- Ecology includes many useful concepts that can be transferred to the field of culture, such as balanced cooperation: existential dangers that come from outside the system; positive and negative feedback, interactions, connections,; patterns.
- Cultural endowers include creating meaning and building social lives, as well as (sometimes) making a profit. If we look at culture as ecology, then the analytical approach requires the identification of cultural value taking into account the multiple and pluralistic value of culture outside the economic as well as including the economic. Culture has social significance and has moral weight by driving the health of the cultural system, creative capacity, the ability to create new meaning, the social and public goods, as well as the earnings which is also important.

Notes

450 UCLG, "Culture 21: Actions."
451 Ibid.
452 Ibid.
453 Ibid.
454 Robert Hewison, "When This Is All Over We Must Reimagine the Infrastructure of the Arts," *The Art Newspaper*, accessed May 3, 2020, https://www.theartnewspaper.com/comment/when-this-is-all-over
455 Ibid.
456 Ibid.
457 Ibid.
458 European Commission, *Green Paper From The Commission on Policy Options for Progress Towards a European Contract Law for Consumers and Businesses*, COM (2010)348 final, Brussels, accessed May 3, 2020, https://eur-lex.europa.eu/LexUriServ/LexUriServ.do?uri=COM:2010:0348:FIN:en:PDF
459 Pau Rausell Köster et al., *Culture as a Factor for Economic and Social Innovation* (2012), accessed May 6, 2020. http://www.uv.es/soste/publications.html
460 Pau Rausell Köster and Raul Abeledo Sanchis, "Main Connections Between Cultural and Creative Activities and the Socio-Economic Space," European Network of Cultural Centres (ENCC), accessed May 5, 2020, https://encc.eu/resources/database/main-connections-between-cultural-and-creative-activities-and-socio-economic
461 Köster et al., *Culture as a Factor for Economic and Social Innovation.*
462 Ibid.
463 Ibid.
464 Ibid.
465 Ibid.
466 Ibid.
467 Frontier Economics, *Creative Industry Spillovers*, 2007, accessed May 6, 2020, https://www.frontier-economics.com.au/category/year/2007/
468 Florida, *The Rise of the Creative Class.*
469 UCLG, "Agenda 21 for Culture."
470 Jason Potts and Stewart Cunningham, "Four Models of the Creative Industries," *Revue d'Économie Politique* 120, no. 1 (2010): 163–180.
471 John Holden, *Ecology of Culture* (Swindon: Arts and Humanities Research Council, 2015), accessed May 9, 2021, http://www.ahrc.ac.uk/documents/project-reports-and-reviews/the-ecology-of-culture/
472 John Nell, *Art of Living* (UK: Harper Collins, 2007).

473 DCMS, *Our Creative Talent, the Voluntary and Amateur Arts in England* (2008), accessed May 9, 2021, https://culturehive.co.uk/wp-content/uploads/2013/04/Our-Creative-Talent.pdf
474 Ibid.
475 Jeffrey L. Koons is an American artist recognized for his work dealing with popular culture.
476 John Holden, *Ecology of Culture*; Samuel Jones is a member of the Senior Executive at Tate London, England, United Kingdom.
477 Holden, *Ecology of Culture.*
478 Denis Owen, *The Science of Ecology?* (Oxford: Oxford University Press, 1980).

8

CASE STUDIES

Research (Local Governments, Cultural Institutions, and Organizations throughout Europe)

Introduction

The research has been focusing on criteria on the level of innovation and development of Creative and Cultural Industries (CCI) in Europe based on the methodology of qualitative research through local governments, cultural institutions, and organizations in Western, Northern, and Central-East Europe. From a human geography point of view, Europe is often described as the "peninsula of peninsulas."[479] The link between these peninsulas has made Europe a dominant economic, social, and cultural force throughout recorded history. Today, Europe is home to citizens with common social, cultural, and economic values. The concept of European culture is generally linked to the classical definition of the Western world.

Western culture is the set of literary, scientific, political, artistic, and philosophical principles that set it apart from other civilizations. The core elements comprise the cultural base of modern Europe. One list of these elements, given by K. Bochmann, includes the following:[480]

- a common cultural and spiritual heritage derived from Christianity, Judaism, the Renaissance, and its Humanism, the political thinking of the Enlightenment, and the French Revolution, and the developments of Modernity, including all types of socialism;
- a rich and dynamic material culture;
- a specific conception of individual respect for human rights and the liberty of the individual;
- a plurality of states; and
- respect for peoples, states, and nations outside Europe.[481]

DOI: 10.4324/9781003336648-10

Western culture, or Western society, is the heritage of social norms, traditional customs, belief systems, political systems, values, artifacts, and technologies of the Western world. The Eastern Europe definition by a United Nations paper adds that "every assessment of spatial identities is essentially a social and cultural construct."[482]

Europe's rich and diverse cultural heritage continues to flourish today. With such a large number of nationalities compacted into such a small area, Europe strongly supports individual cultural identities and products. The European Capitals of Culture program, which began in 1985, has become one of Europe's most important and high-profile cultural events.[483] The goals of the program are local, regional, and global. The program highlights Europe's rich cultural diversity, celebrates its cultural ties, and brings together people from different European backgrounds. In the article, "Social Participation Issues in Becoming a Creative City: Learning from European Capitals of Culture," Professor Anne Gombault suggests that the cultural arena today includes not only all artistic and cultural sectors that place artistic creativity at the heart of their output, like visual arts and heritage, performing arts, cultural industries, but also other industries like design industries, taste industries, leisure industries (including tourism), which incorporate some degree of creation in their production.[484] The "creative industries" are characterized by the nature of their production processes, focused on creation with, as their final product, an object of creation.[485] The structuring of creative industries is intimately linked to the sustainable development of areas, and especially cities, which are now thought of as a kind of creative fertile soil that should be investing in creativity in all its forms, in order to encourage growth.[486] ECOCs are seen as the ideal tool for urban regeneration. Urban regeneration can be defined as the revitalization, the reactivation, and the restoration of a city's heritage and urban spaces with the aim of improving city-dwellers' living environment. Local government representatives try to bring the area's strengths and resources together through partnerships and projects in consultation with the population, economic actors, and political-institutional representatives.[487] The economic dimension is present in the search for impact—"job creation," "return on investment," "tourist income," "marketing the city"—but it is principally applied to local social cohesion. Robert Palmer pointed out that social objectives were not the highest priority for most ECOCs, and that social participation issues require just as much attention as economic issues.[488]

The program has provided a sustained economic boost to cities and regions, raised their international profiles, and enhanced their images in the eyes of their own inhabitants.

The European Union has adopted a multilingual language policy with the goal that everyone should be able to speak at least two languages in addition to their own native tongue.[489] By supporting this policy, the European Union hopes it will strengthen social, educational, professional, and economic ties in Europe and make the continent more competitive in global markets. Europe's cultural products also help unify the region.

The regions in Europe are becoming increasingly connected with cultural projects. The interconnectedness of regions and the cities into a homogenous group regardless of national boundaries, as well as their cooperation on projects in different fields, has become a reality. There are many regions that present themselves with regard to tourism, culture, or economy outside national boundaries, and compete with each other. Projects often involve cross-border cooperation that can enhance the quality and attractiveness of a region. One of the good examples of regional cross-cooperation in Europe is the Great Region. Cultural cooperation has seen intensive development in the Great Region.[490]

The Great Region as a living space of unique cultural diversity and vitality appreciates the increasing number of "crossings of the borders." "Reviving Europe"—between "skill" and "the way of life"—is a reality exercised in this region on a daily basis, Luxembourg has twice received the title of the European Capital of Culture. Luxembourg integrated its neighboring regions into an organization and cultural program. This was the first occasion on which a cross-border region had been defined and presented as a common cultural space. Overall, the result of this Year of Culture, organized through common effort and across borders, was viewed as positive. Those projects involving artists from multiple regions were especially successful, enhancing the preconditions for the implementation of any future cross-border projects. It is also necessary to maintain the existing contacts.[491] "Art at the Border," a joint project by the regions of Lorraine, Rhineland-Palatinate, Saarland, and Wallonia regarding Luxembourg and the Great Region as cultural capitals for 2007, was a positive experience for all participants.

A border, as an existing political and geographical location, can be transformed into an active venue in which, for example, custom outposts, stations, old smugglers' roads, bridges or "no man's land" can become spaces for practicing art. They can also serve as an inspiration, a center for the contents of artistic production. The participating artists were invited to comprehend the artistic value of a border.[492] In recent years, a couple of significant structures have been developed for facilitating and enhancing cultural cooperation in the region. The Great Region is where the first cross-border cultural web portal in Europe has been developed. Plurio.net provides access to current information on artistic and cultural scenes in the neighboring regions. It provides better visibility of cultural happenings in the Great Region as well as invaluable information for those involved. The "Plurio.net" project is developing instruments to enhance cultural cross-border cooperation, as well as displaying the cultural offer of the Great Region.

Apart from making the diversity of the Great Region's cultural offer generally visible, the Plurio.net website uses data transfer to intentionally and transparently introduce this offer to new users and audience groups. It is based on knowledge and experience gained from the projects for developing the Great Region's cultural portals. The experience is then enhanced through the development of special instruments, which are made available to target groups. In a wider context, Plurio.net cooperates with other European cultural portals, securing for itself a stable position in European context and providing visibility of the Great Region's diverse cultural life. The website publishes news concerning happenings organized by institutions and individual artists alike. By selecting topics, times, and places, visitors can navigate around cultural offerings in the German, French, and English language.[493]

In order to understand the Great Region as an interconnected cultural space, it is necessary to develop a strategy for cultural cooperation within the Great Region. The association "Great Region Cultural Space" makes it possible to initiate a dialogue between regional cultural policies in the Great Region in the field of cross-border cooperation, as well as to harmonize and efficaciously manage these policies.[494]

This new association:

- enhances the multilingualism (through culture) and the mobility of the population, artists, and administrative workers, as well as familiarization with the other partial regions;
- promotes the Great Region as a new, unique, existing, interconnected "cultural space";
- increases the extent and quality of cross-border cooperation in the field of culture; and
- makes possible the evaluation of successful cross-border cultural projects.

Specific goals have been defined for cultural workers:

- increasing the mobility of artists and works of art in the Great Region, by informing people about differences in legal and tax-related issues;
- providing information on scholarships and exchange program;
- introducing internship program in cultural institutions and associations;
- providing information on the availability of happenings, including the available means of transport, as well as providing extra buses for large happenings;
- increasing the number of cross-border cultural projects in the Great Region, by intercultural and linguistic mediation through regional coordination;
- improving the coordination of regional funding in the area of cross-border projects, for example by making bilingual documents for application and by providing timely counseling if applying through regional coordinators;
- presenting successful examples in the area of cross-border cultural work;
- informing about competitions and calls for proposals;
- developing strategies for common cultural policy in the Great Region;
- creating transparency in culture by presenting general conditions with all the legal and tax- related differences (using print media, lectures and seminars);
- informing about specific circumstances and cultural or political focal points;
- determining the fields in which cooperation is necessary and potentially successful (topic- oriented round tables of cultural workers; project fairs);
- determining communication strategies;
- structuring the fields of professional culture through the development of networks;
- enhancing information flow and communication between institutions;
- connecting projects from the same domains/thematic areas within the Great Region;

- improving the perception of the Great Region both internally and externally, for example through common external presentation on fairs in and outside the Great Region, etc.[495]

The social dimension of cross-border cultural projects is not to be underestimated. Cultural workers from different countries become acquainted and learn how to respect each other. Prejudices are being eliminated, while numerous similarities are recognized. Regular contact between the neighboring areas across the border, within the Great Region, has become customary. Cultural institutions in the Great Region have seen an increasing number of visitors from the neighboring regions across the border. The audience has started to increasingly accept the cultural offer outside the national boundaries.

Cultural cross-border cooperation has led to the development of new dynamics in the region that can only enhance the artistic quality of the projects. Europe has a large artistic potential that could further be developed through regular cultural cooperation in various regions.[496] Cultural work across national boundaries is rewarding for all participants. The offer for culture fans is becoming more dynamic and diverse.

Professor Fabrice Thuriot's article, "Museums and Globalisation," pointed out the importance of the interdisciplinary and international network regarding cultural politics, heritage, and museums.[497] It showed the complexity of the process, not only through the standardization of Western countries to others in the field of museums and heritage, but also through local adaptations, hybridizations, and specificities. This process has a much greater significance than making deals with politics, religion, society, values, and symbols of the people. This process is not new but is now more widespread with the internationalization of the whole world and digitalization.

He explained that the modernization of French museums has come in part from the US to the French Republic with regard to commercial and pedagogical strategies for tourists and pupils, but the local authorities adapted the new model to their territory with the help of the state.[498] Local sites and authorities have adopted some global methods, especially for communication and programming, with occasional public–private partnerships.[499]

Big museums are duplicating themselves around the world, both outside and/or inside their own countries, albeit with some modifications. Examples include, among others, the Guggenheim, the Hermitage, the Louvre, and the Beaubourg.[500] The digitalization of dates relating to collective memories, histories, and heritages is a new way of sharing values and perhaps of creating "heritage communities" around the world related to cultural diversity.[501]

The need for international management in contemporary culture is increasing due to movements in society which inevitably impact the arts and, consequently, affect cultural institutions and organizations. Increasingly, arts and cultural management is becoming one of the major factors facilitating the mobility and development of society and urbanization at a global level. It enhances the development of the democratization processes in society and, as a result, cultural institutions have become much more open in a bid to keep pace with social changes, while also taking on an active role within them.[502] There is strong demand for an organized system that can ensure balanced development, both within the cultural institutions themselves and between institutions at local and regional levels. Therefore, as we proceed with the intention to continue the advancement and dissemination of knowledge, it is necessary to push for the acquisition of new skills and to call for experiential exchange between cultural practices. In the wider context, cultural management certainly goes beyond local or regional models and in reality, it is located at and beyond European level.[503]

The museums and art galleries have become, not just exhibition spaces, but also centers of art education with education programs that are instrumental in forming and retaining a permanent audience which has access to, and influence over, the content of both the exhibition space and its education program. All experience in this area that can be drawn on is valuable across all levels of society, from workers, young people and those in education to pensioners, local community groups, people with special needs, and so forth.

Funding is also one of the important issues in the context of cultural activity and, because of this, the European Union provides for organized art and cultural management activities at a European level. As the necessity for this becomes more and more inevitable, the local level actually becomes a global level.[504] Contemporary art and culture are an intrinsic part of modern life which brings together aspects of popular culture, modern civilization, and technological development. Worldviews and value systems can be created through art and culture, thereby assisting the development of the human race as well as the advancement of specific ideologies. Therefore, art institutions, organizations, and facilities must actively seek to become open spaces for both artists and society as a whole in order to achieve true significance in a wider context.[505]

The successful engagement with visitors, audience, or participants, is essential to the success of work in the cultural sector. This is true regardless of whether that work is in the domain of the public or the private sector, represents large or small projects, community arts or high art, political or commercial cultural activities, canvas painting, or multimedia installation. A good, well-managed relationship between art and audience not only ensures our financial and public survival, but also makes art meaningful.[506]

We need to encourage our audience to actively engage in cultural activities that we offer them, rather than merely hope that they will turn up. It requires a proactive, planned approach. It is important to understand *the visitor*—

> Who are we talking to? What are they interested in? What messages will they respond to? What do they think of you and your Institution? If we do not have precise and accurate answers to these questions, all further work is based solely on assumptions rather than facts and knowledge. In arts, especially visual arts, there is traditionally widespread opinion that people who

> are interested in our work, are people who "like us"—which means that they understand our references, our way of expression and our world view in general.[507]

The conclusion is that a good relationship with the audience starts with an encounter between strangers and continues through different stages of the development of their relationship to levels of trust and loyalty. We need to develop different relationships with our visitors. The arts are fundamental to our very nature as human beings. They are the expressions of our hopes and fears, as well as our values. The marketing approach is one of fundamental importance for the creation of a long-term sustainable cultural sector, providing it with a leading role in the very center of society, not a place on the edge.

If we concentrate on the practices and processes in the evaluation of the artistic projects, the management and organization of what is required to make culture happen, there seem to be three things that we need to evaluate:

1. the practices and processes of our organization and management
2. the impact on audiences and participants
3. the impact on wider society and the economy

The conclusions and consequences for the work in the cultural sector are worth considering. It is a shame they are not more widely distributed and read. There are two main reasons for the evaluation:

1. to improve what we do
2. to discover the impact of what we are doing

The evaluation can be a liberating experience; it shows we have confidence in what we are doing and are strong enough to accept what evaluation might discover.[508]

The primary role of the cultural institution today is to have an educational impact on society. In this context, educational practices in museums and galleries have been more than present. The second role is the cultural sector as part of a wider spectrum of employment opportunities.[509] The new museums and galleries have become flagship projects for many cities. At the same time, it is arguable that a number of factors, including technology, economic changes, and new social theories, have changed the dynamic of the traditional why of working in museums or galleries. The "institution" can now exist online, in "alternative" adjunct, or "off-site" spaces.

Art has become increasingly linked to the themes of our times—ecology, globalization, communication, and cultural change. The new buildings of the majority of galleries and museums are dedicated to education, learning, and interpretation. Most museums and galleries have dedicated physical spaces for education and learning—a great deal of funding has been allocated to new buildings, or upgrading existing facilities.

The institution works outside its own walls, recognizing the impact of reaching out to an audience, rather than relying on a "visitor" experience as the primary means of engagement. Arts education programs do not focus solely on bringing schoolchildren into a museum; they are also concerned with encouraging, nurturing, and sustaining a critical engagement in the arts as part of everyday life. There is little evidence to suggest that a visit to a museum as a child encourages long-term engagement with culture.

The museums and galleries would continue to be invested in by the government, if there was a clear focus on arts education. Arts have always been linked with a range of agendas: urban regeneration; economic development; social cohesion, etc. At the global level, employment in the creative sector continues to rise.[510] There is a growing spectrum of qualifications and training opportunities available to those working in the arts and cultural sector—delivered by universities, cultural institutions, publicly funded organizations, and agencies.

Art Education Policies

According to Claude Mollard, the French cultural theoretician and cultural engineering ideologist, a cultural system comprises of two intersecting axes with four families on the left and right, top and bottom sides of the axis. On one axis is the cultural market, with its family of creators to its left side and to the right the audience for which art is made. On the vertical axis is cultural policy, with its family of decision-makers on the upper arm and family of agents below. The family of creators comprises of artists, writers, interpretations, and performers of works of art. The audience includes casual and regular "consumers" of works of art and values, as well as the non-audience. The decision-makers are part of all three sectors of culture: in the public one these are the authorities (ministers, directors of cultural institutions, producers); in the private sector they are directors of cultural institutions, banks, industries and corporations financing art production (donors, sponsors, and patrons); and in the third, nongovernmental (civil) sector, the decision-makers are association presidents, foundations, and other nongovernmental organizations (NGOs).[511] The second step, which was very important for developing art educational practice, was that the strategy of education and new personnel policy should include, in addition to additional education and re-education, the shaping of a special philosophy of cultural institutions oriented toward investing in training their personnel as well as establishing special funds within each institution to provide their personnel with the possibility of receiving additional art education and re-education.[512] In this context, precisely formulated, stimulating and restricted criteria for work evaluation, rewards and punishments and a series of other measures to be introduced if the image of personnel capacities is to be changed for the better and adjusted to the new needs of culture and society as a whole are really indispensable.

The challenges of new needs arose alongside new economic, social, and cultural policies. They called for a transformation of the former planning system with a rigid bureaucratic structure into a modern, flexible, and rational one, oriented toward the efficient satisfaction of society's needs as a whole, as well as the individual needs of its component parts. The solution lay in the education of the local administration and in designing on-going training in decision-making and the implementation of decisions. No cultural policy is possible without an educated, capable, and well-organized administration that is able to implement changes, shape cultural policy in accordance with new social demands, and create conditions that will foster the consistent application and also management of changes.[513] Through this provision of art education, audiences become more certain and more reliable.

The conference "Building Creative Capacities for the 21st Century," organized by UNESCO and the Government of Portugal, took place in Lisbon from March 6 to 9, 2006. It addressed issues surrounding the value and importance of art education in contemporary society, as well as presenting strategies for promoting art education policies. The World Conference on Arts Education, "Building Creative Capacities for the 21st Century," was the culmination of a five-year-long international collaboration between UNESCO and its partners in the field of arts education. It was attended by 1,200 participants from over 97 member states.[514] The following themes were discussed: the advocacy and implementation of arts education at policy and governmental level; the impact of arts education on social, cultural, and academic areas; the quality of education relating to teacher training and pedagogical methods; and the promotion of partnerships for implementing arts education programs.

Participants at the conference included representatives of ministries of education and/or culture from UNESCO member states, as well as various experts, practitioners, and researchers. High-level representatives attended the conference and the plenary session on "Defining Priorities for Immediate Action." International NGOs, such as the International Society for Education through Art (InSEA), were identified as UNESCO's main partners.

The arts have an important contributory role in intercultural communication; it should have a cultural base with a focus on local heritage as a source of promoting social relevance and sustainability. Arts education should create spaces of joy, peace, play, leisure, pleasure, and a space for change and exchange. As regards arts education policies: policies on arts education are needed on international, national, regional, and local levels; students (children and young people) have to be at the center of all policies. Teachers have to be educated in social skills and knowledge so that they can use the cultural environment as a resource and bring it into the classroom. A better cooperation between Ministries of Education and Culture is essential. The exchange and cooperation between schools and arts and cultural institutions such as theaters, galleries, and museums are essential for the development of arts education. There need also to be strong interaction between arts specialization schools and general schools, with school-to-school exchanges being a fruitful model.

This European network of art institutions is a network for gathering together educational institutions dealing with art education practice. It is a European platform for encouraging a serious exchange of knowledge, methodologies, experiences, and comparative research programs in the field of art education from a European point of view and through a range of working groups, projects, activities, and events. The partnership aims to: evaluate current art education practice within the four institutions; develop and inform our own practice by exploring new and existing models of arts education; and develop a network of educational partnerships that is sustainable in the long term.[515] Museums and galleries, together with partners in their network, have recognized the importance of developing partners in Europe for the purpose of expanding their exhibitions, outreach, and education programs. The network's partners understand the constant changes taking place in society. They aim to involve these changes in an inclusive way through the development of European educational programs.

The educational goals are:[516]

- to promote the confidence to be in the gallery environment and for young adults and adults and to be self-confident in their personal interpretation of art;
- to prepare for people to extend and increase their experience of the arts through innovative arts projects that engage people at their level of understanding;
- to develop strategic and long-lasting partnerships in the arts and education sector with organizations nationally and internationally which include partners on a European level;
- to invent and implement new educational tools together with European partners that can be used in our institutions and also in the European partners' institutions;
- to work with the Minister for Culture at a local and regional level in order to highlight the benefits of arts education and to secure additional funding;
- to enhance the education department's ability to develop interactive, high-quality arts events that challenge the viewer through the introduction of new and emerging national and international artists; and
- to use the gallery's collection and exhibitions as an educational resource for the benefit of the public in a local, national, and international context.

To develop programs that can enrich and broaden knowledge as well as intercultural understanding and equality, cultural policy has to create strategies for partnership for the arts sector to establish a program that can bring it a level of stability as well as to establish key strategies for funding and development.[517]

In the context of sustainability and the development of partnership and networking, arts education managers have to lead educational programs and also be key elements in promoting the value of the arts in society.

The strategic goals can be defined as follows:

- improvement of communication between national and international partners;
- more effective management;
- improvement of communication and coordination between institutions, both nationally and internationally;

- mobilization of audiences to participate in educational programs;
- to increase activity level and encourage "door opening" toward the audience and the whole art sector (improvements in the quality of technical equipment would be a precondition of this);
- investment in art education programs;
- permanent education of art education staff;
- to support national and international cultural exchange and cooperation—establish partnerships through joint cultural programs;
- to connect local artists with domestic and European peers;
- to encourage and support cooperation between culture, media, and education sectors;
- to establish permanent partnership with the media in processes of defining and implementing cultural values and the mobilization of the audience;
- to build a good art education practice is to invest in new tools, modules, and interactions; and
- to establish a stable, reliable means of funding in order to assure the equitable development of art education practice.

Contemporary art can be an important entry point into the complexities of modern life and it connects the dots between different aspects of popular culture, modern civilization, and developing technologies. Through art, one can acquire a valuable worldview and learn how to question the values that are imposed by society. An understanding of art helps one to mature as an individual and to develop their own opinions.

Case Study Research

This research explores new angles on the concept of cultural development on a wider scale. The case studies in this research have offered a theoretical analysis of the contemporary approach to culture and innovation, as well as to the development of cities, with culture being a factor in the developmental processes. A special emphasis is put on the relationship between culture, innovations, and the economy as a sustainable factor, while clearly stating that a cultural ecosystem contains the economy.

The document *Culture21: Actions* has evaluated that the cultural projects in cities are based on realistic and practical experiences of international organizations, universities, and activists. They represent a dedication of city councils to integrate culture into the process of sustainable development, on both local and global levels. The economy has a great legitimacy when it is adapted to local sources.

In the following document, it is concluded that cultural activism plays an important role in sustainable economic development and creates economic activities. The cultural and economic factors of the environment must be taken into account and developed in parallel. Economic models that aim for cultural sensitivity need to engage in practice that includes collaboration, cooperation, trade, and donations.

All economic models are based on specific cultural values. *Culture21: Actions*, in following an analytic approach, has been focused on the network between the public, market, and cooperative economy, together with the interaction among them, and brings a conclusion that is essential to achieving an environmentally balanced development. The cultural ecosystem should be treated as a system that contains the economy.[518]

In terms of method, the research is based partially upon a qualitative study, centered on the cultural policy dimensions of public cultural governance, cultural institutions, and organizations in Europe, carried out with 30 interviews with professionals on several major themes: place and role of innovation, new modes of governance, relationships with the environment, changing role of institutions, impact of economic and tourism issues, professionalization and education, social changes, and community.

The aim was to study a diversity of examples according to the relevant criteria in relation to the object of research: size of the cultural sector, size of the budget and staff, type of funding and status, presence or lack of an administrator, location in an urban, suburban, or rural setting, etc. The interviews will be partially directive, based on an interview guide. We will analyze case by case, then globally. This research tries to clarify the relationship between culture and innovation. We will analyze innovation facilities based on new technology, creative industries, and institutional research. The research has three focus groups: Northern Europe, Western Europe, and Central and Eastern Europe.

The subject of research will be to monitor the level of innovation through case studies in Europe and can be divided into two groups which contribute to the sustainable development of the cultural sector. They are social and technological, and these two processes are connected. Innovation includes new governance models, consideration of and access to different types of heritage, intergenerational equity, etc. It is thus of paramount importance for urban and rural development, tourism, education, creative industries and cultural heritage professionals to understand how to integrate European culture into sustainable development as the crucial role of social and inclusive innovation.[519]

Social innovation includes the social *processes* of innovation, such as open source methods and techniques, and also innovations which have a social purpose: activism, virtual volunteering, or distance learning.[520] Technical innovation refers to adding the extra steps of developing new services for the public that fulfill unaddressed needs or solve problems that did not exist in the past. Technological innovation, however, focuses on the technological aspects of a product or service. It is important to clarify that innovation is not only driven by technology.[521]

The qualitative research involves collecting and analyzing non-numerical data (e.g., text, video, or audio) to understand concepts, opinions, or experiences. It can be used to gather in-depth insights into a problem or generate new ideas for research.[522] It is also important for qualitative researchers to know how to situate and position themselves in the research setting. It is contended that the self-representations and positionality of researchers can evoke stereotypes that influence the feelings and opinions of the respondents. The intersection of identities and positionalities of researchers has the potential to significantly affect the information provided by the participants.[523]

The strength of qualitative research is its ability to provide complex textual descriptions of professional experience with research facts. It provides information about the "human" side of an issue—that is, the behaviors, beliefs, opinions, and relationships of individuals.[524]

The three most common qualitative methods, explained in detail in their respective modules, are participant observation, interviews, and focus groups. Each method has a specific type of data that we use in this research.

- Participant observation is for collecting data on naturally occurring behaviors in their contexts.
- In-depth interviews are optimal for collecting data on individuals' personal and professionals, perspectives, and experiences, particularly when sensitive topics are being explored.
- Focus groups are effective in eliciting data on the cultural norms of a group and in generating broad overviews of issues of concern to the cultural groups.[525]

The in-depth interviews were focused on three focus groups. Through its multidimensional approach and the flexibility between different perspectives (going from in-depth interviews with the relevant actors of the case studies from direct observations) of three different parts of Europe, this methodology seeks to point as closely as possible to the interaction between culture and innovation.

The case studies are determined by the characteristics of the position, the development of the creative economy and innovation in cities, and how the development of the creative economy is carried out through local governments and innovations and through cultural institutions and organizations. Different sizes of local governments are taken into consideration in order to see the processes of development of innovations and creative industries. Focus groups are divided into ten interviews. It is also important to point out that the policies implemented in the first two focus groups put citizens at the center of development, and, in addition to local resources, citizens are the ones who contribute to the development of the creative economy and innovation through participation in projects at the city level and institutions. In that sense, the first two groups differ from the third focus group, where the above-mentioned policies are not uniform and continuous, and each local self-government and institution must work independently on development and education.

The policies pursued in Western Europe are continuous, while the cultural policies pursued in Eastern and Central Europe do not have the strength of continuity and the implications for the development and they are weaker and uneven, which will be seen later in the analysis itself. Most Western European cities have based their cultural policies directly on the development of creative industries and innovation, thus showing a new image of the city where culture, innovation, and the creative economy are in the balance of development. It is important to point out that local resources provide an excellent basis for the development of the creative economy, as well as innovations that are accompanied by the development of technologies.

The first focus group, consisting of Stockholm, Glasgow, Edinburgh, Dublin, Turku, London, and Eindhoven, belongs to Western Europe and are characterized by the development of innovations in the IT sector such as Stockholm, Edinburgh and the development of creative industries in Glasgow, London, and Eindhoven.

The second group also includes the cities of Western Europe, the city of Rome, Bologna, Brussels and is characterized by the development of social innovation and creative industries, while the city of Reims, Grenoble, Marseilles is characterized by social and technological innovation. The third focus group, which consists of the cities of Ljubljana, Zagreb, Bratislava, Novi Sad and belongs to Central and Eastern Europe, is characterized by social innovation. The city of Bratislava works on creative industries programs but needs greater professionalization of people in the field of culture, which also holds true for Gabrovo. In Belgrade and Skopje, there is a development of innovations that is in its infancy and depends on the culture of politics. The European examples in this study stem from the research belief that selected cities correlate with performance in the field of urban cultural development. The mapping of cities, processed in case studies, was analyzed from the point of view of the effectiveness of local policies in the development of the cultural sector, which together with the citizens were identified in scientific concepts as cities of culture.

The intention is to compare the experiences of the cities processed in the case studies with highly competitive cities from the European continent. In terms of models and role models selected, this book deals with the development of the cultural and innovation sector. The choice of models for comparing the effects of cities from the case studies is limited to the successful European examples in this study. This attitude stems from the research belief that the selected cities are scientifically recognized as cities of successful cultural policies from Europe and the visible weaker development of Eastern European cities, relevant cities for the development of the cultural sector.

The first focus group of the qualitative research includes:

A) Mr Tomas Andersson, Culture Administration, International Relations, External Financing and Sponsorship Strategist, City of Stockholm.
B) Dr Bridget McConnell, Chief Executive Officer, Jill Miller, Director of Culture and Lynda Campbell, Head of Business & Strategy. In 2006, Glasgow City Council created Culture and Sport Glasgow, with the branding name "Glasgow Life," City of Glasgow.
C) Mrs Liz McGettigan, Director, The New Technology and Innovation, Company SOLUS, City of Edinburgh.
D) Mr James E. Doyle, ex-officer of the Dublin City Council and culture expert, City of Brussels and Dublin.
E) Mr Hugh McElveen—InterroBang Ltd, Think Thank Industry, City of Dublin.

F) Mrs Penelope Kenny, Director, ArtsGovernance, Limited Company in the Culture space. City of Dublin.
G) Mrs Penelope Kenny, Board Director and Chair of the Audit and Risk committee, IMMA The Irish Museum of Modern Art, City of Dublin.
H) Mrs Maarit Keto—Seppala, Producer, Dance Theatre ERI, City of Turku.
I) Mr Callum Lee, Managing Director, BOP Consulting, City of London.
J) Mrs Sanne Reiniers, Communications Officer, Cultuur Eindhoven, local government organization, City of Eindhoven.

The second focus group of the qualitative research comprises:

A) Mr Luca Bergamo (Deputy Mayor for Culture's Office of the City of Rome), Vice Mayor in charge of cultural development, City of Rome.
B) Mrs Giorgia Boldrini, Head of Creative Industries, Music and Urban Regeneration Unit, Municipality of Bologna.
C) Mr Esteve Caramés, Head of Culture Program, Institute of Culture Barcelona, Barcelona City Council, City of Barcelona.
D) Mrs Mercedes Giovinazzo, Director, Fundació INTERARTS per a la Cooperació Cultural Internacional (NGO), City of Barcelona.
E) Mr Philippe Kern, Director, KEA European Affairs, Private Research Center, City of Brussels.
F) Mrs Marion Grange Doyard, head of department, cultural development, directorate of culture, Reims City Council, City of Reims.
G) Dr Matthias Rauch, Cultural Innovation Officer, Next Mannheim, City of Mannheim.
H) Mrs Marienne Taillibert, Head of Communications, in charge of sponsorship, At the Museum of Grenoble, City of Grenoble.
I) Mrs Naïk M'SILI—Co-director, Art organization, Instants Vidéo Numériques et Poétiques, City of Marseille.
J) Mr Olaf Ginzel and Mrs Daniela Bekemeier, Founders of the gallery project, 44309 Street//Art Gallery, Dortmund Art Gallery, City of Dortmund.

The third focus group of the qualitative research is as follows:

A) Mrs Katarina Lukyova, culture department, (the local government) *Hlavné mesto Slovenskej republiky Bratislava/ The Capital city of the Slovak republic Bratislava. City of Bratislava.*
B) Mr Dragan Kojic, Director. Novi Sad City Library, City of Novi Sad.
C) Mrs Elena Oranskaia, director, Stichting Art-East+Art-West (NGO), City of Eindhoven / Kiev / Moscow.
D) Mrs Sunčica Milosavljević, Program Director, BAZAART, Representative Association in Culture, City of Belgrade. Mr. Zoran Erić, Curator, Museum of Contemporary Art, City of Belgrade.

E) Mrs Margarita Dorovska, Director, Museum of Humour and Satire, City of Gabrovo.
F) Mrs Dragana Lucija Ratković Aydemir, founder and owner Muze d.o.o./ Muses Ltd., City of Zagreb.
G) Mr Robert Ajdzalovski, Minister of Culture, Local Government for Innovation in Macedonia, City of Skopje.
H) Mrs Anna Micek and Mrs Kamila Biedrońska, Museum of Contemporary Art in Krakow MOCAK, City of Krakow.
I) Mr Blaž Peršin, Director of Museums and Galleries of Ljubljana, City of Ljubljana.
J) Mrs Zsuzsanna Fehér, Ludwig Museum—Museum of Contemporary Art Budapest, City of Budapest.

Notes

479 Europe is the second-smallest continent, and it could be described as a large peninsula or as a subcontinent with "common cultural heritage."
480 Klaus Bochmann, *L'idée d'Europe jusqu'au XXè siècle* (1990) quoted in Jan Berting, *Europe: A Heritage, a Challenge, a Promise* (Delft: Eburon Academic Publishers, 2006), 52. "No two lists of the main constituents of European civilization would ever coincide. But many items have always featured prominently: from the roots of the Christian world in Greece, Rome and Judaism to modern phenomena such as the Enlightenment, modernization, romanticism, nationalism, liberalism, imperialism, totalitarianism."
481 Jan Berting, *Europe: A Heritage, a Challenge, a Promise* (Delft: Eburon Academic Publishers, 2006).
482 United Nations, accessed May 10, 2021, https://www.un.org/
483 "European Capitals of Culture," European Commission, accessed May 9, 2021, https://ec.europa.eu/culture/policies/culture-cities-and-regions/european-capitals-culture
484 Anne Gombault, "Social Participation Issues in Becoming a Creative City: Learning from European Capitals of Culture," *The Creative City: Vision and Execution*, ed. Biljana Mickov and James Doyle (London: Routledge Publishing, 2015).
485 Paris Thomas, "Organisation, processus et structures de la création," *Culture et Prospective* 5, no. 5 (2007): 1–15.
486 Charles, *The Creative City: A Toolkit for Urban Innovators.*
487 Ibid.
488 Robert Palmer, *European Cities and Capitals of Culture: Part I and Part II, Study Prepared for the European Commission* (Brussels: Palmer-Rae Associates, 2004).
489 European Union, European Commission, accessed May 9, 2021, https://ec.europa.eu/info/index_en
490 Luc Braconnier, "Luxembourg and the Great Region: a Cultural Challenge," in *Sustaining Cultural Development, Unified Systems and New Governance in Cultural Life*, ed. James Doyle and Biljana Mickov (London: Routledge Publishing, 2013).
491 Ibid.
492 Ibid.
493 For additional information see www.plurio.net
494 Braconnier, "Luxembourg and the Great Region: a Cultural Challenge."
495 Source and additional information: www.granderegion.net
496 Braconnier, "Luxembourg and the Great Region: a Cultural Challenge."
497 Fabrice Thuriot, "Museums and Globalisation," in *Sustaining Cultural Development: New Governance in Cultural Life*, ed. James Doyle and Biljana Mickov (London: Routledge publishing, 2013).

498 Anne Hertzog et Frédéric Poulard, "Les échanges internationaux comme point d'ancrage de la modernisation et de la diversification des musées français," dans *Patrimoine et mondialisation* (Paris: l'Harmattan, 2008).
499 Martine Regourd et Fabrice Thuriot, "Multiplication des échelles d'intervention et problèmes de coordination Le patrimoine culturel et la souveraineté politique," dans *Patrimoine et mondialisation*, ed. Jean Claude Nemery (Paris: l'Harmattan, 2008).
500 Aurélie Gosselin et Jean-Michel Tobelem, "Concurrence et coopération: vers une uniformisation culturelle? Internationalisation des musées: effet de domination ou coopération culturelle? Le cas de la fondation Guggenheim et du musée de l'Ermitage," dans *Patrimoine et mondialisation*, ed. Jean Claude Nemery (Paris: l'Harmattan, 2008).
501 Ibid.
502 Biljana Mickov, "European Management Models in Contemporary Arts and Culture," in *Sustaining Cultural Development: New Governance in Cultural Life*, ed. James Doyle and Biljana Mickov (London: Routledge Publishing, 2013).
503 Ibid.
504 Ibid.
505 Ibid.
506 Jonathan Goodacre, "The Visitor Appears" in *Sustaining Cultural Development: New Governance in Cultural Life*, ed. James Doyle and Biljana Mickov (London: Routledge Publishing, 2013): 151–162.
507 Ibid.
508 Ibid.
509 S. Hayles, *Art, Education and the Role of Culture Institutions* (Novi Sad: Museum of Contemporary Art Vojvodina, 2010).
510 S. Hayles, *Art, Education and the Role of Culture Institutions.*
511 Sacha Kagan, "A Review of Claude Mollard's 'Cultural Engineering,'" unpublished Paper, Erasmus Universiteit Rotterdam, 2004, accessed May 20, 2021 http://sachakagan.chez-alice.fr/docs/Mollard.pdf
512 Biljana Mickov, "Arts Education Practice," in *Sustaining Cultural Development: New Governance in Cultural Life*, ed. James Doyle and Biljana Mickov (London: Routledge Publishing, 2013): 173–192.
513 Ibid.
514 UNESCO, "Road Map for Arts Education," (The World Conference on Arts Education: Building Creative Capacities for the 21st Century, Lisbon, March 6–9, 2006), accessed May 20, 2021, http://www.unesco.org/new/fileadmin/MULTIMEDIA/HQ/CLT/CLT/pdf/Arts_Edu_RoadMap_en.pdf
515 Biljana Mickov, "Art Education Practice," in *Sustaining Cultural Development: Unified Systems and New Governmance in Cultural Life*, ed. J. E. Doyle and B. Mickov (London: Routledge publishing, 2013).
516 Ibid.
517 Ibid.
518 UCLG, "Culture 21: Actions."
519 "Call: Participatory Approaches and Social Innovation in Culture," EuroAccess Macro-Regions, accessed May 20, 2021, https://www.euro-access.eu/calls/participatory_approaches_and_social_innovation_in_culture
520 Nikola Milosevic, Abdullah Gok, and Goran Nenadic, "Classification of Intangible Social Innovation Concepts" *Natural Language Processing and Information Systems* 12 (2018): 407–418.
521 Wim Naudé and Adam Szirmai "Technological Innovation, Entrepreneurship, and Development," The European Business Review, accessed May 20, 2021, https://www.europeanbusinessreview.com/technological-innovation-entrepreneurship-and-development/
522 Pritha Bhandari, "An Introduction to Qualitative Research," Scribbr, accessed May 20, 2021, https://www.scribbr.com/methodology/qualitative-research/

523 Beverly Mullings, "Insider or Outsider, Both or Neither: Some Dilemmas of Interviewing in a Cross-Cultural Setting," *Geoforum* 30, no. 4 (1999): 337–350; Binaya Subedi, "Theorizing a "Halfie" Researcher's Identity in Transnational Fieldwork," *International Journal of Qualitative Studies in Education* 19, no. 5 (2006): 573–593; Binaya Subedi, "Recognizing Respondents' Ways of Being and Knowing: Lessons Un/Learned in Researching Asian Immigrant and Asian-American Teachers, "*International Journal of Qualitative Studies in Education* 20, no. 1 (2007): 51–71.

524 "Qualitative Research Methods Overview," Family Health International, accessed May 9, 2021, https://course.ccs.neu.edu/is4800sp12/resources/qualmethods.pdf

525 Ibid.

9

THE FIRST FOCUS GROUP OF THE QUALITATIVE RESEARCH

City of Stockholm

Innovation, openness, and connectivity is the way forward to make sure Stockholm remains and develops further as a smart city, continuing on its to being economically, ecologically, and socially sustainable.[526]A smart city is a sustainable city, something which is made possible through connectivity, publicly accessible data, IT platforms that can communicate with each other, sensors and other technologies. Therefore, a strategy for the development of Stockholm as a smart and connected city has been developed in collaboration with the City of Stockholm's employees, residents, businesses, and academia. This strategy was formally adopted by the City Council of Stockholm in 2017. By utilizing Stockholm's favorable conditions, such as well-developed gender equality, widespread IT infrastructure, and the high level of digital maturity, as well as the opportunities for digitalization and the development of new technologies, the City of Stockholm will make life easier and better for everyone who lives, stays, or works in the capital. The core of the strategy's target vision shows the goal of the strategy and the city's digitalization efforts—to provide the highest quality of life for Stockholm's inhabitants and the best entrepreneurial climate.

Stockholm is currently one of the world's most connected cities. Stockholm's fiber solution is constantly contributing to making the city more attractive to businesses in general, and to the tech sector in particular. The goal of the city's fiber network efforts is to build a competition-neutral infrastructure capable of meeting future communication needs, spurring economic activity, diversity and freedom of choice, as well as minimizing disruption on the city's streets. The fiber network in Stockholm is provided and administered by Stokab, a company owned by Stockholm City Council. Culture Administration at the City of Stockholm, Local government organization, municipality. Mr Tomas Andersson, International Relations, External

DOI: 10.4324/9781003336648-11

Financing and Sponsorship Strategist. The Culture Administration is responsible for the main cultural activities in the city which are organized by the municipality. They are responsible for 40 libraries, the Stockholm School of the Arts (with 36,000 children), the Stockholm City Museum, the Medieval Museum, the Liljevalchs Art Gallery, the Stockholm Culture Festival, WeAreSthlm (Northern Europe's largest youth festival), Culture Night and the Stockholmia Publishing House. They also allocate financial aid to independent cultural and voluntary organizations. Through all of their activities, they promote and develop the cultural life of a constantly growing city. The geographic area of programs and activities are realized in the municipality of the City of Stockholm. The service users and target group are primarily the citizens of Stockholm, but also companies, visitors, and tourists.

These services are most often realized through a range of activities, including: book loans (over five million per year), cultural education for young people, 11 million visits that experience a vast variety of culture, and subsidized studios for 600 visual and design artists. These are just a few of the things that the City of Stockholm is doing. The impact of all of the above-mentioned examples is to engage with the audience—to broaden their experience. The development of creative industries and innovation is not good enough. Sweden lacks a strategy on a national, regional, and local level for the creative industries. The city of Stockholm has started a process on developing a strategy for Creative and Cultural Industries (CCI) in the city.

The strengths of the Culture Administration of the City of Stockholm are: The CCI sector is growing at a rapid rate (38% between 2010 and 2017 comparable to an ordinary consumer market's 4% over the same period of time). The Swedish music export is one good example that could serve as a good case for other parts of the sector on how to work and think.

Innovation and Creative and Cultural Industries (CCI): In terms of innovation, the City of Stockholm has a short tradition of strength within the tech industries, ranking number 2 in the world after Silicon Valley in terms of developing unicorns/per capita. That factor should also be borne in mind when considering the developing CCI sector.

The main weakness is a lack of strategy on a national level and it is possible to improve in the current situation with support from the CCI sector with a focus on innovation. The innovative trend in this area is digitalization. The Culture Administration is funded by the city of Stockholm, municipality-wise, yet the Culture Administration has no designated budget for CCI and innovation. The department employs a large number of people with strategy competence. The innovations in the cultural programme are Bibblix—an app for children's book loans at the Digital library unit at the city library; UX design-how people want their libraries; co-creation—the youth festival is co-created with the target group. The work is done at the Event department, which provides an app for experiencing exhibitions at the Art Gallery. This work has carried out by an external consultant.

The Culture Administration cooperates with various administrations such as urban development, the building department, the Stockholm Business Region and

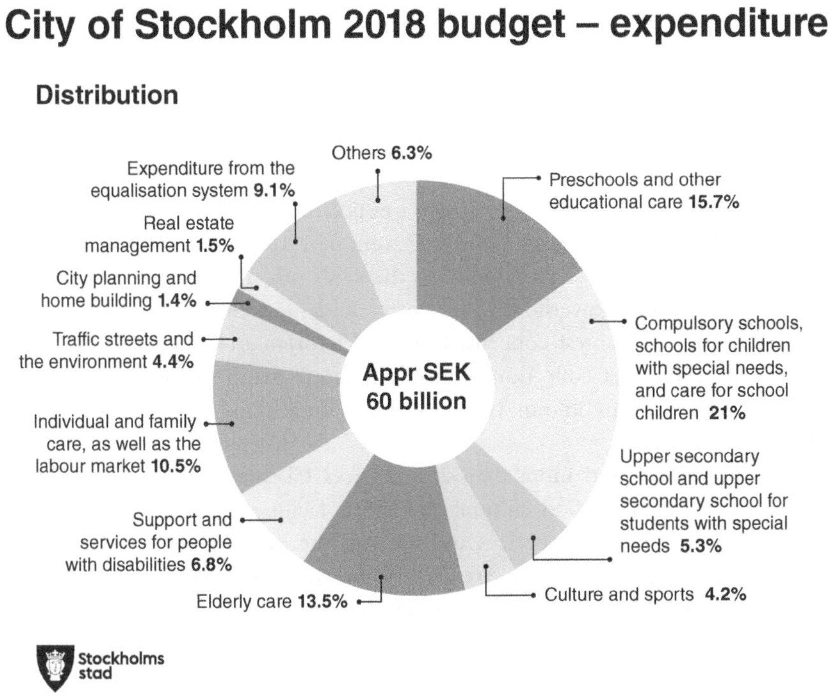

FIGURE 6 City of Stockholm, *Budget expenditure for 2018*, 2018. Available at: https://start.stockholm/

the Visit Stockholm agency within the City of Stockholm. They also collaborate with the state institutions situated in Stockholm on various levels. On an international level, by contrast, they undertake little cooperation. They have recently had an experience exchange with Amsterdam. The international focus is declining due to budget cuts from the city of Stockholm. The costs for both culture and sports are aggregated. The budget for culture within the municipality is 900 million SEK, or approximately €80.32 million.[527]

City of Glasgow

Culture & Sport Glasgow was established on 22 December 2006 by the Glasgow City Council. Its brand name is "Glasgow Life."[528]

Dr Bridget McConnell, Chief Executive Officer, Jill Miller, Director of Culture, Lynda Campbell, Head of Business & Strategy.

In 2007, Glasgow City Council created Culture and Sport Glasgow, a limited company registered in Scotland as a charity with the office of the Scottish Charity Regulator. Glasgow Life delivers cultural (arts, libraries, museums, music, learning, community development) and sports services on behalf of Glasgow City Council. Glasgow Life's remit cuts across a wide variety of policy contexts including: public health, sport and physical activity, tourism, events and destination marketing, culture, heritage, learning, communities and equalities.

It is responsible for leading strategies for: Glasgow's Tourism and Visitor Plan, Sport and Active Legacy Plan, Glasgow's Cultural Plan, Vision for Glasgow Libraries, Glasgow's Events Strategy, Glasgow's Community Learning and Development Plan, and Glasgow's Music Strategy including Glasgow as a UNESCO City of Music. Glasgow is Scotland's largest city; it has a population of around 600,000 and 2.5 million in the city region. Last year there were over 18 million usages of Glasgow Life's services in the city of Glasgow. As the UK's 6th most visited city, Glasgow is Scotland's cultural powerhouse—home to the largest civic museums service in the UK; one of the largest concentrations of Victorian architecture in the world, an extensive public art collection; four of Scotland's five national performing arts companies; a thriving community of visual arts studios and galleries and an unrivalled music scene.

The 160 venues and more than 250 services Glasgow Life manages include a network of neighborhood cultural and sports facilities, a range of community development and learning services and some of the most prestigious buildings in the UK (including: Kelvingrove Art Gallery and Museum; the Burrell Collection; the Emirates Arena and Sir Chris Hoy Velodrome, Glasgow Royal Concert Hall, The Mitchell Library). Glasgow Life takes a leading role in enhancing Glasgow's global profile as a major events and tourist city. The services are used by over 75% of the city's population and by millions of tourists each year. Our services are universal and target the whole population.

The types of activities or services most often realized from April 1, 2017 to March 31, 2018 are: Over 1,126,000 attendances to Arts, Music and Cultural venues and festivals; over 824,000 venue attendances generating £29.8 million to the city's economy; and over 300,000 festival attendances £6.8 million to the city's economy. There were 5 million visits to Glasgow Libraries. Book issues rose to over 2.4 million, including 662,000 issues of children and teenage literature. The expanding library digital offer attracted 1.2 million virtual visits and 340,000 issues of e-Stock.

More than 1.5 million visits across the city's 26 locally based community venues were realized. Many of Glasgow Communities' programs and activities are supported by a volunteering program. There were more than 730 volunteers donating over 36,000 hours of their time to cultural, sporting, and learning programs last year. In the last financial year Glasgow Convention Bureau won 490 new conferences through to 2023 worth £143 million—named the UK's best Convention Bureau for the 12th consecutive year. With an events calendar celebrating world-class cultural and sporting events in state-of-the-art venues, both citizens and visitors to the city can enjoy events all year round. Last year there were attendances at events including: World Pipe Band Championships; World Irish Dance Championships; TOTAL BWF Badminton World Championships; and HSBC Let's Ride. 2020 was a record year for Glasgow Museums—almost four million visits across eight world-class venues. 70% of visitors to Glasgow visit a museum or gallery and 100% of their collection of five million objects is publicly accessible. Glasgow maintained its place as one of the world's top five Ultimate Sports Cities of 2018 and won the award for the world's Best Small City for hosting sporting events for the second time. Glasgow operates the largest civic sports complex in Scotland with 22 gyms and 13 swimming pools. Attendances at the city's sports facilities topped the six million marks for the sixth successive year (6,267,699), and Glasgow Club Fitness Unlimited membership levels ended the year at a record high of 43,611. Innovative practice is embedded in all Glasgow Life services, as evidenced through continued evolution and improvement of programs and activities as well as an extensive list of awards and commendations.

Their Policy & Research team continually assesses all existing and emerging policy and directives from EU, UK and Scottish Governments and they actively contribute to all international enquiries and networks. The most recent has been a consultation with the Scottish Government on the proposed Culture Strategy for Scotland. The strengths of Glasgow Life are: council ownership and revenue funding; historic investment and commitment to culture and sport; local and national government, a charitable mandate; clear vision from Chief Executive; support from Senior Management Team for improved intelligence—move towards reporting outcomes; a specialist, high caliber sectoral workforce; diversity of skills and influence of Board members; a vast network of facilities providing local services and local, national and international reputation.

In 2010 Glasgow Cultural Enterprises transferred to Glasgow Life, bringing the city's music agenda, including the UNESCO commitments, under the overall banner of Glasgow Music. Three additional venues were added to the property portfolio: the Glasgow Royal Concert Hall, City Halls and the Old Fruitmarket. This delivered a £500,000 saving to the City Council. In 2016, as part of the Transforming Glasgow agenda, Glasgow City Council and Glasgow Life's Board approved a merger with the Glasgow City Marketing Bureau (GCMB). On April 1, 2017 GCMB became fully integrated across Glasgow Life and its trading subsidiary and all destination marketing, conference and convention activity became their responsibility, including Glasgow's tourism plan, a key strand of the city's economic strategy. Also, in 2010 the School Library Service transferred to Glasgow Life supporting 29 secondary school libraries and an education outreach service that supports nursery and primary schools.

It helped deliver global events, such as the 2014 Commonwealth Games and the 2015 World Gymnastics Championships and currently heavily involved in 2018 European Championships—all linked to their national and international status rankings.

Scale:

- Usages of Glasgow Life's services have grown from 14.3 million to 18.5 million—an increase of 29%.

- 1st in the UK outside London in the number of: civic museums (Riverside Museum: European Museum of the Year 2013), concert halls, live music performances, live music attendances, cultural production capacity, TV & Film production capacity, Turner Prize Nominees and Winners, Higher Education Cultural Training.
- Named UK's Best Convention Bureau for the 12th consecutive year (Meeting and Incentive Travel Awards)
- Delivering over £130 million economic benefit to the city from conference delegate spend per year
- Glasgow ranked 5th in the list of the world's Ultimate Sporting Cities and 1st in the small city category.
- Achieved a top 4 ranking as one of the world's leading cities for sustainable business tourism
- Attracts 2 m international and domestic visitors spending £482 million- and 20 million day visitors spending £1 billion and supports 31,000 jobs in the city
- Visit and spending by overseas tourists in Glasgow rose to its highest level in 2017 with the number of overseas visitors travelling to Glasgow increasing by nearly a fifth (19%) to 787,000, while expenditure increased by more than a third (36%) to £319 million.

Reach:

- 37% of visits to museums from are from households within Glasgow;
- 43% of Glasgow Club (sport) members are from households in the most deprived areas in Glasgow; and
- 46% Glasgow Library users are from households in the most deprived areas in Glasgow.

The weaknesses of Glasgow life are:

- Over-dependency on council funding
- Reliance on sports' earned income
- Limited ability to fully exploit technology and commercial opportunities
- Lack of diversity in the workforce
- Ongoing building and life cycle maintenance liability
- Embedded culture of reporting outputs

Very few competitors—budget gyms in the city and other venues are available for hire, but there are no other providers of civic museums or libraries. There is no other organization leading the cultural strategy for the city or the tourism strategy.

Glasgow Life are currently looking at extending our partnerships in the city to help use the power of culture and sport to support health interventions, for example social prescribing.

The important sources of financing so far:

		£millions
•	Glasgow Life Gross Budget 2018/19	£111,484
•	Service Fee from Glasgow City Council	£72,679
•	Earned Income	£38,805

Glasgow Life's operating model means that it operates independently from Glasgow City Council and, as one of the largest charities in Scotland, it is in a unique position to make a transformational difference for the people of Glasgow by maximizing the benefits of being a charity. They have a dedicated team who regularly secure funding and sponsorship from external organizations and individual donors. Glasgow Life does not have a separate budget for innovation and creative industries project.

The economic contribution of users and visitors to Glasgow Life venues and events has generated gross value added (GVA) of over £1.5 billion within the Glasgow economy between 2007 and 2017. Glasgow Life leases 132 physical buildings with many of these delivering multiple services such as sport, libraries, and community facilities. They also provide services from play only facilities and therefore deliver services on behalf of the Council from 167 sites. They employ 2,500 staff and have hundreds of volunteers supporting our services across the city.

The Glasgow Life Board is made up of eight Independent Directors, five Partners Directors (Councillors) and the Chief Executive. Its role is to set the strategic direction in achieving Glasgow Life's objectives and ensure the effective operation of Glasgow Life as a Charity.

There is an extensive network of partnerships and formal memorandums of understanding in the city, both in Scotland and internationally.

- Co-located financial services are now available in 11 libraries across the City, generating £2.2 million in financial improvements for the people of Glasgow.
- The Mitchell Library since September now offers a full Citizens' Advice Bureau.
- Jobs and Business Glasgow now offer employability support at 25 libraries across the city.
- Govan Law Centre operates out of three venues (Bridgeton and Parkhead libraries and Netherton Community Centre).
- Revenue and Benefits offer Housing Benefit and Council Tax advice at five libraries across the city.
- The partnership with Macmillan continues to offer a network of support and information services across each of the City's libraries, with nearly 14,000 attendances recorded since its launch.

There are formal memorandums of understanding with the University of Glasgow and the University of Strathclyde. The core cities network extends across the UK.

The most recent partnership was with Berlin, Germany in delivering the inaugural 2018 European Sports Championships.

Innovation: The 160 venues and over 250 services they manage include a network of neighborhood cultural and sports facilities, a range of community development and learning services and some of the most prestigious buildings in the UK. Innovative practice is embedded in all Glasgow Life services, as evidenced through continued evolution and improvement of programs and activities, as well as an extensive list of awards and commendations.

City of Edinburgh

SOLUS UK—company for innovation, City of Edinburgh, UK.

The city of Edinburgh is Scotland's capital—known for its striking architecture and its hilly and compact cityscape. It is famous for its contribution to culture, including the National Galleries of Scotland, the Scottish Poetry Library, the Scottish Chamber Orchestra, and Edinburgh Sculpture Workshop, as well as world-famous city festivals, including the Edinburgh International Festival and the Edinburgh Festival Fringe, the world's largest arts festival. Edinburgh is also a UNESCO City of Literature and was the first ever designated city (awarded in 2004). It exemplifies natural as well as cultural heritage, hosting more listed buildings than anywhere in the world and more trees per person than any other UK city.[529]

SOLUS is a company for library technological innovation research and supplier. The geographic areas of activities are: the UK, Australia and the US. The target groups are librarians, library directors, libraries, cultural services. The services most often realized are: Library apps, social catalogues, and children's learning and literacy apps. Innovation in SOLUS and the impact of it: the company created the UK's first ever library app when Liz McGettigan was Head of City of Edinburgh Libraries. This grew a new online audience and was so popular that it was then adopted by over 90 library authorities in the UK, now followed by over 100 in Australia and 100 in the US. McGettigan is now working to deliver the first ever global social/Netflix-style library catalogue with Australian colleagues. The development of creative industries and innovation: most of the visible effort is from the local community and from organized Council Culture and Leisure Departments, with little to none EU references.

The strengths of the company for innovation are: researching, learning and understanding human behavior, from global activity and adapting to local requirements. When consumers are exposed to superlative customer experiences or faster ways to access something online, they are quick to apply their newly-raised expectations to every other brand or industry and the library is no exception. We are changing as human beings and are becoming increasingly demanding in an expectation economy that is customer-led and data-driven; disruption and innovation have ceased to be a convenience or "some other company's job." Libraries have learned from this and now we know that the library of the future is a very exciting and visually stimulating place; it uses display and interactive technology to expose content and resources of which the public was totally unaware.

SOLUS views innovation in terms of understanding and evolving new business models. Previously, their job was to equalize access and skills to use digital books, while now it implies equalizing access and skills to the new and fast-developing technologies from 3D printing, robotics, coding, and circuit making to self-publishing and augmented reality. The company is good at shaping the future and redesigning the relevant "next" library—the 21st-century people's library. 21st-century public libraries must become learning and digital hubs—one-stop destinations to test drive and learn about the latest technology. They must now be experiential, entrepreneurial, experimental spaces where access to technology enhances opportunities to learn, work, and create. The key innovative and business developments are in applications, technology, augmented reality, children's innovative and interactive technology, and learning and talking to frontline practitioners about customers' interests and demands.

The greatest strength is in the area of innovation technology, while weaknesses are overambition, promotion, and marketing. The company also needs to recruit more staff. The improvement of the current situation would mean to support and drive the national promotion and awareness of innovation, learning and fun in libraries, and cultural services. The main impact of the company is technology and public perception of the library as innovative and cool. As a commercial organization that works in the areas of innovation and research, the company is dependent on local councils being well-funded and/or on them sourcing additional funding from lottery, EU or private sources. The annual budget for innovation is £800,000. SOLUS are a well-resourced commercial company funded by cultural organizations buying or partnering with them on innovation. The company is very well connected across the world and cooperate and present at many conferences on the innovative use of technology to grow audiences.

Innovation: the work of Solus is innovative in shaping the future and redesigning the relevant "next" Library—the 21st-century people library. 21st-century public libraries must become learning and digital hubs. Innovation technology and weakness are overambition, promotion, and marketing. The company also need more staff. The improve of current situation is to support and drive the national promotion and awareness of innovation, learning and fun in libraries and cultural services. The main impact of company is technology and public perception of the library as innovative and cool.

City of Dublin

Dublin City Council

The key highlight of Budget 2019 for Ireland is the cultural sector. The total funding for the arts and culture sector in 2019 were increased by €22.6 m to almost €190 m—an increase of 14% in 2018.[530]

The Arts Plan is the work plan for the Arts Office, a section of, and guided by the CRA Department, Dublin City Council, and based in the Lab; a bespoke arts center in Dublin. It is a unique innovation for the governance office. This plan was a new departure in the development of strategic and sustainable cultural planning for the city. For the first time, the city noted broader cultural actions within its Arts Plan and laid out a vision, in broad strokes, as the basis for actions, rather than detailing the actions themselves. It is this vision that has since taken the project far beyond its initial ambitions.

The Arts Plan led directly to:

- the rewriting of the Cultural Strategy for all areas of the city;
- the adoption of the UNESCO definition of culture & the UNESCO Cultural Rights of the Child;
- the formation of a city-wide policy for Arts, Education and Learning;
- strategic partnerships such as with Business to Arts, which led to the Docklands Development Fund;
- new planning recommendations for cultural infrastructure for the city;
- a schedule for a series of independent city-wide cultural audits;
- an additional one million euro per year for sustainable cultural projects
- a set of European pilot projects including the new EU Funding Unit.

Local cultural policies are formulated in a number of ways: as actions arising from legislation; from the request of the elected representatives of the city council; as a response to a strategic goal of the city council's development plan; on instruction from the Culture and Amenities Department; or from a section within a city council department, which recommends a specific course of action. Examples include policies on cultural heritage and conservation, promoting the designation of Dublin as a UNESCO City of Literature, supporting the national cultural institutions, and facilitating the provision of fit-for-purpose, sustainable cultural infrastructure.

In terms of cultural policy, the weakness is in the lack of interconnectivity to other areas and policies of the Development Plan. More could be done specifically to connect culture to the sections on the economy, development & regeneration, land use and zoning amongst others. Much of the plan is focused on infrastructure which, in some ways, dilutes the impact and potential of a more sustainable approach to city planning.

For example, roughly 65% of the section on Culture and Heritage is heritage-based and forms the entire first ten pages of this section. While of significant benefit to developers and planners, this weighting is disproportioned in terms of the potential of a fully integrated cultural plan for the city. It is anticipated that the incorporation of new recommendations in the plan, such as the greater consideration of issue of sustainability in cultural provision for new developments, will ensure that Dublin City Council is more able to more fully address these issues.

The city council has a Corporate Plan with objectives, priorities, and actions which informs the Culture Recreation and Amenity Department Business Plan and subsequently the Arts Plan. Each of these plans have business unit actions, milestones, and KPI measurements, including outcomes and dependencies (such as resources and partnerships, progress measurements), the usual statistical measures, and a risk register for all actions. The KPIs are classified as "definitive" and are usually specific actions arising, programs delivered, percentage of programs completed.

The results obtained have been detailed in earlier sections. In terms of coherence, the priorities and process used for the Arts Plan were transferred in the preparations for the Cultural Strategy, also authored by Ray Yeates. In addition, the Cultural Strategy is referenced in the Development Plan. The Arts Office also provided contributions and facilitated the wider arts sector in contributing to the plan. In this way the Arts Plan informed the Cultural Strategy, and both the Arts Plan and the Cultural Strategy are informing the Development Plan.

From the beginning, the Arts Plan has paralleled the intent and priorities of Agenda 21 for Culture. In particular, the accord between United Cities and Local Government (UCLG) and UNESCO was complemented in 2015, when the Dublin City Council (DCC) adopted the UNESCO definition of Culture. Namely in its Cultural Strategy arising from the Arts Plan, the City Council affirmed that Culture is: "The set of distinctive spiritual, material, intellectual and emotional features of society or a social group, that encompasses, not only art and literature, but lifestyles, ways of living together, value systems, traditions and beliefs" (UNESCO 2001). In the same document the DCC also adopted the UNESCO Cultural Rights of the Child Charter and with particular reference to this strategy, Article 31. These significant milestones had their genesis in the Arts Plan which stated in 2014 that it, "acknowledged the change driven by major technological advances, by demographic shift and by new forms of social participation and cultural expression" and that "The City Arts Office believes that everyone has a right to access the arts, physically and intellectually, throughout their life."

The economic impacts of the plan are less definitive. The legacy of the bid for the ECoC 2020, arising from the plan, had a greater social impact engaging with more people. It developed capacity and increased funding with an additional one million euros set aside for cultural actions in each of the next four years. In addition, the Cultural Strategy provides for one hundred thousand euros for each of the five electoral areas for national cultural institutions partnering with local neighborhood organizations. One such example is the work of the Chester Beatty Library with a Muslim Community on the south of the city. In addition, a pilot unit is to be set up with the goal of increasing participation in and funding for European projects. The City Council is also looking forward to the work on Cultural and Creative Spillovers published by Tom Fleming's creative consultancy, and funded by the Arts Councils of England and Ireland. The recommendations from this research will go some way to informing the research that Dublin City Council intends to commission in the same area, and will be able to provide more definitive data on the transversal effects of the Arts Plan and the Cultural Strategy.

The plan can be seen in a simplified way as the continuity of the City Council's obligations under the Arts Act 2003, and as such the emergence of another plan will continue to be a responsibility of the City Council. The commitment to the legacy of the bid for ECoC 2020, the creation of the Cultural Strategy and the additions to the Development Plan, alongside the four-year rolling plan of investment in culture and the development of a European Funding Unit, make it clear that at least for the next four years, an unequivocal commitment to the goals outlined in the plan have been made.

Future actions are:

- participation in forums and meetings to raise visibility.
- rebranding all actions of the Arts Plan to confirm its place as an award-winning project.
- launching a local, regional & international PR campaign to celebrate the award.
- program a suitable festival/event at which to publicly celebrate the award.
- inviting cultural attachés and ambassadors from all embassies based in Dublin to a launch night for the award.
- dedicating the first actions to the local and international promotion of Dublin as an Agenda 21 City, specifically to develop a public platform for the citizens of Dublin to engage with Agenda 21 actions, understand the goals of the project and take an active part in its implementation.
- regardless of the award, the city will immediately begin to review the opportunity to become a pilot city for Agenda 21 for Culture.
- if successful, the city will dedicate adequate resources to the management and implementation of the actions of Agenda 21 for Culture.
- re-visiting the Cultural Strategy with a view to augmenting or rewriting the document. The aim will be to include those specific actions and policies that would enhance the Cultural Strategy so that it follows clearly Agenda 21 Actions.
- Match-funding the award and allocating these funds to the specific fulfillment of Agenda 21 Actions.
- hosting a series of expert conferences, alongside an audit of services, to which experts and other pilot cities representatives will be invited to participate, in order to enable the city to learn from these experiences and develop recommendations for best practice.

Innovation: The Arts Plan is the work plan for the Arts Office, a section of, and guided by the CRA Department, Dublin City Council, and based in the Lab—a bespoke arts center in Dublin.[531] It is a unique innovation for the governance office. This plan was a new departure in the development of strategic and sustainable cultural planning for the city. For the first time, the city noted broader cultural actions within its Arts Plan & laid out a vision, in broad strokes, as the basis for actions, rather than detailing the actions themselves.

The Arts Plan changed the way the Arts Office engages with its other sister departments: several interdepartmental partnerships have arisen with; the Area

Offices, Libraries, Planning, Events, Tourism & Sports, & the Intercultural Unit who have previously engaged with the Agenda 21 process. The benefits are: the increased sharing of resources; parallel planning; and the increased recognition of culture as an effective tool for public engagement and sustainable practice. These changes in relationships are, in large part, based on the exchange and sharing of knowledge, resources and networking aimed at increasing opportunities and enhancing projects for mutual benefit.

Arts Governance, City of Dublin

Mrs Penelope Kenny is the Director of ArtsGovernance, a Limited company in the Culture space.[532]

The activities of the company are: consultancy—Governance reviews, financial control, writing: article and books, lecturing and presenting—to universities and professional bodies, company secretarial and directorships in Arts and Cultural organizations. The programs have been realized in Ireland and the UK. The main target groups are: cultural organizations, arts organizations, theaters, galleries, universities, and Arts Councils. The services that the company has been realizing are consulting in governance grants and financial control. Innovation arises from the artistic process, and is applied across other disciplines. In the EU and Ireland, the effort for developing the creative industries is generally good. The strength of the company is in artistic management and governance; in financial directorships; and in reviews and reports. ArtsGovernance is creating an environment for innovation, enabling innovation through good governance, and enabling funding to take place. In addition, the company's strengths lie in: their excellent reputation; their trustworthiness in the sector, their unique expertise; their creation of an environment for innovation; their enabling innovation through good governance; and their enabling funding to take place. The weaknesses are its small size and its limited offering in an expanding market. However, the company operates well in large projects, and is growing through collaboration and selling. The innovative trends that impact the company are artistic and management trends and government policy.

The financing sources for the organization are the Department of Arts Culture Heritage and the Gaeltacht, Ireland. There is no foreign funding and the budget is varied. The economic aspect of the company is that it is often partially state-funded, but can also be in receipt of EU funding. Human resources are consultants, and master's graduates in Cultural Policy Arts Management. Cooperation with institutions, including local and state, is carried out on a domestic level, while cooperation with international institutions is at a very low level.

Innovation: ArtsGovernance is creating an environment for innovation, which enables innovation through good governance and enabling funding to take place. In addition, the strengths are: excellent reputation, trusted in the sector, unique expertise in the sector, creating an environment for innovation, enabling innovation through good governance and enabling funding to take place. The innovative trends which impact company are artistic and management trends and government policy. Innovation arising from artistic process, being applied across other disciplines, and innovation arising from artistic process. The effort for developing the creative industries generally in EU and Ireland are good.

City of Dublin

IMMA, The Irish Museum of Modern Art

The main activities of the Irish Museum of Modern Art (IMMA) are in Ireland and the target groups are Irish visitors and tourists, cultural tourists, and artists. The museum offers exhibitions, talks, lectures, reading groups, collections, and events.

IMMA is a contemporary gallery; it uses innovation from all contemporary art sources around the world, and it holds innovation at the heart of what it does in the contemporary art space.

Accordingly, its staff believe that the development of creative industries and innovations should be an integral part of state policy, and that it should be seen as an essential part of social, educational, and economic policies. Kenny would like to see creative industries being treated as an essential industry and as part of the sustainable and regenerative economic agenda.

IMMA's strengths are that it connects audiences and art, providing an extraordinary space where contemporary life and contemporary art connect, challenge, and inspire one another. They share, develop, and conserve the Irish National Collection of Modern and Contemporary Art for now and the future.

The museum is currently the second most visited free attraction in Ireland. IMMA's program reimagines "the Museum" as an open and participatory space that connects people to contemporary life through art. Surveys show us that our audience comes to IMMA to experience something new and to share knowledge and new thinking. Recent developments in the program have seen IMMA expand beyond the gallery space to incorporate the full site of IMMA's home at the Royal Hospital with a program of live performance, summer festivals, food, and gardening that invites the audience into a direct interaction with creativity, and provides a space for debate, inspiration, and participation.

IMMA is the home of the National Collection of Modern and Contemporary Art. A collection is not just a series of physical objects but also a series of histories and relationships that represent a rich resource of knowledge that, if accessible, holds great potential for a wide range of audiences. IMMA therefore defines its collection as artworks, archive, and data.

We lack an education and learning center: A key objective of IMMA's current strategy is the development of a new Collections Center that will create new forms of physical and digital access to IMMA's Collection, Collection Archive, and Programmatic Archive. Envisioned as both a new building and a new online space, the Collections Center will create a home for the Collection on IMMA's grounds, providing access to the public through visible storage, media banks, accessible photographic and print collections, and education spaces that will facilitate the Collection as a learning tool for all ages. The other institutions in Ireland have been better funded, with bigger collections, and richer donors. The most important thing is to continue to put IMMA on the international stage as an important contemporary art museum.

The contemporary trends are re-imagining the museum; attracting audiences in different ways; developing a new strategy in tandem with objectives of cultural institutions and Arts and cultural policies in Ireland and internationally. We receive an annual grant from the Department of Arts Heritage, Culture and the Gaeltacht, this is our largest source of funding. The annual budget for the IMMA receives around 7 million euros. The Museum has around 100 employees and the director is from the Van Abbe Museum in the Netherlands. International work is important and they are part of the Cultural Institutions network in Ireland, as well as international Museums associations.

Innovation: IMMA is a contemporary gallery; it uses innovation from all contemporary art sources around the world, and it holds innovation at the heart of what it does in the contemporary art space. 'The Museum' is an open and participatory space that connects people to contemporary life through art. Surveys show us that the audience comes to IMMA to experience something new and to share knowledge and new thinking.

Re-imagining the museum; attracting audiences in different ways; developing a new strategy in tandem with objectives of cultural institutions and Arts and cultural policies in Ireland and internationally.

City of Dublin

Think Tank, InterroBang Ltd.

InterroBang does research on, and implements programs for, community empowerment through applied thinking strategies and the arts. The main activities are in Ireland and Europe. The target groups for the activities are disadvantaged and minority communities and individuals. However, they also provide consultancy for businesses and coaching for individuals.

The main activities are problem solving and sustainable decision skills PSSDS strategies. These are conducted through workshops and community art programs.

Decision leadership for community leaders, and "Impostor Syndrome" coaching for individuals are also offered.

They are a service-based company, so innovation means staying abreast of current research and best practice in delivering support to communities. The innovations are the development of unique approaches to PSSDS, the adaption of the approaches of third parties and the blending of a variety of third-party strategies with their research in unique ways. All these innovations are intellectual innovations and are not physical balance sheet assets.

In Ireland, there is a very narrow understanding of creativity in innovation. Projects seem to be evaluated on balance sheet benefits. There seems to be very little understanding of developing metrics to evaluate the social and financial benefits of intangible elements.

InterroBang is engaged in constant research through literature review of other practitioners and academics and through qualitative and quantitative research of their own programs. Over twenty years of research and delivery of education programs inform their services. This gives them a level of expertise that most of their competitors do not have.

InterroBang does not fit the narrow terms of reference for funding. The difficulty with true innovation is there is often little precedent and therefore no funding model for it to fit. This is why they have a commercial arm to the business. It is how they can afford to take on community empowerment projects. They have developed their own funding strategies.

By working with social partners and documenting the efficacy of their interventions, they can slowly influence the government funding culture. Developing metrics to measure intangible benefits is important to advocate for their programs. The innovations are intellectual rather than technological. InterroBang takes funding from the regional government and profit from corporate contracts to subsidize community programs.

As a small company, they partner with experts on a project-by-project basis to meet each project's unique requirements. The web enables international partnerships, so attaining human resources is not an issue. They work closely with many NGOs to inform themselves as to where interventions are most needed and to better understand the needs of those they want to work with. Local government volunteering bodies are also an important partner.

Innovation: The innovations are the development of unique approaches to PSSDS (*System Development Strategy*), adaption of the approaches of third parties and blending a variety of third-party strategies with their research in unique ways. All these innovations are intellectual innovations rather than physical balance sheet assets. The innovations are intellectual rather than technological.

City of London

BOP Consulting, a research and strategy consultancy.

London is a leading creative capital city, which attracts talent and enterprise from all over the world. The creative economy is estimated to provide one in six jobs in London and the creative industries generate around £47 billion for the London economy. It is also one of the city's fastest-growing sectors.

The main activities are research and strategic planning, focusing on culture and the creative industries. The organization is currently active in Europe, Latin America, China, and the Gulf. BOP Consulting have offices in London, Liverpool, Edinburgh, and Shanghai. The target audiences are policy makers, cultural organizations, and any other parties with an interest in developing the cultural sector, e.g., property developers. About 50% of work relates to research and evaluation for policy makers, e.g., Arts Council England, UNESCO and 20–30% relates to strategy and planning, e.g., for the V&A.

The organization is run by the World Cities Culture Forum (20%), which is a knowledge exchange programs and research project.

BOP consulting considers that the EU and others have made significant strides in developing the sector of creative industries and innovation. The EU can be very slow to move, but it can be effective once it does. For example, Creative Europe is very effective in meeting its aims. In the UK efforts have been relatively effective, but there is currently widespread distraction by policy makers who are preoccupied with Brexit.

The strengths of the organization are data and rigorous analysis. The organization is rare in having a chief economist. In terms of innovation, the organization has a bigger data collation and analysis capacity in comparison to other organizations. In addition, it has a wider range of expertise brought together as a result of its network. The BOP has analytical capacity and comfort with data, but also works with so many territories and so many different organizations. Other organizations with the same type of work are cheaper and BOP believes that this is to their advantage. The positive influence of BOP Consultancy's work is the growing use of data and serious policy making. The organization has a team of 25–35, with all of its members educated to degree level or above.

Innovation: In terms of innovation, the organization has a bigger data collation and analysis capacity in comparison to other organizations. In addition, it has a wider range of expertise brought together as a result of their network. BOP has analytical capacity and comfort with data, but also works with so many territories and so many different organizations. BOP consulting thinks that the EU and others have made significant strides in developing the sector of creative industries and innovation. The organization is currently active in Europe, Latin America, China, and the Gulf. BOP Consulting has offices in London, Liverpool, Edinburgh, and Shanghai.

City of Turku

Seppala Tanssiteatteri ERI (Dance Theatre ERI).

The activities of the theater take place mainly in the City of Turku, but it also operates in other parts of Finland every year. Nowadays they do not go abroad as much as they used to. They also find some audiences through the Internet (Vimeo, YouTube, Facebook). The target group is mainly adults, but in the last few years, ERI has performed for children. They also go to many retirement homes with small productions (pro bono). Every year, there are different projects for immigrants and women and children of this group. People can order dance productions for different kind of festivals, happenings, etc. The Dance Theatre ERI is a small company (consisting of seven dancers, one technician and one producer) and they are very productive. ERI uses dance therapy and modern dance in their projects for immigrants and senior citizens. Now in pandemic times, they have used Zoom, telephone, etc., to reach their audiences. In addition, they have dance lessons for children on Zoom after they have watched their performance on YouTube. In the EU, the value of culture—especially modern dance—should be appreciated more.

In the past thirty years, ERI has boldly created a diverse program, including almost 100 productions. The theater presents approximately 130 shows per year, 3–4 of which are premiere performances. ERI is a highly professional dance company. It has, for example, been awarded a prize from the Arts Council of Southwest Finland. ERI has received the esteemed Suomi-prize in recognition for their artistic work. Additionally, the members of the group have received numerous individual grants and awards, such as significant grants from the Finnish Culture Foundation and the Swedish Culture Foundation. The main source of funding is the City of Turku, Ministry of Culture and Education and different cultural foundations.

ERI carries out much work with other cultural organizations. They have a network with local cultural organizations and meetings every month and they also collaborate with other theaters in Finland. Today, however, ERI has less time to cooperate with international institutions

Innovation: ERI uses dance therapy and modern dance in their projects for immigrants and senior citizens. Now in pandemic times, they have used Zoom, telephone, etc., to reach them. In addition, they have dance lessons for children on Zoom after they have watched their performance on YouTube. In the EU, the value of culture—especially modern dance—have to be appreciated more.

City of Eindhoven

Cees Donkers, Urban Architects.[533]

Eindhoven is a modern city that has grown out of the industrial activities of the Philips Company. In the early twentieth century, this industry was the main engine of the developmental and infrastructural growth of a small town which had, through the merging of five local villages in 1920, grown into a large urban area. During the 1990s, production was moved to low-cost labor countries, but at some point, at the beginning of the next decade they discovered that they had retained the "thinking industry." The urgent need for employment and mental strength of the unemployed people has resulted in innovation as a new phenomenon that replaced the small glass lamp, the discovery that marked the nineteenth century in their city. Thus, knowledge has become a new "fuel" for regional development; therefore, in addition to the main commercial port of Rotterdam and the trade port of Amsterdam, the brain port of Eindhoven suddenly emerged.

> Eindhoven had discovered a wealth of knowledge in its institutions and cultural and educational organizations, and in 2003 launched project E+ using the city as a research and educational laboratory. The results of the project were transposed into new development policies, urban designs and social innovations.[534]

Many students, upon graduation, stopped leaving Eindhoven and start joining this new industry based on the new energy of young people. E+ was completed in 2009. After a period of cooperation between the City Council and institutions of culture and education, such as the TU/e and Academy of Design, an ambition to achieve cooperation with private companies evolved. In addition to cooperating with companies within a pyramidal structure of the organization from top to bottom, as the Brainport organization, they wanted to achieve cooperation with those organizations whose structure was reversed, going from the bottom to the top, such as the Virtual Academy of Brabant (www.brabantacademy.nl) which had student organizations on the board. The economic crisis forced them to seek new opportunities and create a new city climate in order to enable young people to establish companies and start their own business. Freelancers have already begun to fill positions in the new market for economic growth. Designers and analysts have the ability to look at things from different angles, to think outside the box, and to create new concepts. As the Philips discovery of the electric light bulb in 1892 is a part of the identity of Eindhoven, this new design, innovation and research, has also become part of its identity, and they are also useful instruments for the development of new economies.

It is SMART to think in different ways, outside the box, within one's own generation, to be the coach and director of the thinking power of young students and to join forces with freelancers in an informal and non-hierarchical network using current technology to support communication with the rest of the world. Donkers enjoys sharing his knowledge with others and receiving good feedback in return. He loves finding a new balance as a surfer in a new (personal) age, riding on the waves of the economic sea and using the winds of innovation. At the end of the twentieth century, the city of Eindhoven was losing parts of her DNA by permitting young, talented students to leave the city after graduation. The knowledge that was built up over several years seemed to flow away to popular Dutch cities, like Amsterdam, and even abroad. Eindhoven was still known as something of a dull town. During the last 15 years, however, the city has slowly transformed into a young, modern and good-looking girl that has become proud of her own beauty. The De Witte Dame (White Lady) building project, in particular, is an icon of this new identity. At the beginning of the 1990s, Donkers organized a city debate called "QAFE" in the Plaza Futura theater to discuss urban issues, including keeping the former Philips buildings alive. The decision of Eindhoven City Council not to demolish it but to re-use it for cultural purposes in the mid-1990s was a historic one. Since then, creative architects, designers, and artists have organized public events and debates about this kind of second life for abandoned and unused buildings in the city following the departure of Philips. The yearly Dutch Design Week in October showcases a lot of these potential new seeds of a creative economy. However, five years ago, the city still seemed to be blind to this new quality. Thus, the social re-use of the local environment can happen in public spaces both outside and inside public buildings. Another good example of how this can be achieved is to share knowledge and to begin international cooperation on the issue of urban design on a European scale.

> Today we find that this urban trend is replicated in various parts of the world. Eindhoven's example of using the city as a laboratory and getting young people involved in questions surrounding urban development to make them think outside the box about social issues is now used in several cities in other countries.[535]

Cultuur Eindhoven—Innovation Policy Governance

This is a local government organization. They are mostly a fund that provides subsidies for cultural organizations. The regions of activities are Eindhoven, Noord-Brabant, and The Netherlands as a whole. The target groups are mostly cultural organizations, professional makers of art and design, and artists. Cultuur Eindhoven arranges funding for cultural activities in Eindhoven. It is important to connect more with each other again after COVID-19. Cultuur Eindhoven is working on organizing activities that can help with that. The all-creative stakeholders have to positively use innovative strengths. The organization is funded by the government and the ministry of the municipality of Eindhoven. The Programma Creatieve Industrie consists of around €350.000 a year, but that funding is due to finish after 2021. At the time of writing, the organization has 11 employees and uses the same equipment as the people in the government of Eindhoven. They work a lot with the municipality, cultural organizations and with several funds. They do not work a lot with international institutions, but provide cultural organizations with the right information on how to connect to international funding.

The Cultuur Eindhoven foundation was founded in June 2015 and is responsible for carrying out the cultural policy of the city of Eindhoven. The city council determines the main themes of the cultural policy and sets the tasks. The assignment is written in the Cultuur brief, which describes the policy to be followed over the next four years. Cultuur Eindhoven invests in art, culture, and creativity for the inhabitants of Eindhoven. On behalf of the city council, Cultuur Eindhoven makes the means available through regulations on basic infrastructure as well as cultural programs and projects. Stichting Cultuur Eindhoven enhances the welfare and well-being of the population and visitors to the city of Eindhoven by stimulating the development of art and culture and increasing the role of art in everyday lives. Stichting Cultuur Eindhoven increases the attraction of the city for its inhabitants, visitors, enterprises, and organizations. The goal of the foundation is to carry out cultural policy, as determined by the city council, in a transparent manner, to enlarge the meaning of art and culture for the city of Eindhoven, her inhabitants and users, in order to stimulate a dynamic and inspiring art and culture climate within the city of Eindhoven, to stimulate creativity and art development within the city of Eindhoven, to advise the council of Eindhoven on cultural policy, to advise (cultural and other) organizations that cover the realization of art, culture, and creativity within the city of Eindhoven, to finance the supply of art and culture within the city of Eindhoven and to offer financial support to legal entities that realize art and cultural projects within the city of Eindhoven, as well as everything else that widely connects with one or the other, links to and/or can be beneficial to this. Cultuur Eindhoven endorses the Code of Cultural Governance. The Code is an instrument for good management and control in the cultural sector. The Code can be consulted on the website.[536]

The pilot projects of the Creative Industry Program are looking for research and experimentation. These are projects around a specific (social) question or need, supported by partners who also commit to further development. The projects are exemplary and can be scaled up to other environments and regions on the basis of evaluation. The blogs contain information about meetings that took place within the Creative Industry Program: GO! VMBO has started, Closing Materials for the Future, Presentations Eindhoven Heritage. Glass Room Plus is an exhibition in libraries aimed towards young people, which provides an insight into how much (personal) data are collected, what happens with it and how one can get a better grip on this with the Data Detox Kit. In this project, designers Joes and Manon joined forces with Fers and ROC Friese Poort to supplement the exhibition with a Digital Moral Compass for young people (16–18 years). With this compass, they want to create urgency, make underlying values tangible and stimulate young people to question their own and each other's digital moral compass (critically and permanently). Publicroam is a Wi-Fi service that allows visitors in public spaces to be online safely via an optimally secured and privacy-friendly Wi-Fi connection. Visitors no longer have to log in again everywhere; rather, they are automatically connected via the guest Wi-Fi of affiliated organizations such as libraries, municipalities, sports complexes or theaters. All visitors have to do is request and activate a Publicroam account the first time they sign on and that is precisely the challenge that Publicroam will tackle together with the designers of Kickoff Lab.

Innovation: The organization came into existence in 2015 as an innovative experiment to make an external organization responsible for the funding of cultural organizations. Therefore, they are an innovative institution. There is always room for more exploration and experimentation. The focus is mainly on deliverables, instead of the experiment. It is necessary to have more room for experimenting and exploration. The organization is good at combining a personal approach as well as a diplomatic one, so they can help cultural partners with their funding. The innovative ways of working are simplicity, approachability, constructiveness, and helpfulness. The creative stakeholders are positively using innovative strengths.

Analysis

In the first focus group of the research, we concluded that innovations are developed in local governments, institutions, and organizations. The development of technology contributes to technological innovation, but social innovation has an important place in the process of development of the cultural sector, and it is interconnected with innovation processes. The City of Stockholm, in terms of innovation, has a short tradition of strength within the tech industries, ranking as number 2 in the world after Silicon Valley in terms of developing unicorns/per capita. This factor should be used when also looking at the developing CCI sector. The main weakness is a lack of strategy at a national level, which is possible to improve in the current situation with support from the CCI sector with a focus on innovation. The innovative trend is digitalization. The Culture Administration is funded by the city of Stockholm, municipality-wise. The Culture Administration does not have a designated budget for CCI and innovation. The department has a high level of people with strategy competence. The innovation in the cultural program are: Bibblix—an app for children's book loans at the Digital library unit at the City library; UX design—how people want their libraries; Co-creation—the youth festival is co-created with the target group at the Event department; an app for experiencing exhibitions at the Art gallery. An external consultant did the work. The Culture Administration cooperates within the city of Stockholm with various administrations such as urban development, building department, Stockholm Business Region and Visit Stockholm. They also collaborate with state institutions situated in Stockholm on various levels. The City of Glasgow—innovative practice is embedded in all Glasgow Life services, as evidenced through continued evolution and improvement of programs and activities, as well as an extensive list of awards and commendations. The city has 160 venues and over 250 services that Glasgow Life manages, including a network of neighborhood cultural and sports facilities, a range of community development and learning services and some of the most prestigious buildings in the UK. The organization Solus from the City of Edinburgh works on the processing of innovation. The work of Solus is innovative in shaping the future and redesigning the relevant "next" Library—the 21st-century people's library. 21st-century public libraries must become learning and digital hubs. Innovation technology and weaknesses are overambition, promotion, and marketing. The company also needs more staff. The improvement of the current situation would mean to support and drive the national promotion and awareness of innovation, learning, and fun in libraries and cultural services. The main impact of the company is technology and the public perception of the library as innovative and cool. The City of Dublin has a new innovative policy which has been adopted for the development of a new approach. The Arts Plan is the work plan for the Arts Office, a section of, and guided by, the CRA[537] Department, Dublin City Council, and based in the Lab; a bespoke arts center in Dublin. It is a unique innovation for the governance office. This plan was a new departure in the development of strategic and sustainable cultural planning for the city. For the first time, the city noted broader cultural actions within its Arts Plan and laid out a vision, in broad strokes, as the basis for actions, rather than detailing the actions themselves. The Arts Plan changed the way the Arts Office engages with its other sister departments. Several interdepartmental partnerships have arisen with the Area Offices, Libraries, Planning, Events, Tourism and Sports, and the Intercultural Unit who have previously engaged with the Agenda 21 process. The benefits are: increased sharing of resources, parallel planning and the increased recognition of culture as an effective tool for public engagement and sustainable practice. These changes in relationships are in large part based on the exchange and sharing of knowledge, resources and networking aimed at increasing opportunities and enhancing projects for mutual benefit. The organization ArtsGovernance from Dublin City is creating an environment for innovation, enabling innovation through good governance and enabling funding to take place. In addition, the strengths are: excellent reputation, trustworthiness in the sector, unique expertise in the sector, creating an environment for innovation, enabling innovation through good governance and enabling funding to take place. The innovative trends that impact the company are artistic and management trends and government policy. Innovation arises from the artistic process being applied across other disciplines. The effort for developing the creative industries in the EU and Ireland is generally good. The IMMA (the Irish Museum of Modern Art) from the City of Dublin is a contemporary gallery—it uses innovation from all contemporary art sources around the world, and it holds innovation at the heart of what it does in the contemporary art space. "The Museum" is an open and participatory space that connects people to contemporary life through art. Surveys show us that our audience comes to IMMA to experience something new and to share knowledge and new thinking. Re-imagining the museum; attracting audiences in different ways; developing a new strategy in tandem with objectives of cultural institutions and Arts and cultural policies in Ireland and internationally. On the other hand, InterroBang Ltd., a think tank in the City of Dublin, is an organization that looks towards innovation in order to develop unique approaches to PSSDS (*System Development Strategy*), adapting the approaches of third parties and blending a variety of third-party strategies with their research in unique ways. All these innovations are intellectual innovations and are not physical balance sheet assets. The innovations are intellectual rather than technological. London's BOP Consulting, in terms of innovation, has a bigger data collation and analysis capacity than is to be found in other organizations. In addition, it has a wider range of expertise brought together as a result of their network. The BOP has an analytical capacity and comfort with data, works with so many territories and so many different organizations. BOP Consulting thinks that the EU and others have made significant strides in developing the sector of creative industries and innovation. The organization is currently active in Europe, Latin America, China, and the Gulf. BOP Consulting has offices in London, Liverpool, Edinburgh, and Shanghai. In terms of innovation, the Dance Theatre ERI in the City of Turku uses dance therapy and modern dance in projects for immigrants and senior citizens. Now, in pandemic times, they have used Zoom, telephone, etc., to reach their audience. In addition, they present dance lessons for children on Zoom after they have watched their performance on YouTube. In the EU, the value of culture—especially modern dance—should be appreciated more. Local government organization Cultuur Eindhoven in the City of Eindhoven came into existence in 2015 as an innovative experiment to make an external organization responsible for the funding of cultural organizations. This is an innovative institution. There is always room for more exploration and experimentation. The focus of work is mainly on deliverables,

TABLE 1 The First Focus Group of Research. Author: Mickov, Biljana. 2021

	Innovation	*Cultural Program (Including Creative and Culture Industries)*	*Budget for Culture Year*
City of Stockholm Culture Department Mr Tomas AnderssonInternational relations—Culture Program	The City ofStockholm, in termsof **innovation**, has a short tradition of strength within thetech industries. Thatfactor have to be used when looking at developing CCI sector as well.	The City of Stockholm promotes and develops the cultural life of a constantly growing city. Regarding the CCI, they have to improve in the current situation with support from the CCI (Creative and Cultural Industries) sector with a focuson innovation.	€80,32 million (2018)
City of Glasgow Dr Bridget McConnell, Chief Executive Officer, Jill Miller, Director of Culture, Lynda Campbell, Head of Business & Strategy.	Innovative practice is embedded in all Glasgow Life services, as evidenced through continued evolution and improvement of programs and activities, as well as an extensive list of awards and commendations.	The 160 venues and over 250 services they manage include a network of neighbourhood cultural and sports facilities, a range of community development and learning services and some of the most prestigious buildings in the UK.	£111,484 million or €129,756 million (2018)
City of Edinburgh UK. *SOLUS UK*—company for innovation. Mrs Liz McGettigan, Director of Digital Library and Cultural Experiences SOLUS UK, City of Edinburg.	Company for research, technological innovation for libraries, and supplier. The services most often realized are: library apps, social catalogues, children's learning and literacy apps.	The company created the UK's first ever library app. This grew a new online audience and was so popular that it was then adopted by over 90 library authorities in the UK. The company is now working to deliver the first ever global social/Netflix style library catalogue.	£800,000 or €931.254 per year.
City of Dublin Mr James E. Doyle former officer Dublin City Council and cultural expert (Brussels)	The Lab; an arts center in Dublin. It is a unique innovation for the governance office. This plan was a new departure in the development of strategic and sustainable cultural planning for the city.	The Arts Plan changed the way the Arts Office engages with its other sister departments: several interdepartmental partnerships, the Area Offices, Libraries, Planning, Events, Tourism and Sports, and the Intercultural Unit who have previously engaged with the Agenda 21 process.	€190 million (2019)

City of Dublin Mrs Penelope Kenny Director, Arts Governance, Limited company in the Culture space.	Creating an environment for innovation and enabling innovation through good governance, as well as enabling funding to take place. Innovation arises from the artistic process, being applied across other disciplines. The effort for developing the creative industries in the EU and Ireland is generally good.	The main target groups are: cultural organizations; arts organizations, theatres, galleries, universities, Arts Councils. The services that the company has been realizing are consulting in governance grants and financial control.	The budget is varied.
City of Dublin IMMA Mrs Penelope Kenny Board Director and Chair of the Audit and Risk committee.	IMMA is a contemporary gallery, it uses innovation from all contemporary art sources around the world, and it holds innovation at the heart of what it does in the contemporary art space. Re-imagining the museum; attracting audiences in different ways; developing a new strategy in tandem with the objectives of cultural institutions and Arts and cultural policies in Ireland and internationally.	A key objective of IMMA's current strategy program is the development of a new Collections Centre that will create new forms of physical and digital access to exhibiting, talks and performances. We would like to see creative industries being treated as an essential industry and part of the sustainable and regenerative economic agenda.	€7 million per year.

(*Continued*)

TABLE 1 (Continued) The First Focus Group of Research. Author: Mickov, Biljana. 2021

	Innovation	*Cultural Program (Including Creative and Culture Industries)*	*Budget for Culture Year*
City of Dublin InterroBang Ltd. Mr Hugh McElveen Think Tank industry	The innovations are the development of unique approaches to PSSDS (System Development Strategy), adaption of the approaches of third parties and blending a variety of third-party strategies with their research in unique ways. All these innovations are intellectual innovations and are not physical balance sheet assets. The innovations are intellectual rather than technological.	The activities are problem solving and sustainable decision skills and PSSDS strategies. These are conducted through workshops and community art programs.	The budget is varied.
City of London BOP consulting Mr Callum Lee Managing Director	In terms of innovation, the organization has a bigger data collation and analysis capacity in comparison to other organizations. In addition, it has a wider range of expertise brought together as a result of their network. BOP has an analytical capacity and comfort with data, but also works with so many territories and so many different organizations.	The target audiences in the program are policy makers, cultural organizations, and any others with an interest in developing the cultural sector, e.g. property developers. About 50% of work relates to research and evaluation for policymakers, e.g. Arts Council England, UNESCO and 20–30% relates to strategy and planning, e.g. for the V&A. The creative economy is estimated to provide one in six jobs in London and the creative industries generate around £47 billion for the London economy. It is also one of London's fastest growing sectors.	The budget is varied. The creative industries generate around £47 billion for the London economy.

City of Turku Dance Theatre ERI Mrs Maarit Keto—Seppala producer	ERI uses dance therapy and modern dance in their projects for immigrants and senior citizens. Now in pandemic times, they have used Zoom, telephone, etc., to reach them. Also, they have dance lessons for children on Zoom after they have watched their performance on YouTube. In the EU, the value of culture—especially modern dance—should be appreciated more.	ERI has boldly created a diverse program, which includes almost 100 productions. The theatre presents approximately 130 shows per year, 3–4 of which are premiere performances.	The budget is varied. ERI is funded by the City of Turku, Ministry of Culture and Education and different cultural foundations.
City of Eindhoven Cultuur Eindhoven Mrs Sanne Reiniers, communications officer Mr Cees Donkers, Urban architect	Cultuur Eindhoven is a new kind of organization within Eindhoven. They came into existence in 2015 as an innovative experiment to make an external organization responsible for the funding of cultural organizations. Therefore, they are an innovative institution. There is always room for more exploration and experimentation.	Cultuur Eindhoven are mostly a fund that provide subsidies for cultural organizations. The regions of activities are Eindhoven, Noord-Brabant, and the Netherlands. Our target groups are mostly cultural organizations, professional makers of art and design and artists. We arrange funding for cultural activities in Eindhoven.	The organization takes funding from the government and the municipality of Eindhoven. The Programma Creatieve Industrie consists of around €350,000 a year.

(*Continued*)

TABLE 1 (Continued) The First Focus Group of Research. Author: Mickov, Biljana. 2021

	Innovation	*Cultural Program (Including Creative and Culture Industries)*	*Budget for Culture Year*
The Qualitative Research Analysis	In the first focus group of the research we conclude that innovations are developed in local governments, institutions and organizations. The development of technology contributes to technological innovation, but social innovation has an important place in the process of development of the cultural sector, and it is interconnected with tech innovation processes. The City of London, City of Glasgow and City of Eindhoven have programs for supporting the Culture and Creative industries CCI, which contribute to the development of a creative economy. The development of creative industries and innovations have to be an integral part of state policy, and it has to be seen as an essential part of social, educational, and economic policies. The future perspective is to see the creative industries being treated as an essential industry and part of the sustainable and regenerative economic agenda.		

instead of the experiment. It is necessary to have more room for experimenting and exploration. The organization is pretty good at combining a personal approach, as well as a diplomatic one in helping cultural partners with their funding. The organization is simple, approachable, constructive, and helpful. The main thing is that all creative stakeholders are positively using innovative strengths.

The City of London, City of Glasgow, and City of Eindhoven have programs for supporting the CCI, which contribute to the development of a creative economy. The development of creative industries and innovations have to be an integral part of state policy, and it has to be seen as an essential part of social, educational, and economic policies. The future perspective is to see the creative industries being treated as an essential industry and part of the sustainable and regenerative economic agenda.

Notes

526 "The Smart City," City of Stockholm, accessed May 9, 2021, https://international.stockholm.se/city-development/the-smart-city/

527 Information on the governance of the city, and the city budget through annual reports (2016 is the latest report on the website) can be found on: "International relation office," City of Stockholm, accessed May 9, 2021, https://international.stockholm.se/

528 Glasgow Life, accessed May 9, 2021, www.glasgowlife.org.uk/

529 "Edinburgh Performing Arts Development (Epad)," World Cities Culture Forum, accessed May 20, 2021, www.worldcitiescultureforum.com/cities/edinburgh/Innovative%20programmes

530 "Minister Madigan Announces Details of €339 Million 2019 Budget Package for Culture, Heritage and the Gaeltacht," Merrion Street, accessed May 9, 2021, https://merrionstreet.ie/en/news-room/releases/minister_madigan_announces_details_of_%E2%82%AC339_million_2019_budget_package_for_culture_heritage_and_the_gaeltacht.html

531 "The Arts Plan," Dublin City Arts Office, accessed May 9, 2021, http://www.dublincityartsoffice.ie/about-the-arts-office/the-arts-plan

532 Arts Governance, accessed May 9, 2021, https://www.artsgovernance.com/

533 Cees Donkers, "Eindhoven – A City as a Laboratory," in *Sustaining Cultural Development: New Governance in Cultural Life*, ed. James Doyle and Biljana Mickov (London: Routledge Publishing, 2013), 225–232.

534 Ibid.

535 Ibid.

536 Cultuur+Ondernemen, accessed May 10, 2021, http://www.governancecodecultuur.nl/

537 "The Arts Plan," Dublin City Arts Office.

10

THE SECOND FOCUS GROUP OF THE QUALITATIVE RESEARCH

City of Rome

Assessorato alla Crescita Culturale di Roma Capitale

The Capital City of Italy, Rome, has a rich legacy in motion pictures dating back to the early 20th century with the creation of the Cinecittà Studios. Home to the largest film production facility in Europe, Rome has become internationally renowned as the hub of Italian cinema. The adopted hometown of Federico Fellini, the so-called "Eternal City" has sustained its reputation as a vibrant city of film, and now supports a large sector with over 1,300 active enterprises in the film industry, generating an annual added value of about €750 million. In addition, Rome's film market has significantly strengthened with strong public–private cooperation. The city welcomes a wide audience of 150,000 people from 25 countries to its International Film Festival, which ranks among the world's top film festivals. Following a week of screenings, the audience is invited to reward the best films with People's Choice Awards. This participative process highlights Rome's steadfast commitment to making the film sector a key driver for social inclusion and cohesion. Local institutions have strongly supported the emergence of cultural and creative industries in recent years. Amongst other supporting programs, the Roma Provincia Creative has established a regional fund to benefit young creative entrepreneurs, as well as a social network to exchange and promote their innovative projects. In the film sector, the Culture and Tourism Department of Rome has developed an urban renewal program to reopen 42 abandoned movie theaters by commissioning small and medium-sized local cooperatives to revitalize urban areas with creativity and innovation.[538]

As a Creative City of Film, Rome envisages: establishing the Italian Audiovisual and Cinema Museum (MuseoItalianodell'Audiovisivo e del Cinema) to both preserve and raise awareness about Italian film heritage, as well as to provide good

DOI: 10.4324/9781003336648-12

practices in film restoration; increasing employment opportunities in the film sector for young entrepreneurs thanks to the Audiovisual Employment Observatory and based on strong public–private partnerships; encouraging cross-cutting approaches to film, music and literature through the E-motion Rome project; cooperating with other Creative Cities of Film to build a common data hub on audiovisual heritage at an international level to nurture intercultural dialogue and appreciation of cultural diversity; fostering the mobility of cinema students within the Unesco Creative City Network (UCCN) through exchange programs operated by the International Film Preservation School; and implementing the Cine-Creative Communities program aimed to promote the film sector in least developed cities as a solid and self-sustainable creative economy.[539]

The contact person, Mr Luca Bergamo (Deputy Mayor for Cultural Office of the City of Rome), is the Vice Mayor in charge of cultural development.

This is a local government organization. The office of the Deputy Mayor for Culture sets out political strategies for the cultural development of the city of Rome, impacting policies concerning cultural activities, cultural institutions, heritage conservation, enhancement and promotion. It acts both through direct action with cultural municipality departments and through relations with regional, national, and international bodies. It primarily gives strategic and operational guidelines to two of the municipality's cultural departments:

1) The Department for Culture ensures coordination, promotion and administrative services in order to support the city's cultural activities generated by local community groups, municipality cultural centers and institutions. It is also responsible for coordinating and supporting the cultural activities of 11 organizations and institutions fully and partially owned by Roma Capital, including the network of Rome's 40 municipal libraries.
2) The Superintendence for Cultural Heritage of Rome manages, maintains, and enhances the archaeological, historical, artistic, and monumental heritage belonging to Roma Capital both in its historical center and across the rest of the city. Under its direct management are ancient to modern heritage attractions, UNESCO sites, historical villas and parks, 21 museums gathered under the network of "Musei in Comune."

The activities are oriented towards the city of Rome, made up of 15 borough municipalities for a total of 1,287 square kilometers. The target groups are: Rome's citizens (permanent and temporary), local, national and international cultural operators/institutions, tourists (it is to be underlined that *this is not a direct target* as there is a specific *Assessorato* in charge of Tourism, although the two *Assessorati*, in charge of Cultural Development and Tourism, are necessarily and obviously interconnected). The *Assessorato* gives guidelines to its administrative offices (the Department for Culture and the Superintendence for Cultural Heritage), which act mainly through public calls, programming of museums, and the coordination of cultural institutions. The municipality deals with innovation and we identified here three innovative local cultural projects and policies that can be featured as examples of the activities being carried out in this field.

The OperaCamion Project (Launched in July 2016)

Building social cohesion in outlying districts via mobile satellites of major cultural institutions

Rome has a complex and disconnected landscape with a mix of urban and rural spaces across a wide area. Findings from a 2016 Eurobarometer survey suggested that 50% of the population of Rome do not trust their own neighbors, further adding to this sense of fragmentation. The touring opera project OperaCamion is aimed towards improving cohesion in communities while allowing a cultural institution based in the city center to reach peripheral areas. OperaCamion consists of a mobile company which aims to bring opera to public squares across Rome. The project is run by Teatro dell'Opera di Roma, in partnership with Rome's municipal libraries, as these are the most widespread cultural institutions in the city. Performances take place close to the local library and are given by the opera's younger singers and its youth orchestra. In 2017, this collaboration allowed more than 10,000 citizens to enjoy free, high-quality opera in their own neighborhood on a summer evening. At the time of writing, eight out of the fifteen Rome sub-municipalities have hosted events and over 30 young musicians have been involved.

The community engagement lasts longer than a single night: the Youth Orchestra and Fabbrica Young Artist Program hold free preparatory encounters in local libraries so that citizens can discuss opera ahead of the performance. At night, there is an informal and festive atmosphere in the square where the performance take place, with citizens gathering long before the show to share anecdotes and knowledge on the opera, as well as bringing chairs, pillows, and food.

The focus of this project is not on creating immediate economic value, but rather on improving the wellbeing of and relationships between local people while developing audiences over time. The process has allowed the institutions involved to analyze the reasons that many people have become detached from opera perceiving it as an "elite" artform. It also offers an opportunity for performers to make the case for opera as relevant to modern audiences, including those who do not normally become involved in cultural events. The work has encouraged the city's cultural institutions to collaborate, move beyond the confines of their buildings, and rethink their activities and mission. This project has attracted praise and significant coverage in the national and international press. This has had a positive impact on public opinion and has generated a view of opera that is not exclusive and inaccessible, but rather genuinely open to new kinds of audience.

From our point of view, the following factors may be seen as the most innovative about this initiative: the experimentation of new solutions and formats to bring high-quality contents in those areas that are furthest from the center where cultural institutions are traditionally located, especially considering Rome's geographical features; the incentive to foster collaboration and networking among the city's cultural institutions to serve local communities, an attitude which is revealed to be essential for the production of the new format of Rome's New Year's Eve celebration; and the informal and festive atmosphere in Opera Camion's squares, in which citizens gather long before the show and share anecdotes and knowledge on the opera, as well as chairs, pillows, and food.

The MIC Card (Launched in Summer 2018)

Valuing Resident Cultural Access in Tourist-Dominated Hotspots

Rome is a magnet for international tourists, but the very success of the visitor economy can make the city's museums and heritage sites expensive and exclusive, pricing local people out of the cultural riches of their own city. Some membership cards already exist for Rome's museums, but these are largely aimed at offering discounts for tourists.

In spring 2018, the city introduced the Musei in Comune (MIC) card, which gives two million citizens unlimited access to the 21 institutions in its civic museums network, Musei in Comune, for a nominal fee. The MIC card offers access to temporary and permanent exhibitions in exchange for a token annual payment of €5. The participating museums are also developing specific programs to welcome citizen audiences, including Notte dei Musei (Night of Museums), Musei in Musica (Museums in Music), and MiX Incontriamoci al museo (MiX 'Let's meet at the museum'). When these events were run in 2017, it was found that approximately 80% of attendees were city residents, of which 70% had never previously taken part in such initiatives. The museums are also aiming to offer a place for amateurs to use their spaces for a much wider range of cultural activities, including dance, theater, music, and rehearsal. The MIC card will therefore help to develop a culture in which visiting a museum is not just an act of consumption, but a route to active participation. This program is run by the Superintendence for Cultural Heritage of Rome, which oversees the network of civic museums, and Zètema Progetto Cultura, the city's cultural service provider. There are future plans to expand the scheme by adding state museums, archaeological sites, and the Vatican museums to the MIC card network. This initiative is the first attempt by any Italian city to offer virtually free museum access with a card that is aimed specifically at citizens, rather than tourists. The accompanying programs of new activities do not just widen audiences but redefine the purpose of museums themselves. They will become livelier places, to be visited by Rome's population as a part of their everyday lives, rather than an exclusive place aimed only at visitors to the city.

As global tourism grows, it is essential for very popular cities to address the trade-offs between the needs of locals and those of international visitors. Rome's evolving initiative has the potential to lead the way for other cities which need to strike a similar balance.

The following factors are the most innovative about this initiative: it is the first city attempt in Europe to allow citizens (and not just tourists) to access museums for free with the payment of a symbolic nominal fee of 5€/year; rethinking museums as real public places and transforming them into everyday life common spaces might be a revolutionary city cultural policy as it ignites changes both in the behavior of citizens and in the Public Administration.

Seasons of Rome (Launched in April 2017)

Promoting Contemporary and Scientific Culture in an Ancient City

Rome is renowned around the world for its history, but often under-appreciated for its modern cultural offer which includes artistic communities, scientific research, and hundreds of cultural organizations. Since 2017, the Municipality of Rome has promoted and co-ordinated the Seasons of Rome, three main programming seasons to highlight the city's contemporary offer. The spring season is dedicated to science; the summer is focused on activities to develop a stronger sense of community by living and reinterpreting open and public spaces; and the autumn is devoted to contemporary cultural production. This program is led by the Municipality of Rome's Department of Cultural Affairs, in partnership with the city's 15 boroughs, and work is chosen through public calls for scientists and artists. The three seasons are backed by an annual budget of €2.5 million which is shared among private cultural operators and civil society, and also by the activities of public institutions, research, and education centers. Some of this funding is annual, but part of the budget supports the development of three-year city-wide projects, aimed to have an impact both on specific neighborhoods and on the wider reputation of the city: projects range from a science van that reaches peripheral piazzas to a new free festival of independent music, and from performances in underground stations' halls to theatrical storytelling in city parks.

The first two programming seasons, in the summer and autumn of 2017, generated over 1,600 events and drew around half a million people to each season. The work has also strengthened Rome's cultural ecosystem as a whole, encouraging a wide spectrum of cultural actors from a range of very different fields to work together. This has expanded the concept of what a cultural event can look like, in particular acknowledging that engaging with science and acquiring new knowledge are creative processes. As stated above, some festival activity has attracted three-year funding, allowing operators to produce more considered and effective projects and reducing a tendency for programming to be fragmentary and episodic. The festival has allowed the city to consciously spread events right across Rome, highlighting geographic features beyond the center and promoting activities closer to where the city's citizens actually live. Finally, the Seasons of Rome project has forged many new alliances between cultural workers and the city government: 70% of the contributors appointed for the first season on science communication were participating for the first time in a municipally organized festival.

The following factors are the most innovative about this initiative: structural mechanism and an incentive for the all-year-round distribution of cultural planning throughout the city. In the case of the Estate Romana/Roman Summer, as of

2017 three-year projects were also introduced: a number of projects were selected in accordance with criteria that allow operators to plan over a longer period of time, with a guarantee of the funding from the municipality, new project parameters for cultural operators, fostering their relationship with the city, its territories' and citizens' well-being, a new reading of the city itself through the convergence of public/private initiatives, an entire city that, by making public and private converge, builds synergies and join the efforts, with a view to offering a new reading of itself.

The main objective of their cultural policies is to implement art. 27 of 1948's Universal Declaration of Human Rights:

> *Article 27: Right to participate in cultural life:*
>
> - *Everyone has the right freely to participate in the cultural life of the community, to enjoy the arts and to share in scientific advancement and its benefits.*
> - *Everyone has the right to the protection of the moral and material interests resulting from any scientific, literary or artistic production of which he is the author.*

Most cities are currently far from developing and implementing policies which aim at the fullest, freest and most equal participation in cultural life of the community where people live. In the case of Rome municipality, it is the institution's commitment to foster innovative trends having a positive impact on Roman citizens' well-being and cultural life: the City of Rome is creating a new data observatory aimed at measuring cultural participation and its impact on citizens' trust and wellbeing. This work will be enriched by a cross-analysis of Big Data and will be increasingly intertwined with the objectives and targets of the administrative departments, a growing number of active citizens are creating cultural experiences at grassroots level. The city is seeking to find a balance which encourages this development, while ensuring that public spaces remain shared by all, and using cultural institutions to make sure that communities are also linked into broader co-operative networks. New activity forms are emerging, which are built around provisional structures, or which need no new built structure at all. Examples include urban scientific walks and the rise of "urban stages" such as streets, metro stations, and building façades which can be used for a temporary cultural intervention.

Rome receives mainly local financial revenue (taxation) and government funds. There is also an increasing role of cultural patronage, and sponsorships from private organizations. There is no specific budget line dedicated to innovation and creative industries.

The staff of the Deputy Mayor for Culture's Office is composed of 16 people (both internal to the City of Rome and external) with skills ranging from communication to international relations, from infrastructure expertise to project management of events, and from strategic development to core issues know-how of the administrative machinery. However, the real resources committed to develop the cultural policies set out from the Deputy Mayor's office are the employees from the abovementioned cultural departments, cultural institutions, and municipal libraries. Rome has a record of excellent international cooperation.

Innovation: The municipality deals with innovation and we identified three innovative local cultural projects and policies that can be featured as examples of the activities being carried out in this field: the experimentation of new solutions and formats to bring high-quality contents in those areas that are furthest from the centre where cultural institutions are traditionally located, especially considering Rome's geographical features; the incentive to foster collaboration and networking among the city's cultural institutions to serve local communities, an attitude which reveals to be essential for the production of the new format of Rome's New Year's Eve celebration; and the informal and festive atmosphere in Opera Camion's squares, in which citizens gather long before the show and share anecdotes and knowledge on the opera, as well as chairs, pillows, and food. The most innovative aspects of this initiative are that Rome is the first city attempt in Europe to allow citizens (and not just tourists) to access museums for free with the payment of a symbolic nominal fee of 5€/year; rethinking museums as real public places and transforming them into everyday life common spaces might be a revolutionary city cultural policy as it ignites changes both in the behavior of citizens and in that of the Public Administration. The City of Rome's commitment to foster innovative trends is having a positive impact on Roman citizens' wellbeing and cultural life: The City of Rome is creating a new data observatory aimed at measuring cultural participation and its impact on citizens' trust and wellbeing. This work will be enriched by a cross-cultural analysis of Big Data and will be increasingly intertwined with the objectives and targets of the administrative departments, A growing number of active citizens are creating cultural experiences at the grassroots level. The city is seeking to find a balance which encourages this development, while ensuring that public spaces remain shared by all, and using cultural institutions to make sure that communities are also linked into broader co-operative networks, new activity forms are emerging which are built around provisional structures, or which need no new built structure at all. Examples include urban scientific walks and the rise of "urban stages" such as streets, metro stations and buildings façades which can be used for a temporary cultural intervention.

City of Bologna

Municipality of Bologna—INCREDIBOL! —l'INnovazione CREativa DI BOLogna (Bologna's Creative Innovation) Project

Based on interview with Giorgia Boldrini, Head of Creative Industries, Music and Urban Regeneration Unit, Municipality of Bologna.

INCREDIBOL! is a project managed and co-ordinated by the local government of the city (Comune di Bologna) in close collaboration with, and supported by, the Emilia-Romagna regional government. INCREDIBOL! (Bologna's Creative

Innovation) is a project started in 2010 to promote creative and cultural professions and industries in the Emilia-Romagna region. Those activities could be summarized as:

- a recurrent call to promote the creation of start-ups in the creative and cultural sector;
- a recurrent call to foster the internationalization of regional creative companies;
- a consulting desk service (upon appointment only);
- premises and venues owned by the Municipality of Bologna and given on gratuitous loan to cultural entities and creative professionals;
- info and opportunities published on the official website www.incredibol.net, on the Facebook page and under the "creative" section of www.emiliaromagnastartup.it;
- organization of free workshops, public meetings, networking and b2b events, etc.; and
- special and pilot projects on specific topics (e.g., videogames and cultural heritage, creative spillover, etc.) and participation in European projects, networks and international activities about ICC.

Moreover, the project is based on a regional public–private network offering guidance, training, ad hoc consulting services according to the needs of the winners of the main call. The programs have been covering the whole Emilia-Romagna region since 2010. The INCREDIBOL! project is addressed to all cultural and creative entrepreneurs and professionals based in Emilia-Romagna. However, some of the activities are specifically designed for those under 40 years of age. At the time of writing, the projects mostly launch calls for benefits as grants, spaces, exchange, etc. However, the Help Desk (for advice or information) is frequently used.

The INCREDIBOL! project deals with innovation in several ways, including:

- promoting and supporting new business ideas in the field of cultural and creative enterprises (since 2010);
- testing new methods of generating innovation through creative spillovers (European project URBACT Creative Spin, 2013–2015);
- creating winning processes within the Public Administration using, at best, no financial resources (since 2010–ongoing);
- more attention on creative spillovers and on cultural-based creativity and non-technological innovation for developing creative industries in Europe.

The strengths are: an integrated approach, multilevel governance, tailor-made solutions, and friendly communication. In comparison with others, the municipality is better at promoting creativity-based regeneration of public heritage. The weakness in the scheme is a lack of growth: with more political commitment, they could have developed a strong regional network; with more commitment from project partners, they could have offered more opportunities to the creative sector in the region. The Municipality of Bologna thinks that they are in the top 10 and that they do not have competitors.

The positive impact of the project is more commitment at the political level on the topic of Creative Industries as drivers for social innovation, wellbeing, and less emphasis on economic growth.

The funding sources of the INCREDIBOL! project are domestic: from the Municipality of Bologna and the Emilia-Romagna Region. In the past, projects have also received small contributions from two local banking foundations. For 2018, the budget available for the INCREDIBOL! project was €200,000 in cash and about €400,000 in non-monetary value (e.g., personal, real estate, etc).

The Municipality of Bologna has permanent premises, employees, computers and equipment of various kinds. The human resources of the INCREDIBOL! project are public employees.

The INCREDIBOL! project is coordinated by the Municipality of Bologna and supported by the Emilia-Romagna Region in conjunction with around 30 public and private partners.

The network is composed by around 30 partners as training bodies, legal and business consultants, micro-credit consultants, and specialized institutions.

Innovation: The INCREDIBOL! project is promoting and supporting new business ideas in the field of cultural and creative enterprises, testing new methods of generating innovation through creative spillovers (European project URBACT Creative Spin), and creating winning processes within the Public Administration using at best not financial resources. More attention on creative spillover and on cultural-based creativity and non-technological innovation for developing creative industries in Europe is needed.

1. *Culture as a Byword for Urban Development: The Italian Experience*[540] by Mauro Felicori[541]

In Italy, the burgeoning public debt has served only to postpone this adjustment, which now stares us in the face. In the meantime, globalization has brought new challenges—and not only for the industrial and financial world to which state-funded public institutions, unlike the market-oriented cultural industry, are scarcely able to respond.

But it is right at the end of the 1970s that expenditure on culture became a focus of interest for government, especially local government. It is with *Estati Romane*—the brainchild of the late lamented Renato Nicolini[542]—(but also, in the field of cultural heritage, with the queues to see the Riace bronzes) that Italian towns, regardless of their size, geographical location or political hue, discover that it can be profitable, in terms of building consensus for both politicians and administrators, to use public funds to offer low-cost events. No more niggling distinctions between *high* culture and *pop* culture, but a new focus on events that come across as unique, unrepeatable, and for *special* people. Such events are aimed at the new social subject brought into existence by mass education: a new urban *middle class* which—we note as an aside—was instrumental in bringing about first the students' protest movement of the 1970s, followed by the backlash and the hedonistic Italian society of the 1980s, then the revamping of the Italian Republic in the 1990s and, finally, the current institutional crisis.

Fresh spending on culture, therefore, is from its very start a precarious exercise; it is funded by borrowing money on the market, and is frittered away in short-lived initiatives; alternatively, where it does produce new cultural institutions (contemporary art galleries, for the most part), it often generates recurrent expenditure that will last forever. It is as if culture and its growth had been funded with a mortgage.

What we call today *public cultural policies* are therefore a recent (perhaps 40 years old?) and fragile product. Given that these premises were clear from the beginning, it would have taken far-sighted and disciplined rulers to grasp rapidly that, in order to sustain great ambitions in conditions of penury, sobriety, rigor, an aptitude for efficiency and a sharp distinction between the public and the private were called for. Instead, cultural policies have been the forum where the very opposite has taken place, beginning with the use of public resources to promote assorted political careers.

The political class and official institutions must promise to regard culture as the citizens' own right, a necessity in advanced societies, on a par with education, health care and social care; an asset in collective and individual wealth, a measure of wealth and happiness; a powerful engine of economic development; and a strong cement for social cohesion and inclusion. Accordingly, they must allocate resources commensurate with the new-found social significance of this model.

2. *The Four Challenges*

These are the four challenges (i.e., the four conditions to regain legitimacy) which will be faced by cultural policies in the next few years:

1. There has to be a sustained commitment to broadening the public that participates in cultural events; this cannot be limited to the well-educated without raising serious issues of legitimacy in drawing on public expenditure. The challenge within the challenge here concerns the *new Italian citizens*, for whom cultural inclusion must be planned to go hand in hand with the acquisition of other fundamental rights. In other words, the process of including immigrant workers (of both genders) and their families must cease to be considered the sole remit of social and educational services, and become the result of a commitment that cuts across all branches of administration, including those cultural institutions which are to be found everywhere, such as public libraries and museums.

   Over the past half-century or so, Italian society has made great strides in promoting the availability of cultural products. With mass education in place since the early 1960s, widespread cultural offerings followed suit from the late 1970s. "However, Italian society has come to rest on its laurels, without setting itself new challenges; cultural institutions have merely recorded the growing level of education, without contributing anything. Museums have an important role to play, leaving behind their past as institutes for collecting, safeguarding and (occasionally) conducting research, to become *culture factories, communication engines*, to highlight both their ultimate purpose and the importance of deploying state-of-the-art information and communication technologies."

2. The debate on how to "do" culture must take *efficiency* into account. Cultural institutions face the same problems as public bodies generally do in making efficient use of resources, albeit hidden behind the beguiling word *culture*, which justifies and lends legitimacy to everything.[543] In the same way as energy saving is the prime new energy source, efficiency must become the prime new resource of cultural institutions. It is peculiar how no one seems capable of defining the terms of the problem adequately: on the one hand, we wish for a culture that is regarded as an economic asset, while, on the other hand, we refuse to scrutinize it as if it were one; on the one hand, we demand that culture be considered an investment, while on the other we recoil from any attempt to assess its performance and improve its output. We imagine that expenditure on culture is always unquestionably positive, and the same applies to the *efficiency* of cultural activities.

> However, a cultural enterprise is certainly not the same as a company offering goods or services. The output of a cultural institute is never measured in monetary terms, it is always a cultural product! The *turnover* of a museum is not the revenue shown in its balance sheet, but rather how much its visitors have managed to learn. However, this does not mean that the need to identify objectives and seek to improve them over time should be overlooked, but not—of course—in terms of turnover or profit, but rather in terms of number of visitors, spectators, guided tours; knowledge that has been passed on, and the ability to promote social inclusion.[544]

"Instead, cultural institutions have always displayed an extraordinary talent for escaping evaluation. Unfortunately, behind the idea that *culture cannot be measured* hide all sorts of inefficiencies."[545]

3. Expenditure on culture needs to boost its economic value, proving itself to be a driving force of economic growth, especially in those of our towns that are genuine repositories of culture and boast a valuable asset in the form of a vibrant *creative class*. For three decades we have been talking of "Creative Cities" and the crucial role played by the so-called *cultural and creative industries*. Indeed, over the past few years this debate has achieved a certain popularity also in Italy, while at the European Union level the word "culture" has been included within the new *Creative Europe* program. The recognition of the sector's importance as an engine for growth and source of cohesion and social innovation needs to be matched in the very near future by specific and courageous policies and initiatives.

> We need policies oriented towards the production of art, not only towards the consumption of culture, with suitable attention being paid to the exportability of art products, to the global appeal of creative enterprise (as is the case in any economic sector), and to the intersection between culture and tourism; this is essential if we are to make the most of our historic and artistic assets while ensuring the vitality and international appeal of contemporary production. We need policies which equate urban development with culture, where culture is an object of consumption but also becomes investment, industrial policy, and strategic planning.[546]

We need culture to become central in the economic planning of our cities. This is the dawn of a new era, in which culture must bind with and promote the growth of productive activities and trade; it must concern itself with old town centers, with the quality of the urban environment, with social welfare. So numerous are the possible combinations that mayors should not delegate this function; on the contrary, they should make full use of it so that it can inform all local government policies—a process which the British, with their extraordinary ability to express complex ideas succinctly, refer to as *cultural planning*: culture as the leavening of all urban policies. "We need to be able to stop using the culture budget as an easy tool to buy political consensus, and accept the risk of arts as investment."[547]

4. Culture must revert to being a technical discipline and stop being the battlefield of political entrepreneurs looking for consensus. "We need to restore autonomy and dignity to culture professionals, as is already the case for the health sector, law and order, public works—all sectors where the importance of public structures possessing technical expertise is widely recognized." [548]The reforms carried out in the 1990s, which were intended to separate political decision-making and administrators have failed, but a culture budget despotically administered by politicians, without technical expertise to counterbalance it, is doomed to short-termism, the pursuit of safe options, the lowest common denominator, the very opposite of a drive to innovate as part of a far-reaching strategy.

More generally, we need to replace a model in which taxpayers fund cultural institutions *indirectly* through tax collection and the allocation of revenue to cultural institutions, thus fostering their dependence on the political system, with a model in which, by making expenditure on cultural pursuits tax-deductible and detoxifying culture, citizens fund *directly* and collectively their cultural life, thus freeing if from political influence.

Finally, a word about European policies. The European Union (EU) would appear to be the only organization where subsidiarity is being applied. As a matter of fact, it considers cultural policies as something over which the individual member states have jurisdiction. Therefore, in line with the principle of subsidiarity, the EU does not make it one of the mainstays of its activity, limiting itself to funding cooperation programs among its member states, as if there were still a need for it. But today's hot topic is competition and cooperation among continental systems—an area which national governments struggle to control, and one that should be covered by the EU Commission, in response to the requirement that Brussels calls *European value added.* It is possible to imagine a Union that commits resources and channels them to promoting European culture across the globe.

In the last few years, a new player has appeared on the Italian subsidiarity scene, the so-called *fondazioni di origine bancaria.*[549] Here too we face the problem of determining their rightful place in the organization of culture, and the tasks they could take on in partnership with local government institutions, municipal bodies, and universities. Their most valuable contribution could stem from their independent nature. Indeed, the law and, more recently, the Constitutional Court have established that *fondazioni* must cooperate with, but not be subordinate to, elected powers, and local elected powers in particular.

Thus, this choice will give the best results if the *fondazioni* succeed in making the most of their *aristocratic* nature, avoiding the lure of local, short-term consensus, and emphasizing long- range strategies, making those choices that elected institutions, caught up in the daily political fray, are all too often incapable of making. If we disapprove of bending culture to the needs of short-term political gain, this would be even less acceptable for a *fondazione* that has no need for it. *Fondazioni di origine bancaria* must therefore resist the temptation to ape the style and (limited) horizons of a town council's department for culture, and place themselves firmly in that other space, over and beyond, where scientific research and genuine artistic endeavor often aspire to be.

City of Barcelona

Based on interview with Mr Esteve Caramès, Director of Cultural Sectors, Institut de Cultura de Barcelona.

The Barcelona Institute of Culture is part of the local government of the city of Barcelona. The main activity of the Institute is to develop local cultural policies for the city. The programs and activities are directed towards the Barcelona municipality. The target group of service users are Barcelona's population, local cultural sectors and cultural industries. The Institute has different service activities, including cultural funding, the production of cultural projects, and the development of cultural policy strategies.

Innovation is an aspect of everyday action. The Institute monitors action with data indicators, evaluates actions systematically and introduces constant innovation in its programs and projects.

To develop creative industries and innovation, it is necessary to establish a more integral approach to EU projects. The strength of the Institute is proximity of dimensions, contact with local cultural stakeholders and capacity of interaction. The Barcelona Institute of Culture is better than others in terms of monitoring and evaluating innovation. Partners from the EU view the Institute of Culture as a strong actor in the dynamic creative field and international projection. The weakness of the Institute's work is budget capacity. Other partners from the EU work better in the field of integral assessment of cultural policies. To improve the current situation would mean to continuously develop strategic planning and data. Big Data, decentralized policy making and digital advancement have all had a positive impact on the Institute. The funding of the Barcelona Institute of Culture comes from tax revenues and there are no separate budgets for creative industries and innovation. At the time of writing, the Institute has 420 employees. The local government is fully connected, both internationally and locally.

Cultural policies have been at the center of development strategies of Barcelona City[550] over the past 30 years. Since 1979, when the first democratic local government was formed, the City Council has been promoting ambitious policies in order to encourage and facilitate citizens' involvement in the creation and implementation of cultural policies at the city level, as well as to strengthen the role of the city's cultural institutions such as the Foundation Joan Miró, the Antoni Tàpies Foundation and the Picasso Museum. A strong cultural identity of the city, in which Catalan and Spanish cultural traditions are intertwined, is based primarily on the extensive network of cultural entities and associations. There is no doubt that this solid network is the foundation for the promotion and implementation of ambitious policies in the field of culture at the city level, and that is exactly what Barcelona's cultural policy seeks to promote during this period. As a key element in the promotion of the urban transformation of Barcelona, a young and innovative cultural profile of the city was identified. Shortly after the 1992 Olympics, the promotion of Barcelona as the center of culture has become one of the basic strategies. This period saw the opening of some of the main cultural institutions of the city, such as the Centre for Contemporary Culture of Barcelona (CCCB), the Museum of Contemporary Art (MACBA), and a new concert hall, L'Auditori. At that time the cultural sector made an important contribution to the city's economic growth, as stated in the text of the first Strategic Plan for Culture, presented in 1999. The significant development of major cultural events and festivals were also characteristic of this period. The Universal Forum of Cultures, under the auspices of UNESCO, was held in Barcelona in 2004, symbolizing the end of the city's cultural platform presentation.

The new momentum in the development of cultural strategy has been defined only recently. There are several essential elements that define a new context: the city is becoming increasingly diverse; the relevant performance and influence of cultural sector activities have already become unanimously recognized; the constant multiplication of communication channels has increased the opportunities, as well as risks, to massively communicate cultural projects; the excellent geographical position of the city attracts a large number of tourists and visitors to cultural institutions and facilities; and, finally, a significant growth in the creative sector of the city has been recorded. Based on these facts, it seemed justified and appropriate to reshape and adapt cultural strategy of the city in accordance with these elements for the following years.

Based on the "Agenda 21," Barcelona promoted the transformation of its cultural strategy in 2006. The document "The Second Strategic Plan for Culture" was the result of the cooperation and contribution of 400 local cultural representatives. The three main messages of this document referred to: encouragement of access and participation in local cultural programs; the promotion of outstanding artistic productions, as a basis for cultural projects at the city level; and a strengthening of the relationships within the cultural sector of Barcelona, in order to more effectively organize the available resources for culture at the city level.

The basic direction of activities is to strengthen support for production projects in the fields of culture and the arts. Traditionally, the promotion of local cultural development was based on the policies of promotion and support for art exhibitions: striving for more museums, more festivals, more cultural centers, etc. However, a modern and ambitious cultural capital in the present day must take into consideration the existence of a dynamic artistic community within its frame—the existence of a solid base consisting of musicians, performers, and visual artists, generates the appearance and the presence of new projects and new opportunities, which are feeding a dynamic cultural sector.

Barcelona, as a cultural capital, have to emphasize and underline its support for local cultural creators. This is the primary aim of the Barcelona Art Factory, which will provide 20,000 square meters of public venues exclusively for arts and cultural production, such as rehearsal spaces for dancers and theater groups, a music center, a studio for visual artists or spaces for circus performers to hone their skills.

As the cultural dynamics of any city is based on the work and abilities of its cultural and artistic community, the importance and relevance of culture at the city level is based on the results of the performance of its largest cultural institutions, such as major museums, concert halls, opera, and influential festivals. The exceptional quality of these institutions within Barcelona reflects the exceptional quality of artistic production at the local level.

The city's main cultural institutions, such as the MACBA, the Lliure Theatre, the Natural History Museum, and CCCB, are all currently in the process of reform in order to enable their programs to comply with the requirements of new services they have to offer. This program represents the basis for the future positioning of Barcelona as an international Capital of Culture, in which the development of the largest and most influential cultural institutions in the city plays a key role. The fourth main direction in the development strategy is the introduction of innovations in the field of development, as well as the presentation of new ways and means, for the creation of local cultural policies at the city level. It is clear that this, more complex cultural system requires a much better performance of the cultural administration. The fact is that it is no longer possible to plan cultural policies with one sole voice; instead, it is necessary that the redefinition of the development orientation includes means of contrast and discussion.

The aim of this text is to briefly explain the highlights of innovations in Barcelona's cultural policies over recent years. A further and more extensive description of this theme should also have included issues such as strategic policies with regard to the restoration of the urban memory as a major step to strengthen local cultural heritage, or measures to support the local cultural industry, such as the recent creation of the Design Hub Barcelona. However, it should also be mentioned that there are still important challenges to be covered, such as the issue of the development of arts educational programs, the formation of the cultural strategy for the development of the urban area, or a more active involvement of partners from the private sector in the process of shaping and creating local cultural projects.

To keep innovation at the core of the city's cultural policies, it is in any case necessary to place culture at the center of urban development strategies, to carry out individual programs based on the cultural dimension possessed by every city, and, finally, it is necessary to integrate the diversity of cultural institutions and cultural programs into a single, comprehensive strategy. The contemporary context, characterized by changes and complexities, requires the application of cultural policies that can create a more comprehensive future.

The Decidim Project

Decidim is a digital infrastructure for participatory democracy, built entirely and collaboratively as free software.[551] More specifically, Decidim is a web environment (*framework*) produced in *Ruby on Rails* that allows users to create and configure a website platform or portal, to be used in the form of a social network, for democratic participation. The portal allows any organization (local city council, association, university, NGO, trade union, neighborhood or cooperative) to create massive democratic processes for strategic planning, participatory budgeting, collaborative regulatory design, urban space design and elections. It also enables the organization of in-person meetings, signing up for them, the publication of minutes, proposing points for agendas and receiving notifications of the results. Decidim can also help in organizing governing bodies, councils or assemblies, the convening of consultations and referendums or channeling citizen or member initiatives to impact different decision-making processes. Overall, Decidim makes it possible to digitally structure a complete system of participatory democratic governance for any organization. Equality in the political participation of citizens is one of the fundamental principles of any democratic system and the platform has to ensure equal opportunities with respect to not only the uses and functions, but also the access rights. In this sense, the entity in charge of the platform assumes the commitment to promote actions that advance in the direction of providing access and support to the platform for all citizens alike. Giving tools and resources appropriate to the platform is available to anyone who wants to use them.

Innovation: Innovation is a part of everyday action. The Institute monitors action with data indicators, evaluates actions systematically, and introduces constant innovation in programs and projects. To develop creative industries and innovation, a more integral approach to EU projects is necessary. The strength of the Institute is proximity of dimensions, contact with local cultural stakeholders and capacity of interaction. The Barcelona Institute of Culture is better than others in terms of the monitoring and evaluation of innovation. Partners from the EU view the Institute of Culture as a strong actor in the dynamic creative field and international projection.

City of Barcelona

Based on interview with Mercedes Giovinazzo, Director, Fundació INTERARTS per a la Cooperació Cultural Internacional (NGO), Barcelona.

The INTERARTS Foundation is a private agency/non-governmental organization/civil society organization. The foundation is contributing to human development through culture, support for the design of cultural policies, promoting knowledge and information in the field of culture, and advocating for the role of culture in public governance and network at European and international levels.

The areas of activities are Europe, Latin America and the Caribbean, and Africa. The users and target group of work are CSOs (civil society organizations) of the cultural sector.

INTERARTS deploys its work in the following activity areas:

- Development cooperation: INTERARTS designs and implements international development cooperation projects with a cultural dimension. They believe that culture is both a driver and an enabler of human sustainable development.
- Consultancy: INTERARTS provides consultancy services, for both private and public entities. It puts the knowledge acquired in its different activity areas at the disposal of public and private operators.
- Knowledge transfer: INTERARTS develops training and information activities, including seminars and conferences. Through their trainee program, they host students from a number of international higher education centers. Through their web and social media channels they provide continuous information on their activities and on topics relevant for the cultural sector.
- Applied research: INTERARTS defines itself as a laboratory of ideas and a center for applied research. They focus on emergent issues of relevance for the cultural sector and for cultural policies.
- Networking & Advocacy: INTERARTS has always been active in European cultural networks. They consider that networking strengthens their organization and enables them to take part in on-going debates on issues of crucial interests for the cultural sector, advocating for a major role of culture in European governance.
- INTERARTS has done pioneer research, consulting and training work in areas such as cultural rights, international cooperation and development by introducing culture as a key factor, connections between culture and economy, culture and sexual and reproductive health, and more.

- INTERARTS sets the benchmark for the cultural sector, especially in relation to cultural policies. It does this in close collaboration with other key players, both within Europe and internationally.
- INTERARTS adapts innovative instruments to its internal administration procedures and also to its internal, as well as external, communication policies. This has been done in close collaboration with specialized professionals in each of the specified areas.

Examples of innovative tools include the following:

- Enterprise Resource Planning specific to INTERARTS: the system was developed through the collaboration of INTERARTS, accountants, information technology staff, etc.;
- models for cross-checking the technical activities and management costs;
- an internal control system for the expenditures and project activities;
- predictive models for the general budget and analytical budget;
- control and management systems for the activities carried out abroad;
- a specialized social platform for the cultural and creative sector, which will include a social feature to facilitate contacts and the setting up of projects;
- work experience program abroad for INTERARTS employees;
- the establishment of a visiting research fellow in INTERARTS, which allowed it to invite renowned professionals, especially university professors;

These innovative aspects help INTERARTS achieve its objectives, and maintain the organization's international reputation and positioning among the professional circles and the general public. Innovative elements are intended to help the organization's development and sustainability in the long run. Investing in developing the organization's potential in international public relations is understood as crucially important given that this is considered a major asset to ensure the organization's capacity to adapt quickly to a rapidly changing environment.

At a local level, the City of Barcelona has deployed efforts to support innovation, in particular through its @22 urban development project. In the @22 district, but also elsewhere in the city, it has developed a network of art factories, mostly in dismissed locations. The Spanish Ministry of Culture as a directorate responsible for cultural industries.

INTERARTS has a very strong network of partners (individual experts/organizations). It also has the capacity to manage large-scale projects. It has an important capacity to adapt to external challenges. The networking and management capacities are really strong, and the weakness is that the foundation depends on funding for projects. The foundation is a unique organization.

To improve, INTERARTS has to work on diversifying their sources of funding. The total operational budget for 2021 was €4,152,121.28.

The breakdown structure between different external funders is as follows: Services: 81% European Union, 19% Russian Federation. Grants: 100% European Union. The innovation and creative industries depend on the on-going projects.

INTERARTS's organizational structure is formed by:

- The Board—currently composed of 10 individual members who are highly competent and experienced in a diverse range of complementary sectors (ranging from the cultural to the financial). The Board takes all major strategic decisions, including the approval of the annual accounts and operational budgets. It also discusses the future development of the organization.
- The Executive Committee—composed of three board members (Chair, Vice-chair and Secretary) and two staff members (Director and General Manager). The Committee is mandated by the Board to follow up on the implementation of the organization's activities and to make the necessary ad hoc decisions.
- Executive team—consists of 8 full-time staff members, highly competent professionals coming from a diverse cultural and professional background.
- External collaborators, who are recruited on a project basis, for short time periods.
- Interns—between two and four work with INTERARTS each quarter. They are selected on the basis of individual applications. For each intern there is a prior agreement with the university in the framework of their post-graduate studies. The period of the internship can be prolonged up to six months. Remuneration is foreseen. Selection is done on the basis of qualification and experience.

INTERARTS rents an independent office (200 square meters) with meeting facilities (two meeting rooms for 10 and 50 persons respectively) in the center of Barcelona, on the last floor of an office building. The premises have two large terraces, one equipped for lunches and coffee-breaks. INTERARTS owns its own equipment: 15 independent work stations each with a PC equipped with Windows, Office, A3, Acrobat Professional, specifically tailored to meet the needs of the organization, Microsoft Exchange, EXO Platform; 4 laptops; 2 tablets; 2 servers with capacity for remote access, periodical back-up system; digital telephones and smart phones; large band-width (ADSL and Optical fiber): videoconference system; Skype premium and Go-to-meeting; flat mega screen for television, projections and other audiovisual support; documentation center.

Cyberkaris, INTERARTS's newsletter, was first launched in a paper edition in 2000. It is an important and well-known communication tool, and it is currently distributed electronically to its subscribers on different continents (Europe, Latin America and Africa) in three languages (Catalan, Spanish, English).

Currently, INTERARTS manages over 10 web pages, 20 social networks and a YouTube channel. The main websites are: interarts.net, fomecc.org, campuseuroamericano.org, decides.pro, smedwia.eu, smedcv.net, culturalbase.eu, cultureatworkafrica.net, mcpbroker.eu, culturalrights.net, culture-ks.org, and netcher.eu.

The main partners of INTERARTS are international organizations, state, and local public administrations (in particular, all those departments which are directly or indirectly responsible for culture and cultural cooperation), private foundations, nongovernmental organizations, universities, etc.

INTERARTS's stakeholders are mainly the same as the partners already mentioned; to these may be added the culture sector's professionals in the larger sense, which includes cultural entrepreneurs and other public entities such as chambers of commerce, ministerial departments responsible for education, labor, health, trade, and industries, etc.

Innovation

The specific innovative tools include:

- Enterprise Resource Planning specific to INTERARTS: the system was developed through the collaboration of INTERARTS, accountants, information technology staff, etc.
- models for cross-checking the technical activities and management costs;
- an internal control system for the expenditures and project activities;
- predictive models for the general budget and analytical budget;
- control and management systems for the activities carried out abroad;
- a specialized social platform for the cultural and creative sector, which will include a social feature to facilitate contacts and the setting up of projects;
- work experience program abroad for INTERARTS employees; and
- visiting research fellow in INTERARTS: inviting renowned professionals, especially university professors.

These innovative aspects help INTERARTS achieve its objectives, and maintain the organization's international reputation and positioning among the professional circles and the general public. Innovative elements are intended to help the organization's development and sustainability in the long run. Investing in developing the organization's potential in international public relations is understood as crucially important given that this is considered a major asset to ensure the organization's capacity to adapt quickly to a rapidly changing environment.

At the local level, the City of Barcelona has deployed efforts to support innovation, in particular through its @22 urban development project. In the @22 district, but also elsewhere in the city, it has developed a network of art factories, mostly in dismissed locations. The Ministry of Culture of Spain has a directorate responsible for cultural industries.

City of Brussels

Based on interview with Mr Phillipe Kern, Director of KEA European Affairs, (NGO) private research center, KEA European Affairs, City of Brussels.

Brussels is the administrative, commercial, and financial heart of Belgium, and the majority of national services and institutions are based in the city.[552] Brussels is, in addition, a major European tourist and cultural attraction, functioning simultaneously as a regional metropolis and an international center. The last-named role has flourished since the city became host to the European Communities.

Phillipe Kern is the Director of the KEA European Affairs (NGO), a private research center. The focus of their activities is cultural policy. The area of activities is mainly the European Union.

The service users are mainly public authorities in the EU. The organization covers studies and research, as well as the management of EU projects.

The innovation in the organization are projects on art and science, the impact of culture on innovation and creative spillovers in cities. The developing creative industries and innovation vary from one public authority to the other; in general, however, greater awareness on the importance of cultural investment for attractiveness and economic development is needed.

The strength of the organization is its multinationalism, and its ability to provide comparative analysis across countries. KEA can directly communicate with policy makers and influence them through reports. An additional strength is a good understanding of law and policies.

The weakness of the organization is that there are too many researchers with shoestring budgets. The donors and funding bodies for the organization are EU institutions (Commission, Parliament, EIF). The annual budget depends on the project budget received from their donors. The organization has six full-time employees. The international cooperation is realized as an extensive international network through years of collaboration and active presence on social media.

Innovation:

The innovations in the organization are projects on art and science, the impact of culture on innovation, creative spillovers in cities. The developing creative industries and innovation vary from one public authority to the other, but, in general, greater awareness on the importance of cultural investment for attractiveness and economic development is needed.

City of Marseille

Based on interview with Naïk M'Sili, Co-director, Instants Vidéo Numériques et Poétiques, City of Marseille

Marseille is at a turning point in its history.[553] The cradle of a unique type of multiculturalism, France's second-largest city, is undergoing significant expansion. These days, Marseille is known not only for its southern lifestyle, but also as a dynamic and evolving area, taking its place as a top-flight Mediterranean and global city. Marseille was named "European City of the Year" at the "2014 Urbanism Awards." A city on the doorstep of the calanques, in 2015 it also joined National Geographic's list of the top 10 seaside cities to visit. Attracted by the city's dynamic appeal, many investors now wish to set up business operations in Marseille. The City of Marseille and the Aix-Marseille-Provence Metropolis are committed to anticipating and supporting urban and economic projects. This will therefore help entrepreneurs and galvanize employment. More than an open-air museum overlooking 26 centuries of history, Marseille offers a big cultural life. A factor of attractiveness and synonymous with a quality living environment, the offer is very diverse and the spectacle is permanent.

Instants Vidéo Numériques et Poétiques, City of Marseilles, is an association under the 1901 Law (NGO). The main topics of the organization are video arts. Their project *Thought & practice of images* follows two priorities that overlap, interact and enrich one another, and whose links are inseparable and unbreakable: one is artistic and the other in related to cultural and poetical rights. The organization's activities on the artistic level are: curating (exhibitions and screenings); representing artworks and intermediating; expertise sharing: mentoring artists and organizations; co-creation & support of festivals, jurying at festivals, awarding diplomas, organizing conferences, lectures; exchanging knowledge through publications, workshops, symposiums; holding an annual international festival (32nd edition in 2019).

Activities in the realm of cultural and poetical rights are: image education and participation—video art awareness workshop, a conversation tour of exhibitions, popular art galleries, the *Programm'actors* collaborative project; art, citizenship & civil society: collective commitments with REF (Euromed network France), Ligue de l'Enseignement (Popular education), Territoires Solidaires: co-organization of workshops (Libyan, Syrian youths), public encounters, forums, panel discussions...); de-compartmentalisation/cultural biodiversity. The areas of programs are France and worldwide. The organization is interested in addressing the activities to a very diverse panel of persons from civil societies: the youth, adults and seniors; cultural operators, artists and persons who are not used to meeting with contemporary arts; women, men, non-binary persons, trans persons; racialized persons, persons in exile, or in a situation of vulnerability, disabled persons, intellectuals, persons in an economically-strong position; students, workers, unemployed, etc.

The organization has different activities, such as:

- the international Festival Les Instants Vidéo and the Palestinian Biennale;
- curatorial activities; and
- actions for a cultural biodiversity.

The Instants Vidéo Numériques et Poétiques believes that today, in our global world in which the person (and the future of the planet) is no longer at the center, to innovate is a question of attitude—a form of thinking. It is the translation of solidarity, sharing, collaboration. The mission of cultural organizations is therefore to

> recognize every single person's cultural identity, to have the person at the centre of political and public policies again, to reaffirm the principles of freedom and human dignity, and to work concretely to bring humanity together. Cultural rights is at the same time a concept, a posture, a process.
>
> *(Patrice Meyer-Bish)*

Innovation is in all the projects and actions they have organized.

Additionally, the organization thinks that institutions are making a big confusion between "innovation" and "technological tools." For instance, today the EU, the region and local institutions all ask for "Digital projects," as if it is *the* solution to all crises. Another example is the EU making an effort to support only very big organizations, and forcing smaller ones to disappear.

The organization's strengths are the beliefs that better cohabitation is possible, that (international) cooperation is necessary, and that human beings are the solution. To never stop asking themselves how to innovate and what for, and to link it not only with their own actions, but as a part of a building of our society. The supporting and presenting of high-quality art works are also a big strength. They work on strongly lobbying for their projects and for the commitments to cultural rights and sustainable human development, in which ethics are the driving force in order to include three axes, the social, economic and ecological axes, and the issue of Cultural Rights as a process.

The project is funded by France: Ministry of Culture, Regional Council South, Département des Bouche du Rhône, City of Marseille. The annual budget for the projects is €110,000.

They have two "contract workers" (*intermittent du spectacle*), a full-time employee, two civic volunteer services and thirty volunteers. The Instants Vidéo Numériques et Poétiques is committed to long-term local to international cooperation, having built a constellation of diverse partners like:

- festivals & biennales
- producers & distributors
- those engaged in artistic creation: artists, ateliers, foundations
- spaces for art presentations: museums, galleries, theatres, public spaces, restaurants and shops, art & new technologies centers, mediatheques, and libraries
- public institutions—embassies and consulates, cultural institutes, municipalities
- ducation and training—universities, schools of art, cinema and design
- media—web TV, magazines, radio

The Instants Vidéo Numériques et Poétiques is committed to different forms of actions, including:

- sharing of expertise—co-creation of festival, artists & other professional intermediation, mentoring of artists and organizations, conferences, jurying in festivals;
- artistic curatorship—exhibitions, screening programs, representing and intermediation; and knowledge sharing through publications, workshops, lectures, archives, and digital libraries.

Innovation: The mission of cultural organizations is, therefore, to

> recognize every single person's cultural identity, to have the person at the centre of political and public policies again, to reaffirm the principles of freedom and human dignity, and to work concretely to bring humanity together. … Cultural rights are at the same time a concept, a posture, a process.
>
> *(Patrice Meyer-Bish)*

Innovation is in all the projects and actions they have organized.

The organization thinks that institutions are making a big confusion between "innovation" and "technological tools." For instance, today the EU, the region and local institutions all ask for "Digital projects," as if it is *the* solution to all crises. Another example is the EU making an effort to support only very big organizations, and forcing smaller ones to disappear.

City of Reims

Based on interview with Mrs Marion Grange Doyard, head of department, cultural development, directorate of culture, City of Reims.

Reims, the *City of Art and History*, has a lot to offer.[554] In addition to its art deco architecture and its Gallo-Roman ruins, one can visit its museums and learn more about the history of the city. As a cultural city, Reims has a lot to offer in terms of culture and art. Music, dance, theater, circus, or opera—there is something for everyone. Shows and concerts at La Cartonnerie; dance, music and circus shows at the Manège, scène nationale-Reims; classic and contemporary plays at La Comédie; a rich lyrical program (operas, operettas, ballets…) at l'Opéra de Reims. The city of Reims has two cinemas, one of which is located on the famous Place d'Erlon in the heart of the city.

The public service missions for culture are:

- books and reading: three media libraries and four libraries, museums: one fine arts, four historic;
- artistic education: one conservatory of music, dance, theatre;
- scientific culture: one planetarium;
- heritage protection, enhancement and restoration;
- creation, dissemination and amateur practices: three dedicated venues;
- summer activities, art practice workshops, exhibitions;
- arts and culture education in schools;
- support for events, festivals (subsidies);
- support for the five labeled cultural structures (CDN, SMAC, CNCM, Opera House, national stage); and
- information, communication.

The users are residents and associations.

The innovation is seeing the implementation of a citizen and professional consultation approach through to write a cultural guidelines diagram (2019–2023), and preparing a bid for the European Capital of Culture. The strength of Reims is the richness and diversity of cultural proposals on the territory, associated with cooperation and structuring. The weakness is the large size of the community and the offer in the territory generating a certain inertia. Different policies depend on the communities, which choose to favor certain areas of action.

The situation can be improved with the cooperation of actors. A city is financed by state grants but also by the various taxes collected. A patronage policy is committed to restoring heritage. There is no specific budget for creative industries. The budget for culture is €31 million. They cooperate with the state, the region, the department, and development is underway with European institutions as part of the CEC application.

Innovation: Innovation is seeing the implementation of a citizen and professional consultation approach through to write a cultural guidelines diagram (2019–2023), and preparing a bid for the European Capital of Culture. The strength of Reims is the richness and diversity of cultural proposals on the territory, associated with cooperation and structuring. The weakness is the large size of the community and the offer in the territory generating a certain inertia. Different policies depend on the communities, which choose to favor certain areas of action.

City of Grenoble

Based on interview with Mrs. Marianne Taillibert, Museum of Grenoble, Head of Communication, in charge of sponsorship.

The Grenoble Museum is a municipal museum. The Grenoble Museum is a fine arts museum created at the end of the 18th century, making it now more than 200 years old. Its collections cover a long period of the history of art—from the 12th century until the most contemporary tendencies of the 21st century. Every year, the museum organizes three temporary exhibitions: two within the museum (to enhance the collections and to give an account of contemporary creation) and one outside the walls, in a district of the city of Grenoble (to reach out to the public who do not come to the museum). Numerous activities and events (visits, workshops, evening events, conferences, etc.) are offered to the widest possible audience.

The museum is located in the heart of the city of Grenoble, but it extends to the region Auvergne Rhône Alpes and beyond. The public is very varied—30% are group visits and 70% are individual visitors; 30% are under the age of 26; 40,000 schoolchildren visit; 40% are inhabitants of the Metropolis. The public is: people within proximity, amateur, leisure, school, tourist, early childhood, works councils, etc. The museum also offers facilities for people with disabilities and those who are socially or culturally excluded.

Activities in the museum are: free visits to the exhibitions and collections, guided tours, workshops for young people, night visits for students, visits to the sculpture park, readings and shows based on the works of art. The associations Musée en musique and Les Amis du musée offer a program of 40 concerts in the auditorium. The first offers 40 concerts in the auditorium and short musical sessions in the exhibitions, while the second offers about 30 lectures and cultural outings. Spaces (auditorium, large gallery, patio) are rented for events organized by external parties, the *bibliothèque, restaurant et boutique indépendants.*

Innovations: the first pioneer was the curator Andry Farcy who, as early as 1920, brought modern art to the Grenoble Museum (Picasso, Matisse, and many others). As such, the Grenoble Museum was historically the first museum of modern art in France and its collection remains quite exceptional in the European museum landscape. It is also one of the first museums, twenty years ago, to have made exhibitions outside the walls (in public places in the neighborhood—library, social center, youth center, hospital—an immersion that gives rise to a work of construction with the actors of the neighborhood). Another innovation is the "Nocturnes pour les étudiants" (Night Performances for Students) where the young people are the mediators of an evening around a work of their choice—more than 3000 students were present.

Other innovations in the reception of the public are partnerships with actors in the social field (e.g. Secours Populaire) for dedicated receptions of families at the museum.

The innovation came more from the museum teams than from the outside. It would be interesting to better inform and sensitize the teams on innovative techniques and approaches and to put in touch the innovative industries and companies with the cultural actors.

The strengths are a collection of masterpieces that continues to grow; a dynamic program of temporary exhibitions; a wide range of services offered to the public; a good reputation; the attachment of the public to their museum; a location in the heart of the city. The exhibition programs attract a diverse public, from amateurs to first-time visitors. The other actors perceive this dynamic that has allowed them to develop loyalty and to increase the number of visitors. The weakness is digital mediation and enhancing the value of the permanent collections.

To improve the current situation, the museum has to develop a partnership policy, and tourism even if Grenoble is not a touristic destination. In addition, a presentation of innovations could raise awareness among the teams. Sources of funding are the City of Grenoble (budget voted by the city council) with more than 95%; a subsidy from the Department of Isère; very occasional aid from the Ministry of Culture; and sponsorships (club of companies whose sponsorship is directed mainly towards the acquisition of works). There is no budget dedicated to innovation. The museum has partnerships with major national museums (Musée du Louvre, Centre Pompidou, Musée d'Orsay, Musée Picasso, etc.) and international museums for the programming of exhibitions. The museum establishes local partnerships with the school and university world, as well as with economic, social, and tourist organizations, in order to develop and diversify its policy of welcoming the public.

Innovations: The first pioneer was the curator Andry Farcy who, as early as 1920, brought modern art to the Grenoble Museum (Picasso, Matisse, and many others). As such, the Grenoble Museum was historically the first museum of modern art in France and its collection remains quite exceptional in the European museum landscape. It is also one of the first museums, twenty years ago, to have made exhibitions outside the walls (in public places in the neighborhood—library, social center, youth center, hospital— an immersion that gives rise to a work of construction with the actors of the neighborhood). Another innovation is the "Nocturnes pour les étudiants" (night performances for students) where the young people are the mediators of an evening around a work of their choice—more than 3000 students were present.

Other innovations in the reception of the public are partnerships with actors in the social field (e.g. Secours Populaire) for dedicated receptions of families at the museum.

There are free visits to the exhibitions and collections, guided tours, workshops for young people, night visits for students, visits to the sculpture park, readings and shows based on the works of art. The associations Musée en musique and Les Amis du musée offer a program of 40 concerts in the auditorium. The first offers 40 concerts in the auditorium and short musical sessions in the exhibitions, while the second offers about 30 lectures and cultural outings. Spaces (auditorium, large gallery, patio) are rented for events organized by external parties, *bibliothèque, restaurant et boutique indépendants*. The innovation came more from the museum teams than from the outside. It would be interesting to better inform and sensitize the teams on innovative techniques and approaches and to put in touch the innovative industries and companies with the cultural actors.

City of Mannheim

Based on interview with Mr. Matthias Rausch, Head of Innovation department, Next Mannheim.

The City of Mannheim[555] is a regional center with a rich cultural offering. Mannheim is recognized for its institutionally established cultural sector (museums, theaters, festivals, cinemas) and lively independent creative scene. Mannheim's Cultural Office supports many projects and serves as a consultant, moderator, supporter, cooperation partner and promoter of cultural and artistic initiatives from the visual and performing arts, to film, photography, literature, music and pop culture. Mannheim's multitude of intercultural activities plays a constructive role in shaping the strategic objectives of the city, based on being "open for urbanity, open for others, open for creativity, and open for commitment."

Music is deeply etched into Mannheim's history. A long-standing leader and innovator, Mannheim has an extraordinary infrastructure for music. The "Mannheim Music Model"—Mannheim's support network—has received particular attention. Mannheim sees music as a driver for artistic, economic, educational, and urban policy development.

The added value: introducing other UNESCO Cities of Music to the "Mannheim Music Model" through a new project called "Delegation Tour"; actively participating in the UCCN's Annual Meetings while designing innovative and effective working methods and strategies both for the seven creative fields and the global Network;[556] initiating a music-literature symposium "Twin Cities Project" with Edinburgh and Glasgow; organizing an international symposium for young culture managers; continuing to support candidate cities to the UCCN in the field of music; and increasing the international scope of Mannheim's music festivals.

Mannheim has an impressive vibrant city life. Mannheim offers an attractive and dynamic environment for start-ups and corporate networks. Mannheim enjoys an outstanding position as a business location. Economic strength, employment development, quality of life, retail trade, or real estate market—amongst the largest German cities Mannheim is always ranked as one of the front-runners in current city comparisons.

Next Mannheim is a public company that is owned 100% by the City of Mannheim. It supports the entire start-up ecosystem, including entrepreneurs in the cultural and creative industries.

In the cultural urban development department, of which Rausch is head, there are three main objectives: to initiate and promote interdisciplinary projects at the intersection of art/culture, business, technology and science; to initiate and support place making projects primarily through creative interventions; to support the entire realm of night culture and night-time economy through the position of the first night mayor in Germany and the activities are at the city of Mannheim and region.

The stakeholders are the entire realm of the cultural and creative industries, culture, as well as stakeholders from the fields of business, entrepreneurship, technology, and science.

Next Mannheim works on several innovation projects. It has initiated innovation projects at the intersection of music and medicine (technology), where it cooperated with the University Hospital Mannheim, the Fraunhofer Institute IAO, several music industry stakeholders and artists and musicians. It realized projects in the oncological day-care unit of the hospital and developed a prototype for neurosurgeries where people are brought back into consciousness during the operation and a person is communicating with them in order not to harm the language center of the brain, for instance.

Next Mannheim is also working on the topic of urban sound design, investigating the question of what role music and sound can play in the urban environment and in urban development. Moreover, the company is developing projects that are looking to integrate artistic thinking in entrepreneurial contexts.

The support for the cultural and creative industries in Mannheim has been exceptional. This has a lot to do with the mayor, Dr Peter Kurz, who has supported culture and the creative industries. Mannheim has put into place a unique support structure, particularly for music and the music industry, which is considered a best practice nationally and internationally and which played a big part in Mannheim being accepted into the UNESCO Creative Cities network. There are fairly strong regional networks supporting culture and the cooperation with the state of Baden-Württemberg has also brought several projects in Mannheim to fruition.

Mannheim has also greatly benefited from the EU in terms of financial support for the numerous hubs that the city has built during the last almost 20 years (mostly EFRE funds).

Moreover, Next Mannheim thinks that the EU funding schemes have increasingly become better at identifying and supporting the central role of the cultural and creative industries with regard to their innovation potential also for other sectors and industries. Rausch believes that both more sector-specific support and more support for cross-innovation and co-creative projects is needed. What has largely been overlooked on the EU level is a structured support for the intersection of culture/cultural and creative industries and urban development, an aspect that has been paramount in Mannheim.

Transcending silos and working at the intersection of disciplines. Seeing and using the creative industries as drivers of innovation also for other sectors and industries. The strength is vast support infrastructure both in terms of hubs and detailed support structures for creative industries, particularly music. We have there is a lack of sufficient monetary funds and better funding and more budgets are required. More participatory projects and an even better integration of a broad range of different stakeholders is also necessary. The innovative trends are cross-innovation and co-creation. The main funds are provided by the city of Mannheim, but it usually also brings in funds from partners and sponsors in order to realize projects. The department has an annual budget around of €50,000 in total.

Next Mannheim cooperates with a large number of companies and institutions, both on a local, regional and state and international level. It has cooperated on various levels with the EU and has projects at national, state, regional and local levels. These are too numerous to elaborate here in detail, but Rausch would be happy to share them during a conversation.

Innovation: Next Mannheim works on several innovation projects. It has initiated innovation projects at the intersection of music and medicine (technology), where it cooperated with the University Hospital Mannheim, the Fraunhofer Institute IAO, several music industry stakeholders and artists and musicians. The company realized projects in the oncological day-care unit of the hospital and developed a prototype for neurosurgeries where people are brought back into consciousness during the operation and a person is communicating with them in order not to harm the language center of the brain, for instance. The support for the cultural and creative industries in Mannheim has been exceptional. This has a lot to do with the mayor, Dr Peter Kurz, who has supported culture and the creative industries. Mannheim has put into place a unique support structure, particularly for music and the music industry, that is considered a best practice nationally and internationally and which played a big part in Mannheim being accepted into the UNESCO Creative Cities network.

There are fairly strong regional networks supporting culture and the cooperation with the state of Baden-Württemberg has also brought several projects in Mannheim to fruition.

The strengths of the company are transcending silos and working at the intersection of disciplines. Seeing and using the creative industries as drivers of innovation also for other sectors and industries. The strengths are a vast support infrastructure both in terms of hubs and detailed support structures for creative industries, particularly music. The innovative trends are cross-innovation and co-creation.

City of Dortmund

Based on interviews with Mr Olaf Ginzel and Mrs Daniela Bekemeier, directors of FG DESIGN UG.

Dortmund is the 8th-largest city in Germany and a vibrant center within the Ruhr area.[557] In the course of its history, Dortmund has had many titles – Free Imperial City, Hanseatic City, center of industry, football capital—but one thing has remained constant: its function as a driver of change across the region. Dortmund is now a city of medium-sized companies and an important reference for technology, digitization, education, and services. It has transformed from a "city of coal, steel and beer" into a high-technology location, which people from many different cultures like to call home. Dortmund is known today for its lively multicultural community, its start-ups, and its innovative entrepreneurs. The city has embraced its industrial heritage and made it an integral part of its attractiveness. The city's inhabitants enjoy an attractive mix of green areas, commercial and leisure areas, and residential spaces.

Investment in culture is important for its own sake, but culture is also key to any progress in sustainable and resilient cities. Culture is an engine for urban economic development and contributes directly to enhancing the quality of life of citizens. It is increasingly at the heart of local development agendas, and its connection to other areas is becoming more evident. This is also a clear trend at EU level, which is reflected in more and more transversal European policies and programs where culture is connected to other policies. Dortmund promotes cultures a means of social change: using culture to improve relationships between people; promoting links between creative industries and culture; and exchanging best practice for improving quality of life through cultural experiences and development.[558]

Olaf Ginzel and Daniela Bekemeier, are founders of the Gallery Project and Olaf is the Managing Director of FG DESIGN UG (FG DESIGN UG is the legal registered company name behind the gallery project. It exhibits international artists, all active in the genre of urban contemporary art and contemporary art).

The area of activities are: local (Dortmund, Germany) and regional (NRW, Germany). From a gallery perspective, it mainly has global clients.

The target groups are: people interested in art; people interested in contemporary art; people interested in urban art, street art, graffiti, etc. The gallery is active in: solo and group shows, art fairs from time to time, pop-up shows outside its location and region, online and social media presentations and promotion of its activities and artists' art presentations, active collaboration with a non-profit organization, realizing urban projects like mural paintings, workshops, etc. The organization does not know how to define innovation.

For the gallery's non-profit urban projects, it applied for governmental (local or regional) funding multiple times. In some cases, even funding from the EU had been applied. In general, the bureaucratic efforts must be cut down to make it possible for small institutions like the gallery to participate.

The main competitors of the gallery are active in a national or European context and, when compared on that level, the company faces disadvantages because of its location in Germany and, unfortunately, the city (Dortmund). The main competitors have a straighter profile and due to larger teams, they are probably much more active in terms of social media representation. Improving the situation would imply looking for more global networking via social media in order to raise larger awareness on the company's profile and on what it is doing, as well as trying to find a co-financing investor. The innovative trends for the gallery are global community networking, Instagram, etc. The gallery has private financing with help from the bank. The budget is €40–50,000 per year. The international cooperation is quite limited because of bureaucracy.

Innovation: The innovative trends for gallery are global community networking, social networks and platforms (Instagram, Twitter, Facebook, etc.), visitors and citizens interested in art. The company does not know how to define innovation. To improve the situation and innovation would imply looking for more global networking via social media in order to raise larger awareness on the company's profile. It needs to have a straighter profile in terms of innovation and be much more active regarding social media representation.

Analysis: In the second focus group of the research, we conclude that innovations are developed in local governments, institutions, and organizations. The development of technology contributes to technological innovation, but social innovation is in the first position in the process of development of the cultural sector supported by technological innovation, and it is connected with tech innovation processes. The City of Rome deals with innovation through innovative local cultural projects and developing innovation through creative industries and tourism. The municipality deals with innovation and we identified three innovative local cultural projects and policies that can be featured as examples of the activities being carried out in this field. The experimentation of new solutions and formats to bring high-quality contents in those areas that are furthest from the centre where cultural institutions are traditionally located, especially considering Rome's geographical features. The incentive to foster collaboration and networking among the city's cultural institutions to serve local communities is an attitude which has revealed to be essential for the production of the new format of Rome's

New Year's Eve celebration. The informal and festive atmosphere of the Opera Camion's squares, on which citizens gather long before the show and share anecdotes and knowledge on the opera, as well as chairs, pillows, and food. The most innovative aspect of this initiative is that Rome is the first city attempt in Europe to allow citizens (and not only tourists) to access museums for free with the payment of a symbolic nominal fee of 5€/year. Rethinking museums as real public places and transforming them into everyday life common spaces might be a revolutionary city cultural policy as it ignites changes both in the behavior of citizens and in the public area. The City of Rome's commitment to foster innovative trends is having a positive impact on Roman citizens' wellbeing and cultural life. The City of Rome is creating a new data observatory aimed towards measuring cultural participation and its impact on citizens' trust and wellbeing. This work will be enriched by a cross-analysis of Big Data and will be increasingly intertwined with the objectives and targets of the administrative departments. A growing number of active citizens are creating cultural experiences at grassroots level. The city is seeking to find a balance that encourages this development, while ensuring that public spaces remain shared by all, and is using cultural institutions to make sure that communities are also linked into broader co-operative networks. New activity forms are emerging, which are built around provisional structures, or which need no new built structure at all. Examples include urban scientific walks and the rise of "urban stages" such as streets, metro stations and building façades, which can be used for a temporary cultural intervention. The City of Bologna, through the project INCREDIBOL!, is focusing more attention on creative spillovers and on culturally-based creativity and non-technological innovation for developing creative industries in Europe. Project INCREDIBOL! is promoting and supporting new business ideas in the field of cultural and creative enterprises, testing new methods of generating innovation through creative spillovers (European project URBACT Creative Spin), creating winning processes within the Public Administration using little to no financial resources. The city places more attention on creative spillovers and on culturally-based creativity and non-technological innovation for developing the creative industries in Europe. The City of Barcelona includes innovation as part of everyday action. To develop creative industries and innovation, a more integral approach to EU projects is necessary. Innovation is a part of everyday action. The Institute monitors action with data indicators, evaluates actions systematically and introduces constant innovation in programs and projects. The strength of the Institute is the proximity of dimensions, contact with local cultural stakeholders and capacity of interaction. The Barcelona Institute of Culture is better than others in monitoring and evaluating innovation. Partners from the EU view the Institute of Culture as a strong actor in the dynamic creative field and international projection.

An example is the Decidim project[559]—a digital infrastructure for participatory democracy, built entirely and collaboratively as free software. More specifically,

Decidim is a web environment (a *framework*) produced in *Ruby on Rails* that allows users to create and configure a website platform or portal, to be used in the form of a social network for democratic participation. The portal allows any organization (local city council, association, university, NGO, trade union, neighborhood, or cooperative) to create massive democratic processes for strategic planning, participatory budgeting, collaborative regulatory design, urban spaces design, and elections. It also enables the organization of in-person meetings, signing up for them, the publication of minutes, proposing points for the agenda and receiving notifications of the results. Decidim can also help organize governing bodies, councils or assemblies, the convening of consultations and referendums or channeling citizen or member initiatives to impact different decision-making processes. Overall, Decidim makes it possible to digitally structure a complete system of participatory democratic governance for any organization. Equality in the political participation of citizens is one of the fundamental principles of any democratic system, and the platform not only has to ensure equal opportunities with respect to the uses and functions, but also access right. In this sense, the entity in charge of the platform assumes the commitment to promote actions that advance in the direction of providing access and support to the platform for all citizens alike. Giving tools and resources appropriate to the platform is available to anyone who wants to use it.

The specific innovative tools for the program of the Barcelona INTERARTS organization are: Enterprise Resource Planning specific to INTERARTS (the system was developed through the collaboration of INTERARTS, accountants, information technology staff, etc.); models for cross-checking technical activities and management costs; an internal control system for the expenditures and project activities; predictive models for the general budget and analytical budget; control and management systems for the activities carried out abroad; a specialized social platform for the cultural and creative sector, which will include a social feature to facilitate contacts and the setting up of projects; a work experience program abroad for INTERARTS employees; and visiting research fellows in INTERARTS (inviting renowned professionals, especially university professors). These innovative aspects help INTERARTS achieve its objectives, and maintain the organization's international reputation and positioning among professional circles and the general public. Innovative elements are intended to help the organization's development and sustainability in the long-run. Investing in developing the organization's potential in international public relations is understood as crucially important given that this is considered a major asset to ensure the organization's capacity to adapt quickly to a fast-changing environment. At a local level, the City of Barcelona has deployed efforts to support innovation, in particular through its @22 urban development project. In the @22 district, but also elsewhere in the city, it has developed a network of art factories, mostly in dismissed locations. The Ministry of Culture of Spain has a directorate responsible for cultural industries. The City of Brussels has creative spillover projects in the city. The innovations in the organization are projects on art and science, the impact of culture on innovation and creative spillovers in cities. The developing creative industries and innovation vary from one public authority to the other, but, in general, greater awareness on the importance of cultural investment for attractiveness and economic development is necessary. The City of Marseille supports innovation in the projects and actions they have organized. The mission of cultural organizations is therefore to

> recognize every single person's cultural identity, to have the person at the centre of political and public policies again, to reaffirm the principles of freedom and human dignity, and to work concretely to bring humanity together. ... Cultural rights are at the same time a concept, a posture, a process.
>
> *(Patrice Meyer-Bish)*

The organization thinks that institutions are making a big confusion between "innovation" and "technological tools." For instance, nowadays, the EU, the region and local institutions all ask for "Digital projects," as if it is *the* solution to all crises. Another example is the EU making an effort to support only very big organizations, and forcing smaller ones to disappear. In the City of Reims, the innovation is seeing through the implementation of a citizen and professional consultation approach to write a cultural guidelines diagram (2019–2023), and prepare a bid for the European Capital of Culture. The strength of Reims is the richness and diversity of cultural proposals on the territory, associated with cooperation and structuring. The weakness is the large size of the community and the offer in the territory, which can generate a certain inertia. Different policies depend on the communities, which choose to favor certain areas of action. The City of Grenoble implements social innovation in terms of partnerships with actors in the social field. We analyzed the first pioneer of the Grenoble Museum, the curator Andry Farcy, who, as early as 1920, brought modern art to the Grenoble Museum (Picasso, Matisse and many others). As such, the Grenoble Museum was historically the first museum of modern art in France and its collection remains quite exceptional in the European museum landscape. It is also one of the first museums, twenty years ago, to have made exhibitions outside the walls (in public places in the neighborhood—library, social center, youth center, hospital—an immersion that gives rise to a work of construction with the actors of the neighborhood). Another innovation is the "Nocturnes pour les étudiants" (Night Performances for Students) where the young people are the mediators of an evening around a work of their choice—more than 3000 students were present. Other innovations in the reception of the public are partnerships with actors in the social field (e.g. Secours Populaire) for dedicated reception of families at the museum, free visits to the exhibitions and collections, guided tours, workshops for young people, night visits for students, visits to the sculpture park, readings, and shows based on works of art. The associations Musée en musique and Les Amis du musée offer a program of 40 concerts in the auditorium. The first offers 40 concerts in the auditorium and short musical sessions in the exhibitions, while the second offers about 30 lectures and cultural outings. Spaces (auditorium, large gallery, patio) are rented for events organized by external parties, *bibliothèque, restaurant et boutique indépendants*. The innovation came more from the museum teams than from the outside. It would be interesting to better inform and sensitize the teams on innovative techniques and approaches and to put in touch innovative industries and companies with cultural actors. The City of Mannheim is developing projects that are looking to integrate artistic thinking in entrepreneurial contexts. It is working on several innovation projects. It has initiated innovation projects at the intersection of music and medicine (technology), where it cooperated with the University Hospital Mannheim, the Fraunhofer Institute IAO, several music industry stakeholders and artists and musicians. It realized projects in the oncological day-care unit of the hospital and developed a prototype for neurosurgeries where people are brought back into consciousness during the operation and a person is communicating with them in order not to harm the language center of the brain, for instance. The support for the cultural and creative industries in Mannheim has been exceptional. This has a lot to do with the mayor, Dr Peter Kurz, who has supported culture and the creative industries. Mannheim has put into place a unique support structure, particularly for music and the music industry, which is considered a best practice nationally and internationally and which played a big part in Mannheim being accepted into the UNESCO Creative Cities network.

There are fairly strong regional networks supporting culture and cooperation with the state of Baden-Württemberg has also brought several projects in Mannheim to fruition.

The strengths are transcending silos and working at the intersection of disciplines and seeing and using the creative industries as drivers of innovation also for other sectors and industries. The strength is a vast support infrastructure in terms of both hubs and detailed support structures for creative industries, particularly music. The innovative trends are cross-innovation and co-creation. In the City of Dortmund, the innovative trends for the gallery are global community networking, social networks and platforms (Instagram, Twitter, Facebook, etc.), and the visitors and citizens interested in art. The company does not how to define innovation. To improve the situation and innovation means looking for more global networking via social media in order to raise larger awareness on its profile. It needs to have a straighter profile in terms of innovation and be much more active regarding social media representation.

The City of Rome, City of Mannheim and City of Bologna have programs to support the Cultural and Creative Industries (CCI), which contribute to the development of a creative economy. The developing creative industries and innovation vary from one public authority to the other, but in general, greater awareness on the importance of cultural investment for attractiveness and economic development is necessary.

TABLE 2 The Second Focus Group of Research. Author: Mickov, Biljana. 2021

	Innovation	*Culture Program (Including Culture and Creative Industries)*	*Budget for Culture Year*
City of Rome Mr Luca Bergamo Ex. Deputy Mayor for Cultural Office of the City of Rome) is the Vice Mayor in charge of cultural development.	City of Rome fosters innovative trends having a positive impact on Roman citizens' well-being and cultural life. The municipality deals with innovation through innovative local cultural projects.	Local institutions have strongly supported the emergence of cultural and creative industries in the past five years. Opera Camion project: *Building social cohesion in outlying districts via mobile satellites of major cultural institutions*, The MIC Card project: *Valuing resident cultural access in tourist dominated hotspots*, Seasons of Rome project: *Promoting contemporary and scientific culture in an ancient city*	€2.5 million per year. The Creative Economy (film industry) generates around €750 million.
City of Bologna Mr Mauro Felicori Mrs Giorga Boldrini Head of Creative Industries, Music and Urban Regeneration Unit, Municipality of Bologna.	Project INCREDIBOL! • promoting and supporting new business ideas in the field of cultural and creative enterprises. • testing new methods of generating innovation through creative spillovers (European project URBACT Creative Spin) • creating winning processes within the Public Administration using little to no financial resources. More attention on creative spillovers and on cultural-based creativity and non- technological innovation for developing the creative industries in Europe.	The INCREDIBOL! project is coordinated by the Municipality of Bologna and supported by the Emilia-Romagna Region in conjunction with around 30 public and private partners. The network is composed of around 30 partners as training bodies, legal and business consultants, micro- credit consultants and specialized institutions. The Municipality in the competing with others are better in creativity-based regeneration of public heritage.	The budget is varied. For innovative projects in creative industries: €200,000.

(*Continued*)

TABLE 2 (Continued) The Second Focus Group of Research. Author: Mickov, Biljana. 2021

	Innovation	*Culture Program (Including Culture and Creative Industries)*	*Budget for Culture Year*
City of Barcelona Mr Esteve Caramès Director for Cultural Sectors, Institut de Cultura de Barcelona.	The innovation is part of everyday action. The Institute monitors action with data indicators, evaluates actions systematically and introduces constant innovation in the programs and projects. To develop the creative industries and innovation a more integral approach to EU projects is necessary.	The programs and activities are directed towards the Barcelona municipality. The target group of service users are Barcelona's population, local cultural sectors and cultural industries. The Institute has different service activities like cultural funding, production of cultural projects and cultural policy strategic development.	€164,285,632 (2020).
City of Barcelona INTERARTS **Mercedes Giovinazzo**, Director, Fundació INTERARTS per a la Cooperació Cultural Internacional (NGO), Barcelona.	Innovative elements/tools are intended to help the organization's development and sustainability in the long-run. These innovative aspects help INTERARTS achieve its objectives, and maintain the organization's international reputation and positioning among the professional circles and the general public.	The areas of activities are Europe, Latin America and the Caribbean, Africa. The users and target group of work are CSOs (civil society organizations) of the cultural sector. INTERARTS activity areas: • Development cooperation: INTERARTS designs and implements international development cooperation projects with a cultural dimension.	€1,863,206 (2017/2018).

City of Brussels Phillipe Kern, Director of KEA European Affairs, (NGO) private research center, KEA European Affairs, City of Brussels.	The innovations in the organization are projects on art and science, impact of culture on innovation, creative spillovers in cities. The developing creative industries and innovation vary from one public authority to the other, but in general greater awareness on the importance of cultural investment for attractiveness and economic development is needed.	The topic of activities is cultural policy. The area of activities is mainly the European Union. The service users are mainly public authorities in the EU. The organization covers studies and research, and management of EU projects.	The budget is varied. The donors and funding bodies for our organization are EU institutions (Commission, Parliament, EIF).
City of Marseille Mrs Naïk M'SILI—Co-director, Instants Vidéo Numériques et Poétiques, City of Marseille	The mission of cultural organizations is to "recognize every single person's cultural identity, to have the person at the center of political and public policies again, to reaffirm the principles of freedom and human dignity, and to work concretely to bring humanity together… Cultural rights is at the same time a concept, a posture, a process." (Patrice Meyer-Bish). Innovation is in all the projects and actions it has organized.	Instants Vidéo Numériques et Poétiques work on strongly lobbying for its projects and for the commitments to cultural rights and sustainable human development. The Instants Vidéo Numériques et Poétiques is committed to: • sharing of expertise co-creation of festivals, artists & other professional intermediation, mentoring of artists and organizations, conferences, jurying at festivals; and • artistic curatorship exhibitions, screening programs, representing and intermediation, knowledge sharing through publications, workshops, lectures, archives and digital libraries.	€110,000 per year.

(*Continued*)

TABLE 2 (Continued) The Second Focus Group of Research. Author: Mickov, Biljana. 2021

	Innovation	*Culture Program (Including Culture and Creative Industries)*	*Budget for Culture Year*
City of Reims Mrs Marion Grange Doyard, head of department, cultural development, directorate of culture, City of Reims.	Innovation is seeing through the implementation of a citizen and professional consultation approach to write a cultural guidelines diagram (2019–2023), and prepare a bid for the European Capital of Culture. The strength of Reims is the richness and diversity of cultural proposals on the territory, associated with cooperation and structuring.	Reims has a lot to offer in terms of culture and art—Music, dance, theatre, circus or opera: there is something for everyone. There is no specific program for development of creative industries.	€31 million
City of Grenoble Mrs Marianne Taillibert, Museum of Grenoble, Head of communication, in charge of sponsorship, City of Grenoble.	The Grenoble Museum was historically the first museum of modern art in France. The Night Performances for Students where young people are the mediators of an evening around a work of their choice • more than 3000 students were present. Other innovations in the reception of the public: partnerships with actors in the social field (e.g., Secours Populaire) for dedicated receptions of families at the museum.	The Grenoble Museum collections cover a long time of the history of art, from the 12th century until the 21st century. Every year, it organizes three temporary exhibitions: two within the museum (to enhance the collections and to give an account of contemporary creation) and one outside the walls, in a district of the city of Grenoble (to reach out to the public who do not come to the museum).	The budget voted by the city council - more than 95%; subsidy from the Department of Isère; very occasional aid from the Ministry of Culture; sponsorships (club of companies whose sponsorship is directed mainly towards the acquisition of works). No specifically budget for innovation.

City of Mannheim Dr Matthias Rauch, cultural innovation officer, Next Mannheim	Next Mannheim is working on several innovation projects. It has initiated innovation projects at the intersection of music and medicine (technology). It realized projects in the oncological day- care unit of the hospital and developed a prototype for neurosurgeries where people are brought back into consciousness during the operation and a person is communicating with them in order not to harm the language center of the brain, for instance. It is also working on the topic of urban sound design, investigating the question of what role music and sound can play in the urban environment and in urban development. Next Mannheim is developing projects that are looking to integrate artistic thinking in Entrepreneurial contexts.	The support for the cultural and creative industries in Mannheim has been exceptional. This has a lot to do with the mayor, Dr Peter Kurz, who has supported culture and the creative industries. Mannheim has put into place a unique support structure, particularly for music and the music industry that is considered a best practice nationally and internationally and which played a big part in Mannheim being accepted into the UNESCO Creative Cities network.	€50,000 per year.
City of Dortmund Olaf Ginzel & Daniela Bekemeier Directors of FG DESIGN UG, the legal registered company name behind the gallery project.	The innovative trends for the gallery are global community networking, social networks and platforms (Instagram, Twitter, Facebook, etc.) the visitors and citizens interested in art do not how to define innovation	The programs are the exhibitions of international artists, all active in the genre of urban contemporary art and contemporary art.	€40,000–50,000 per year.

(*Continued*)

TABLE 2 (Continued) The Second Focus Group of Research. Author: Mickov, Biljana. 2021

	Innovation	*Culture Program (Including Culture and Creative Industries)*	*Budget for Culture Year*
Analyses of Qualitative Research	In the second focus group of the research, we conclude that innovations are developed in local governments, institutions, and organizations. The development of technology contributes to technological innovation, but social innovation is in the first position in the process of development of the cultural sector supported by technological innovation, and it is connected with tech innovation processes. The City of Rome deals with innovation through innovative local cultural projects and developing innovation through creative industries and tourism. The City of Bologna, through the project INCREDIBOL! is placing more attention on creative spillovers and on culturally-based creativity and non-technological innovation for developing creative industries in Europe. The City of Barcelona includes innovation as part of everyday action—monitoring action with data indicators, evaluating actions systematically and introducing constant innovation in programs and projects. To develop creative industries and innovation, a more integral approach to EU projects is necessary. The City of Brussels has creative spillover projects in the city. The City of Marseille supports innovation in projects and actions it has organized. In the City of Reims, the innovation is seeing through the implementation of a citizen and professional consultation approach to write a cultural guidelines diagram (2019–2023) and prepare a bid for the European Capital of Culture. The City of Grenoble implements social innovation in terms of partnerships with actors in the social field. The City of Mannheim is developing projects that are looking to integrate artistic thinking in entrepreneurial contexts. The City of Rome, City of Mannheim and City of Bologna have programs to support the CCI, which contribute to the development of a creative economy. The developing creative industries and innovation vary from one public authority to the other, but in general, greater awareness on the importance of cultural investment for attractiveness and economic development is necessary.		

Notes

538 "Rome," UNESCO Creative Cities Network, accessed May 10, 2021, https://en.unesco.org/creative-cities/rome
539 "Rome," UNESCO Creative Cities Network.
540 First published as *La cultura sinonimo di sviluppo urbano* in *Un'Agenda per le città. Nuove visioni per lo sviluppo urbano*, ed. Walter Vitali, Il Mulino 2014.
541 In collaboration with Giorgia Boldrini, Mauro Felicori (an Italian official linked to the world of art and culture, from October 2015 until October 2018, general manager of the Royal Palace of Caserta after having been a director of the Municipality of Bologna since 1986), since 2018, has been the director of Ago Modena Fabbriche Culturali.
542 Renato Nicolini (1942 – 2012), was an Italian architect, politician and playwright, well known in Italy and abroad as the creative mind behind the popular *Estate Romana*, a series of open-air cultural events organized by the Rome town council, when Nicolini was in charge of cultural activities, from 1977 to 1986. The program included films, theatre, concerts and literary events, and attracted vast crowds to the city monumental sites from Rome and beyond.
543 Mauro Felicori, "Culture as a Byword for Urban Development: The Italian Experience," in *The Creative City*, ed. James Doyle and Biljana Mickov (London: Routledge, 2015), 125–131.
544 Ibid.
545 Ibid.
546 Ibid.
547 Ibid.
548 Ibid.
549 Fondazione di origine bancaria: "A *foundation of banking origin* is a legal construct established by the Amato Law of 1990 in the context of the privatization and de-specialization of the Italian banking industry. The 1990 Law modernized the structure of banking institutions introducing the joint stock model and vesting bank shares in the *fondazione*. In essence, traditional state-controlled banking institutions were hived off into a joint stock company which would assume responsibility for banking operations and a *fondazione* which owned and managed the shares and pursued philanthropic goals." (Source: Jacopo Crivellaro, *Fumbling Foundations? The case of the Fondazione di Origine Bancaria in Italy*, Centre for Commercial Law and Financial Regulation, University of Reading, Working Paper, accessed March 19, 2021, https://www.reading.ac.uk/web/FILES/CCLFR/crivellaro_fondazionibancarie.pdf)
550 Esteve Caramés, "Barcelona's Cultural Policies Behind the Scenes New Context, Renewed Strategies," in *Sustaining Cultural Development, Unified Systems and New Governance in Cultural Life*, ed. James Doyle and Biljana Mickov (London: Routledge Publishing, 2013), 29–35.
551 "General Description and Introduction to How Decidim Works," Decidim, accessed April 27, 2021, https://docs.decidim.org/en/features/general-description/
552 Alex Papadopoulos, "Brussels," *Encyclopedia Britannica*, accessed May 10, 2021, https://www.britannica.com/place/Brussels
553 Marseille, accessed May 9, 2021, https://www.marseille.fr/
554 Tourist Office of Grand Reims, accessed May 10, 2021, https://www.reims-tourism.com/
555 "Mannheim," UNESCO Creative Cities Network, accessed May 9, 2021, https://en.unesco.org/creative-cities/mannheim
556 "Creative Cities Network Annual Meeting," UNESCO Creative Cities Network, accessed May 9, 2021, http://www.unesco.org/new/en/culture/themes/creativity/creative-cities-network
557 "Dortmund," Eurocities, accessed May 9, 2021, https://eurocities.eu/cities/dortmund/
558 "Culture and Creativity," Eurocities, accessed May 9, 2021, https://eurocities.eu/goals/culture-and-creativity/
559 "General Description and Introduction to How Decidim Works," Decidim.

11

THE THIRD FOCUS GROUP OF THE QUALITATIVE RESEARCH

City of Bratislava

Culture Department, City of Bratislava (the local government) Hlavné mesto Slovenskej republiky Bratislava/The capital city of the Slovak Republic Bratislava.

Bratislava is the cultural heart of Slovakia. Owing to its historical multicultural character, the city's local culture is influenced by various ethnic groups. Bratislava has numerous theaters, museums, galleries, concert halls, cinemas, film clubs, and foreign cultural institutions. The Bratislava City Council is the Department of Culture, Education, Sport and Youth. It coordinates organizations (the Bratislava City Gallery, the Bratislava City Museum, the Bratislava City Library, etc.), deals with the organization or coordination of city happenings, the agendas of grant programs for cultural happenings (exhibitions, books, theatre and dancing performances, etc.), agendas for the protection of cultural heritage, collaboration and communication with organizations and institutions from other governments, and cooperation with the Bratislava Tourist Board. The activities of the Department of Culture, Education, Sport and Youth are carried out on the territory of the capital city, Bratislava.

The target groups for culture are organizations include the Bratislava City Gallery, the Bratislava City Museum, the Bratislava City Library, the Institution for the Protection of Culture Heritage, the Bratislava Tourist Board, the Bratislava Center for Culture and Information; art schools, leisure centers, the Zoo.

The users are citizens and professional public. The local government realized the agenda for cultural grants, administrative services for citizens, professionals, and cultural organizations.

The innovation is reflected in the participation of organizations in a project with the mobile phone application KnowSpot, which provides users with information about historic buildings or interesting places either on- or offline. In order to improve the innovative and creative industries sector, it is necessary for professionals

DOI: 10.4324/9781003336648-13

to be given increased financial resources, for a reduction in the costs of information being distributed in urban spaces and for more space to be provided for these activities.

The strengths of the Culture Department are: multicultural history, rich history and tradition of arts, many institutions and organizations for culture, large spaces for cultural professionals—strong community, big interest from public, active citizens, strong space in art education—art schools with high quality.

The weaknesses of the Culture Department are: disregard for cultural heritage, weak position for young art professionals, insufficient spaces, weak collaboration between the city, region and state, weak reflection of the cultural and professional critics in media space and weak communication between art professionals with institutions.

Other local culture departments in Europe have more money for art professionals and achieve better communication between the city, region and state, as well as between professionals and institutions. Improving the situation implies developing discussions with professionals for culture.

Culture in Bratislava is financed from the city budget, which is approved by the Bratislava City parliament. Other sources of funding include project funding from the European Union (EU) and the Ministry of Culture of the Slovak Republic. The city budget for culture in 2019 was €7,200,284.

Employees, students (the trainee program), external consultants, contracted workers all work in the organization. The Culture Department of the City of Bratislava and cultural organizations work with partners from foreign countries on several projects. It is a member of the cultural forum EUROCITIES, and is working on agreement with fellow European countries such as Austria, Poland, and Italy, among others.

Innovation: The innovation is reflected in the participation of organizations on a project with the mobile phone application KnowSpot, which provides users with information about historic buildings or interesting places either on- or offline. In order to improve the innovative and creative industries sector, it is necessary for the professionals to be given more financial resources, costs of propagation for information in urban spaces to be lowered and more space for these activities to be provided. To improve the situation implies developing discussions with professionals for culture. The Culture Department of the City of Bratislava and cultural organizations work with partners foreign countries on several projects. It is a member of the cultural forum EUROCITIES, and is working on an agreement with Austria, Poland, Italy, etc.

City of Novi Sad

Novi Sad City Library (Gradska biblioteka u Novom Sadu).

City of Novi Sad—European Capital of Culture in 2022. For decades, Novi Sad has built its uniqueness on the foundations of its multicultural character and numerous cultural and educational institutions.

The basic function of the City of Novi Sad Library is to collect, process, preserve, and lend books, periodicals, non-book material and other sources of information. In addition, it provides free and open access to human knowledge and information, self-education, and formal education at all levels; it educates its members to use different sources of information independently and promotes books and reading. The activities of the library are carried out in the urban area and the suburbs of Novi Sad. The users are 25,000 library members, each of whom pay an annual membership. The members are citizens of Novi Sad (children, youth, adults, elderly citizens). As a parent library for 250 libraries in the South Backa District, the library promotes projects, and also monitors and develops library activities, so the users are also these libraries. Over 300 librarians from Serbia and the wider Balkan region attend accredited seminars which the library organizes at least once a year. Other than that, there are 30,000 visitors of the programs, 69,350 visitors of the internet page and 54,200 visitors of the Facebook page for the City Library.

The target groups are made up of a number of groups: primarily young people between the ages of 15 and 30 (students in high schools and universities), children, members of marginalized social groups, technological innovation fans, etc. The services offered by the library include: book lending, reservations, information service upon user's request; thematic database search, use of popular scientific literature and reference collection, free internet access, photocopying, scanning, printing, saving material to various electronic media or emailing; use of sets for learning the English and German language, foreign languages learning programs; the use of the Local History Collection; book home delivery service for specific categories of users; cultural and educative programs for adults; workshops and educational contents for children and youth, programs for the quality use of spare time; and librarians' professional specialization programs.

The innovation projects and processes promoted by the library are: the digitalization of the Local History Collection; library on the beach during summer, on the banks of the Danube; book home delivery service for the elderly, the sick, the pregnant, and for those who are unable to come to the library due to the severe invalidity or other causes; the "Language Drama Lab," a festival of English-language drama; Democratization of Digitalization (a service for the self-use of the smartphone), new library branch for young people with maker-space and many contemporary contents. These actions have had many a number of impacts on the organization: an increased number of library users, increased consciousness of the importance of the library, bringing the library closer to young people, easier and more comfortable usage of the cultural heritage, etc.

Programs for the Development of Innovation and Creative Industries

There are many programs for cultural development and the library is a part of the EUTEKA network, conducted by the Delegation of the European Union for Serbia. The library has also taken part in certain activities of EUROPEANA projects. It has a diverse cooperation with members of EUNIC.

IPA projects are a very potent way of fund raising, but also very demanding in procedures. Regarding European projects, pre-financing, finding partners, as well as certain areas of project management, there are insurmountable difficulties, especially when the state's place a ban on new employment.

The strengths of the library are: that a large percentage of the employed are professionals (71%); that it possesses a large selection of library materials and has access to a huge amount of information; that it is well-equipped with IT technology; that it has a stable source of financing, a long tradition, and, as a formal institution, that it represents an eligible partner; that competences are clearly divided within the systematization of jobs when the core business is concerned; that there is a good tracking of business results when the core business is concerned; and that it is a well-known institution.

The library of Novi Sad tries to involve young people in its activities and offers them a chance to create their own cultural development. It has extended its field of competence to diverse areas, such as electronic media, formal and informal education in arts and computers, and programming. It plans to equip a workshop for maker space. The library has a practice of engaging volunteers. In addition, it has a long tradition, formal institutionalization, visibility and well-educated human resources in certain areas of expertise.

The weaknesses are: inadequate space for performing activities (old building, lack of storage space and space for performing activities); lack of motivation and lack of interest of employees due to the lack of reward and punishment practices; an insufficient number of employees to pursue activities outside the core business, a lack of skills required for modern business (knowledge of foreign languages, IT skills, project management); stable funding according to the annual plan, which prevents flexibility within the financial process; the mismatch in the systematization of jobs with the needs of the modern library (unclear job descriptions and situations in which "one does everything, ten do nothing"); complicated procedures and rigid administration; insufficient links with other cultural institutions in the city; and inadequate monitoring of the results for the activities concerning modern business.

There is no competition for the core business in the local area. Regarding culture and programs in general, the library's competition is better in project management and focusing on fewer, well-selected ones. The situation could be reduced by cutting down the number of activities, orienting toward fewer of them, and building a purpose-built library.

Digitalization and online services are the innovative trends that would help make the virtual library accessible to remote users and youth. More extensive engagement of volunteers would also improve its work. The sources of funding are the Ministry of Culture and Information, and the Provincial Secretariat for Culture, Public Information and Relations with Religious Communities. Among the foreign donors are the British Council and a number of embassies, but these donations are mostly in the form of books.

The average annual budget for innovation is 2,000,000 RSD (€170.000). The library is well equipped in technological resources. There are 80 employees, with

57 of them being professionals (librarians). Most of them have studied Serbian literature and language, and all of them have passed the professional exams. The library is well connected to organizations of all types, on local, national, and international levels. Its international cooperation is mainly centered around the library branch "Anica Savic Rebac," which contains library materials in 12 foreign languages and conducts programs with members of EUNIC.

Innovation: The innovation projects and processes are: the digitalization of the Local History Collection; library on the beach during summer, on the banks of the Danube; book home delivery service for the elderly, the sick, the pregnant, and for those who are unable to come to the library due to severe invalidity or other causes; the "Language Drama Lab," festival of drama in English; Democratization of Digitalization (service for self-use of the smart phone); and a new library branch for young people with maker-space and many contemporary contents. The impacts of these actions are many: an increased number of library users, increased consciousness of the importance of the library, bringing the library closer to young people, easier and more comfortable usage of the cultural heritage, etc. The Library of Novi Sad tries to involve young people in its activities and offers them a chance to create their own cultural development. The library has extended its field of competence to diverse areas, including electronic media, formal and informal education in arts and computers, and programming. It plans to equip a workshop for makers' spaces. The library has a practice of engaging volunteers. It also has a long tradition, formal institutionalization, visibility, and well-educated human resources in certain areas of expertise.

Cities of Kiev/Moscow/Eindhoven

Stichting Art-East+Art-West (NGO)[560]

The organization has been developing cultural projects, curating exhibitions and consulting governmental and private institutions on strategic cultural issues (art, design, landscape architecture). The areas of the projects are: the Netherlands, Russia, Ukraine. The target group of activities are the general public, architects, designers, and art professionals. The most frequent services are exhibitions and consultations on cultural activities. The innovation present in the 2014 exhibition in Moscow, Dialog with Water, in which the organization showed a new ecological approach to solving the problems of flooding. It also included innovation in the assignment for exhibitions of Creative Ukraine at Dutch Design Week. In Oranskaia's opinion, the result was weak.

The projects on innovations and creative industries are very well developed. In the region of Eindhoven, the organization is doing a very good job, especially in comparison to Eastern European countries. Oranskaia thinks paying more attention to the EU neighboring countries with creative potential and different view would help produce new innovative ideas.

The strengths of the organization are in the area of understanding differences in mentalities and knowledge of problems and strengths in different countries, which allows it to introduce the right solution to the problem. The organization is innovative in terms of combining the Eastern European and Dutch approaches. Other organizations and cultural institutions perceive that the organization has experience in different fields, such as cultural projects and the knowledge of different mentalities. The weaknesses of the organization are a lack of ability to accumulate finances for the projects, establishing/maintaining the relationship with foundations and distributing the subsidies. Usually, there is support for projects but they do not come to fruition. Improvement in the organization would entail make better networking with local organizations and greater cooperation with other people from Eindhoven.

The innovative trend that positively impacts the organization is cooperation between designers and scientists.

The main sources of funding for the organization are as follows: the Ministry of Foreign Affairs and Ministry of Economics in the Netherlands; the Enterprise Europe Network; the Ministry of Foreign Affairs of Ukraine; the Ukrainian Institute; and private companies in the Netherlands, Russia, and Ukraine.

The annual budget is €20,000–50,000.

The governmental institutions are mostly quite cooperative, while international institutions think that the foundation is too small. The organization has partners/employees for every project, computers and other electronic devices and no permanent employees. The organization maintains very good contacts with professionals in art, design and architecture in the Netherlands, Russia, and Ukraine. For every separate project it consults experts in the necessary fields.

Innovation: The innovative trend that positively impacts the organization is cooperation between designers and scientists. This innovation was present, for example, in the 2014 exhibition in Moscow, "Dialog with Water," in which it showed a new ecological approach to solve problems of flooding. It also included innovation into the assignment for exhibitions of Creative Ukraine during the Dutch Design Week. In Oranskaia's opinion, the result was weak. The projects on innovations and creative industries are very well developed. In the region of Eindhoven, the organization is doing a very good job, especially in comparison with Eastern European countries. Oranskaia thinks paying more attention to the neighboring EU countries with creative potential and a different view would help produce new innovative ideas.

The organization is innovative in terms of combining the Eastern European and Dutch approaches. Other organizations and cultural institutions perceive that the organization has experience in different fields such as cultural projects and knowledge of different mentalities.

City of Belgrade

Museum of Contemporary Art Belgrade, City of Belgrade

Belgrade is the center of culture and art of Serbia.[561] It is in this city that the most notable artists create, where over 11.000 theatrical performances, exhibitions, concerts, performance events, and other artistic programs are presented and where prominent authors in the world of art are hosted. Belgrade is the center of the highest state and national institutions of culture and art. These include: the Serbian Academy of Arts and Sciences, the National Library of Serbia, the National Museum, the National Theatre, and the University of Arts. It is Belgrade where the most significant works of architecture are located, with Kalemegdan accommodating the Belgrade Fortress, cultural monuments and other immovable cultural treasures, numerous archaeological sites with remnants of developed civilizations and culture on the territory of Belgrade from prehistory until today. The City of Belgrade is the founder of 30 cultural institutions (12 theatres, 8 institutions for the protection of cultural values, 4 libraries, and 6 cultural centers and galleries) and, at the same time, contributes to the implementation of schedules and scheduled attractions of institutions and artistic associations. The Secretariat of Culture within the City Administration is in charge of the areas of culture and art. The museum is a modern institution that organizes exhibitions, musicological activities of preservation of the cultural heritage, talk programs, educational programs, etc.

The Secretariat operates in Serbia and in collaboration with its counterpart institutions in Europe. The target groups are schoolchildren, the art community, people with disabilities, general public, etc. The activities are guided tours, children and youth club workshops, talks related to the topics of the exhibitions, artists' talks, etc.

Innovation is not a tangible concept that could be analyzed in the case of this museum. It does not deal with the creative industries. The strengths are a good technical team, in-house graphic designers and the quality of its publications. The problems, which can be described in terms of the extent to which they hamper innovation, are that the museum needs to educate staff, since it is the most important understaffed institution, and that employees, in general, do not speak any foreign languages. The museum has a partner institution. Its donors are the Ministry of Culture and Information, Serbia and ERSTE Foundation, Austria. The annual budget is €70,000–90,000 annually for all programs.

The museum has different departments.[562] It has solid but not up-to-date technical equipment for exhibitions. In addition, it has good connections and partnerships with a number of local institutions such as the Museum of Contemporary Art of Vojvodina, the only other museum of this kind in Serbia. It has also had a number of collaborations with international institutions, including Tate Modern, Stedelijk Museum, Artium-Basque Museum, etc.

Innovation: Innovation is not a tangible concept that could be analyzed in the case of this museum. The innovation can be seen through the programs that the institution delivers over the course of a year.

BAZAART, Representative Association in Culture, Belgrade

BAZAART is an association.[563] It is involved in a range of artistic and cultural activities: theater and drama, culture, education, community art work and advocacy. It realizes its program principally in Serbia and the Western Balkans region, as well as cooperating with partners from Europe through EU-funded projects (and other donors) The target groups and members are: artists, cultural operators, and educators.

The service users are the general public (through events and productions); the expert public—that is, other artists and many teachers (through training schemes, conferences, workshops, published manuals, etc.); and children and youth (through creative workshops and productions).

The target groups of the association are the same as the above (service users). The most realized programs of the association are: development of drama texts (scripts) for school-aged and young audiences; theatre-in-education productions; workshops—both creative and educational, mostly for the young; organizing horizontal education workshops (exchange among colleagues—artists and teachers); accredited training in drama/theater-based methodologies for learning and education, for teachers, approved by the Institute for Educational Development of Serbia; organizing annual national conferences with international participation on topics of inter-sectorial cooperation of culture and education; organizing a festival of children's theatre creativity "Theatre in the Park"; the publication of manuals, compendia, collections of dramas etc., which are made available free for download; and different advocacy activities, aiming at the advancement of cultural and educational policies.

BAZAART develops new methodologies for learning through drama and theater. Under the auspices of the IDEAL project, it invented the Intercultural Learning through Drama methodology, which is published on-line and widely implemented by the association and others. Another example is the "Tolerant Classroom" collection of workshops, which aim to promote tolerance, inclusion, and cooperation among schoolchildren (both available on the website for BAZAART). Also, drama texts are staged across the region.

All BAZAART's products (methods, plays, books) aim for better socialization and improvement of empathy among youth and in schools and communities. The association also promotes cultural models which are accessible to all. This goes really slowly. With regard to the innovations, mechanisms should be established as to how to mainstream them in general cultural and educational systems. The decision-makers have practically no contact with the "base" practice. This should be changed first.

The strengths of this organization include: expertise, activism, talent, vision, and contacts. Also, the organization has better management capacities, which enhance its impact. It has been seen as an innovator, expert, and visionary. The weakness of the organization is the small number of people and hence its limited operational capacities, as the association does not have working space for workshops, rehearsals, and productions, and has unstable financing.

In an operational sense, if the association succeeds in getting a larger project, it can rent the space and hire the staff. In terms of impact, it can improve the competences of teachers, artists, and cultural operators for co-operating on solving social issues. In the order of importance, the issues it addresses are: the democratization of society; the modernization of cultural, and educational systems; better financing for the civic sector; and the establishment of a university program in theatre and/or cultural education.

The main donors for the organization are: the Ministry of Culture, the Ministry of Education, the City of Belgrade, the EU, and other international donors. The annual budget of the organization changes from year to year. It is very small—from domestic funds, no more than €4.000 per year. In the association, there are no employees at the moment, only volunteers. The human resources are artists, teachers, and activists. The organization cooperates with other civil society organizations (CSOs); it has initiated the establishment of a platform for theatre education organizations. With institutions, cooperation is formal—they allow the organization to use their space and technical resources for the annual conference. The association is also developing cooperation contacts with the ministries.

Innovation: BAZAART develops new methodologies for learning through drama and theater. In the IDEAL project, it invented the Intercultural Learning through Drama methodology, which is published on-line and has been widely implemented by the organization and others. Another example is the "Tolerant Classroom" collection of workshops, which aims to promote the development of tolerance, inclusion, and cooperation among schoolchildren (both available on the BAZAART website). Also, drama texts are staged across the region. As for innovations, mechanisms have to be established as to how to mainstream them in general cultural and educational systems. The decision-makers have practically no contact with the "base" practice. This have to be changed first. BAZAART has been seen as an innovator, expert, and visionary. The weakness of the association is its small scale and hence its limited operational capacities. The association does not have working space for workshops, rehearsals and productions, and has unstable sources of funding.

City of Gabrovo

Museum of Humour and Satire,[564] *City of Gabrovo*

The Museum of Humour and Satire is a museum for humor, cartoons, comic strips, contemporary art, contemporary culture, jokes and storytelling, and carnivals. The main activities of the museum are realized in the City of Gabrovo and its surroundings. In addition it stages travelling exhibitions, and programs which are implemented both nationwide and internationally. The target groups for the museum are tourists and local audiences. The museum has different activities, including: exhibitions, events, and educational programs (workshops, cinema, performances, lectures, discussions, concerts). In terms of innovation policy, the museum has been dealing with change, but not really innovation. Introducing change in institutions that are conservative by nature, such as museums, is a slow and difficult process. Some projects have been considered innovative without essentially being such. Both change and innovation are a matter of communication; however, innovation is often too far ahead to be possibly communicated.

Governments in the region are generally well designed for innovation. Both innovation and entrepreneurial approaches require systematic investment in human capital, which is quite a contradiction in aging and demographically endangered areas.

The strengths of the museum are the unique profile of the institution in terms of organizational ethos: institutional ambition, boldness and the strong international network. In the level of innovation in comparison with others, the museum does not shy away from difficult topics and humor offers a good context to address taboos and subjects that society generally does not feel comfortable with. Actually, the main strength is humor and having fun.

The weakness is scaling activities and quick development, which is very difficult in a very narrow job market. Professional mobility is very unusual in Bulgaria, so the museum is unable to attract experts from elsewhere either. It has done better than other institutions in terms of the level of networks. To improve the museum, it needs a physical environment for the museum and its visibility. Innovative trends to improve the museums would entail making increased use of digital content. The sources of financing for the museum are: the local government, the Ministry of Culture, foundations, and Creative Europe. The average budget for innovation and cultural projects is €20,000 euro for more innovative work. The museum has 26 employees, the usual museum facilities and more than 5000 square meters of exhibition and administrative space. In terms of cooperation, the museum has a good institutional network, but there is much to be improved. It works very well with all local organizations and businesses.

Innovation: In terms of innovation policy, the museum has been dealing with change, but has not really been innovative. Introducing change in institutions that are conservative by nature, such as museums, is a slow and difficult process. Some projects have been considered innovative without essentially being such. Both change and innovation are a matter of communication; however, innovation is often too far ahead to be possibly communicated. Governments in the region are generally well designed for innovation. Both innovation and entrepreneurial approaches require systematic investment in human capital, which is quite a contradiction in an aging and demographically endangered areas.

City of Zagreb

Muze d.o.o./Muses Ltd., Zagreb, Croatia

The Muze d.o.o./Muses Ltd. is an organization for consulting and managing in the areas of culture and tourism. The main activities involved are: linking knowledge in the area of cultural heritage protection, (eco)museology and heritage interpretation, cultural policies and cultural tourism with cultural management skills, the Muze/Muses team acts as a partner in the process of quality planning and professional management of heritage interpretation across Croatia and internationally. The area of activities are Croatia and neighboring countries. The target groups are:

the public sector (municipalities, tourist boards, museums and libraries, interpretation centers, national parks and nature parks…); non-governmental sectors (NGOs in the field of cultural and natural heritage); and the private sector (B2B: architects, designers, investors in the field of culture and heritage).

The types of activities that the Muses organize are: strategy and management of destinations, attractions, institutions and projects; organizational development of a destination, attraction, institution or project; cultural development, interpretation and branding of a destination, attraction, institution or project; setting up museums and interpretation centers; and the establishment of both permanent and temporary exhibitions.

Innovation is at the heart of all activities in the Muses. The organization has a strong team, always a step ahead, a European dimension in the interpretation of heritage, creative associates. The strengths of the organization are innovation, reliability, methodology, thoroughness, passion, teamwork, and a knowledge of work processes.

In terms of innovation, it has strong foundations in theory, a selection of creative collaborators, extensive work with clients, and great practical experience. Most of the Muses' business is based on projects financed by the public sector. It wants to reinforce B2B activities. The Muses are better at the knowledge-based consulting, while the competitors have a different approach based on design and less on heritage interpretation planning.

To improve the current situation, the Muses are working to raise awareness of the importance of the interpretation of heritage as a discipline that is crucial to the sustainable use and sustainability of heritage at all. Innovation comes from understanding the heritage substance and the Muses both interpret and understand the audience's place in creative platforms of its collaborators (architects, designers, IT, artists, etc.) In the period from 2013 to 2015, the Muses team worked on the development of the interpretation and presentation of nature in conjunction with the EU Natura 2000 Integration Project (the budget was €1,000,000.00). The project was led by the Ministry of Environmental and Nature Protection (today: the Ministry of Environmental Protection and Energy), and integration into the EU Natura 2000 European ecological network was one of the conditions of Croatia's accession to the European Union. The project is financed by a loan from the World Bank and it was the first project in Croatia to systemically address natural heritage interpretation planning. Over a three-year period, thirty different interpretation plans were developed. The budget depends on the projects; the museum and interpretation center exhibitions budget ranges from €500,000.00 to

€5,000,000,00. The Muses have eight employees (managers in tourism and culture, ethnologists, cultural anthropologists, art historians, musicologists, etc.).

The Muses are a member of both Interpret Europe (IE) and the Supervisory Committee. Other colleagues are managing staff—IE coordinator for social media. The Muses are the founders and members of the NGO Interpret Croatia and members of ICOM.

Innovation: In terms of innovation, the Muses have strong foundations in theory, the selection of creative collaborators, extensive work with clients, and great practical experience. The others perceive their strength through innovation, reliability, methodology, thoroughness, passion, teamwork, and knowledge of work processes.

Innovation is at the heart of all activities undertaken by Muze d.o.o. The organization has a strong team, is always a step ahead, and adds a European dimension to the interpretation of heritage. Most of the Muses business is based on projects financed by the public sector. It wants to reinforce B2B activities. The Muses are better at knowledge-based consulting, while the competitors have a different approach based on design and less on heritage interpretation planning.

To improve the current situation, the Muses are working to raise awareness of the importance of the interpretation of heritage as a discipline that is crucial to the sustainable use and sustainability of the heritage at all. Innovations come from understanding the heritage substance and the Muses interpret as well as understand the audience's place in the creative platform of their collaborators (architects, designers, IT, artists, etc.)

City of Skopje

Republic of Macedonia Local government for innovation in Macedonia

There is no specific policy on innovation. Innovations are the introduction of lines for interdisciplinary projects, for the independent cultural sector, for participatory projects, and an ingrained strategy for the creative industries. There was small funding for the creative industries, but the government stopped it to do a new strategy for the development of the creative industries. The funding available mostly depends on the people who are to be found at the top of the ministry.

The main problem is the weak capacity of public administration, the lack of interministerial cooperation, the poor monitoring of implementation, the lack of evaluation, and so on. The cultural democracy is the strong point, since they have opened institutions to citizens, trade union organizations and the like. The ministry uses European funds within the framework of what is envisaged for cooperation. NGOs are better at promoting partnerships. For institutions, this is still a relatively rare occurrence. The budget of the Ministry of Culture amounts to approximately 2.6% of the total budget (some €70 million). Of that, about €25 million is purely program money, while some €40 million is spent on the so-called cultural infrastructure, construction projects, including the erection of new buildings, and the maintenance of existing ones.

Innovation: There is no specific policy on innovation. Innovations are the introduction of lines for interdisciplinary projects, for the independent cultural sector, for participatory projects and an ingrained strategy for the creative industries. The main problem is the weak capacity of public administration, the lack of interministerial cooperation, the poor monitoring of implementation, the absence of evaluation, etc. Cultural democracy is one of their strong points, as they have opened institutions to citizens.

City of Krakow

Museum of Contemporary Art in Krakow MOCAK, City of Krakow

The two most important aims of the Museum of Contemporary Art MOCAK are to present the art of the two last decades in the context of the post-war avant-garde and conceptual art as well as clarifying the rationale behind the creation of art by highlighting its cognitive and ethical value and its relationship with everyday reality.

The target groups for activities are the citizens of Krakow, tourists, families, students, and people who are interested in art. The main programs are the exhibitions. The aim of the gallery is to present and support contemporary art and artists, in particular art from the past two decades. The Museum of Contemporary Art in Krakow MOCAK was established in February 2010, the same year that the first works found their way into the Collection. During the eight years of the museum's existence, it has succeeded in acquiring

4787 works (with 1188 distinct inventory numbers) by 296 Polish and international artists. One of the main objectives of the expansion of the collection is to achieve the museum's statutory objectives by collecting and presenting Polish art from the second half of the 20th century against the background of world art. Just as important are the presentations of the main trends of contemporary art and the popularization of the achievements of the leading artists across diverse audiences.

Through its activities, MOCAK's Education Department (MOCAK-edu) promotes the idea of a society open to art, in which everyone, regardless of age or social status, can join in the discussion. It organizes interactive meetings with contemporary art and its creators, collectors and commentators. The educational projects prepared by the museum enable their participants to explore the universe of art and try their hand at creative activities. MOCAK-edu offers workshops for various age groups, from kindergarten pupils to seniors. The museum's educational projects are meant not only to make their participants open and sensitive to art from the youngest age but also to prove that it is never too late for education. The museum organizes workshops and museum lessons tailored to the needs of both younger and older audiences. MOCAK's educational projects are geared towards various social groups, including people with disabilities, teachers and educators, people from smaller towns and those subject to various forms of social exclusion. It focuses, in particular, on the inhabitants of Zabłocie and Podgórze, its closest neighbors, in order to transform the district into a space that is friendly to contemporary art. MOCAK not only organizes meetings with artists, but also invites them to join the museum's artistic projects. The participants have already had an opportunity to draw comic strips or paint murals together with the artists. The projects take place both in the museum and in the city, while educational classes are also conducted in other institutions, schools and kindergartens.

In essence, MOCAK is innovative in terms of its thinking. It is place for young people and is the museum of contemporary art. The projects, exhibitions, and collaborating artists are innovative. Due to that, innovation is a topic of significant interest. It is also interested in technological innovation. As an example, MOCAK has prepared a mobile app which is designed to help visitors plan their visit to the museum and serve as a guide around the exhibitions. The navigation was possible thanks to QR codes and innovative HG Beacon device. All the projects are undertaken by the museum with diverse audiences in mind. The publications produced will provide information, highlighting the origin and significance of the works and events presented and placing them in a wider context. The institution considers it an important challenge to reduce prejudice against very recent art.

The strengths are the exhibitions (which are challenging, intelligent and interesting), beautiful presentation of art works, a beautiful building (well placed in the history and location), interesting, diverse and well-organized museum lessons, friendly staff, and a great café and bookstore. To improve its work, MOCAK is developing its offer and activities. The innovative digital and new media are promising tools for culture and the art world.

The budget is varied and the museum has been financed by: the Minister of Culture and National Heritage (www.gov.pl/web/kultura), Fundusze Europejskie (www.funduszeeuropejskie.gov.pl), EFRR (www.ec.europa.eu/regional_policy/index.cfm/pl/funding/erdf/), Województwo Małopolskie (www.rpo.malopolska.pl), Krakow City (www.bip.krakow.pl), and the National Centre For Culture (www.nck.pl/en). MOCAK has a very qualified team. The museum houses the Departments of Art, Art Knowledge, Publications, Promotion, IT, Administration, Accounts, Technical Service, the Library and MOCAK Bookstore. It collaborates with many organizations in Krakow, Poland and abroad.

Innovation

Through its activities, MOCAK-edu promotes the idea of a society open to art, in which everyone, regardless of age or social status, can join the discussion. It organizes interactive meetings with contemporary art and its creators, collectors and commentators. The educational projects prepared by the museum enable their participants to explore the universe of art and try their hand at creative activities. MOCAK-edu offers workshops for various age groups, from kindergarten pupils to seniors. The museum's educational projects are not only meant to make their participants open and sensitive to art from the youngest age but also to prove that it is never too late for education. The museum organizes workshops and museum lessons tailored to the needs of both younger and older audiences. MOCAK's educational projects are geared towards various social groups, including people with disabilities, teachers and educators, people from smaller towns and those subject to various forms of social exclusion. It focuses, in particular, on the inhabitants of Zabłocie and Podgórze, their closest neighbors, in order to transform the district into a space that is friendly to contemporary art. MOCAK not only organizes meetings with artists, but also invites them to join the museum's artistic projects. The participants have already had an opportunity to draw comic strips or paint murals together with the artists. The projects take place both in the museum and in the city, while educational classes are also conducted in other institutions, schools and kindergartens.

MOCAK is innovative in thinking. It is a place for young people and it is the museum of contemporary art. The projects, exhibitions, and collaborating artists are all innovative. Accordingly, innovation is a topic of significant interest. MOCAK is also interested in technological innovation. As an example, MOCAK has prepared a mobile app designed to help visitors plan their visit to the museum and serve as a guide around the exhibitions. The navigation was possible thanks to QR codes and innovative HG Beacon device. All the projects are undertaken by the museum with diverse audiences in mind. The publications produced will provide information bringing closer the origin and significance of the works and events presented and placing them in contexts. The institution considers it an important challenge to reduce prejudice against very recent art. To improve its work, MOCAK is developing its offer and activities.

City of Ljubljana

Museums and Galleries of Ljubljana,[565] Slovenia

The institution is a local publicly-founded institution for the presentation and collection of the art history of the city and the presentation of contemporary visual art in its galleries. The main aim is to present and discuss the broad topic of history in terms of what is contemporary urban life in the city—the capital of Slovenia. The institution presents exhibitions and workshops which explore the past and its influences on our contemporary way of life. Different practices from programs for schools and for the wider public provide the opportunity to put in focus all aspects of today's problems.

The program and activities are realized mostly in Ljubljana, but also operate on an international level. The activities are exhibitions in the local environment, but the institution is strongly present in many European projects, which are also founded by EU programs.

The target groups are schools, university students, local communities, tourists and, of course, interested institutions and scientists from both home and abroad. The Museums and Galleries of Ljubljana have public guided tours, workshops, and round tables. They present different exhibitions at home and abroad and are also involved in different programs for tourists, which represents about 40 percent of the visitors.

In terms of innovation, the Museums and Galleries of Ljubljana are increasingly involved in different presentation schemes, which also include new models of presentation of the exhibitions, especially work with the young public. They have organized special programs for children who have become their co-workers in preparing an exhibition. This program is called "Museum from Close," in which young collaborators become curators, PR experts, etc. They are given an opportunity to watch how museums function and what is important in their work.

The institutions are strongly convinced that new models of practices must be a part of the sustainable development of the work of museums and galleries. To improve work, the institutions have their own network called RogLab, which is a creative platform for creative processes. On this platform, creative industries are connected with new models of creativity and practical labs for emerging creative productions. The Museums and Galleries are strongly involved in the local community and collaboration with the NGO sector. They are also strong in processes of making alliances with international partners.

Institutions have good relations with different communities and, because of that, they also have a reputation of being open institutions connected to life in the city. The strengths are a good standard of human resources and a relatively strong position in the local community. The weaknesses are a lack of resources from the private sector and not enough new digital orientation, which is needed for the future. The competitors may be better at improving social media practices. The Museums and Galleries have to improve digital competitiveness and organization of their work environment. It is important to follow new possibilities in the digital world and to improve social inclusion. The Museums and Galleries of Ljubljana use funding from the Ministry of Culture, City of Ljubljana, EU funds, private sponsors, and donators. The annual budget for innovation and projects is €150,000. The institutions employ approximately 56 people and, in addition, 15 students. International cooperation is really active with a big range of cooperation in Slovenia and abroad with government institutions and NGOs. They are partners in numerous networks and international cooperation.

Innovation: In terms of innovation, the Museums and Galleries of Ljubljana are increasingly involved in different presentation schemes, which also include new models of presentation of exhibitions, especially work with the young public. They have organized special programs for children, who become their co-workers in preparing an exhibition. This program is called "Museum from Close," in which young collaborators become curators, PR experts, etc. They are given an opportunity to watch and operate how museums function and what is important in their work. The institutions are strongly convinced that new models of practices must be a part of the sustainable development of museum and galleries work. To improve work, institutions have their own network called RogLab, which is a creative platform for creative processes. On this platform, creative industries are connected with new models of creativity and practical labs for emerging creative productions. The Museums and Galleries are strongly involved in the local community and in collaboration with the NGO sector. They are also strong in processes of making alliances with international partners. The Museums and Galleries have to improve digital competitiveness and organization of their work environment. It is important to follow new possibilities in digital world and to improve social inclusion.

City of Budapest

Ludwig Museum—Museum of Contemporary Art Budapest,[566] Hungary

The museum co-organizes contemporary exhibitions (between seven and eight exhibitions a year) and related professional and public programs. The collection is based on a donation from the Ludwig couple and is constantly growing with new artworks from the 1960s to the present.

The area of museum activities is Central Europe.

The museum's target audience is primarily young people (an average age of 28 years), students receiving art education, other students, and families. According to its surveys, the audience visiting the museum is highly educated and comes primarily from Budapest, while ca. 20% are tourists. Special attention is paid to museum education programs, and there are special programs for disadvantaged people. The activities are contemporary temporary exhibitions and permanent exhibitions, symposiums, exclusive programs for visitors, family programs, scientific conferences, the restoration of art works, museum pedagogy, library service, and marketing communication.

The innovation policies of the museum include the following: multimedia exhibitions—yearly 1–2 exhibitions with these kind of artworks (the public is increasingly looking for these exhibitions and demanding media and interactive works, guided tours with mobile applications—developed for the permanent exhibition, with every visitor getting a code for it with the purchased ticket, but it is not particularly popular); new programs for people with disadvantages (not only for blind or people with wheelchairs but for mentally disabled or homeless people too. The museum conducted special research on this topic and one of its colleagues is constantly developing these kind of methods); projects and programs outside the museums; scientific research on the restoration and preservation of media art works—international scientific conferences are organized every year.

To improve the work, the universities of design can do much because they have the opportunity to combine science and art with practice. Fehér thinks that these initiatives should be supported, as well as cooperation in the spirit of co-creation.

The main strengths of the Ludwig Museum—Museum of Contemporary Art are the following: professionalism in researching, collecting, presenting, mediating and propagating contemporary art; open-mindedness towards new ideas and perspectives; diversity in terms of the exhibited artists and artworks; the hosting of events and activities, as well as in terms of the presentation of the applied arts; that it is active in finding new partners, cooperative parties, and sponsors. The museum is better than others for the fact that, with a small budget and few employees, it is implementing a program that is equivalent to that of other Western European museums. The staff are very creative and very ambitious. In Hungary, working at the Ludwig Museum is very prestigious. It has many progressive projects, and partners from all over the world.

The strength is the high quality of its exhibitions, visual branding, interesting programs. The weaknesses are the low salaries, and that there are very few staff available for publications and research. The museum cannot plan for the long term; it always focuses only on the realization of the given exhibition. It does not have the capacity to develop long-term projects. Regarding this, the competition institutions are better in terms of long-term projects.

To improve the situation, the museum has to have online communication, fundraising and new technologies. The innovative trends that improve its work are companies seeking collaborations with cultural institutions. The source of funding is the government. There is no special budget for innovation, but the museum tries to make some developments every year: ca. €20,000.

At the time of writing, there are 44 people working at the museum—half are technical-financial staff and the other half are art historians and educators. The collection is in a MuseumRia database, which exports data to the museum's web page. This software is also used as a management system. International cooperation is well developed. The Ludwig Museum collaborates with the Palace of Arts, who are based in the same building, a concert hall and dance theater, with a free ticket to the museum. It collaborates with other Ludwig Museums across the world, and is also a member of the International Committee for Museums and Collections of Modern Art (CIMAM). The museum also collaborates with art universities and other cultural institutions.

Innovation: The innovation policies of the museum include: multimedia exhibitions—yearly 1– 2 exhibitions with these kind of artworks (the public is increasingly looking for these exhibitions and demanding media and interactive works, guided tours with mobile applications—developed for the permanent exhibition, with every visitor getting a code for it with the purchased ticket, although this has not proved to be too popular); new programs for people with disadvantages (not only for blind or people with wheelchairs but for mentally disabled or homeless people too. The museum conducted special research on this topic and one of its colleagues is constantly developing these kind of methods); projects and programs outside of the museums; scientific research on the restoration and preservation of media art works—international scientific conferences organized every year.

To improve innovation, the universities of design can do a lot because they have the opportunity to combine science and art with practice. Fehér thinks that these initiatives should be supported, as well as cooperation in the spirit of co-creation.

The collection is in a MuseumRia database, which exports data to the web page. This software is also used as a management system. To improve the situation, the museum has to have online communication, fundraising, and new technologies. The innovative trends that improve its work are companies seeking collaborations with cultural institutions.

Analysis

In the third focus group of the research of Central–Eastern Europe, we conclude that innovations are not a priority of development for local governments, institutions and organizations, mostly because cultural policy is not currently being fully implemented. It is clear that innovation is not on the list of priorities, mostly because of the policy makers that coordinate public institutions. The innovation in the programs appeared in independent associations—in the program activities, social innovation is dominant. The development of technology contributes to technological innovation, but social innovation has an important place to play in the process of development of the cultural sector, and it is interconnected with tech innovation processes. In the local government of the City of Bratislava, innovation is seen in the participation of organizations on project with the mobile phone application KnowSpot, which provides users with information about historic buildings or interesting places either on- or offline. To improve the innovative and creative industries sector, it is necessary for the professionals to be given increased financial resources, the costs of propagation for information in urban spaces to be lowered and more space for these activities to be provided. The improvement of the situation implies developing discussions with professionals for culture. The Culture Department of the City of Bratislava and cultural organizations work with partners from foreign countries on several projects; they are members of the culture forum EUROCITIES, and are working on an agreement with Austria, Poland, Italy, etc. Bratislava is the cultural heart of Slovakia. Owing to its historical multicultural character, local culture in the city is influenced by various ethnic groups. Bratislava has numerous theaters, museums, galleries, concert halls, cinemas, film clubs, and foreign cultural institutions. The City of Novi Sad is the European Capital of Culture in 2022. Innovation has to be a part of local culture policy. For decades, Novi Sad has built its uniqueness on foundations of its multicultural character and numerous cultural and educational institutions. The City of Novi Sad Library has innovation projects and processes: digitalization of the Local History Collection; library on the beach during summer, on the banks of the Danube; book home delivery service for the elderly, the sick, the pregnant, and for those who are unable to come to the library due to severe invalidity or other causes; the "Language Drama Lab," festival of drama in English; Democratization of Digitalization (service for self-use of the smartphone); and a new library branch for young people with makers' spaces and many contemporary contents. The impacts of these actions are many: an increased number of library users, increased consciousness of the importance of the library, bringing the library closer to young people, easier and more comfortable usage of cultural heritage, etc. Concerning innovation, the Library of Novi Sad tries to involve young people in its activities and offers them a chance to create their own cultural development. It has extended its field of competence to diverse areas, such as electronic media, formal and informal education in arts and computers, and programming. The library plans to equip a workshop for makers' spaces. It has a practice of engaging volunteers. In addition, the library has a long tradition, formal institutionalization, visibility and well-educated human resources in certain areas of expertise. In the Cities of Kiev/Moscow/Eindhoven the organization Stichting Art-East+Art-West (NGO)[567] has been developing cultural projects, curating exhibitions, and consulting governmental and private institutions on strategic cultural issues (art, design, landscape architecture). The areas of the projects are the Netherlands, Russia, and Ukraine. The target group of activities are the general public, architects, designers, and art professionals. The most realized services are exhibitions and consulting services with innovation processes. The innovative trend that has the most positive impact for the organization is the cooperation between designers and scientists. Innovation was present in the 2014 exhibition in Moscow, "Dialog with Water," in which it showed a new ecological approach to solve the problems of flooding. The organization also included innovation in an assignment for exhibitions of Creative Ukraine during Dutch Design Week. The result of the project was weak, but the projects with regard to innovations and creative industries are very well developed in the region of Eindhoven. The organization is doing a very good job, especially in comparison with Eastern European countries. The organization believes that paying more attention to the neighboring EU countries with creative potential and different viewpoints would help produce new and innovative ideas. The organization is innovative in terms of combining the Eastern European and Dutch approaches, and the other organizations and cultural institutions perceive that the organization has experience in different fields of cultural projects, as well as some knowledge of different mentalities. At the Museum of Contemporary Art Belgrade, in the City of Belgrade, innovation is not a tangible concept that could be analyzed in the case of the museum. Innovation can be seen through the programs that the institution delivers over the course of a year. On the other hand, the Belgrade association BAZAART develops new methodologies for learning through drama and theater. In the IDEAL project, it invented the Intercultural Learning Through Drama methodology, which is published on-line and widely implemented by the association and others. Another example is the "Tolerant Classroom" collection of workshops, which aims to promote tolerance, inclusion and cooperation among schoolchildren (both available on the website). In addition, drama texts are also staged across the region. With regard to innovations, mechanisms have to be established as to how to mainstream them in general cultural and educational systems. The decision-makers have practically no contact with the "base" practice. This has to be changed first. BAZAART has been seen as an innovator, expert, and visionary. The weaknesses are the small number of people and hence the limited operational capacities, the absence of working space for workshops, rehearsals and productions, and unstable financing. In terms of innovation for the City of Gabrovo's Museum for Humour and Satire, it has been dealing with change, rather than actual innovation. Introducing change in institutions which are conservative by nature, such as museums, is a slow and difficult process. Some projects have been considered innovative without essentially being such. Both change and innovation are a matter of communication; however, innovation is often too far ahead to be possibly communicated. Governments in the region are generally well designed for innovation. Both innovation and entrepreneurial approaches require systematic investment in human capital, which is quite a contradiction in aging and demographically endangered areas. In the City of Zagreb, The Muze d.o.o./Muses Ltd. is an organization for consulting and managing in culture and tourism. In terms of innovation, it has strong foundations in theory, selection of creative collaborators, extensive work with clients, and substantial practical experience. The others perceive the company's strength through innovation, reliability, methodology, thoroughness, passion, teamwork, and the knowledge of work processes. Innovation is at the heart of all activities in the Muses. The organization has a strong team, is always a step ahead, adds a European dimension to the interpretation of heritage, and has creative associates. Most of the Muses' business is based on projects financed by the public sector. It wants to reinforce B2B activities. The Muses are better at knowledge-based consulting, while the competitors have a different approach based more on design and less on heritage interpretation planning. To improve the current situation, the Muses are working to raise awareness of the importance of the interpretation of heritage as a discipline that is crucial to sustainable use and the sustainability of heritage overall. Innovation comes from understanding the heritage substance and the Muses interpret this as understanding the audience's place in the creative platform of their collaborators (architects, designers, IT, artists, etc.) In the City of Skopje, Republic of Macedonia, there is no specific policy with regard to innovation. Innovations are the introduction lines for interdisciplinary projects, for the independent cultural sector, for participatory projects and an ingrained strategy for the creative industries. The main problem is the weak capacity of public administration, the lack of interministerial cooperation, poor monitoring of implementation, no evaluation, etc. The cultural democracy is the strong point; they have opened institutions for citizens. The Museum of Contemporary Arts in the City of Krakow, through its activities within MOCAK's Education Department (MOCAK-edu), promotes the idea of a society open to art, in which everyone, regardless of age or social status, can join in the discussion. It organizes interactive meetings with contemporary art and its creators, collectors, and commentators. The educational projects prepared by the museum enable participants to explore the universe of art and try their hand at creative activities. MOCAK-edu offers workshops for various age groups, from kindergarten pupils to seniors. The museum's educational projects are not only meant to make their participants open and sensitive to art from the youngest age, but also to prove that it is never too late for education. The museum organizes workshops and museum lessons tailored to the needs of both younger and older audiences. MOCAK's educational projects are geared towards various social groups, including people with disabilities, teachers and educators, people from smaller towns, and those subject to various forms of social exclusion. It focuses especially on the inhabitants of Zabłocie and Podgórze, its closest neighbors, in order to transform the district into a space that is receptive to contemporary art. MOCAK not only organizes meetings with artists, but also invites them to join the museum's artistic projects. The participants have already had an opportunity to draw comic strips or paint murals together with the artists. The projects take place both in the museum and in the city, while educational classes are also conducted in other institutions, schools and kindergartens. MOCAK is innovative in thinking. As stated above, it is a place for "young" people and is the museum of contemporary art. The projects, exhibitions, and collaborating artists of the museum are innovative. Accordingly, innovation is a topic of significant interest. It is also interested in technological innovation. To take just one example, MOCAK has prepared a mobile app designed to help visitors plan their visit to the museum and serve as a guide around the exhibitions. The navigation was possible thanks to QR codes and the use of an innovative HG Beacon device. All of the projects are undertaken by the museum with diverse audiences in mind. The publications produced will provide information bringing closer the origin and significance of the works and events presented and placing them in context. The institution considers it an important challenge to reduce prejudice against the most contemporary of art. It offers exhibitions (which are challenging, intelligent and interesting), art works that are beautifully presented, a beautiful building (well placed in terms of the history and location), interesting, diverse and well-organized museum lessons, friendly staff, a great café and bookstore. To improve its work, the museum is developing its offer and activities. In terms of innovation in the City of Ljubljana, the Museums and Galleries of Ljubljana are becoming increasingly involved in different presentation schemes, which also include new models of presentation of the exhibitions, especially work with a young public. They have organized special programs for children who became their co-workers in preparing an exhibition. This program is called "Museum from Close," in which young collaborators become curators, PR experts, etc. They are given the opportunity to watch how a museum functions and what is important in its work. The institutions are strongly convinced that new models of practices must be a part of the sustainable development of the work of museums and galleries. To improve their work, the institutions have their own network called RogLab, which is a creative platform for creative processes. On this platform, creative industries are connected with new models of creativity and practical labs for new emerging creative productions. The museums and galleries are strongly involved in the local community and collaboration with the NGO sector. They are also strong in processes of making alliances with international partners. The museums and galleries have to improve both digital competitiveness and the organization of their work environment. It is important to follow new possibilities in the digital world and to improve social inclusion. The Ludwig Museum in the City of Budapest has innovation policies through multimedia exhibitions—there are 1–2 annual exhibitions featuring these kinds of artworks. The public is increasingly looking for these exhibitions and demanding media and interactive works, guided tours with mobile applications, developed for the permanent exhibition, with every visitor getting a code for it with the purchase ticket (not too popular). Other innovation policies are new programs for people with disadvantages (not only for blind or people with wheelchairs but for mentally disabled or homeless people too. The museum conducted special research on this topic and one of its colleagues is constantly

TABLE 3 The Third Focus Group of Research

	Innovation	*Culture Program (Culture and Creative Industries)*	*Budget Over Year*
City of Bratislava Mrs Katarina Lukyova, culture department, City of Bratislava (the local government)	Innovation is seen in the participation of organizations on projects with the mobile phone application KnowSpot, which provides users with information about historic buildings or interesting places online or offline.	It deals with the coordination of organisations (Bratislava City Gallery, Bratislava City Museum, Bratislava City Library, etc.), organization or cooperation in city happenings, the agenda of grant program for culture happenings (exhibitions, books, theatre and dancing performances, etc.).	€7,200,284 per year.
City of Novi Sad Mr Dragan Kojic, director. Novi Sad City Library	The innovation projects and processes: digitalization of the Local History Collection; library on the beach during summer, on the bank of the Danube; the "Language Drama Lab," festival of drama in English; Democratization of Digitalization (service for self-use of the smart phone); new Library branch for young people with maker space and many contemporary contents.	Programs for the development of innovation and creative industries: There are many programs for the cultural development; the library is a part of the EUTEKA network, conducted by Delegation of the European Union for Serbia. It also took part in certain activities of EUROPEANA projects. The library has a diverse cooperation with members of EUNIC.	€170,000 per year.
City of Eindhoven/ Kiev/Moscow Mrs. Elena Oranskaia, director, Stichting Art- East+Art- West (NGO)	The innovative trend that positively impacts the organization is cooperation between designers and scientists. The organization is innovative in terms of combining the Eastern European and Dutch approaches. Other organizations and cultural institutions perceive that the organization has experience in different fields of cultural projects, and knowledge of different mentalities.	The projects on innovations and creative industries are very well developed. In the region of Eindhoven, the organization is doing very good job, especially if in comparison with Eastern European countries.	€20,000–50,000 per year.

City of Belgrade Mrs Sunčica Milosavljević, programme director, BAZAART, Representative Association in Culture, Belgrade.	The organization develops new methodologies for learning through drama and theatre. It invented the Intercultural Learning Through Drama methodology, which is published on-line and widely implemented by the organization and others. Another example is the "Tolerant Classroom" collection of workshops, for the development of tolerance, inclusion and cooperation among schoolchildren (both available on the website).	Development of drama texts (scripts) for school stage and young audiences; Theatre-in-Education productions; workshops—creative and educational, mostly for the youth; organizing education workshops (exchange among colleagues—artists and teachers); accredited trainings in drama/theatre based methodologies for learning and education, for teachers, approved by the Institute for Educational Development of Serbia; national conferences with international participation, on topics of inter- sectorial cooperation.	€4000 per year.
City of Belgrade Mr Zoran Erić The main curator the Museum of Contemporary Art.	Innovation is not a tangible concept that could be analyzed in the case of the Museum of Contemporary Arts Belgrade.	The museum is a modern institution that organizes exhibitions, musicological activities of the preservation of cultural heritage, talk programs, education, etc.	Budget of the museum €70,000 to 90,000
City of Gabrovo Margarita Dorovska, director, Museum of Humor and Satire	In terms of Innovation policy, the museum has been dealing with change, not really innovation. Introducing change in institutions conservative by nature, such as museums, is a slow and difficult process. Some projects have been considered innovative without essentially being such. Both change and innovation are a matter of communication, however, innovation is often too far ahead to be possibly communicated.	The museum has different activities such as: exhibitions, events and educational programs (workshops, cinema, performances, lectures, discussions, concerts).	€20,000

(*Continued*)

TABLE 3 (Continued) The Third Focus Group of Research

	Innovation	*Culture Program (Culture and Creative Industries)*	*Budget Over Year*
City of Zagreb Mrs Dragana Lucija Ratković Aydemir, founder and owner Muze d.o.o. / Muses Ltd., Zagreb, Croatia.	Innovation is at the heart of all activities in Muze d.o.o. The organization has a strong team, is always a step ahead, adds a European dimension to the interpretation of heritage, and has creative associates. The strengths of the organization are innovation, reliability, methodology, thoroughness, passion, teamwork, and knowledge of work processes.	The main activities are linking knowledge in the area of cultural heritage protection, (eco)museology and heritage interpretation, cultural policies and cultural tourism with cultural management skills, the Muses team acts as a partner in the process of quality planning and professional management of heritage across Croatia and internationally.	The budget depends on the projects; museum and interpretation centers exhibitions budgets are from €500,000 to €5,000,000.
Republic of Macedonia, State Ministry of Culture Mr Robert Ajdzalovski, Minister of Culture, Local government for innovation in Macedonia.	There is no specific policy on innovation. Innovations are the introduction of lines for interdisciplinary projects, for the independent cultural sector, for participatory projects and an ingrained strategy for the creative industries.	The cultural democracy is its strong point, it has opened institutions to citizens, trade union organizations and the other culture projects.	€25 million per year.

City of Ljubljana Mr. Blaž Peršin, Director of Museums and Galleries of Ljubljana, Slovenia	In terms of innovation, the Museums and Galleries of Ljubljana are more and more involved in different presentation schemes, which also includes new models of the presentation of exhibitions, especially work with the young public. They have organized special programs for children who became their co-workers in preparing an exhibition.	The Museums and Galleries of Ljubljana have public guided tours, workshops, and round tables. They present different exhibitions home and abroad and are also involved in different programs for tourists, which represent about 40 percent of total visitors.	€150,000 per year
Mrs Anna Micek and Kamila Biedrońska, Museum of Contemporary Art in Krakow MOCAK, City of Krakow.	In essence, MOCAK is innovative in thinking. It is a "young" place (9 years old) and is the museum of contemporary art. The projects, exhibitions and collaborating artists are innovative. Due to that, innovation is a topic of significant interest. The museum is also interested in technological innovation.	The two most important aims of the Museum of Contemporary Art MOCAK's are presenting the art of the two last decades in the context of the post-war avant-garde and conceptual art, and clarifying the rationale of creating art by highlighting its cognitive and ethical value and its relationship with everyday reality.	Budget is varied; funded by the Minister of Culture and National Heritage, Fundusze Europejskie, Województwo Małopolskie, Krakow City, National Centre For Culture.
City of Budapest **Mrs Zsuzsanna Fehér**, Ludwig Museum—Museum of Contemporary Art Budapest, Hungary	The multimedia exhibitions—yearly 1–2 exhibition with these kinds of artworks. The public is increasingly looking for these exhibitions and demanding media and interactive works. There are also guided tours with mobile applications, developed for the permanent exhibition, with every visitor getting a code for it with the purchase ticket (not too popular).	The programs are contemporary temporary exhibitions and permanent exhibitions, symposiums, exclusive programs for visitors, family programs, scientific conferences, restoration of art works, museum pedagogy, library service, marketing communication.	€20,000

(*Continued*)

TABLE 3 (Continued) The Third Focus Group of Research

	Innovation	*Culture Program (Culture and Creative Industries)*	*Budget Over Year*
The Qualitative Research Analysis	In the third focus group of the research of Central–Eastern Europe we conclude that innovations are not a priority of development for local governments, institutions and organizations mostly because cultural policy is not fully implemented. It is clear that innovation is not on the list of priorities, mostly because of the policy makers that coordinate public institutions. The innovation in programs appeared in independent associations—in the program activities, social innovation is dominant. The development of technology contributes to technological innovation, but social innovation has an important place in the process of development of the cultural sector, and it is interconnected with tech innovation processes. The City of Ljubljana, City of Eindhoven/Kiev/Moscow and City of Zagreb have programs for supporting the cultural and creative industries CCI including innovation, which contribute to economic development		

developing this kind of methods, projects and programs outside of the museums, and scientific research on the restoration and preservation of media art works—international scientific conferences are organized every year. To improve innovation, the universities of design can do a lot because they have the opportunity to combine science and art with practice. The museum thinks that these initiatives should be supported, as well as cooperation in the spirit of co-creation. The collection is in a MuseumRia database, which exports data to the web page. This software is also used as a management system. To improve the situation, the museum has to have online communication, fundraising and new technologies. The innovative trends that improve its work are companies seeking collaborations with cultural institutions.

Notes

560 Stichting Art-East+Art-West, accessed May 9, 2021, https://www.arteastartwest.nl/nl/3/contact.html
561 "Culture and Art," City of Belgrade, accessed May 10, 2021, https://www.beograd.rs/en/discover-belgrade/201038-culture-and-art/
562 Museum of Contemporary Art Belgrade, accessed May 10, 2021, www.msub.org.rs
563 BAZAART, accessed May 10, 2021, http://bazaart.org.rs/
564 Museum House of Humour and Satire, accessed May 10, 2021, www.humorhouse.bg
565 Museum and Galleries of Ljubljana, accessed May 10, 2021, https://mgml.si/en/
566 Ludwig Museum, "Museum of Contemporary Art Budapest," accessed May 10, 2021, https://www.ludwigmuseum.hu/en
567 Stichting Art-East+Art-West, accessed May 9, 2021, https://www.arteastartwest.nl/nl/3/contact.html

PART III

Analysis of Case Studies in Europe

The cultural ecosystem should be treated not as merely a segment of the economy, but rather as a system that contains the economy. The interconnectedness of cultural systems and other segments of sustainable development must be taken into account. The study analyses cities and their cultural development through innovation processes which take into account social innovation, project innovation, cross-innovation, and environmental sustainability. The study offers an analysis of the contemporary approach to culture and innovation, as well as to the development of cities, with culture being a pivotal factor in the developmental processes.

The thesis offers a theoretical and practical analysis of the contemporary approach to culture and innovation, with a special emphasis on the relationship between culture, innovations, and the economy as an indispensable sustainability factor, while clearly stating that a cultural ecosystem contains the economy.

> The evaluation of cultural projects in cities is based on realistic and practical experiences of international organizations, universities and activists. They represent a dedication of city councils to integrate culture into the process of sustainable development, both on local and global level.[568]
>
> The evaluation of cultural projects in cities is based on realistic and practical experiences of international organizations, universities and activists. They represent a dedication of city councils to integrate culture into the process of sustainable development, both on local and global level.[569]

To attain sustainability, the economy must produce the values on which it is based, and which consider the culture of the specific environment. The economy has a great legitimacy and dynamic when it is adapted to local sources.[570] Cultural activism plays an important role in sustainable economic development and creates

DOI: 10.4324/9781003336648-14

economic activities, entrepreneurship, and jobs, adding to the attractiveness of cities and contributing to the development of tourism. However, economic models,[571] that priorities quick development do not work in the long run and are not beneficial to local environments. Cultural and economic factors of the environment must be taken into account and developed in parallel. In the following document, it is emphasized that

> Economic models that aim at cultural sensitivity need to engage in implementation practice that includes collaboration, cooperation, trade and donations. All economic models are based on specific cultural values. An effective link between the public, market and cooperative economy, together with the reciprocity among them, is essential to achieving a decentralized, environmentally balanced development.[572]

It is essential to distinguish artists and professionals in the cultural sector, ensure access to their work, promote corporative responsibility, and implement adequate support for cultural projects. There are mechanisms for cultural project support, such as microloans and sponsorships. Cities and regions should maintain mixed economic programs that maximize donations for cultural projects. Partnership between people from culture and business fields is also important, together with systemic innovations and knowledge transfer. "Tourism needs to be linked to this cultural ecosystem, by means of implementing cultural routes. Business organizations such as chambers of commerce possess special programs related to cultural politics of cities."[573] When it comes to developing cities and regions, a priority should be made of restoring public spaces for cultural happenings and art-related activities that would represent the social unity of a city, as well as strengthening the city's cultural identity based on a network of cultural entities and associations.[574] Clearly, it is this firm network that forms a basis for the promotion and implementation of ambitious cultural policies on a city level. The study points out that as a key factor in the promotion of urban change, an innovative cultural profile of the city should be defined, together with the transformation and opening of new cultural institutions. This would be the contribution of the cultural sector to economic development.

This study aims to understand processes *from the Innovative Culture Policies to the Economy and Innovation* and to exchange knowledge of innovation and experience between different cultural institutions and environments in Europe and the UK.

It is crucial to highlight the concept that shows a clear vertical connection between different experiences of innovation regarding strategic plans for the development of culture, which, in effect, reinforce a horizontal cultural organization regarding innovation policies.

This study analyzes regional and local cultural policies and examines how the relationship between innovation and new design contributes towards raising standards while also stimulating development, new thinking, and the relationship of local governments towards cultural institutions. It also investigates the significance of networking, the value of collaborative partnerships, and developments in the field of creative industries and, lastly, it provides an evaluation of specific innovative cultural projects.

This book encompasses a wide range of case studies dealing with topics of innovative sustainable cultural development in different cultural institutions in cities and regions. It also includes various examples of cultural innovation with respect to the environment, combined with theories and practice of innovative development contributed to by leading professionals specializing in this area. It is clearly unnecessary to emphasize the importance of innovative cultural development. Essentially, contemporary culture itself speaks about the crucial questions of our time and the immense changes in the environment of global identity. Innovation stands in direct correlation with the cultural policy and strategy of a particular city or region. The role of cultural policy is to encourage the structuring of cultural projects (art projects and equipment, for example) that can have a powerful impact on society. Furthermore, cultural policy enables an equitable apportionment of cultural facilities in a particular city or region; it makes it possible to clearly balance the impartial reasons that may exist either in favor of or against certain cultural projects; and, finally, to encourage artistic creativity.

> Innovative cultural development at both regional and national levels in a modern society must be transversal. All dimensions of the city or territory (social, educational, economic, touristic) are interconnected and culture should connect with each of them. By means of clear cultural policy, innovation should incorporate contemporary innovative approach, digitalization, new ideas, creative processes and technologically sophisticated media. It should also take into consideration the presentation of culture which aims to facilitate cultural exchange between contrasting communities while simultaneously preserving the specific characteristics of place, traditional values and architectural heritage.[575]

In order to ensure future innovation and attain certain levels of stability, it is important to present new models that can be implemented, especially in strategic cultural planning. This early part of the twenty-first century, and perhaps this decade in particular, will almost certainly be an epoch of networking that will give rise to the advancement of myriad agendas and platforms that will seek to further cultural research and development. Networking provides the space in which information turns into knowledge and knowledge into innovation; making it the laboratory of the present.[576] Because of this, the networks that exist both within and between regions and cities have evolved to become conceptual, programmatic, and organizational in order to cater for this new kind of cultural sector. Innovative management and the management of these three elements of cultural sector networking brings with it certain complexities. We still require some room for research and laboratory-style experimentation. The local becomes global, and one of the reasons for this is the technological advancement of recent times which compels us to share, exchange, and communicate. There are now some platforms available to cultural managers which are incredibly inexpensive and yet which have the ability to enable global improvements in innovative cultural management through the exchange of innovative models and their transfer into other environments, which can then be implemented at a local level.[577] Without these new technologies we cannot expect artistic creativity to maintain the high standards of innovation required of it in order to achieve balanced development across the various sectors of society. However, the effective management of the tripod of this new governance system is a complex exercise. The majority of cities have based their cultural policies on key principles: cultural identity, cultural diversity, creativity, innovation, and the participation of citizens in cultural life. More than ever before, we now need dedicated places for interchange, centers of transference, spaces for experimentation and cultural laboratories. The objective of this thesis is to present examples of innovative cultural policy in action and the experiences of its practitioners. The research has been done using methods of qualitative research, including three focus groups based on the characteristics of development, innovation and creative industries. In the first focus group of the qualitative research, we conclude that innovations are developed in local governments, institutions, and organizations. The development of technology contributes to technological innovation, but social innovation plays an important place in the process of development of the cultural sector, and is interconnected with innovation processes. The City of Stockholm, in terms of innovation, has a short tradition of strength within the tech industries, currently ranking number two in the world after Silicon Valley in terms of developing "unicorns" per capita. That factor should also be used when looking at developing the Creative and Cultural Industries (CCI) sector. The main weakness is a lack of strategy on a national level, but it is possible to improve in the current situation with support from the CCI sector with a focus on innovation. The innovative trend is digitalization. The Culture Administration is funded by the city of Stockholm, municipality-wise. The Culture Administration does not have a designated budget for CCI and innovation. However, it is staffed by a large number of people with strategy competence. The innovations in the cultural programmes are as follows: Bibblix—an app for children's book loans at the Digital library unit at the city library; UX design—how people want their libraries; Co-creation—for example, the youth festival is co-created with the target group; in the Event department, an app for experiencing exhibitions at the art gallery, created by an external consultant. Within the City of Stockholm, the Culture Administration cooperates with various administrations such as urban development, the building department, the Stockholm Business Region, and the Visit Stockholm agency. It also collaborates with state institutions situated in Stockholm on various levels. In Scotland, the Culture Department in the City of Glasgow has embedded innovation policy and innovative practice in all Glasgow Life services, as evidenced through continued evolution and improvement of programs and activities, as well as an extensive list of awards and commendations. The city has 160 venues and it also manages over 250 services, including a network of neighborhood cultural and sports facilities, a range of community development and learning services and some of the most prestigious buildings in the UK. The organization SOLUS from the

City of Edinburgh is currently working on the processing of innovation. The work of SOLUS is innovative in terms of shaping the future and redesigning the relevant "next" library—the 21st-century people's library. These 21st-century public libraries must become learning and digital hubs. Innovation technology and weaknesses are overambition, promotion, and marketing. The company also needs to recruit more staff. Improvement of the current situation would involve supporting and driving the national promotion and awareness of innovation, learning and fun in libraries and cultural services. The main impact of the company to date is technology and the public perception of the library as being innovative and cool.

The City of Dublin has a new innovative policy which has been adopted for the development of a new approach. The Arts Plan is the work plan for the Arts Office, a section of, and guided by, the CRA Department of Dublin City Council, and based in the Lab; a bespoke arts center in Dublin.[578] It is a unique innovation for the governance office. This plan was a new departure in terms of the development of strategic and sustainable cultural planning across the city. For the first time the city noted broader cultural actions within its Arts Plan and laid out a vision, in broad strokes, as the basis for actions, rather than detailing the actions themselves. The Arts Plan changed the way in which the Arts Office engages with its other sister departments: several interdepartmental partnerships have arisen with, among others, the Area Offices, Libraries, Planning, Events, Tourism & Sports & the Intercultural Unit, who have previously engaged with the Agenda 21 process. The benefits of this approach include: an increased sharing of resources, parallel planning and the increased recognition of culture as an effective tool for public engagement and sustainable practice. These changes in relationships are, in large part, based on the exchange and sharing of knowledge, resources and networking aimed at increasing opportunities and enhancing projects for mutual benefit. The organization ArtsGovernance, from Dublin City, is creating an environment for innovation, enabling innovation through good governance and enabling funding to take place. The strengths of this approach are: excellent reputation, trustworthiness in the sector, unique expertise in the sector, creating an environment for innovation, enabling innovation through good governance and enabling funding to take place. The innovative trends that can impact upon the company include artistic and management trends and government policy. Innovation arises from the artistic process being applied across other disciplines. The effort for developing the creative industries in EU and Ireland is generally good. The Irish Museum of Modern Art (IMMA), based the City of Dublin, is a contemporary gallery, which uses innovation from all contemporary art sources around the world and has innovation at the heart of what it does in the contemporary art space. "The Museum" is an open and participatory space that connects people with contemporary life through art. Surveys show that the audience comes to IMMA to experience something new and to share knowledge and new thinking. Strengths are re-imagining the museum; attracting audiences in different ways; developing a new strategy in tandem with objectives of cultural institutions and Arts and cultural policies in Ireland and internationally. On the other hand, the think-tank in the City of Dublin, InterroBang

Ltd., is an organization whose innovation is reflected in the development of unique approaches to PSSDS (*System Development Strategy*), adaption of the approaches of third parties and the blending of a variety of third-party strategies with its research in unique ways. All these innovations are intellectual innovations, rather than being physical balance sheet assets. The innovations are intellectual rather than technological.

In terms of innovation, London's BOP Consulting has a bigger data collation and analysis capacity in comparison with other organizations. In addition, it has a wider range of expertise brought together as a result of its network. The BOP has an analytical capacity and comfort with data, but also works with many territories and many different organizations. BOP Consulting acknowledges that the EU and others have made significant strides in developing the sector of creative industries and innovation. The organization is currently active in Europe, Latin America, China, and the Gulf. BOP Consulting have offices in London, Liverpool, Edinburgh, and Shanghai.

The Dance Theatre ERI in the City of Turku uses dance therapy and modern dance in projects for immigrants and senior citizens. Now in pandemic times, it has used Zoom, telephone, etc, to reach them. Also, ERI has dance lessons for children on Zoom after they have watched their performance on YouTube. In the EU, the value of culture—especially modern dance—should be appreciated more. Cultuur Eindhoven in the City of Eindhoven is a local government organization that came into existence in 2015 as an innovative experiment to make an external organization responsible for the funding of cultural organization. This is an innovative institution. There is always room for more exploration and experimentation. The focus of the work is mainly on deliverables, rather than on the experiment itself. The organization is pretty good at combining a personal and a diplomatic approach, thus helping cultural partners with their funding. The organization is simple approachable, constructive, and helpful. The main thing is that all creative stakeholders are positively using innovative strengths. The City of London, City of Glasgow and City of Eindhoven have programs for supporting CCI, which contribute to the development of a creative economy. The development of creative industries and innovations should be an integral part of state policy, and it should be regarded as an essential part of social, educational, and economic policies. The future perspective is to see the creative industries being treated as an essential industry and part of the sustainable and regenerative economic agenda. In the second focus group involved in the research, we conclude that innovations are developed in local governments, institutions, and organizations. The development of technology contributes to technological innovation, but social innovation is in the first position in the process of development of the cultural sector supported by technological innovation, and it is connected with tech innovation processes. The City of Rome deals with innovation through innovative local cultural projects and developing innovation through creative industries and tourism. The municipality deals with innovation and we identified three innovative local cultural projects and policies that can be featured as examples of the activities being carried out in this field. The experimentation of new solutions and formats to bring high-quality contents into those areas that are furthest from the center where cultural institutions are traditionally located, especially taking into account Rome's geographical features. The incentive to foster collaboration and networking among the city's cultural institutions to serve local communities is an attitude which has revealed to be essential for the production of the new format of Rome's New Year's Eve celebration. The informal and festive atmosphere of the Opera Camion's squares, on which citizens gather long before the show and share anecdotes and knowledge on the opera, as well as chairs, pillows, and food. The most innovative aspect of this initiative is that Rome is the first city attempt in Europe to allow citizens (and not only tourists) to access museums for free with the payment of a symbolic nominal fee of 5€/year.

Rethinking museums as real public places and transforming them into everyday common spaces might be a revolutionary city cultural policy as it ignites changes both in the behavior of citizens and in the PA one. The City of Rome's commitment to foster innovative trends is having a positive impact on Roman citizens' well-being and cultural life. The City of Rome is creating a new data observatory aimed towards measuring cultural participation and its impact on citizens' trust and well-being. This work will be enriched by a cross-analysis of Big Data and will be increasingly intertwined with the objectives and targets of the administrative departments. A growing number of active citizens are creating cultural experiences at grassroots level. The city is seeking to find a balance that encourages this development, while ensuring that public spaces remain shared by all, and is using cultural institutions to make sure that communities are also linked into broader co-operative networks. New activity forms are emerging, which are built around provisional structures, or which require no new built structure at all. Examples include urban scientific walks and the rise of "urban stages" such as streets, metro stations, and building façades, which can be used for a temporary cultural intervention. The City of Bologna, through the project INCREDIBOL!, is focusing more attention on creative spillovers and on culture-based creativity and non-technological innovation for developing creative industries in Europe. Project INCREDIBOL! is promoting and supporting new business ideas in the field of cultural and creative enterprises, testing new methods of generating innovation through creative spillovers (European project URBACT Creative Spin), and creating winning processes within the Public Administration (PA) using little to no financial resources. The city places more attention on creative spillovers and on culture-based creativity and non-technological innovation for developing the creative industries in Europe. The City of Barcelona includes innovation as part of its everyday action. To develop creative industries and innovation, it is necessary to introduce a more integral approach to EU projects. Innovation is a part of everyday action. The Institute monitors action with data indicators, evaluates actions systematically, and introduces constant innovation in programs and projects. The strength of the Institute is the proximity of dimensions, contact with local cultural stakeholders and capacity of interaction. The Barcelona Institute of Culture has better than others in terms of monitoring and evaluating innovation. EU partners view the Institute of Culture as a strong actor in the dynamic creative field and international projection. One example is the Decidim project[579]—a digital infrastructure for participatory democracy, built entirely and collaboratively as free software. More specifically, Decidim is a web environment (a framework) produced in Ruby on Rails, which allows users to create and configure a website platform or portal, to be used in the form of a social network for democratic participation. The portal allows any organization (local city council, association, university, nongovernmental organization (NGO), trade union, neighborhood, or cooperative) to create massive democratic processes for strategic planning, participatory budgeting, collaborative regulatory design, urban spaces design, and elections. It also enables the organization of in-person meetings, signing up for them, the publication of minutes, proposing points for the agenda and receiving notifications of the results. Decidim can also help organize governing bodies, councils or assemblies, the convening of consultations and referendums or channeling citizen or member initiatives to impact different decision-making processes. Overall, Decidim makes it possible to digitally structure a complete system of participatory democratic governance for any organization. Equality in the political participation of citizens is one of the fundamental principles of any democratic system, and the platform not only has to ensure equal opportunities with respect to the uses and functions, but also access rights. In this sense, the entity in charge of the platform assumes the commitment to promote actions that advance in the direction of providing access and support to the platform for all citizens alike. Giving tools and resources appropriate to the platform is available to anyone who wants to use it.

The specific innovative tools for the program of the Barcelona INTERARTS organization are: Enterprise Resource Planning specific to INTERARTS (the system was developed through the collaboration of INTERARTS, accountants, information technology staff, etc.); models for cross-checking technical activities and management costs; an internal control system for the expenditures and project activities; predictive models for the general budget and analytical budget; control and management systems for the activities carried out abroad; a specialized social platform for the cultural and creative sector, which will include a social feature to facilitate contacts and the setting up of projects; a work experience program abroad for INTERARTS employees; and visiting research fellows in INTERARTS (inviting renowned professionals, especially university professors). These innovative aspects help INTERARTS achieve its objectives, and maintain the organization's international reputation and positioning among professional circles and the general public. Innovative elements are intended to help the organization's development and sustainability in the long run. Investing in developing the organization's potential in international public relations is understood as crucially important given that this is considered a major asset to ensure the organization's capacity to adapt quickly to a rapidly-changing environment. At a local level, the City of Barcelona has deployed efforts to support innovation, in particular through its @22 urban development project. In the @22 district, but also elsewhere in the city, it has developed a network of art factories, mostly in run-down locations. The Ministry of Culture of Spain has a directorate responsible for cultural industries.

The City of Brussels has creative spillover projects in the city. The innovations in the organization are projects on art and science, the impact of culture on innovation and creative spillovers in cities. The developing creative industries and innovation vary from one public authority to the other; in general, however, greater awareness on the importance of cultural investment for attractiveness and economic development is necessary. The City of Marseille supports innovation in the projects and actions they have organized. The mission of cultural organizations is therefore to

> recognize every single person's cultural identity, to have the person at the center of political and public policies again, to reaffirm the principles of freedom and human dignity, and to work concretely to bring humanity together. … Cultural rights are at the same time a concept, a posture, a process.
>
> *(Patrice Meyer-Bish)*

The organization thinks that institutions are making a big confusion between "innovation" and "technological tools." For instance, at present, the EU, the region, and local institutions all ask for "Digital projects," as if it is the solution to all crises. Another example is the EU making an effort to support only very big organizations, and forcing smaller ones to disappear. In the City of Reims, for example, the innovation is seeing through the implementation of a citizen and professional consultation approach to write a cultural guidelines diagram (2019–2023), and prepare a bid for the European Capital of Culture. The strength of Reims is the richness and diversity of cultural proposals on the territory, associated with cooperation and structuring. The weakness is the large size of the community and the offer in the territory, which can generate a certain inertia. Different policies depend on the communities, which choose to favor certain areas of action. The City of Grenoble implements social innovation in terms of partnerships with actors in the social field. We analyzed the first pioneer of the Grenoble Museum, the curator Andry Farcy, who, as early as 1920, brought modern art to the Grenoble Museum (Picasso, Matisse and many others). As such, the Grenoble Museum was historically the first museum of modern art in France and its collection remains quite exceptional in European terms. It is also one of the first museums (some 20 years ago) to have made exhibitions outside the walls (in public places in the neighborhood—library, social center, youth center, hospital an immersion that gives rise to a work of construction with the actors of the neighborhood). Another innovation is the "Nocturnes pour les étudiants" (Night Performances for Students), where young people are the mediators of an evening around a work of their choice; on one occasion more than 3000 students were present. Other innovations in the reception of the public are partnerships with actors in the social field (e.g. Secours Populaire) for dedicated reception of families at the museum, free visits to the exhibitions and collections, guided tours, workshops for young people, night visits for students, visits to the sculpture park, readings, and shows based on works of art. The associations Musée en musique and Les Amis du musée offer a program of 40 concerts in the auditorium. The first offers 40 concerts in the auditorium and short musical sessions in the exhibitions, while the second offers about 30 lectures and cultural outings. Spaces (auditorium, large gallery, patio) are rented for events organized by external parties, libraries, restaurants and independent shops. The innovation came more from the museum teams than from the outside. It would be interesting to better inform and sensitize the teams on innovative techniques and approaches and to put in touch innovative industries and companies with cultural actors.

The City of Mannheim is developing projects that are looking to integrate artistic thinking in entrepreneurial contexts. It is working on several different schemes. It has initiated innovation projects at the intersection of music & medicine (technology), where it cooperated with the University Hospital Mannheim, the Fraunhofer Institute IAO, several music industry stakeholders, and individual artists and musicians. It realized projects in the oncological day-care unit of the hospital and developed a prototype for neurosurgeries where people are brought back into consciousness during the operation and a person is communicating with them in order not to harm the language center of the brain, for instance. The support for the cultural and creative industries in Mannheim has been exceptional. This has a lot to do with the support of the mayor, Dr Peter Kurz, who has supported culture and the creative industries. Mannheim has put into place a unique support structure, particularly for music and the music industry, which is considered a best practice, both nationally and internationally, and which played a big part in Mannheim being accepted into the UNESCO Creative Cities network. There are fairly strong regional networks supporting culture and cooperation; the state of Baden-Württemberg has also brought several projects in Mannheim to fruition. Transcending silos and working at the intersection of disciplines. Seeing and using the creative industries as drivers of innovation also for other sectors and industries. The strength is a vast support infrastructure in terms of both hubs and detailed support structures for creative industries, particularly music. The innovative trends are cross-innovation and co-creation. In the City of Dortmund, the innovative trends for the gallery are global community networking, social networks and platforms (Instagram, Twitter, Facebook, etc.), and the visitors and citizens interested in art. The company does not how to define innovation. To improve the situation and innovation means looking for more global networking via social media in order to raise larger awareness on its profile. It needs to have a straighter profile in terms of innovation and to be much more active regarding social media representation. The City of Rome, City of Mannheim and City of Bologna have programs to support the CCI, which contribute to the development of a creative economy. The developing creative industries and innovation vary from one public authority to the other; in general, however, greater awareness on the importance of cultural investment for attractiveness and economic development is necessary.

In the third focus group of the research of Central-Eastern Europe, we conclude that innovations are not generally a priority of development for local governments, institutions and organizations, mostly because cultural policy is not fully implemented. It is clear that innovation is not on the list of priorities, mostly because of the policy makers that coordinate public institutions. The innovation in the programs appeared in independent associations in the program activities, social innovation is dominant. The development of technology contributes to technological innovation, but social innovation has an important place in the process of development of the cultural sector, and it is interconnected with tech innovation processes. In the local government of the City of Bratislava, innovation is seen in the participation of organizations on project with the mobile phone application KnowSpot, which provides users with information about historic buildings or interesting places online or offline. In order to improve the innovative and creative industries sector, it is necessary that professionals to be given more financial resources, for the costs of marketing to be reduced and for more spaces for these activities to be provided. The improvement of the situation implies developing discussions with professionals for culture. The Culture Department of the City of Bratislava and cultural organizations work with partners from foreign countries on several projects; they are members of the culture forum EUROCITIES, and are working on an agreement with Austria, Poland, and Italy, among others. Bratislava is the cultural heart of Slovakia. Owing to its historical multi-cultural character, local culture is influenced by various ethnic groups. Bratislava has numerous theaters, museums, galleries, concert halls, cinemas, film clubs, and foreign cultural institutions. The City of Novi Sad is the European Capital of Culture in 2022. This city shows how innovation has to be a part of local culture policy. For decades, Novi Sad has built its uniqueness on the foundations of its multicultural character and its numerous cultural and educational institutions. The City of Novi Sad Library has a number of innovation projects and processes: digitalization of the Local History Collection; library on the beach during summer, on the bank of the Danube; book home delivery service for the elderly, the sick, the pregnant, and for those who are unable to come to the library due to severe invalidity or other causes; the "Language Drama Lab," a festival of drama in English; Democratization of Digitalization (service for self-use of the smart phone); and a new library branch for young people with maker spaces and many contemporary contents. The impacts of these actions are many: an increased number of library users; increased consciousness of the importance of the library; bringing the library closer to young people; easier and more comfortable usage of cultural heritage, etc. Concerning innovation, the Library of Novi Sad tries to involve young people in its activities and offers them a chance to create their own cultural development. It has extended its field of competence to diverse areas, such as electronic media, both formal and informal education in arts and computers, and programming. The library plans to equip a workshop for makers' spaces. It has a practice of engaging volunteers. In addition, the library has a long tradition, formal institutionalization, visibility and well-educated human resources in certain areas of expertise. In the Cities of Kiev/Moscow/Eindhoven the organization Stichting Art-East+Art-West (NGO)[580] has been developing cultural projects, curating exhibitions, and consulting governmental and private institutions with regard to strategic cultural issues (art, design, landscape architecture). The areas encompassed by the projects are the Netherlands, Russia, and Ukraine. The target groups of the activities are the general public, architects, designers, and art professionals. The most frequently realized services are exhibitions and consultations with innovation processes. The innovative trend that has had the most positive impacts on the organization is the cooperation between designers and scientists. For example, innovation was present in the 2014 exhibition in Moscow, "Dialog with Water," in which it showed a new ecological approach to solve problems of flooding. The organization also included innovation in an assignment for exhibitions of Creative Ukraine during Dutch Design Week. The result of the project was weak, but the projects on innovations and creative industries are very well developed in the region of Eindhoven. The organization is doing a very good job, especially in comparison with Eastern European countries. The organization believes that paying more attention to the neighboring EU countries with creative potential and different views would help in the production of new innovative ideas. The organization is innovative in terms of combining the Eastern European and Dutch approaches, and the other organizations and cultural institutions perceive that the organization has experience in different fields of cultural projects, and knowledge of different mentalities. At the Museum of Contemporary Art Belgrade, in the City of Belgrade, innovation is not a tangible concept that could be analyzed in the case of the museum. Innovation can be seen through the programs that the institution delivers over the course of a year. On the other hand, the Belgrade association BAZAART develops new methodologies for learning through drama and theatre. During the IDEAL project, it invented the Intercultural Learning Through Drama methodology, which is published on-line and widely implemented by the association and others. Another example is the "Tolerant Classroom" collection of workshops, which aims to promote tolerance, inclusion, and cooperation among schoolchildren (both of which are available on the website for BAZAART). In addition, drama texts are staged across the region. With regard to innovations, mechanisms should be established as to how to mainstream them into general cultural and educational systems. The decision-makers have practically no contact with the "base" practice. This has to be changed first. BAZAART has been regarded as an innovator, expert, and visionary. The weaknesses are the small number of people and hence limited operational capacities, no working space for workshops, rehearsals and productions, and unstable financing. In terms of innovation for the City of Gabrovo Museum for Humour and Satire, it has been dealing with change, not really innovation. Introducing change in institutions which are conservative by nature, such as museums, is a slow and difficult process. Some projects have been considered innovative without essentially being such. Both change and innovation are a matter of communication; however, innovation is often too far ahead to be possibly communicated. Governments in the region are generally well designed for innovation. Both innovation and entrepreneurial approaches require systematic investment in human capital, which is quite a contradiction in aging and demographically endangered areas. In the City of Zagreb, The Muze d.o.o./Muses Ltd. is an organization for consulting and managing in culture and tourism. In terms of innovation, it has strong foundations in theory, selection of creative collaborators, extensive work with clients, and great practical experience. The others perceive the company's strength through innovation, reliability, methodology, thoroughness, passion, teamwork, and knowledge of work processes. Innovation is at the heart of all activities in the Muses. The organization has a strong team, is always a step ahead, adds a European dimension to the interpretation of heritage, and has creative associates. The majority of the business of the Muses is based on projects financed by the public sector. It wants to reinforce business-to-business (B2B) activities. The Muses are better at knowledge-based consulting, while the competitors have a different approach based on design and less on heritage interpretation planning. To improve the current situation, the Muses are working to raise awareness of the importance of the interpretation of heritage as a discipline that is crucial to sustainable use and sustainability of heritage overall. Innovation comes from understanding the heritage substance and the Muses interpret this as understanding the audience's place in the creative platform of their collaborators (architects, designers, IT, artists, etc.) In the City of Skopje, Republic of Macedonia, there is no specific policy on innovation. Innovations are the introduction lines for interdisciplinary projects, for the independent cultural sector, for participatory projects and an ingrained strategy for the creative industries. The main problem is the weak capacity of public administration, the lack of interministerial cooperation, poor monitoring of implementation, no evaluation, etc. Cultural democracy is the strong point, as they have opened institutions for citizens. Through its activities within MOCAK's Education Department, the Museum of Contemporary Arts in the City of Krakow promotes the idea of a society open to art, in which everyone, regardless of age or social status, can join the discussion. It organizes interactive meetings with contemporary art and its creators, collectors, and commentators. The educational projects prepared by the museum enable participants to explore the universe of art and try their hand at creative activities. MOCAK-edu offers workshops for various age groups, from kindergarten pupils to seniors. The museum's educational projects are not only meant to make their participants open and sensitive to art from the youngest age, but also to prove that it is never too late for education. The museum organizes workshops and museum lessons tailored to the needs of both younger and older audiences. MOCAK's educational projects are geared towards various social groups, including people with disabilities, teachers and educators, people from smaller towns and those subject to various forms of social exclusion. It focuses, in particular, on the inhabitants of Zabłocie and Podgórze, its closest neighbors, in order to transform the district into a space that is friendly to contemporary art. MOCAK not only organizes meetings with artists, but also invites them to join the museum's artistic projects. The participants have already had an opportunity to draw comic strips or paint murals together with the artists. The projects take place both in the museum and in the city, while educational classes are also conducted in other institutions, schools, and kindergartens. MOCAK is innovative in thinking. It is a place targeted at young people and is the museum of contemporary art. The projects, exhibitions, and collaborating artists of the museum are innovative. Due to that, innovation is a topic of significant interest. It is also interested in technological innovation. As an example, MOCAK has prepared a mobile app designed to help visitors plan their visit to the museum and serve as a guide around the exhibitions. The navigation was possible thanks to QR codes and innovative HG Beacon device. All the projects are undertaken by the museum with diverse audiences in mind. The publications produced will provide information bringing closer the origin and significance of the works and events presented and place them in contexts. The institution considers it an important challenge to reduce prejudice against very recent art. It offers exhibitions (challenging, intelligent, and interesting), art works that are beautifully presented, a beautiful building (well placed in the history and location), interesting, diverse and well-organized museum lessons, friendly staff, a great café, and bookstore. To improve its work, the museum is developing its offer and activities. In terms of innovation in the City of Ljubljana, the Museums and Galleries of Ljubljana are becoming more and more involved in different presentation schemes, which also include new models of presentation of the exhibitions, especially work with a young public. They have organized special programs for children who became their co-workers in preparing an exhibition. This program is called Museum from Close, in which young collaborators become curators, PR experts, etc. They are given the opportunity to watch how a museum functions and what is important in its work. The institutions are strongly convinced that new models of practices must be a part of sustainable development of the work of museums and galleries. To improve work, the institutions have their own network called RogLab, which is a creative platform for creative processes. On this platform, creative industries are connected with new models of creativity and practical labs for new emerging creative productions. The Museums and Galleries are strongly involved in the local community and collaboration with the NGO sector. They are also strong in processes of making alliances with international partners. The Museums and Galleries have to improve digital competitiveness and organization of their work environment. It is important to follow new possibilities in the digital world and to improve social inclusion. The Ludwig Museum in the City of Budapest has innovation policies through multimedia exhibitions – annually, there are between 1 and 2 exhibitions featuring these kinds of artworks. The public is increasingly looking for these exhibitions and demanding media and interactive works, guided tours with mobile applications, developed for the permanent exhibition, with every visitor getting a code for it with the purchase ticket (not too popular). Other innovation policies are new programs for people with disadvantages (not only for blind or people with wheelchairs but also for mentally disabled or homeless people). The museum conducted special research on this topic and one of its colleagues is constantly developing these kinds of methods, projects, and programs outside of the museums, and international conferences focusing on scientific research about the restoration and preservation of media art works are organized on an annual basis. To improve innovation, the universities of design can do a lot because they have the opportunity to combine science and art with practice. The museum thinks that these initiatives should be supported, as well as promoting cooperation in the spirit of co-creation. The collection is in a MuseumRia database, which exports data to the webpage. This software is also used as a management system. To improve the situation, the museum has to have online communication, fundraising and new technologies. Those companies that improve their with innovative trends have to be in collaboration with cultural institutions.

Notes

568 UCLG, "Culture 21: Actions."
569 Ibid.
570 UCLG, "Agenda 21 Culture."
571 UCLG, "Culture 21: Actions."
572 Ibid.
573 Ibid.
574 Esteve Caramés, "Barcelona's Cultural Policies Behind the Scenes New Context, Renewed Strategies," in *Sustaining Cultural Development, Unified Systems and New Governance in Cultural Life*, ed. James Doyle and Biljana Mickov (London: Routledge Publishing, 2013):, 29–35.
575 UCLG, "Culture 21: Actions."
576 Biljana Mickov and James Doyle, "Introduction," in *Sustaining Cultural Development: Unified Systems and New Governance in Cultural Life*, ed. James Doyle and Biljana Mickov (London: Routledge Publishing, 2013), 1–15.
577 UCLG, "Agenda 21 for Culture."
578 "The Arts Plan," Dublin City Arts Office.
579 "General Description and Introduction to How Decidim Works," Decidim.
580 Stichting Art-East+Art-West, accessed May 9, 2021, https://www.arteastartwest.nl/nl/3/contact.html

12
DISCUSSION

The empirical hypothesis of this study is that the elements we investigate are consequentially related. The relations between culture, social development, economy, and environmental sustainability are causal-consequential and have to be balanced; when there is a change in relation to cultural policy, the social, economic context changes and they are interconnected. The cultural sector is an important element in addition to the economic, social, and environmental dimensions of sustainable development, and should be included as one of the dimensions that support sustainability. Sustainable development itself balances environmental protection, social progress, the economy, and stability both today and for the future. It is a vision of sustainable development with three dimensions: economy, social inclusion, and ecological balance. The conclusion is based on a balance between culture, environment, social values, and economic sustainable development with a focus on innovation policy.

Based on the arguments of the case studies, it can be seen that the development by the research criteria between the presented groups are different. The results of the research throughout Europe indicate a balanced link between innovation, culture, and the economy. It also shows that cultural policy has to be in correlation with innovation in the cultural sector. The development of creative industries contributes to the sustainable economy, creates new jobs, and brings stability to cultural sector. Innovation through the local governments, institutions, and cultural organization has been present through cultural projects, art management, the IT sector, and social innovation. One of the cities in Europe that has this strategy is the City of Eindhoven, a medium-sized town with a constant innovative development process. However, if we consider instead the City of Barcelona,[581] we will see the systematic local development of culture based on a strategic plan for culture and innovation. The Barcelona City Council has a systematic management approach for cultural development.

DOI: 10.4324/9781003336648-15

We would like to point out that local development does not mean the loss of input by the state government. It only means that culture development is equable. Every city has to find the best way for change and face new challenges. The answer to that is to "be extremely innovative and try to implement your ideas." A strategic plan for culture that has to be evaluated after a few years with the analysis of the results is increasingly important. Further, it is important that a regional government has strategic plans for the cities in the region in relation to the cultural sector. The regional—city context is the key to development at the state level.

The creative people are present everywhere: in art, business, and architecture, and in both small and big companies. Innovative ideas are original values for business, art, and culture. Also, a new innovative idea is a response to the fast-changing times we are living in at present. Change is actually an essential ingredient for any innovation project. But we need to have the ability to be agile and to make changes quickly; it is therefore important to listen to your own feelings too, and, on that basis, to make decisions regarding which way to go. The competition in that sense becomes stronger, but the quality of innovation is much better. The important issue is also how people become happier in creative processes. Citizens will have a new opportunity for change and success. To attract the citizens to cultural events, we have to create a good program and we have to feel what people like and to listen to their needs. Thus, the visitors are significant and the processes of involving them in cultural activities needs to be systematic. We have to find a way to attract them as well as to understand what they are interested in. We cannot be passive viewers; instead, we have to be innovative in order to include more people in cultural activities. It does not matter if it is a museum, theatre, or a city library. Interesting programs, education programs, and attractive information are among the elements that can help in attracting more visitors. The mutual trust between cultural professionals and citizens has to be built in order to serve and feel what the citizens expect from us. We must know what kind of feelings they have and how to make them interested in becoming a part of art expression. That means not only entertainment but also a learning process and innovative development (for both the professionals and the citizens). The right and clear information is the main tool necessary to get people informed about the happenings in the cultural field in their city. If we look at that task from a managerial position, it is clear that a complete digitalization of the sector can make information accessible.

In order to attract citizens to cultural activities through institutions and open space artistic projects, we have to provide good information (that is, comprehensive marketing). There are so many different kinds of exhibitions, festivals, and theatre shows which are seeking the right audience. We believe that it is crucial to make a good balance between cultural projects and citizens' interest.

The analysis supports the theory that innovation implies new ideas that make a difference: "The creation and implementation of new processes, products, services and methods of delivery which result in positive social and/or economic outcomes for the citizenry."[582]

> Economic models that aim at cultural sensitivity need to engage in implementation practice that includes collaboration, cooperation, trade and donations. All economic models are based on specific cultural values. An effective link between the public, market and cooperative economy, together with the reciprocity among them, is essential to achieving a decentralized, environmentally balanced development.[583]

The data suggest that full innovation processes lead to improved functioning of local governance, institutions, and arts organizations. It also suggests that the development of creative industries has to be the priority in state policy in order to bring stable development to the culture sector.

The statistics shown in the *Orange Economy* by Felipe Buitrago support us "to share essential knowledge" and innovation.[584] His work is largely concerned with the creative economy. The strongest facts/statistics relating to the Cultural Economy are the following: the global, cultural and creative economy is currently worth $4.3 trillion every year; creative goods and services are a more resilient investment than oil; for example, oil exports, as reported by OPEC, contracted by 40% in 2009 while creative goods and service only contracted by 12% in the same period; similarly, the entertainments industry, at the core of the cultural economy, was worth 230% of the oil exports for all OPEC countries in 2009; more than 25,000,000,000 songs have been downloaded since the launch of iTunes in 1998, at an average of 99 cents per song; Box Office and Merchandising for the 10 most successful Broadway musicals brought in 26.9 billion compared with China's expenditure of 25 billion on the Three Gorges dam; the Cirque du Soleil is an acrobatic theatre company employs more than 5,000 people, and reports a yearly turnover of over $800 million; it is estimated that the Rio Carnival attracted over 850,000 visitors in 2012, and they contributed $628 million in consumption to the country's economy; the 12th Ibero-American Theatre Festival of Bogotá in 2010 estimates an overall attendance of 3.9 million people; nine of the Artists at the 2015 Venice Biennale created works that sold for over $1 million; in 2015, over 6 million people visited the Tower of London, with Chester Zoo coming a close second with 4.6 million.

In the post-Covid[585] period we have to consider that the effects of the crisis and the drop in investment in the sector will affect the production of cultural goods and services and their diversity in the years to come. In the absence of public support and recovery strategies, the cultural and creative sectors will have a negative impact on cities and regions in terms of jobs, levels of innovation, citizen well-being, and the diversity of communities. Digitalization, coupled with emerging technologies such as virtual realities, can create new forms of cultural experience, dissemination, and new business models with market potential. With the lockdown, many public and private providers moved content online for free in order to keep audiences engaged and satisfy the increased demand for cultural content. The lockdown and social distancing measures have also made evident the importance of arts and culture for people's mental well-being.

The cities and regions may consider cultural and creative sectors as well as cultural participation as a driver of social impact in its own right and throughout the economy. The sector is already an economic driver and source of innovation. In many cities and regions, specializations in the cultural and creative sectors are evolving, making new skills of creation and pro-social behavioral changes. The current crisis and the social distancing measures are likely to have long-lasting effects on culture. It is clear from the study outlined above that it is important to support the innovation capacity of cultural and creative sectors.

Notes

581 "Barcelona Cultura," Barcelona Institute of Culture.
582 Mark Evans et al., Innovation in Local Government.
583 UCLG, "Culture 21: Actions."
584 Felipe Buitrago Restrepo and Iván Duque Márquez, *The Orange Economy an Infinite Opportunity* (Washington: Inter-American Development Bank, 2013).
585 "Culture shock: COVID-19 and the cultural and creative sectors", OECD, accessed May 15, 2021, https://www.oecd.org/coronavirus/policy-responses/culture-shock-covid-19-and-the-cultural-and-creative-sectors-08da9e0e/

13
CONCLUSION

The study analyses the theoretical and practical approach to culture and innovation. Joseph Schumpeter defined innovation as encompassing new products, processes, raw materials, management methods, and markets.[586]

The economy has to produce the values on which it is based and build a sustainable ecosystem. Cultural and economic factors of the environment must be taken into account and developed in parallel. The cultural ecosystem should not be treated as merely a segment of the economy, but rather as a system that contains the economy.[587] The interconnectedness of cultural systems and other segments of sustainable development must be taken into account. The thesis analyses cities, and their cultural development through innovation processes that take into account social innovation, project innovation, cross-innovation, and environmental sustainability. The study offers an analysis of the contemporary approach to culture and innovation, as well as to the development of cities, with culture being a pivotal factor in developmental processes. Sustainable development and culture are connected since culture contributes to society's understanding and appreciation of the natural resources and, because of that, plays an essential role in the promotion of economic progress in a fair society. Sustainable development balances environmental resource protection, social progress, the economy, and stability now and for the future. It is a vision of sustainable development with three dimensions: the economy, social inclusion and environmental balance.[588]

The key points of the thesis are cultural policy development with aspects of innovation that have an impact on the development of culture and creative industries in cities throughout Europe that ensure sustainable development processes. The case studies show with the facts that the cultural ecosystem contains the economy. The relations between culture, social development, economy, and environmental sustainability are causal-consequential and have to be balanced. The cultural sector is an important element in addition to the economic, social, and environmental

DOI: 10.4324/9781003336648-16

dimension of sustainable development, and should be included as one of the dimensions that support stable sustainability. The topic is relevant for the professionals, academic work, and researchers.

To attain sustainability, the economy has to produce the values on which it is based, and which consider the culture of the specific environment. The economy is in a good state if its policy promotes the use of local resources.[589] Cultural activism plays an important role in sustainable economic development and creates economic activities, entrepreneurship, and jobs, adding to the attractiveness of cities and contributing to the development of tourism.[590] Cultural and economic factors of the environment have to be taken into account and developed in parallel. In the following document it is emphasized that

> Economic models that aim at cultural sensitivity need to engage in implementation practice that includes collaboration, cooperation, trade and donations. An effective link between the public, market and cooperative economy, together with the reciprocity among them, is essential to achieving a decentralized, environmentally balanced development.[591]

The cultural ecosystem should not be treated as merely a segment of the economy, but rather as a system that contains the economy. Therefore, the interconnectedness of cultural systems and other segments of sustainable development must be taken into account.

Cities and regions have to maintain mixed economic programs that maximize donations for cultural projects. Partnership between people from culture and business fields is also important, together with systemic innovations and knowledge transfer. "Tourism needs to be linked to this cultural ecosystem, by means of implementing cultural routes. Business organizations such as chambers of commerce possess special programs related to cultural politics of cities."[592] When it comes to developing cities and regions, a priority has to be made of restoring public spaces for cultural happenings and art-related activities that would represent the social unity of a city, as well as strengthening the city's cultural identity based on a network of cultural entities and associations.[593] Clearly, it is this firm network that forms a basis for the promotion and implementation of ambitious cultural policies on a city level. Charles Landry concludes that some vast cities are wonderful and loveable, while others are depressing. Similarly, some smaller cities are a delight and convenient, while others are small-minded and limiting. The cultural sector is the main chain that can make city life good for the people. In his book *Psychology and the City*, Landry states that the cycle of influencing and being influenced by the city impacts our mind, and our emotional state impacts the city with untold effects.[594]

> It is astonishing that psychology, the study exploring the dynamics of feeling and emotion, has not been taken sufficiently seriously as an urban discipline, not only by psychology itself but also urban decision makers, since it seeks to understand why we act the way we do.[595]

People are those who define the city and they have personality, identity and make the city.

Digitalization is changing society and social life, culture, connectivity, the economy, and cities.[596] Smart city ideas or evolving collaborative governance models are among the responses to digitalization through which improvements to our quality of life are possible by making life more citizen-centric, more local, more convenient, or efficient.[597] Cities matter like never before, in spite of increased virtual interactions.

Revolutionary technology has also changed the role of culture in people's lives. Instead of being passive consumers of culture, today we all take on positions such as producers and consumers, authors and readers, performers, and spectators all of the time.[598] This all creates the sense of individual and collective identity and people define themselves by what they choose to watch, read, and listen. All of these processes explain why culture has become more important to cities and increasingly important in the world of politics and policy. New technology is completely transforming the ways of doing and creating. This is crucial to the ecosystem of humans. Connectivity between cities is important in terms of economy and creative industries as a driver of those industries. The policy approach is that the job of city governance is to *enable* people to be a part of culture and to improve their ability to learn from culture, and also to create the culture of today and the future. It is about drawing attention to the capacity of people to use cultural places for themselves. The city will flourish both socially and economically. The conclusion is that city governments can make a rich cultural life for everyone.[599]

The innovations are unavoidable; they improve creative processes. Moreover, innovations encourage the creative sector in all directions; they include novelties in processes and services, and are an effective way for things to be carried out. Some theorists believe that innovations are more economic and social in nature, rather than a technological term, but also that they are intertwined and closely linked. If we observe the sector of culture, it is very important, in the context of cultural policies in cities in particular. Innovations contribute to an increased visibility of urban cultural development, and they also put citizens at the center of innovative process development, allowing them to create innovations by themselves.

> Innovative cultural development at both regional and national levels in a modern society must be transversal. All dimensions of the city or territory (social, educational, economic, touristic) are interconnected and culture should connect with each of them. By means of clear cultural policy, innovation should incorporate contemporary innovative approach, digitalization, new ideas, creative processes and technologically sophisticated media. It should also take into consideration the presentation of culture which aims to facilitate cultural exchange between contrasting communities while simultaneously preserving the specific characteristics of place, traditional values and architectural heritage.[600]

In order to ensure future innovation and attain certain levels of stability, it is important to present new models that can be implemented, especially in strategic cultural planning. This early part of the twenty-first century, and perhaps this decade in particular, will almost certainly be an epoch of networking that will give rise to the advancement of myriad agendas and platforms that will seek to further cultural research and development. Networking provides the space in which information turns into knowledge and knowledge into innovation, making it the laboratory of the present.[601] There is a direct effect of the IT sector—as platforms are increasingly used, different forms and possibilities are developing. The creative industries have additional digital forms, which means that this kind of innovation is accelerating more and developing further. This is digital innovation, and it affects the social context. The cultural policy is the one that has to regulate it. At this time, there many challenges in the functioning of the cultural sector caused by the pandemic—culture must undoubtedly be developed with the help of innovative processes. The action is to continue research and development of innovations for the purpose of cultural policy that focuses on humanity at the center of development for the benefit of all.

We are witnessing quick changes in the economy, education, and resource systems—all through the intensive development of networks and technology. These are very fast times.

Culture is increasingly becoming one of the major factors in the development of society and cities on a global level. It intensifies both democratization and development. One of our tasks is definitely to give a perspective of an extreme future; to give possible answers to the development of society, cultural industries and businesses, i.e., the creators of the extreme future.

Those who make decisions are increasingly coming to realize that priority must be given to the innovators and representatives of the creative industry. These are the people who envision the future; they aspire to make our lives more pleasant and strive to make business and the traditional industries more profitable.

Modern times bring a new approach to the development and setting of the cultural policy system of a city. We are in a time when systems change quickly: the financial model is changing, and so are both economy and technology. This is a very fast-moving time, which forces us to change. The answer to these challenges is innovation.

Technology, talent, and tolerance are the features that make a city attractive for creative people. Only with these elements can an innovative environment develop. To create an environment that is appropriate for modern society, the city has to have a stable policy in the cultural sector. All of the steps forward, as well as making the culture of space more modern, are directly related to art and urban planning. The balance between practice and research has to be constantly present, and in this relation, art achieves its real meaning. The cities of the future will require maximum creativity; the infrastructure has to be set in an excellent way. It is a need of the new society.

Based on the research in three focus groups through the cities of Europe, which was conducted in the work, and based on the characteristics of the development of innovations and creative industries, the following can be concluded. The focus groups are based on the characteristics of development of innovation and creative industries in Europe. In the first focus group of the research, the conclusion is that innovations are developed in local governments, institutions, and organizations. The development of technology contributes to technological innovation, but social innovation has an important place to play in the process of development of the cultural sector, and it is interconnected with tech innovation processes. The City of London, City of Glasgow and City of Eindhoven all have programs supporting the Cultural and Creative industries (CCI), which contribute to the development of a creative economy. The development of creative industries and innovations should be an integral part of state policy, and it should be seen as an essential part of social, educational and economic policies. The future perspective is to see the creative industries being treated as an essential industry and part of the sustainable and regenerative economic agenda. The conclusion drawn from the second focus group of the research is that innovations are developed in local governments, institutions, and organizations. The development of technology contributes to technological innovation, but social innovation is in the first position in the process of development of the cultural sector supported by technological innovation, and its connected with tech innovation processes. The City of Rome deals with innovation through the promotion of innovative local cultural projects and developing innovation through creative industries and tourism. The City of Bologna, through the project INCREDIBOL!, is seeking for more attention to be paid to creative spillovers and cultural-based creativity and non-technological innovation for developing creative industries in Europe. The City of Barcelona includes innovation as a part of everyday action. The monitoring action with data indicators evaluates actions systematically and introduces constant innovation into its programs and projects. To develop creative industries and innovation, a more integral approach to EU projects is necessary. The City of Brussels has creative spillover projects in the city. The City of Marseille supports innovation in the projects and actions they organize. Similarly, in the City of Reims, the innovation is seeing through the implementation of a citizen and professional consultation approach to write a cultural guidelines diagram (2019–2023), and is preparing a bid for the European Capital of Culture. The City of Grenoble implements social innovation in terms of partnerships with actors in the social field and the City of Mannheim develops projects that are looking to integrate artistic thinking in entrepreneurial contexts. The developing creative industries and innovation vary from one public authority to another; in general, however, what is needed is greater awareness about the importance of cultural investment for attractiveness and economic development. Finally, in the third focus group of the research, that focused on Central and Eastern Europe, the conclusion is that innovations are not a priority of development in local governments, institutions, and organizations, principally because cultural policy is not fully implemented. It is clear that innovation is not on the list of priorities, mostly because of the policy makers that coordinate public institutions. The use of innovation in programs appears in the work of independent associations; in the program activities, social innovation is dominant. The City of Ljubljana, the Cities of Eindhoven, Kiev and Moscow and the City of Zagreb have programs for supporting the CCI, including innovation, which contributes to economic development. In order to achieve the sustainability of the cultural sector, the development of creative industries and innovations should become an integral part of state policy, and it should be seen as an essential part of social, educational, and economic policies.

Innovation has to be positioned at the center of development; it is one of the basic strategies. In order to transform the urban profile and the international presentation of a city, it is crucial to mobilize enormous amounts of collective enthusiasm. As the key element of promoting urban transformation, a cultural profile of a city should be set. The role of art is, without doubt, great and necessary, both in the sense of aesthetics and art and in the sense of urban development and connecting a number of city segments. Cultural institutions and creative centers are among such segments. The cultural platform of a city has to be harmonized, stable, and strategically set. The successful and attractive cities of the future will be those that are run by people who really understand the new needs of their citizens. The key factors in these terms are tolerance, diversity, a dynamic market, excellent urban infrastructure, the educational system, and of course, culture. The need for management in modern culture is increasing due to social mobility, which inevitably affects art and, equally, cultural institutions. Cultural institutions become much more open; they keep up with social changes and take an active role in this process. They are a significant factor in securing the sustainability of a society. There is a strong need for an organized system that will provide equable development. With the aim of continuing progress in knowledge, the search for new skills in activities—that is, an exchange of experiences in cultural practice—is necessary. Within a wider context, management in culture exceeds local borders. Modern art and culture are important additions to contemporary life and they connect aspects of popular culture, modern civilization, and the technology of development. Through art, a perspective of the world of values and all open questions is made, a process which helps us to develop human prosperity and specific thinking.

Politicians and policy makers must now consider factors such as the economy, culture, social inclusion, environment protection, and the balance between them if they wish to achieve a more sustainable practice. To raise the status of sustainability we have to create a balance between these elements. Ways of thinking are changing so quickly that we have to change.

Pragmatism in creativity, business, and culture represents an interest for all of us in the future. It is clear and important that there will be an unavoidable fusion in the future between art and technology within a human context in terms of creativity, expression, emotion, and new ideas. We are perhaps at the beginning of a new age. We live in times of creativity and innovation. Standard models are no longer recognizable. Creativity is the core of ability in culture. Innovation in any sense is an important segment of present times in the post-industrial world, which is being virtually impacted by changes in global culture, where importance is given to the innovators in the creative industries and their representatives with the aim of creating a much more satisfied society.

Notes

586 Schumpeter, *Capitalism, Socialism and Democracy.*
587 UCLG, "Culture 21: Actions."
588 Rio+20 took place in June 2012, on the 20th anniversary of the first UN Conference on Environment and Development (UNCED), also known as the Earth Summit, at which the concept of "sustainable development" was introduced to the international agenda.
589 UCLG, "Agenda 21 for Culture."
590 UCLG, "Culture 21: Actions."
591 Ibid.
592 Ibid.
593 Esteve Caramés, "Barcelona's Cultural Policies Behind the Scenes New Context, Renewed Strategies," in *Sustaining Cultural Development, Unified Systems and New Governance in Cultural Life*, ed. James Doyle and Biljana Mickov (London: Routledge Publishing, 2013), 29–35.
594 Charles Landry, *Psychology & the City: The Hidden Dimension* (Gloucestershire: Comedia Publisher, 2017).
595 Ibid.
596 Charles Landry, *The Digitized City: Influence & Impact 2016.* https://charleslandry.com/themes/the-digitized-city/
597 Ibid.
598 Ibid.
599 John Holden, "How We Value Arts and Culture," in *Sustaining Cultural Development, Unified Systems and New Governance in Cultural Life*, ed. James Doyle and Biljana Mickov (London: Routledge Publishing, 2013).
600 UCLG, "Culture 21: Actions."
601 Biljana Mickov and James Doyle, "Introduction," in Sustaining Cultural Development: Unified Systems and New Governance in Cultural Life, ed. James Doyle and Biljana Mickov (London: Routledge Publishing, 2013), 1–15.

BIBLIOGRAPHY

Agenda 21 for Culture. "#CULTURECOVID19." n.d. Accessed May 15, 2021. http://www.agenda21culture.net/culturecovid19

Art Forum., *Innovation and Creativity in Europe*, Brussels, 2009. www.encatc.com, http://www.cityfutures2009.com/PDF/89_M_Kostres_Atanackovic_Jelicic.pdf

Bakhshi, Hasan, Radhika Desai, and Alan Freeman. *Not Rocket Science: A Roadmap for Cultural R&D*. London: Mission Models Money, 2010.

Bakhshi, Hasan, Alan Freeman, and Peter Higgs. *A Dynamic Mapping of the UK's Creative Industries*. London: Nesta, 2013.

Bakhshi, Hasan, Alan Freeman, and Jason Potts. *State of Uncertainty, Innovation Policy Through Experimentation*. London: NESTA, 2011.

Bakhshi, Hasan, Ian Hargreaves, and Juan Mateos-Garcia. *A Manifesto for the Creative Economy*. London: Nesta, 2013.

Bakhshi, Hasan, and Erin McVittie. "Creative Supply Chain Linkages and Innovation: Do the Creative Industries Stimulate Business Innovation in the Wider Economy?" *Innovation: Management, Policy & Practice* 11, no. 2 (2009): 169–189.

Barcelona Art Factories programme. n.d. Accessed April 18, 2020. http://www.bcn.cat/fabriquesdecreacio/ca/

"Barcelona Cultura." Barcelona Institute of Culture. n.d. Accessed May 10, 2021. http://barcelonacultura.bcn.cat/en/culture-institute

Benghozi, Pierre-Jean, Elisa Salvador, and Jean Paul Simon, *Models of ICT Innovation. A Focus on the Cinema Sector. European Union Report*. Luxembourg: Publications Office of the European Union, 2015: 9–14.

Béraud, Phillipe. "Les industries de territoire : énergie, réseaux, culture." *Les Cahiers du CERCI* 4, no. 1. (2009): 221–257.

Béraud, Phillipe, Viviane Du Castel, and Frank Cormerais. "Open Innovation, Economy of Contribution and the Territorial Dynamics of Creative Industries." *Journal of Innovation Economics & Management* 2, no. 10 (2012): 81–105.

Berger, Thor, and Carl Benedict Frey. *Bridging the Skills Bap*. London: Institute for Public Policy Research, 2006: 40–42.

Berting, Jan. *Europe: A Heritage, a Challenge, a Promise*. Delft: Eburon Academic Publishers, 2006.

Bhandari, Pritha. "An Introduction to Qualitative Research." Scribbr. n.d. Accessed May 20, 2021 https://www.scribbr.com/methodology/qualitative-research/

Bloomfield, Jude, and Franco Bianchini. *Planning for the Intercultural City*. Bournes Green: Comedia, 2004.

Bochmann, Klaus. *L'idée d'Europe jusqu'au XXè siècle*, (1990) quoted in Jan Berting. *Europe: A Heritage, a Challenge, a Promise*. Delft: Eburon Academic Publishers, 2006.

Bomsel, Olivier, Anne-Gaëlle Geffroy, and Gille Le Blanc. *When Internet Meets Entertainment: The Economics of Digital Media Industries*. Paris: Presses de l'Ecole des Mines, 2006.

Braconnier, Luc. "Luxembourg and the Great Region: A Cultural Challenge." In *Sustaining Cultural Development, Unified Systems and New Governance in Cultural Life*, edited by James Doyle and Biljana Mickov. London: Routledge publishing, 2013.

Breckon, Jonathan. *Better Public Services Through Experimental Government*. London: Alliance for Useful Evidence, 2015.

Bujinac, Davor. "Creative Industries." In *Sustaining Cultural Development, Unified Systems and New Governance in Cultural Life*, edited by James Doyle and Biljana Mickov. London: Routledge publishing, 2013.

Camuffo, Dario. *Microclimate for Cultural Heritage*. Amsterdam: Elsevier, 1998.

Cañigueral, Albert. "Hacia una economía colaborativa responsable." *Oikonomics* 6 (2016): 16–27.

Caramés, Esteve. "Barcelona's Cultural Policies Behind the Scenes New Context, Renewed Strategies." In *Sustaining Cultural Development, Unified Systems and New Governance in Cultural Life*, edited by James Doyle and Biljana Mickov, 29–35. London: Routledge publishing, 2013.

Cassar, May. "Sustainable Heritage: Challenges and Strategies for the Twenty-First Century." *APT Bulletin: Journal of Preservation Technology* 40, no.1 (2009): 3–11.

Côme, Thierry. *Management de la diversité culturelle: quels enjeux en Europe?* coll. « Identités et cultures en Europe » T. Côme, L. Meskova, dir. Bruxelles: Editions Bruylandt, 2012.

Comune di Bologna. "Open Data." n.d. Accessed May 15, 2021, http://dati.comune.bologna.it/

Cultural Heritage in Action. n.d. Accessed April 8, 2020. http://www.cultureforcitiesandregions.eu/

Davos Declaration, 2018. Accessed April 7, 2020. https://www.newsd.admin.ch/newsd/message/attachments/51119.pdf

Decidim. n.d. Accessed April 5, 2020. https://www.decidim.barcelona/

Demsetz, Harold. "The Theory of the Firm Revisited." In *The Nature of The Firm: Origins, Evolution and Development*, edited by Oliver Williamson and Sidney Winter. New York: Oxford University Press, 1991.

Doyle, James. "An introduction to the Cultural Economy." In *Culture, Innovation and the Economy*, edited Biljana Mickov and James Doyle. London: Routledge Publishing, 2019: 1–2.

Doyle, James, and Biljana Mickov. "On Creativity." In *The Creative City: Vision and Execution*. London: Routledge Publishing, 2015.

Dukić, Dušan. *Klimatologija*. Beograd: Geografski fakultet, 2006.

"Ecology of culture." n.d. http://www.ahrc.ac.uk/documents/project-reports-and-reviews/the-ecology-of-culture/, Accessed May 9, 2021.

Ehrlich, Paul, and John Holdren. "Impact of Population Growth." *Science* no. 3977 (1971): 1212–1217. https://faculty.washington.edu/stevehar/Ehrlich.pdf

EuroAccess. "Call: Participatory Approaches and Social Innovation in Culture." Macro-Regions. n.d. Accessed May 20, 2021. https://www.euro-access.eu/call/participatory_approaches_and_social_innovation_in_culture

European Center for Creative Economy. n.d. Accessed May 10, 2021, www.e-c-c-e.de

European Commission. *Preserving Our Heritage, Improving Our Environment, Volume I – 20 Years of EU Research Into Cultural Heritage*. Luxembourg: Publications Office of the European Union, 2008.

European Commission. *Green Paper Audit Policy: Lessons from the Crisis*. COM(2010) 561 final, Brussels, 2010. Accessed April 9, 2020. https://www.europarl.europa.eu/meetdocs/2009_2014/documents/com/com_com(2010)0561_/com_com(2010)0561_en.pdf

European Commission. *Cultural Awareness and Expression Handbook*. Luxembourg: Publications Office of the European Union, 2016.

European Commission. *A Renewed EU Agenda for Higher Education*. COM/2017/0247 final, Brussels, 2017. Accessed April 7, 2020. https://eur-lex.europa.eu/legal-content/EN/TXT/?uri=COM%3A2017%3A247%3AFIN

European Commission. *A Credible Enlargement Perspective for and Enhanced EU Engagement with the Western Balkans*. COM(2018)65 final, Strasbourg, 2018. Accessed April 8, 2020. https://eur-lex.europa.eu/legal-content/EN/TXT/?uri=CELEX%3A52018DC0065

European Commission. *The New European Agenda for Culture*, 2018. Accessed April 7, 2020. https://ec.europa.eu/culture/policy/strategic-framework_en

European Commission, "Intercultral Dialogue." n.d. Accessed April 7, 2020. https://ec.europa.eu/culture/policy/strategic-framework/intercultural-dialogue_en

European Commission. "European Capitals of Culture." n.d. Accessed May 9 2021. https://ec.europa.eu/culture/policies/culture-cities-and-regions/european-capitals-culture

European Commission. "Smart Cities." n.d. Accessed May 9, 2021. https://ec.europa.eu/info/eu-regional-and-urban-development/topics/cities-and-urban-development/city-initiatives/smart-cities_en

European Commission. "Social Innovation." n.d. Accessed May 9, 2021. https://ec.europa.eu/growth/industry/policy/innovation/social_en

European Commission. "Glossary: Lisbon Strategy." Eurostat Statistics Explained. n.d. Accessed April 5, 2020. https://ec.europa.eu/eurostat/statistics-explained/index.php/Glossary:Lisbon_Strategy

European Commission. "Links Between Natural and Cultural Heritage." n.d. Accessed April 8, 2020. https://ec.europa.eu/environment/nature/natura2000/management/links_natural_cultural_heritage_en.html

European Commission. *Green Paper From The Commission on Policy Options for Progress Towards a European Contract Law for Consumers and Businesses*, COM(2010)348 final, Brussels. n.d. Accessed May 3, 2020. https://eur-lex.europa.eu/LexUriServ/LexUriServ.do?uri=COM:2010:0348:FIN:en:PDF

European Council. "Bratislava Declaration and Roadmap." n.d. Accessed April 7, 2020. http://www.consilium.europa.eu/en/press/press-releases/2016/09/16/bratislava-declaration-and-roadmap/

European Council Conclusion. Brussels, 2017. Accessed April 7, 2020. https://www.consilium.europa.eu/en/press/press-releases/2017/12/14/european-council-conclusions-external-relations/

European Union. European Commission. n.d. Accessed May 9, 2021. https://ec.europa.eu/info/index_en

Eurostat, *ESSnet-Culture Final Report*. Luxembourg: Eurostat, 2012: 57. Accessed April 5, 2020. https://ec.europa.eu/assets/eac/culture/library/reports/ess-net-report_en.pdf

Eurostat. "Category: Culture." European Commission. n.d. Accessed April 8, 2020. https://ec.europa.eu/eurostat/statistics-explained/index.php/Category:Culture

Evans, Mark, Chris Aulich, Anne Howard, and Megan Peterson. *Innovation in Local Government: Defining the Challenge, Making the Change*. Australian center for Local Government; Sydney: University of Technology, 2013.

Family Health International. "Qualitative Research Methods Overview." n.d. Accessed May 9, 2021. https://course.ccs.neu.edu/is4800sp12/resources/qualmethods.pdf

Felicori, Mauro. "Culture as a Byword for Urban Development: The Italian Experience." In *The Creative City*, edited by James Doyle and Biljana Mickov. London: Routledge, 2015.

Florida, Richard. *The Rise of the Creative Class*. USA: Basic Books Publisher, 2019.

Frontier Economics. *Creative Industry Spillovers*, 2007. Accessed May 6, 2020. https://www.frontier-economics.com.au/category/year/2007/

Frontiers Economics. *Comparative Analysis of the UK's Creative Industries*. Report to the DCMS, 2006. Available at: www.eukn.org/dsresource?objectid=149334&type=org

Gibson, Chris, and Natasha Klocker. "Academic Publishing as a Creative Industry, and Recent Discourses of Creative Economies: Some Critical Reflections." *Area* 36, no. 4 (2004): 423–434.

Glaeser, Edward. *Triumph of the City*. New York: Penguin Press, 2011.

Glaveski, Steve. "Innovation in Local Government." Collective Campus. n.d. Accessed April 18, 2020. www.collectivecampus.io/blog/innovation-in-local-government

Gombault, Anne. "Social Participation Issues in Becoming a Creative City: Learning from European Capitals of Culture." In *The Creative City: Vision and Execution*, edited by Biljana Mickov and James Doyle. London: Routledge publishing, 2015.

Goodacre, Jonathan. "The Visitor Appears." In *Sustaining Cultural Development: New Governance in Cultural Life*, edited by James Doyle and Biljana Mickov. London: Routledge Publishing, 2013: 151–162.

Gosselin, Aurélie et Jean-Michel Tobelem. "Concurrence et coopération: vers une uniformisation culturelle? Internationalisation des musées: effet de domination ou coopération culturelle? Le cas de la fondation Guggenheim et du musée de l'Ermitage." In *dans Patrimoine et mondialisation*, edited by is Jean Claude Nemery. Paris: l'Harmattan, 2008.

Government of the United Kingdom. "Department for Digital, Culture, Media & Sport (DCMS)." n.d. Accessed March 30, 2020. https://www.gov.uk/government/organisations/department-for-digital-culture-media-sport/about

Hall, Michael, Tim Baird, Michael James, and Yael Ram. "Climate Change and Cultural Heritage: Conservation and Heritage Tourism in the Anthropocene." *Journal of Heritage Tourism* 11, no. 1 (2015): 10–24.

Hamilton, Ron, and Helen Crabbe. "Environment, Pollution and Effects." In *The Effects of Air Pollution on Cultural Heritage*, edited by John Watt, Johan Tidblad, Vladimir Kucera, and Ron Hamilton, 1–28. New York: Springer, 2009.

Hayles, S. *Art, Education and the Role of Culture Institutions*. Novi Sad: Museum of Contemporary Art Vojvodina, 2010.

Hertzog, Anne et Frédéric Poulard. " Les échanges internationaux comme point d'ancrage de la modernisation et de la diversification des musées français." In dans *Patrimoine et mondialisation*. Paris: l'Harmattan, 2008.

Hesmondhalgh, David, and Andy Pratt. "Cultural Industries and Cultural Policy." *International Journal of Cultural Policy* 11, no. 1 (2005): 1–14.

Hewison, Robert. "When This Is All Over We Must Reimagine the Infrastructure of the Arts." *The Art Newspaper*. n.d. Accessed May 3, 2020. https://www.theartnewspaper.com/comment/when-this-is-all-over

Holden, John. *Capturing Cultural Value: How Culture Has Become a Tool of Government Policy*. London: Demos, 2004.

Holden, John. *Cultural Value and the Crisis of Legitimacy*. London: Demos, 2006.

Holden, John. *The Future of the City*. Chicago: University of Chicago, 2011.

Holden, John. "How We Value Arts and Culture." In *Sustaining Cultural Development, Unified Systems and New Governance in Cultural Life* edited by James Doyle and Biljana Mickov. London: Routledge Publishing, 2013.

Houghton, John. *Global Warming. The Complete Briefing*. Cambridge: Cambridge University Press, 2006.

Kagan, Sacha. "A review of Claude Mollard's 'Cultural engineering'." Unpublished paper, Erasmus Universiteit Rotterdam, 2004. Accessed May 20, 2021. http://sachakagan.chez-alice.fr/docs/Mollard.pdf

KEA. *The Economy of Culture in Europe*. Bruxelles: KEA European Affairs, 2006.

KEA. *Mapping the Creative Value Chains: A Study on the Economy of Culture in the Digital Age*. Luxembourg: Publications Office of the European Union, 2017.

KEA European Affairs. *The Impact of Culture on Creativity*. Brussels: Author, 2009.

KEA European Affairs. n.d. Accessed April 20, 2020. https://keanet.eu/

Kenny, Penelope. "The Business of Arts Consultancy: A Personal Analysis of the History, Growth and Opportunities for Business in Arts Consultancy." In *Culture, Innovation and the Economy*, edited by Biljana Mickov and James Doyle. London: Routledge publishing, 2018: 7–10.

Kirton, Michael. "Adaptors and Innovators: A Description and Measure." *Journal of Applied Psychology* 61, no. 5 (1976): 622–629.

Köster, Pau Rausell, and Raul Abeledo Sanchis. "Main Connections Between Cultural and Creative Activities and the Socio-Economic Space." European Network of Cultural Centres (ENCC). n.d. Accessed May 5, 2020. https://encc.eu/resources/database/main-connections-between-cultural-and-creative-activities-and-socio-economic

La 27e Région. "A Lab to Transform Public Policies." n.d. Accessed April 21, 2020. http://www.la27eregion.fr/en/

La chambre d'eau. n.d. Accessed May 10, 2021. www.lachambredeau.com

Lämmer-Gamp, Thomas. "Creative Industries, Policy Recommendations - Promotion of Cross- Innovation from Creative Industries." Berlin: Institute for Innovation and Technology, 2014.

Landry, Charles. *The Creative City: A Toolkit for Urban Innovators*. London: Earthscan, 2000.

Landry, Charles. *The Fragile City*. Gloucestershire: Comedia publisher, 2014.

Landry, Charles. *Psychology & the City: The Hidden Dimension*. Gloucestershire: Comedia publisher, 2017.

Landry, Charles. *The Civic City in a Nomadic World*. Rotterdam: nai010 publishers, 2017.

Martí, Grau Jordi, and Carles Giner Camprubi. "If the Agenda 21 for Culture is the Answer, What Was the Question?" In *Report 5: Cities, Cultures and Developments A Report that Marks the Fifth Anniversary of Agenda 21 for Culture*. Barcelona: UCLG, 2009.

Marti, Jordi. "If Agenda 21 for Culture is the Answer: What Was the Question." In *Sustaining Cultural Development, Unified Systems and New Governance in Cultural Life*, edited by James Doyle and Biljana Mickov, 37–43. London: Routledge publishing, 2013.

Maslin, Mark. *Global Warming. A Very Short Introduction*. Oxford: Oxford University Press, 2004.

McElveen, Hugh. "Transformations: numérique et art dans un environnement urbain (Urbain, Humain, Art et Technologie)." *dans Innovation culturelle et transformation des villes*, edited by Biljana Mickov et Fabrice Thuriot, 213–233. Paris: L'Harmattan, 2019.

McGettigan, Liz. "Smart Libraries Make Smart Communities Make Smart Cities." In *Culture, Innovation and the Economy*, edited by Biljana Mickov and James Doyle. London: Routledge publishing, 2019.

Mickov, Biljana. "Arts Education Practice." In *Sustaining Cultural Development: New Governance in Cultural Life*, edited by James Doyle and Biljana Mickov, 173–192. London: Routledge publishing, 2013.

Mickov, Biljana. "European Management Models in Contemporary Arts and Culture." In *Sustaining Cultural Development: New Governance in Cultural Life*, edited by James Doyle and Biljana Mickov. London: Routledge publishing, 2013.

Mickov, Biljana. "Networking and the Creative Impetus." In *Creative Cities: Vision & Execution*, edited by James Doyle and Biljana Mickov, 1–2. London: Routledge publishing, 2019.

Mickov, Biljana, and James Doyle. "Introduction" in *Sustaining Cultural Development: Unified Systems and New Governance in Cultural Life*, edited by James Doyle and Biljana Mickov, 1–15. London: Routledge publishing, 2013.

Mickov, Biljana et Fabrice Thuriot. dir. *Innovation culturelle et transformation des villes.* Coll. Gestion de la Culture. Paris: L'Harmattan, 2019.

Miles, Ian, and Lawrence Green. *Hidden Innovation in the Creative Industries*, Research Report. London: NESTA, 2008.

Milosevic, Nikola, Abdullah Gok, and Goran Nenadic. "Classification of Intangible Social Innovation Concepts." *Natural Language Processing and Information Systems* 12 (2018): 407–418.

Montalto, Valentina, Carlos Jorge Tacao Moura, Sven Langedijk, and Michaela Saisana. *The Cultural and Creative Cities Monitor: 2017 Edition.* Luxembourg: Publications Office of the European Union, 2017. Accessed April 8, 2020. https://ec.europa.eu/jrc/en/publication/eur-scientific-and-technical-research-reports/cultural-and-creative-cities-monitor-2017-edition

Mullings, Beverly. "Insider or Outsider, Both or Neither: Some Dilemmas of Interviewing in a Cross-Cultural Setting." *Geoforum* 30, no. 4 (1999): 337–350.

Naudé, Wim, and Adam Szirmai. "Technological Innovation, Entrepreneurship, and Development." The European Business Review. n.d. Accessed May 20, 2021. https://www.europeanbusinessreview.com/technological-innovation-entrepreneurship-and-development/

Nell, John. *Art of Living.* UK: Harper Collins, 2007.

NESTA. *Creative Growth: How the UK Can Develop World Class Creative Businesses.* London: NESTA, 2006.

NESTA. *Creating Innovation: Do the Creative Industries Support Innovation in the Wider Economy?* London: NESTA, 2008.

NESTA. "20 Tools for Innovating in Government." 2019. Accessed April 20, 2020. https://media.nesta.org.uk/documents/20_Tools_Innovating_Government.pdf

NESTA. n.d. Accessed April 20, 2020. https://www.nesta.org.uk/

Nypan, Trond. *Cultural Heritage Monuments and Historic Buildings as Value Generators in a Post-Industrial Economy.* Oslo: Directorate for Cultural Heritage, 2006.

Ochoa, George, Jennifer Hoffman, and Tina Tin. *Climate: The Force That Shapes our World and the Future of Life on Earth.* London: Rodale International, 2005.

OECD. *The Value of Culture and the Creative Industries in Local Development*, 2018. Accessed April 10, 2020. https://www.oecd.org/cfe/leed/2018-SACCI-Handbook.pdf

Owen, Denis. *What is Ecology?* UK: Oxford University Press, 1980.

Palmer, Robert. *European Cities and Capitals of Culture: Part I and Part II, Study Prepared for the European Commission.* Brussels: Palmer-Rae Associates, 2004.

Parrish, David. n.d. Accessed May 10, 2021. www.davidparrish.com

Perez-Alvaro, Elena. "Climate Change and Underwater Cultural Heritage: Impacts and Challenges." *Journal of Cultural Heritage* 21 (2016): 842–848.

Perry, Jim, and Charlie Falzon. *Climate Change Adaptation for Natural World Heritage Sites - A Practical Guide*. World Heritage Papers Series, no. 37. Paris: UNESCO World Heritage Centre, 2014.

Pesqueur, Bernard. "Le tournant territorial de l'économie globale." *Espaces et sociétés* 1–2, 125–125 (2006): 17–32.

Pivac, Tatjana, Ivana Blešić, and Tamara Kliček. "Impact On Tourism Development - The Case Study Of The Creative Industries Cluster Of Vojvodina." In *Tourism & Management Studies Intenational Conference*, ToSEE – Tourism in Southern and Eastern Europe, Opatija, Croatia, May 4–6, 2017. DOI: 10.20867/tosee.04.47

Polasky, Stephen, Catherine Louise Kling, Simon Levin, Stephen R. Carpenter, Gretchen C Daily, Paul R. Ehrlich, Geoffrey M. Heal, and Jane Lubchenco. "Role of Economics in Analyzing the Environment and Sustainable Development." *Proceedings of the National Academy of Sciences*, 116, no. 12 (2019): 5233–5238. Accessed May 9, 2020, https://www.pnas.org/content/116/12/5233

Potts, Jason, and Stewart Cunningam. "Four Models of the Creative Industries." *Revue d'Economie Politique*. 120, no. 1 (2010): 163–180.

Pratt, Andy. "The Cultural Economy. A Call for Spatialized 'Production of Culture' Perspectives." *International Journal of Cultural Studies* 7, no. 1 (2004): 117–128.

Reba, Darko. "Culture and Innovation in Open City." *Lecture at the Conference on Culture and Innovation, Institute of Culture Vojvodina*, Novi Sad, Serbia, October 29, 2019.

Reba, Darko, Milica Vračarić, and Olivera Marković. *Cultural Developments Planning and Innovations at Urban Open Spaces, In progress: Laboratory of Culture21 – Innovation in Culture Sector*. Belgrade: Službeni glasnik, 2020.

Regourd, Martine et Fabrice Thuriot. "Multiplication des échelles d'intervention et problèmes de coordination Le patrimoine culturel et la souveraineté politique" dans *Patrimoine et mondialisation*, edited by Jean Claude Nemery. Paris: l'Harmattan, 2008.

Reuvers, A. J., J. W. A. van den Berg, and C. A. Smolders. "Formation of Membranes by Means of Immersion Precipitation: Part I. A Model to Describe Mass Transfer During Immersion Precipitation." *Journal of Membrane Science* 34, no. 1 (1987): 45–65.

Rogers, Mark. *The Definition and Measurement of Innovation*. Melbourne: Melbourne Institute of Applied Economic and Social Research, 1998.

Rykwert, Joseph. *The Seduction of Place*. Oxford: Oxford University Press, 2000.

Sabbioni, Cristina, Peter Brimblecombe, and May Cassar. *The Atlas of Climate Change Impact on European Cultural Heritage, Scientific Analysis and Management Strategies*. London: Anthem Press, 2012.

Sabbioni, Cristina, May Cassar, Peter Brimblecombe, and Roger-Alexandre Lefèvre. *Vulnerability of Cultural Heritage to Climate Change*, European and Mediterranean Major Hazards Agreement (EUR-OPA). Strasbourg, November 20, 2008.

Sacco, Pier Luigi. *Culture 3.0: A New Perspective for the EU 2014–2020 Structural Funds Programming*, 2011. European Expert Network on Culture (EENC).

Schumpeter, Joseph. Capitalism, Socialism and Democracy. New York: Harper, 1950.

Scott, Allen. The Cultural Economy of Cities. London: Sage, 2000.

Scott, Allen. "Creative Cities: Conceptual Issues and Policy Questions." *Journal of Urban Affairs* 28, no. 1 (2006): 1–17.

Senge, Peter. *The Fifth Discipline: The Art and Practice of the Learning Organisation*. New York: Doubleday, 1990.

Shogren, Jason, and Laura Taylor. "On Behavioral-Environmental Economics." *Review of Environmental Economics and Policy* 2, no. 1 (2008): 26–44. Accessed May 10, 2020. https://ideas.repec.org/a/oup/renvpo/v2y2008i1p26-44.html

Subedi, Binaya. "Theorizing a "Halfie" Researcher's Identity in Transnational Fieldwork." *International Journal of Qualitative Studies in Education* 19, no. 5 (2006): 573–593.

Subedi, Binaya. "Recognizing Respondents' Ways of Being and Knowing: Lessons Un/Learned in Researching Asian Immigrant and Asian-American Teachers." *International Journal of Qualitative Studies in Education* 20, no. 1 (2007): 51–71.

The United Nations Educational, Scientific and Cultural Organization (UNESCO). "UNESCO in Brief - Mission and Mandate." n.d. Accessed May 6, 2020. https://en.unesco.org/about-us/introducing-unesco

The Work Foundation. *Staying Ahead: The Economic Performance of the UK's Creative Industries.* London: The Work Foundation, 2007.

Thomas, Paris. "Organisation, processus et structures de la création", *Culture et Prospective* 5, no. 5 (2007): 1–15.

Throsby, David. *Economics and Culture.* London: Cambridge University Press, 2001.

Thuriot, Fabrice. "Museums and Globalisation." In *Sustaining Cultural Development: New Governance in Cultural Life*, edited by James Doyle and Biljana Mickov. London: Routledge Publishing, 2013.

UCLG. "Agenda 21 for Culture." n.d. Accessed May 6, 2020. http://www.agenda21culture.net/

UNCTAD. *Economy: Towards Informed Policymaking.* Geneva: UNCTAD, 2008. Accessed April 5, 2020, https://unctad.org/en/docs/ditc20082cer_en.pdf

UNCTAD. *Creative Economy Report 2010 – Creative Economy: A Feasible Development Option.* Geneva: UNCTAD, 2010. Accessed April 5, 2020. https://unctad.org/en/Docs/ditctab20103_en.pdf

UNCTAD. *Creative Economy Report 2008 – The Challenge of Assessing the Creative* 2004.

UNCTAD. "Global creative economy shows resilience, growth – report." n.d. Accessed May 8, 2021. https://unctad.org/news/global-creative-economy-shows-resilience-growth-report

UNESCO. *The 2005 Convention on the Protection and Promotion of the Diversity of Cultural Expressions.* Paris: UNESCO, 2005.

UNESCO. "Road Map for Arts Education." *The World Conference on Arts Education: Building Creative Capacities for the 21st Century*, Lisbon, March 6–9, 2006. Accessed May 20, 2021. http://www.unesco.org/new/fileadmin/MULTIMEDIA/HQ/CLT/CLT/pdf/Arts_Edu_RoadMap_en.pdf

UNESCO. *Case Studies on World Heritage and Climate Change.* Paris: UNESCO World Heritage Centre, 2007.

UNESCO. *Creative Economy Report - Widening Local* Development Pathways, 2013 Special Edition.

United Cities and Local Governments (UCLG). *Culture 21 Actions: Commitments on the Role of Culture in Sustainable Cities.* Bilbao: UCLG, 2015. Accessed May 6, 2020. http://www.agenda21culture.net/documents/culture-21-actions

United Nations. n.d. Accessed May 10, 2021. https://www.un.org/

United Nations Conference on Trade and Development (UNCTAD). *Creative Economy Outlook: Trends in International Trade in Creative Industries*, 2018. Accessed April 10, 2020. https://unctad.org/en/pages/PublicationWebflyer.aspx?publicationid=2328

United Nations University (UNU). "The Environment and Sustainable Development." n.d. Accessed May 9, 2021. https://archive.unu.edu/esd/ESDtext.pdf

Van den Leo, Berg, Roy Drewett, Leo H. Klaassen, Angelo Rossi, and Cornells H.T. Vijverberg. *A Study of Growth and Decline.* UK: Pergamon publishing, 1982.

Varbanova, Lidia. *International Entrepreneurship in the Arts.* London/New York: Routledge, 2016.

Virtual Museum Transnational Network. n.d. Accessed May 15, 2021. www.v-must.net

Vitálišová, Katarina and Fabrice Thuriot ed., with Anna Vaňová, Mária Uramová, Ľudmila Mešková, Soňa Čapková, Kamila Borseková, Thierry Côme, and Thomas Hélie. *Creative Potential in the Cities and its Exploitation in the Sustainable Development.* Faculty of Economics, Matej Bel University in Banská Bystrica, Slovakia, with the CRDT of the Faculty of Law and Political Science of the University of Reims Champagne-Ardenne (URCA), 2019: 148.

Vitálišová, Katarina, Anna Vaňová, Mária Uramová, Soňa Čapková, Kamila Borseková, Fabrice Thuriot, Thierry Côme, and Thomas Hélie. "Innovations in the Cultural and Creative Local Development." *Acta aerarii publici* 15, no. 2 (2018): 41–55.

Wilson, Nick, Jonathan Gross, and Anna Bull. *Towards Cultural Democracy: Promoting Cultural Capabilities for Everyone.* London: King's College London, 2017.

INDEX

Pages in *italics* refer figures, **bold** refer tables and pages followed by n refer notes.

action plans 20, 22–23
advertising 63, 110, 114
Africa 6, 17
Agenda 21; city regeneration 16; for Culture 12–16, 40, 51, 69, 71, 123, 190; Dublin 157–159; open city 13; power 13
Ajdzalovski, R. 144, **242**
Amato Law (Italy, 1990) 217n549
Amsterdam 164–165; experience exchange with Stockholm 149
Andersson, T. 142, 147, **170**
art 33; connection with technology 42–43; 'crucial for city' 43; open space as works of 43
art galleries 63, 135–136, 138, 185, 232–233
artificial intelligence (AI) 47
Arts Act (Ireland, 2003) 157–158
Arts Council (England) 157, 163
Arts Council (Ireland) 157
arts education 3, 18, 20, 118n405, 134, 191; policies 136–139
Arts Governance (Dublin) 143, 159–160, **171**; activities 159; funding 159; innovation 159–160; services 159; strengths and weaknesses 159; target groups 159
arts organizations 103–105
Asia 6, 17, 37, 44
Assessorato alla Crescita Culturale di Roma Capitale 176
Athens 44–45
Atlas of Climate Change (Sabbioni *et al.*, 2012) 54, 56n188
augmented reality (AR) 47, 50n168, 106
Australia 80, 154
Aydemir, D. L. R. 144, **242**

Bakhshi, H. 79, 91, 115n329
banking 188, 217n549
Barcelona 8, 13, 36, 74, 143, 188–195, 207–208, **212**, **216**, 253–254, 263, 271; cultural capital role 190; cultural development (systematic management approach) 24; cultural institutions 189–190; cultural policies 189–190; economic growth (cultural sector contribution) 189
Barcelona Art Factory 69, 190
Barcelona, @22 urban development project 193, 195
Barcelona City Council 69–70, 189
Barcelona Culture Department 48n92
Barcelona, Decidim Project 13, 74, 191–192
Barcelona, Design Hub Barcelona 191
Barcelona Institute of Culture 143; activities 188; funding 189; innovation 188–189, 191–192; strength 191–192; target users 188

Barcelona, INTERARTS 143, 192–195; activities 192–193; communications network 194; funding 193; innovative tools (examples) 193, 195; networking 193; newsletter 194; office and equipment 194; organizational structure 194; partners 194–195; purpose 192; reach (geographical) 192; stakeholders 195; target users 192
Barcelona Olympics (1992) 189
Barcelona, Strategic Plan for Culture: 1999 189; 2006 190
Barcelona, UNESCO Universal Forum of Cultures (2004) 189
Basque country 84
Bekemeier, D. 143, 205
Belgrade 42, 142–143, 223–226, 237, **241**, 258
Belgrade, BAZAART 224–226; activities 224; budget 226; funding 226; innovation 226; Intercultural Learning through Drama 225–226; learning methodologies 225; products 225; reach (geographical) 224–225; service users 225; strengths and weaknesses 225; target groups 225; Tolerant Classroom workshops 225–226
Belgrade, Museum of Contemporary Art 223–224; activities 224; budget 224; collaborations 224; departments 224; funding 224; innovation 224; strengths and weaknesses 224; target groups 224
Belgrade, Secretariat of Culture 224
Bergamo, L. 143, 177
Berlin 99, 154
Bianchini, F. 31, 49n114
Bibblix 148, 168
Biedrońska, K. 144, **243**
big data 181, 189
Bilbao 69, 72, 81n254
Bilbao, Guggenheim Museum 84, 99
Bochmann, K. 129
Bogotá, Ibero-American Theatre Festival 265
Boldrini, G. 143, 182, 217n541
Bologna 142–143, 182–188, 207, 210, **211**, **216**, 253, 271
Bologna City Council 36
Bologna, Creative Innovation Project (2010–) 182–184; activities 183; funding 184; human resources 184; innovation 184; positive impact 184; strengths and weaknesses 183–184
BOP Consulting 143, 169, **172**, 252; activities 162–163; innovation 163; strengths 163
brands 64; place branding 67
Bratislava 142–143, 236, **240**, 257
Bratislava City Council: funding 219; innovation 218–219; strengths and weaknesses 219; target groups 218; users 218
Brexit 163
British Council 97, 221
Broadway musicals 265
Brussels 142–143, 195–196, 208–209, **213**, **216**, 255, 271
Budapest 144, 239, **243**, 245, 260–261
Budapest, Ludwig Museum of Contemporary Art: activities 234; budget 235; funding 235; innovation 234–235; networking 235; range (geographical) 234; staff 235; strengths and weaknesses 234–235; target audience 234; webpage 235; young people 234
Buitrago Restrepo, F. 265
Bulgaria 226–227
business of arts 103–105

Campbell, L. 142, 149, **170**
Caramés, E. 26–27, 48n92, 143, 188
Central and Eastern Europe focus group 140–144, 218–245, 256–261, 271–272; analysis 236–245, **240–244**; budgets **240–244**; innovation **240–244**; members 143–144; *see also* focus groups
Central and Eastern Europe focus group (places): Belgrade 142–143, 223–226, 237, **241**; Bratislava 142–143, 218–219, 236, 240; Budapest 144, 234–235, 239, 243, 245; Gabrovo 142, 144, 226–227, 237–238, 241; Kiev 222–223, 237, 240, 244; Krakow 144, 230–232, 238–239, 243; Ljubljana 142, 144, 232–233, 239, 243–244; Moscow 222–223, 237, 240, 244; Novi Sad 142–143, 219–222, 236–237, 240; Skopje 142, 144, 229, 238; Zagreb 142, 144, 227–229, 238, 242, 244
central government 59, 73
chambers of commerce 2, 23, 67, 248, 268
Chester Zoo 265
China 78, 265; economic rise (role of experimentation) 80
cinema 90–91, 108, 176
Cirque du Soleil 265

cities 6, 93, 96–97, 142, 248–250, 264–270; cultural profiles 272; culture 'pillar of sustainable development' 30; double layer of networks 122; inclusive (smart cultural sector) 105–106; key factors 272; low-and middle-income 106–107; revitalization 68–69; technologies and innovation 43–46; *see also* European Capitals of Culture
cities today 10–19; Agenda 21 for Culture 12–16; challenge 16; innovation (benefits for cities) 16–18; innovation and cultural policy 16–18; plan for culture 12–16; regeneration (role of culture) 16; research projects (investment necessary) 16
citizen participation 33, 35
city councils 1, 139
city governments 60, 80
city landscape, innovation and technologies 'becoming connected' 41–42
civil society 60, 70–72, 180
civil society organizations (CSOs) 52, 192, 226
climate change 52, 74, 56n188; culture, innovation, and 53–55
climate, definition 53
clocks 42
clusters 66–67, 96, 106
Coalition for Cultural Diversity 41
Colombia 75
commercial culture 14, 21
communication, theme of our times 135
competitive advantage 65, 94, 112
connectivity 15, 269; role 28
consultancy and consulting services 97, 192
Copenhagen 44, 108
copyright 29
Cork 108
corporate governance requirements 103–104
corporate social responsibility 23, 73
COVID-19 pandemic 55, 164, 166, 265–266, 270
creative cities (Europe) 106–108
Creative Cities of Film 176–177
Creative Cities Monitor 106
creative city 11, 18n43, 23, 111, 125
Creative City (Landry and Bianchini, 1995) 87, 115n310
creative class 18n41, 186
creative economy 29, 63, 122, 141; culture and 121–245; future 114; global value 265; UNCTAD definition 122
Creative Europe 163, 186
creative industries 28–30, 34, 125, 142, 263; definitions 90, 95–96, 101, 110; development 'has to be priority' 265; digital forms 270; interaction (four types) 111; interdependent with culture, arts, creativity 101; new technologies 96–97; 'not sector, but structural part of economy as whole' 125; public policy of economy 90–91; spillover effects and cross-innovation 108–111; structuring 130; terminological analysis 90; territorial anchoring 111–113
creative industries (innovation and development) 83–119; creative cities (Europe) 106–108; cultural economy 97–105; smart cultural sector (inclusive cities) 105–106
Creative Industries Mapping Documents (UK, 1998, 2001) 85
Creative Industries Task Force (UK) 85
creative space 33–41
creative tourism, definition 67–68
Creative Ukraine 222
creative value chains 66
creativity 6, 11, 22, 24; 'complex process' 85; 'core of capability in culture' 20, 22, 272; dimensions 86; relations with innovation 77–78; six pillars 65; strategic plans for culture 25; territorial dimension 87
Croatia 227–229
Croatia, Ministry of Environmental Protection 228
cross-innovation 108–111, 247; happens in two ways 109
cultural activism 1, 268; role 247–248
cultural change, theme of our times 135
cultural concept, definition 89
Cultural and Creative Cities Monitor (Montalto *et al.*) 93, 107–108, 117n399
cultural and creative industries (CCIs) 66, 91, 110, 112, 129, 168, **170–174**, 175–176, 183, 186, 250, 271–272; definition 63; Mannheim 203–204; Stockholm 148
cultural and creative sector (CCS) 65, 86, 92–94, 101, 106–108, 193, 195, 208, 254, 265–266; contribution to GDP and employment 107, 118n401
cultural development: benefits 6; innovative 4, 7–8, 269; new system 'should begin immediately' 6; strategies 5
cultural diplomacy 39–40

cultural diversity, closely related to 'natural diversity' 52
cultural ecology (anthropological term) 125
cultural economy 97–105; business of arts 103–105; economic potential 87
cultural ecosystems 2, 23, 67, 71–72, 121–123, 140, 247–248; 'contain economy' 268; Rome 180
cultural governance, horizontal *versus* vertical 6
cultural heritage 53–54
cultural identity 248, 250, 268
cultural industries 12, 20; definition 29
cultural institutions 3, 7, 17–18, 25, 27, 32–33, 35, 37, 71, 105–106, 129–146, 187, 223, 248–249, 264, 272; efficiency 'prime new resource' 186; important questions 38–39; primary role 135; vision (external and internal) 39
cultural management 17, 250
cultural needs, satisfaction of 'main purpose of economic system' 124–125
cultural organizations: mission 197; small 27
cultural participation 37, 92–93, 266; barriers 93
cultural planning 13, 187
cultural policy 3, 10, 27, 32, 34–35, 52, 60, 136, 193, 236, 249, 270; aim 8; basis 40; capable administration required 137; challenges 5, 185–187; definition 49n144; experimental government 78–80; indispensable role 4; innovation and 16–18; innovation in local governments 63–82; principles 5; role 7; social and technical innovation 59
cultural policy analysis 20–23; action plan 22–23
cultural portals 131
cultural practice 12; diversification 8
cultural products, definition 89
cultural projects 31, 247–248; positioning 28
cultural rights 197; 'substantial part' of human rights 125
cultural sector 33–34, 140, 142; economic and social value 123–128; evaluation (three things, two reasons) 135; investment in research projects 4; quality-of-life determinant 10; smart (inclusive cities) 105–106
Cultural Sector and Sustainable Economic Development: aim 2, 7; background and research 7–8; case studies 3, 7, 139–144, 263; analysis 247–273; conclusion 267–273; content 7; discussion 263–266; hypothesis 2, 263; key points 267–268; methodology 2–3; objective 1, 8, 250, 267; research objectives and questions 3–6; themes 2; thesis 5
cultural system (Mollard) 136
cultural values 121, 124–125
culture 263; 'cannot be measured' 186; causal relationship with social development, economy, environmental sustainability 2; complexity and diversity 12; connection with sustainable development 267–268; contemporary (Rome) 180–182; contribution to GDP and employment (EU) 98; and creative economy 121–245; dimensions 83; ecology of 125–127; 'essential fourth pillar of sustainable city' 6; expenditure 186–187; 'fundamental element within society' 3–4; importance 15; international partner cooperation 39; major factor in development of society 270; 'must stop being battlefield' 187; pillar of city development 15; 'powerful driver of economic activity' 93; principle of as creative tool 16; provides skills for other sectors of economy 86; repositioning 16; role in city regeneration 16; role in European societies 83–84; soft power 108; strategic plans 25, 264; territorial dimension 87
culture, innovation, development 20–50; action plan 22–23; building creative space 33–41; building open space as works of art 43; cultural policy analysis 20–23; intersectoral cooperation 35; networking and innovation 23–33; new ideas 33–41; open city 41–43; technologies and innovation as programs in cities 43–46; transformations (digital art in urban environment) 46–47
culture of engineering (Landry) 12
Culture Strategy for Scotland (proposed) 151
Culture 21, Actions 70–72, 81n254, 139
Cunningham, S. 125

Decidim *see* 'Barcelona, Decidim Project'
decision-making 60, 74, 76, 136–137
delivery, definition 89
democracy 11, 13, 60
design 107–108, 122
Deutsche Bank Research 90

development 3; culture, innovation, and 20–50
digital age 96, 100, 105, 114
digital art, urban environment 46–47
digital media 46–47
digital world 96, 106, 233, 239, 260; real world 114
digitalization 6, 11, 17, 22, 26, 29, 34–36, 39, 66, 105–106, 133, 147–148, 168, 220–222, 249, 265, 269
Disneyland 44
diversity 12, 31, 272
Donkers, C. 164–165, **173**
Dorovska, M. 144, **241**
Dortmund 143, 205–206, 210, **215**, 256
Dortmund, FG DESIGN UG: activities 205–206; funding 206; innovative trends 206; target groups 205; weaknesses 206
Doyard, M. G. 143, 199
Doyle, J. E. 142, **170**
Drucker, P. 78, 82n281
Dublin 142–143, 155–162, 168–169, **170–172**, 251–252; cultural and creative spillovers 157; cultural program **170–172**; innovation **170–172**; UNESCO City of Literature 156
Dublin, Chester Beatty Library 157
Dublin, Irish Museum of Modern Art (IMMA) 143, 160–161, 169, **171**, 251; funding 161, **171**; innovation 161; key objective 160–161; recent developments 160; strengths and weaknesses 160; target groups 160; trends 161
Dublin City Council (DCC) 155; benefits 159; cultural policies (formulation) 156; future actions 158; innovation 158–159; UNESCO definition of culture adopted (2015) 157; weakness 156
Dublin City Council, Arts Office 157–159
Dublin City Council, Arts Plan 156–159, **170**
Dublin City Council, Corporate Plan 156–157
Dublin City Council, Cultural Strategy 157–158
Dublin City Council, Culture, Recreation, Amenity (CRA) Department 156–158
Dutch Design Week 165, 222–223

E+ project (Eindhoven, 2003–2009) 164–165
Earth 52–53
ecology 65, 68; theme of our times 135
economic development 248, 271; cultural sector (particular contribution) 2
economic growth 69; culture 'driving force' 186
economy 2, *21*, 263
ecosystems 51–52, 68–69; *see also* cultural ecosystems
Edinburgh 142, 154–155, 168, **170**, 203, 251; attributes 154; cultural program **170**; innovation **170**; UNESCO City of Literature 154
Edinburgh Libraries 154
education 6, 8, 17, 60, 94, 107, 185, 264
Eindhoven 24, 108, 142–143, 164–167, **173–174**, 175, 222–223, 237, **240**, **244**, 252, 257–258, 263, 271–272; brain port 164; cultural program **173**; innovation **173**; innovation policy governance 166–167; urban development questions 166; young people 167
Eindhoven, Brainport organization 165
Eindhoven, Code of Cultural Governance 167
Eindhoven, Cultuur Eindhoven (2015–) 143, 166–167, 169, **173**; funding 166, 173; goal 166–167; innovation 167; responsibilities 166; target groups 166
Eindhoven, De Witte Dame building project 165
Eindhoven, Programma Creatieve Industrie 166–167
Eindhoven, Publicroam 167
Eindhoven, QAFE city debate (1990s) 165
Eindhoven City Council 165–166
elites and elitism 14, 21, 27, 34, 178
Emilia-Romagna region 182–184
employment 68, *98–99*, 99, 107, 136, 164, 265; United Kingdom (2010) 101
employment creation 112, 121, 123
entertainment 264
entertainment industry, comparison with oil sector (2009) 265
entrepreneurs and entrepreneurship 72, 97, 107, 111
environment *21*, 22, 33; sustainable development 51–57
Erić, Z. **241**
Ernst & Young Global Limited 63
ESSnet-Culture 90–91
Essen 107
Estate Romana (Roman Summer) 180–181
EU Natura 2000 Integration Project 228
EUNIC 220, 222
Eurobarometer 178

Europe 7, 10, 28–29, 34, 37, 44, 80, 248; creative cities 106–108; culture (role) 83–84; heritage sector employment 100; local governments and cultural institutions 129–146
European Agenda (2007) 92
European Capitals of Culture (ECoCs, 1985–) 63–64, 92, 130; Dublin bid (2020) 157–158; expenditure 99–100
European Commission 93, 95, 109–110, 118n401, 188; Green Paper (2010) 110–111, 118n419
European Competitiveness Report 118n401
European Innovation Scoreboard 65
European Structural and Investment Funds 92
European Union 13, 38, 84, 86, 90–91, 98, 134, 154, 159, 163–164, 187–188, 193, 196, 206, 222, 225; creative economy's contribution to GDP (2014) 63; cultural trade surplus and employment (2016) 94; economic sectors (indicators, 2012–2019) *99*; employment by economic activity (2008–2017) *98*; 'forcing smaller organizations to disappear' 198–199; GDP (cultural contribution) 94; Green Paper (2010) 124, 127n458; multilingual language policy 130, 132
EUTEKA network 220
Evans, M. 80, 81n240
experimental government 78–80

Facebook 163, 183, 220
fairs 43–44
Farcy, A. 201–202
fashion 108, 110, 122
Fehér, Z. 144, **243**
Felicori, M. 184–187, 217n541
Fellini, F. 176
Finland 163
Fleming, T. 157
flooding 222–223
Florida, R. 11, 18n41, 125; *Rise of Creative Class* (2019) 87, 115n309
focus groups 140–141, 250; *see also* Northern Europe focus group
fondazioni di origine bancaria (foundations of banking origin) 188, 217n549
France 28; castles and abbeys (profits, 2006) 99; museum modernization 133
France, 27e Région 75
Frontier Economics: report (2007) 125, 127n467
funding 14, 27, 103, 124, 132, 138, 152, 162
Gabrovo 142, 144, 237–238, **241**, 258
Gabrovo, Museum of Humour and Satire 226–227; activities 226; budget 227; funding 227; innovation 226–227; networking 227; strengths and weaknesses 227; target groups 226
gastronomy 52, 68
Gates, W. 46
gender equality 71, 147
Germany 31, 110
Ginzel, O. 143, 205
Giovinazzo, M. 143, 192
Glasgow 107–108, 142, 149–154, 168, **170**, **174**, 175, 203, 250, 252, 271; cultural program **170**; employment 152; global events 151; innovation 170; sport 151; tourism 151–152; UNESCO City of Music 150; universities 153
Glasgow City Council 149, 151, 153
Glasgow City Marketing Bureau (GCMB) 151
Glasgow Club Fitness Unlimited 151
Glasgow Communities 150
Glasgow Convention Bureau 150, 152
Glasgow Cultural Enterprises 151
Glasgow, Culture and Sport Glasgow 149
Glasgow Life 142, 149–151, 168, 170, 250; composition 153; digital library 150; funding 153, **170**; innovation 154; leases of buildings 153; networking 153–154; one of largest charities in Scotland 153; operating model 153; public use of services (2017–2018) 150; reach 152; scale 151–152; strengths 151–152; weaknesses 152
Glasgow Life, Board 151
Glasgow Life, Policy & Research 151
Glasgow Life, School Library Service 151
Glasgow Museums 150–151
Glasgow Music 151
Glasgow, Transforming Glasgow 151
Global Alliance 29
global identity 4, 7
globalization 15, 30, 64, 109, 133, 184; theme of our times 135
Gombault, A. 130
Google 37–38
governance *21*
Great Region 131–133; cultural workers (specific goals) 132–133; social dimension 133
Grenoble 142, 200–202, 209–210, **214**, **216**, 255–256, 271
Grenoble Museum 143, 200–202; activities 200–201; funding 201; innovation

201–202; partnership policy 201; strengths and weaknesses 201; users 200
Gross Domestic Product (GDP) 94–95, 98, 100; generated by travel and tourism 100; UK (contribution of creative economy, 2010) 101
Guggenheim Foundation 133, 145n501

Hall, P. 87
Hamburg, Reeperbahn 46
health 123, 152
HealthLab 75
heritage, 'continuously renewing itself' 86
heritage sector 99; employment 100
Hewison, R. 123–124
Hidden Innovation in Creative Industries (Miles and Green, 2008) 88–89, 115n318
high art: 'intertwined with popular art' (Holden) 14
high culture 21, 184
history 52, 55; 'always connected with modern times' 44
Holden, J. 13–14, 35, 49n129; culture 'organism' (rather than 'mechanism') 65
Howkins, J. 122, 122n448
human capital 77, 87, 93, 97, 108, 125
human rights 129; cultural rights 'substantial part' of 125
Hungary 234–235

iTunes (1998–) 265
IBM 37
ideas 114, 121, 125
Impact of Global Climate Change on Material Heritage (EU project, 2004–2007) 54
INCREDIBOL! 182–188; *see also* Bologna
information and communications technology (ICT) 44, 84, 91, 96, 107, 115n328, 142, 147
information-knowledge-innovation continuum 4, 35, 249
innovation 140, 263–264, 271–272; contribution to creative accessibility 111; 'core of capability in culture' 20; creative industries and 83–90; cultural policy 16–18, 63–82; culture, and development 20–50; 'has to be positioned at center of development' 272; local government and 59–119; 'new ideas that make difference' 264; notion of intent 23–24; as programs in cities 43–46; relations with creativity 77–78; Schumpeter's definition 7
innovation laboratories 74–75
Innovation in Local Government (Evans *et al.*, 2013) 80, 81n240
Innovazione Creativa di Bologna (2010–) 182–184
Inside-Out process 109
intellectual property (IP) 15, 89–90, 101, 108
intellectual property rights (IPRs) 22, 29, 88, 112–113, 115n314
intercultural city 31
International Committee for Museums and Collections of Modern Art (CIMAM) 235
international development cooperation 192
International Film Preservation School 177
International Network of Cultural Policy 41
International Society for Education through Art (InSEA) 137
internet 13, 15, 29, 88, 125, 163, 220
Interpret Europe (IE) 228
InterroBang Ltd 142, 161, 169, **172**, 251–252; activities 161; commercial arm to business 162; constant research 162; funding 162; innovation 161–162; international partnerships 162
intersectionality, culture and tourism 187
interviews 2–3, 140, 182, 192, 196, 199–200, 202; in-depth 141
invention *versus* 'innovation' 77
Ireland, budget (2019) 155, **170**
Ireland, Department of Arts, Culture, Heritage, Gaeltacht 159, 161
Italy: challenges 185–187; culture as byword for urban development 184–185; culture funding 185
Italy, Constitutional Court 188

Jones, S. 126
Jowell, Sir Roger 79

Kassel, Documenta modern art exhibition 99
KEA 66, 143, 195–196; *Economy of Culture in Europe* (2006) 83–87, 114n298; focus of activities 196; funding 196; innovation 196; report (2009) 65; service users 196; strengths and weaknesses 196
Kenny, P. 143, 159–160, **171**
Kern, P. 143, 195–196
Keto, M. 143, **173**
key performance indicators (KPIs) 157
Kiev 222–223, 237, **240**, **244**, 257–258, 272

Kirton, M. 77
KnowSpot 218–219
knowledge spillover 109; definition 66
knowledge transfer 109, 192
Kojic, D. 143, **240**
Koons, J. 126
Krakow 144, 238–239, **243**, 259–260
Krakow, Museum of Contemporary Art (MOCAK, 2010–) 230–232; activities 230; aims 230; Education Department (MOCAK-edu) 230–231; educational projects 230–231; funding 231; innovation 230–232; strengths and weaknesses 231; target groups 230
Kurz, P. 203–204

Landry, C.: *Creative City* (2000) 18n43, 118n423; *Fragile City* (2014) 10; *Psychology and City* (2017) 11, 268
language 130–131
leadership roles 76
Lee, C. 143, **172**
Leuven 108
libraries 25, 32, 105, 148, 150, 152–153, 168, 177–178; Edinburgh 154–155
lifelong learning 60, 94
lighting 43, 46
Lisbon, Building Creative Capacities (conference, 2006) 137
Lisbon Strategy 84, 115n302
Ljubljana 142, 144, 239, **243–244**, 260, 272
Ljubljana, Museums and Galleries 232–233; activities 232; aim 232; budget 233; funding 233; innovation 232–233; Museum from Close program 232–233; range (geographical) 232; RogLab network 233; strengths and weaknesses 233; sustainable development 233; target groups 232
local authorities 33, 133
local governments 21, 23–24, 29, 31, 52, 59–119, 129–146, 236; culture policy (innovation) 63–82; innovation in 63–78; innovations (two groups) 59; joint projects 71–72
London 42, 85, 142–143, 162–163, 169, **174**, 175, 252, 271; cultural program **172**; innovation 172
London, Tate Modern Gallery 126
London, Tower of London 265
Lukyova, K. 143, **240**
Luxembourg 131

M'Sili, N. 143, 196
MacArthur Foundation 80
Macedonia: Ministry of Culture **242**; budget 229; EU funding 229; innovation 229
Madrid, Prado Museum 34
Mannheim 143, 210, **215–216**, 256, 271
Mannheim, Cultural Office 202
Mannheim, Next Mannheim 143, 203–205; cultural urban development department 203; funding 204; innovation 203–204; objectives 203; stakeholders 203; strengths 205; urban sound design 203
Mannheim Music Model 202–204
mapping 47, 69, 71, 85, 96
marketing 26–27, 105, 264
Marseille 142, 209, **213**, **216**, 255, 271; European City of Year (2014) 196
Marseille, *Instants Vidéo Numériques et Poétiques* 143, 196–199; activities 197–198; funding 198; innovation 198–199; partners 198; reach (geographical) 197; staffing 198; strengths 198; target users 197; Thought and Practice of Images project 197
Martí Grau, J. 8, 9n26
McConnell, B. 142, 149, **170**
McElveen, H. 46, 142, **172**
McGettigan, L. 142, 154, **170**
Mexico 75
Meyer-Bish, P. 197
Micek, A. 144, **243**
middle class 184–185
millennium development goals (MDGs) 51
Miller, J. 142, 149, **170**
Milosavljević, S. 143, **241**
MKW Wirtschaftsforschung GmbH 100
Mollard, C. 136
Mons 107
Moscow 222–223, 237, **240**, **244**, 257–258, 272
multi-culturalism 32, 83–84, 196, 205, 219
multi-level governance 60, 70
Museo Italiano del Cinema 176–177
Muses Ltd 227–229; activities 227–228; budget 228; innovation 228–229; networking 228; range (geographical) 227; strengths and weaknesses 228–229; target groups 227–228
museums 35, 39, 63, 133–136, 138, 152; role 185–186; Rome 179–180; 'turnover' 186
music 108, 114, 148, 151–152, 202–205
Muze d.o.o. *see* Muses Ltd

Nantes 107
National Geographic 196
national governments 60, 65
Nell, J., *Art of Living* (2007) 125
NESTA (UK) 88–89; focus 76; innovation tools 73; local government's new role 73; *Manifesto for Creative Economy* (2013) 101; report (2019) 73–76, 82n257
Netherlands 164–167, 222–223, 237
Network for Cultural Diversity 41
network society 8, 12
networking 4, 7, 10, 35, 138, 192, 248–249, 270; impetus on local culture actors 67; and innovation 23–33
networks 33–34, 38, 122
New European Agenda for Culture 91–95, 100; economic dimension (connecting factors) 94; innovation models 93; objectives 92; social dimension 92
new ideas 33–41
niche markets 97
Nicolini, R. 184, 217n542
non-governmental organizations (NGOs) 60, 136, 162, 192, 195, 197, 222, 233
Noord-Brabant 166
Northern Europe focus group 140, 142–143, 147–175, 250–252, 271; qualitative research analysis 167–175, **170–174**; *see also* Western Europe focus group
Northern Europe focus group (places): Dublin 155–162, 168–169, **170–172**; Edinburgh 154–155, 168, **170**; Eindhoven 164–167, 173; Glasgow 149–154, 168, 170; London 162–163, 169, 172; Stockholm 147–149, 167–168, 170; Turku 163–164, 169, 173
not-for-profit sector 123–124
Novi Sad 42, 142–143, 236–237, **240**, 257
Novi Sad, European Capital of Culture (2022) 219
Novi Sad City Library 219–222; activities 220; employees 221–222; function 220; funding 221; innovation 220, 222; programs for development of innovation and creative industries 220–222; strengths and weaknesses 221; target groups 220; users 220; young people 221
Nypan, T. 98

OPEC 265
open city 13, 22; culture and innovation 41–43
open innovation 111–113
open-space artistic projects 264
opera 178–179
Orange Economy (Buitrago and Duque, 2013) 265
Oranskaia, E. 143, 222–223, **240**
Organization for Economic Co-operation and Development (OECD) 93, 97, 118n405
Owen, D.: *Science of Ecology* (1980) 126

Palmer, R. 130
Paris 108
Paris, Beaubourg [*Centre Georges Pompidou*] 133
Paris, Eiffel Tower 42, 50n151
Paris, Louvre 34, 133
pedestrians 42, 46
Peršin, B. 144, **243**
Philips Company 164–165
planning, bottom-up 24, 48n85
platforms, agendas, networks (trilogy) 5
Plurio (cross-border cultural web portal) 131
Podgórze 230
Pokémon Go 47, 50n168
Potts, J. 125
pragmatism 22, 37, 272
Prague, Astronomical Clock 50n153
private sector 15, 31, 60, 70, 124, 134, 136, 191
privatization 71, 217n549
problem-solving 76–77, 80, 140
problem-solving and sustainable decision skills (PSSDS) 161–162, 169, **172**, 252
professionals 28, 35–36; skills required 94
Program for International Student Assessment (PISA) 93
psychology 11, 268
public administration 184, 229
public participation 5, 22; broadening 185
public policy 27, 29, 40, 60, 70, 75, 90–91, 107, 185
public relations 90, 193
public sector 15, 38, 70, 73–74, 76, 80, 134
public space 2, 32, 37, 42–47 *passim*, 52, 55, 70, 106, 165, 167, 180–182, 198, 207, 248, 253, 268
public-private partnerships 133, 177, 181, 183
publishing sector 39, 114

qualitative research 2, 129, 140–141, 162, 250; methods 141; strength 141
quality of life 10–11, 93, 205, 269

randomized controlled trials (RCTs) 78
Rausch, M. 143, 202, 204, **215**
Reba, D. 41, 50n148
regional governments 24–25, 29, 60, 264
regions 28, 38, 40, 96–97, 106, 122, 134, 164, 248–249, 265–266, 268; transcending national boundaries 130–131; *see also* Great Region
Reims 142–143, 199–200, 209, **214**, **216**, 255, 271; culture (public service mission) 199; funding 200; innovation 200; strengths and weaknesses 200; users 200
Reiniers, S. 143
research and development (R&D) 64, 84, 90–91, 192, 270
Rogers, M. 77
Roma Capital 177
Roma Provincia Creative 176
Rome 43–45, 142–143, 176–182, 184, 206–207, 210, **211**, **216**, 217n542, 252–253, 271; cinema 176; contemporary and scientific culture (promotion) 180–182; financing 181; innovation 182; outlying districts (mobile satellites of major cultural institutions) 178–179; social cohesion 178–179; tourist-dominated hotspots (resident cultural access) 179–180; urban stages 182
Rome, *Assessorati* 176–178
Rome, Cinecittà Studios 176
Rome, Creative City of Film 176
Rome, Department for Culture 176–177, 180
Rome, Deputy Mayor for Culture's Office 177, 181–182
Rome, Fabbrica Young Artist Program 178
Rome, International Film Festival 176
Rome, Musei in Comune (MIC) 177, 179–180, 182
Rome, New Year's Eve Celebration 179, 182
Rome: *Opera Camion* (project, 2016–) 178–179, 182
Rome, Seasons of Rome (2017–) 180–182
Rome, Superintendence for Cultural Heritage 177, 179
Rome, Teatro dell'Opera 178
Rome, Youth Orchestra 178
Rome, Zètema Progetto Cultura 179
Rotterdam, Schouwburgplein market 36
Ruby on Rails 191, 208, 254
rural areas 93–94, 107
Russian Federation 193, 222–223, 237
Sacco, P. L.: culturalization of economy 64
Saint Petersburg, Hermitage Museum 133
Schumpeter, J. 7, 267
science, Rome 180–182
Seppala Tanssiteatteri ERI (ERI Dance Theatre) 143, 163–164, 169, **173**, 252; awards 164; funding **173**; innovation 164
Serbia 220, 223–226
short-termism 187–188
Silicon Valley (California) 96, 148, 168, 250
SITRA (Sweden) 75
Skopje 142, 144, 229, 238, 259
Slovak Republic 218–219
Slovak Republic, Ministry of Culture 219
Slovenia 232–233
SMART, explanation 22
smart city 11, 59, 87, 147, 269; definition 61n205
social capital 16–17
social change 17, 205
social cohesion, outlying districts (mobile satellites of major cultural institutions) 178–179
social development 2, 263; pillars 41
social inclusion *21*, 25, 33, 60, 61n206, 83, 176, 185–186, 263, 272; participation in cultural life 'key aspect' 123
social innovation 59–60, 70, 140, 142, 167, 206, 236, 247, 250, 271; definition 61n206
social innovation in culture: definition 59
social interactions 47, 53
social media 105, 196, 206, 233
society, sustainable development (cultural ideas 'fourth pillar') 37
socio-economic space 124–125
software 191; open-source 36
SOLUS UK 154–155, 168, **170**, 250–251; budget 155, **170**; creative industries (development) 154; innovation 154–155; main impact 155; strengths and weaknesses 154–155
South Korea 75
Soviet Union, 'pathological inability to experiment' 79
Spain, Ministry of Culture 193, 195
spillover effects 108–111
state governments 65, 80
statistics 95, 107, 117n377, 157
STEM *versus* STEAM 93
stereotypes 140–141

Stichting Art-East+Art-West (NGO) 222–223; activities 222; budget 223; funding 223; innovation 222–223; services 222; strengths and weaknesses 222–223; target groups 222
Stockholm 142, 147–149, 175n527; cultural program **170**; culture budget 149, 170; developing strategy for creative industries 148; engagement with audience 148; expenditure (2018 budget) *149*; fiber network 147; innovation 148, 167–168, 170; tech strength 148; weakness 168
Stockholm, Culture Administration 148–149, 168, **170**, 250
Stockholm City Council 147
Stockholm City Library, digital unit 148
Stokab (company) 147
strategic partnerships 20, 33
subsidiarity principle 187–188
sustainable development 1, 4, 22, 71–72, 121, 123, 125, 130, 139, 247, 249; connection with culture 267–268; culture 'fourth pillar' 27, 33, 48n95; dimensions 263; environment and 51–57; new square *21*; origins of concept 273n588

Taillibert, M. 143, 200
technical innovation, definition 60–61
technological advancement 167, 249; effects 5
technologies 11, 33, 84, 105, 121, 168, 250, 269; connection with art 42–43; duration 'significant fact' 44–45; as programs in cities 43–46
technologies-innovations-arts: essential issues 45–46
theme parks 44, 89
Thuriot, F.: networks (interdisciplinary and international) 133
tolerance 270, 272
tourism 1–2, 17, 22–23, 39, 72, 98–100, 107, 121–123, 140, 201, 248, 268; annual growth rate 100; culture 'main driving force' 98; employment (2011) 100; employment by economic activity (2008–2017) *98*; Glasgow 150; 'powerful driver of economic activity' 93
traffic 42, 61n205
training 60, 94, 136–137
transparency 103–104, 132
trust 26–27, 80, 113, 121, 135, 178, 182
Turkey 100
Turku 142–143, 163–164, 169, 252; cultural program **173**; innovation 173

Ukraine 222–223, 237
Ultimate Sports Cities, Glasgow 151–152
Umeå 108
United Arab Emirates (UAE) 100
United Cities and Local Government (UCLG) 8n1, 81n254, 157
United Kingdom 7, 73, 75, 79, 87, 159, 163, 248; creative economy 85, 101–102, *102*, 123
United Kingdom, Department for Culture, Media, Sport (DCMS) 88, 90, 126
United Nations: Rio+20 (2012) 273n588; UNCED (1992) 51, 273n588; UNCTAD 29, 97, 122; UNESCO 3, 29, 38, 41, 48n105, 49n144, 97, 110, 137, 154, 163, 189; UNESCO Cities of Music 203; UNESCO Creative City Network (UCCN) 177, 203–204; UNESCO Cultural Rights of Child 156–157; Universal Declaration of Human Rights (1948) 181; UN Settlements Programme (UN-Habitat) 13; UN 2030 Agenda for Sustainable Development 95
United States 44, 80, 133, 154
University of Valencia 124
urban development 187; culture as byword for 184–185; joined politics needed 37; promotion (essential factor) 2
urban environment, digital art 46–47
urban planning 29, 37
urban regeneration 31, 68, 107, 130, 272
urbanism 35, 38
urbanization 6, 17, 34, 133
user interface, definition 89
Utrecht 108

Varbanova, L.: *International Entrepreneurship in Arts* (2016) 77–78, 82n280
Venice 42, 265
Vienna, Prater (amusement park) 44
Vimeo 163
Virtual Academy of Brabant 165
Virtual Museum Transnational Network 36
virtual reality 105, 265
visitors 26–27, 63, 264; importance of understanding 134–135; *see also* tourism
visual arts 122

water 54
websites 104, 191

Western culture 129–130
Western Europe focus group 140–143, 176–206, 252–256, 271; analysis 206–210, **211–216**; budgets 211–215; cultural and creative industries 211–216; innovation 211–216; members 143; *see also* Central and Eastern Europe focus group
Western Europe focus group (places): Barcelona 143, 188–195, 207–208, **212**, **216**; Bologna 143, 182–188, 207, 210–211, 216; Brussels 143, 195–196, 208–209, 213, 216; Dortmund 143, 205–206, 210, 215; Grenoble 143, 200–202, 209–210, 214, 216; Mannheim 143, 202–205, 210, 215–216; Marseille 143, 196–199, 209, 213, 216; Reims 143, 199–200, 209, 214, 216; Rome 143, 176–182, 206–207, 210–211, 216
works of art *versus* 'cultural goods and services' 85–86
World Bank 228
World Cities Culture Forum 163
World Intellectual Property Organization 97

Yeates, R. 157
youth employment 63
YouTube 163–164, 194

Zabłocie 230
Zagreb 142, 144, 227–229, 238, **242**, **244**, 258–259, 272
Zoom 164

For Product Safety Concerns and Information please contact our EU representative GPSR@taylorandfrancis.com Taylor & Francis Verlag GmbH, Kaufingerstraße 24, 80331 München, Germany